Course	General Sociology
Course Number	**SOC 120**
	Gina Benedict
	University Of Tennessee
	SOCIOLOGY

http://create.mheducation.com

This McGraw-Hill Create text may include materials submitted to
McGraw-Hill for publication by the instructor of this course.
The instructor is solely responsible for the editorial content of such
materials. Instructors retain copyright of these additional materials.

ISBN-10: 1121064019   ISBN-13: 9781121064010

Contents

Credits

"What has sociology got to do with me or with my life?" As a student, you might well have asked this question when you signed up for your introductory sociology course. To answer it, consider these points: Are you influenced by what you see on television? Do you use the Internet? Did you vote in the last election? Are you familiar with binge drinking on campus? Do you use alternative medicine? These are just a few of the everyday life situations described in this book that sociology can shed light on. But as the opening excerpt indicates, sociology also looks at large social issues. We use sociology to investigate why thousands of jobs have moved from the United States to developing nations, what social forces promote prejudice, what leads someone to join a social movement and work for social change, how access to computer technology can reduce social inequality, and why relationships between men and women in Seattle differ from those in Singapore.

Sociology is, simply, the scientific study of social behavior and human groups. It focuses on social relationships; how those relationships influence people's behavior; and how societies, the sum total of those relationships, develop and change.

The Sociological Imagination

In attempting to understand social behavior, sociologists rely on a particular type of critical thinking. A leading sociologist, C. Wright Mills, described such thinking as the **sociological imagination**—an awareness of the relationship between an individual and the wider society, both today and in the past (Mills [1959] 2000a). This awareness allows all of us (not just sociologists) to comprehend the links between our immediate, personal social settings and the remote, impersonal social world that surrounds and helps to shape us. Kelsey Timmerman certainly used a sociological imagination when he studied foreign garment workers.

A key element in the sociological imagination is the ability to view one's own society as an outsider would, rather than only from the perspective of personal experiences and cultural biases. Consider something as simple as sporting events. On college campuses in the United States, thousands of students cheer well-trained football players. In Bali, Indonesia, dozens of spectators gather around a ring to cheer on roosters trained in cockfighting. In both instances, the spectators debate the merits of their favorites and bet on the outcome of the events. Yet what is considered a normal sporting event in one part of the world is considered unusual in another part.

The sociological imagination allows us to go beyond personal experiences and observations to understand broader public issues. Divorce, for example, is unquestionably a personal hardship for a husband and wife who split apart. However, C. Wright Mills advocated using the sociological imagination to view divorce not as simply an individual's personal problem but rather as a societal concern. Using this perspective, we can see that an increase in the divorce rate actually redefines a major social institution—the family. Today's households frequently include stepparents and half-siblings whose parents have divorced and remarried. Through the complexities of the blended family, this private concern becomes a public issue that affects schools, government agencies, businesses, and religious institutions.

The sociological imagination is an empowering tool. It allows us to look beyond a limited understanding of human behavior to see the world and its people in a new way and through a broader lens than we might otherwise use. It may be as simple as understanding why a roommate prefers country music to hip-hop, or it may open up a whole different way of understanding other populations in the world. For example, in the aftermath of the terrorist attacks on the United States on September 11, 2001, many citizens wanted to understand how Muslims throughout the world perceived their country, and why. From time to time this textbook will offer you the chance to exercise your sociological imagination in a variety of situations.

 use your sociological imagination

You are walking down the street in your city or hometown. In looking around you, you can't help noticing that half or more of the people you see are overweight. How do you explain your observation? If you were C. Wright Mills, how do you think you would explain it?

Sociology and the Social Sciences

Is sociology a science? The term **science** refers to the body of knowledge obtained by methods based on systematic observation. Just like other scientific disciplines, sociology involves the organized, systematic study of phenomena (in this case, human behavior) in order to enhance understanding. All scientists, whether studying mushrooms or murderers, attempt to collect precise information through methods of study that are as objective as possible. They rely on careful recording of observations and accumulation of data.

Table **1-1**   Sections of the American Sociological Association

Aging and the Life Course	Ethnomethodology and Conversation Analysis	Political Economy of the World-System
Alcohol, Drugs, and Tobacco	Evolution, Biology, and Society	Political Sociology
Animals and Society	Family	Population
Asia and Asian America	History of Sociology	Race, Gender, and Class
Body and Embodiment	Human Rights	Racial and Ethnic Minorities
Children and Youth	International Migration	Rationality and Society
Collective Behavior and Social Movements	Labor and Labor Movements	Religion
Communication and Information Technologies	Latino/a Sociology	Science, Knowledge, and Technology
Community and Urban Sociology	Law	Sex and Gender
Comparative and Historical Sociology	Marxist Sociology	Sexualities
Crime, Law, and Deviance	Mathematical Sociology	Social Psychology
Culture	Medical Sociology	Sociological Practice and Public Sociology
Economic Sociology	Mental Health	Teaching and Learning
Education	Methodology	Theory
Emotions	Organizations, Occupations, and Work	
Environment and Technology	Peace, War, and Social Conflict	

The range of sociological issues is very broad. For example, sociologists who belong to the Animals and Society section of the ASA may study the animal rights movement; those who belong to the Sexualities section may study global sex workers or the gay, bisexual, and transgendered movements. Economic sociologists may investigate globalization or consumerism, among many other topics.

Source: American Sociological Association 2010b.

Think about It

> Which of these topics do you think would interest you the most? Why?

Sociology is the scientific study of social behavior and human groups.

Of course, there is a great difference between sociology and physics, between psychology and astronomy. For this reason, the sciences are commonly divided into natural and social sciences.

Natural science is the study of the physical features of nature and the ways in which they interact and change. Astronomy, biology, chemistry, geology, and physics are all natural sciences. **Social science** is the study of the social features of humans and the ways in which they interact and change. The social sciences include sociology, anthropology, economics, history, psychology, and political science.

These social science disciplines have a common focus on the social behavior of people, yet each has a particular orientation. Anthropologists usually study past cultures and preindustrial societies that continue today, as well as the origins of humans. Economists explore the ways in which people produce and exchange goods and services, along with money and other resources. Historians are concerned with the peoples and events of the past and their significance for us today. Political scientists study international relations, the workings of government, and the exercise of power and authority. Psychologists investigate personality and individual behavior. So what do *sociologists* focus on? They study the influence that society has on people's attitudes and behavior and the ways in which people interact and shape society. Because humans are social animals, sociologists examine our social relationships with others scientifically. The range of the relationships they investigate is vast, as the current list of sections in the American Sociological Association suggests (Table 1-1).

Let's consider how different social scientists would study the impact of the earthquake that hit Port-au-Prince, the capital of Haiti, in 2010. Historians would stress Haiti's economic exploitation as a colony of France, and its resulting poverty today. Economists would discuss ways to rebuild Haiti's economy, perhaps by diversifying it. Environmental ecologists would treat Haiti and its neighbor, the Dominican Republic, as a single ecosystem, the island of Hispaniola. Psychologists would study individual cases of emotional stress caused by the traumatic event. And political scientists would study the short-term prospects for the nation's governance, which might include trustee status under the United Nations.

What approach would sociologists take? They might consider the possibility of reversing Haitians' generation-long migration from the countryside to the capital city, by making life in rural areas more sustainable. They might study the use of new media, such as Twitter, to funnel donations to charities. They might conduct short- and long-term research on the adoption of Haitian orphans by U.S. families, many of them White. Or they might evaluate current and potential U.S. policy toward Haitian immigrants, refugees, and deportees.

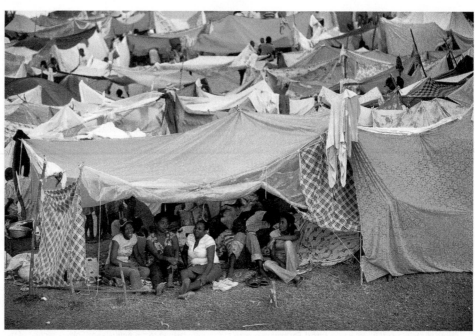

The earthquake that hit Haiti in January 2010 may have lasted only a few minutes, but the social impact on the small, impoverished island nation will last many years. This "temporary" tent city shelters 20,000 people whose homes were destroyed, and for whom there is still no permanent housing.

Sociologists would take a similar approach to studying episodes of extreme violence. In April 2007, just as college students were beginning to focus on the impending end of the semester, tragedy struck on the campus of Virginia Tech. In a two-hour shooting spree, a mentally disturbed senior armed with semi-automatic weapons killed a total of 32 students and faculty at Virginia's largest university. Observers struggled to describe the events and place them in some social context. For sociologists in particular, the event raised numerous issues and topics for study, including the media's role in describing the attacks, the presence of violence in our educational institutions, the gun control debate, the inadequacy of the nation's mental health care system, and the stereotyping and stigmatization of people who suffer from mental illness.

Besides doing research, sociologists have a long history of advising government agencies on how to respond to disasters. Certainly the poverty of the Gulf Coast region complicated the huge challenge of evacuation in 2005. With Hurricane Katrina bearing down on the Gulf Coast, thousands of poor inner-city residents had no automobiles or other available means of escaping the storm. Added to that difficulty was the high incidence of disability in the area. New Orleans ranked 2nd among the nation's 70 largest cities in the proportion of people over age 65 who are disabled—56 percent. Moving wheelchair-bound residents to safety requires specially equipped vehicles, to say nothing of handicap-accessible accommodations in public shelters. Clearly, officials must consider these factors in developing evacuation plans (Bureau of the Census 2005f).

Sociological analysis of the disaster did not end when the floodwaters receded. Long before residents of New Orleans staged a massive anticrime rally at City Hall in 2007, researchers were analyzing resettlement patterns in the city. They noted that returning residents often faced bleak job prospects. Yet families who had stayed away for that reason often had trouble enrolling their children in schools unprepared for an influx of evacuees. Faced with a choice between the need to work and the need to return their children to school, some displaced families risked sending their older children home alone. Meanwhile, opportunists had arrived to victimize unsuspecting homeowners. And the city's overtaxed judicial and criminal justice systems, which had been understaffed before Katrina struck, had been only partially restored. All these social factors led sociologists and others to anticipate the unparalleled rise in reported crime the city experienced in 2006 and 2007 (Jervis 2008; Kaufman 2006).

Throughout this textbook, you will see how sociologists develop theories and conduct research to study and better understand societies. And you will be encouraged to use your sociological imagination to examine the United States (and other societies) from the viewpoint of a respectful but questioning outsider.

Sociology and Common Sense

Sociology focuses on the study of human behavior. Yet we all have experience with human behavior and at least some knowledge of it. All of us might well have theories about why people become homeless, for example. Our theories and opinions typically come from common sense—that is, from our experiences and conversations, from what we read, from what we see on television, and so forth.

In our daily lives, we rely on common sense to get us through many unfamiliar situations. However, this commonsense knowledge, while sometimes accurate, is not always reliable, because it rests on commonly held beliefs rather than on systematic analysis of facts. It was once considered common sense to accept that the earth was flat—a view rightly questioned by Pythagoras and Aristotle. Incorrect commonsense notions are not just a part of the distant past; they remain with us today.

Contrary to the common notion that women tend to be chatty compared to men, for instance, researchers have found little difference between the sexes in terms of their talkativeness. Over a five-year period they placed unobtrusive microphones on 396 college students in various fields, at campuses in Mexico as well as the United States. They found that both men and women spoke about 16,000 words per day (Mehl et al. 2007).

Similarly, common sense tells us that in the United States today, military marriages are more likely to end in separation or divorce than in the past due to the strain of long deployments in Iraq and Afghanistan. Yet a study released in 2007 shows no significant increase in the divorce rate among U.S. soldiers over the past decade. In fact, the rate of marital dissolution among members of the military is comparable to that of nonmilitary families. Interestingly, this is not the first study to disprove the widely held notion that military service strains the marital bond. Two generations earlier, during the Vietnam era, researchers came to the same conclusion (Call and Teachman 1991; Karney and Crown 2007).

Like other social scientists, sociologists do not accept something as a fact because "everyone knows it." Instead, each piece of information must be tested and recorded, then analyzed in relation to other data. Sociologists rely on scientific studies in order to describe and understand a social environment. At times, the findings of sociologists may seem like common sense, because they deal with familiar facets of everyday life. The difference is that such findings have been *tested* by researchers. Common sense now tells us that the earth is round, but this particular commonsense notion is based on centuries of scientific work that began with the breakthroughs made by Pythagoras and Aristotle.

What Is Sociological Theory?

Why do people commit suicide? One traditional common-sense answer is that people inherit the desire to kill themselves. Another view is that sunspots drive people to take their lives. These explanations may not seem especially convincing to contemporary researchers, but they represent beliefs widely held as recently as 1900.

Sociologists are not particularly interested in why any one individual commits suicide; they are more concerned with identifying the social forces that systematically cause some people to take their own lives. In order to undertake this research, sociologists develop a theory that offers a general explanation of suicidal behavior.

We can think of theories as attempts to explain events, forces, materials, ideas, or behavior in a comprehensive manner. In sociology, a **theory** is a set of statements that seeks to explain problems, actions, or behavior. An effective theory may have both explanatory and predictive power. That is, it can help us to see the relationships among seemingly isolated phenomena, as well as to understand how one type of change in an environment leads to other changes.

The World Health Organization (2006) estimates that some 900,000 people commit suicide every year. More than a hundred years ago, a sociologist tried to look at suicide data scientifically. Émile Durkheim ([1897] 1951) developed a highly original theory about the relationship between suicide and social factors. Durkheim was primarily concerned not with the personalities of individual suicide victims but rather with suicide rates and how they varied from country to country. As a result, when he looked at the number of reported suicides in France, England, and Denmark in 1869, he also noted the total population of each country in order to determine the rate of suicide in each nation. He found that whereas England had only 67 reported suicides per million inhabitants, France had 135 per million and Denmark had 277 per million. The question then became "Why did Denmark have a comparatively high rate of reported suicide?"

Durkheim went much deeper into his investigation of suicide rates. The result was his landmark work *Suicide*, published in 1897. Durkheim refused to accept unproved explanations regarding suicide, including the beliefs that inherited tendencies or cosmic forces caused such deaths. Instead, he focused on social factors, such as the cohesiveness or lack of cohesiveness of religious, social, and occupational groups.

Durkheim's research suggested that suicide, although it is a solitary act, is related to group life. He found that people without religious affiliations had a higher suicide rate than those who were affiliated; the unmarried had much higher rates than married people; and soldiers had a higher rate than civilians. In addition, there seemed to be higher rates of suicide in times of peace than in times of war and revolution, and in times of economic instability and recession rather than in times of prosperity. Durkheim concluded that the suicide rates of a society reflected the extent to which people were or were not integrated into the group life of the society.

Émile Durkheim, like many other social scientists, developed a theory to explain how individual behavior can be understood within a social context. He pointed out the influence of groups and societal forces on what had always been viewed as a highly personal act. Clearly, Durkheim offered a more *scientific* explanation for the causes of suicide than that of inherited tendencies or sunspots. His theory has predictive power, since it suggests that suicide rates will rise or fall in conjunction with certain social and economic changes.

Of course, a theory—even the best of theories—is not a final statement about human behavior. Durkheim's theory of suicide is no exception. Sociologists continue to examine factors that contribute to differences in suicide rates around the world and to a particular society's rate of suicide. They have observed that

Las Vegas has a suicide rate that is twice the national average. Sociologists suspect that the rapidly expanding city lacks a sense of community cohesiveness.

in Las Vegas, for example, the chances of dying by suicide are strikingly high—twice as high as in the United States as a whole. Noting Durkheim's emphasis on the relationship between suicide and social isolation, researchers have suggested that Las Vegas's rapid growth and constant influx of tourists have undermined the community's sense of permanence, even among longtime residents. Although gambling—or more accurately, losing while gambling—may seem a likely precipitating factor in suicides there, careful study of the data has allowed researchers to dismiss that explanation. What happens in Vegas may stay in Vegas, but the sense of community cohesiveness that the rest of the country enjoys may be lacking (Wray et al. 2008).

MODULE 1 | Recap and Review

Summary

Sociology is the scientific study of social behavior and human groups. In this module, we examine the nature of sociological theory and the work of some of the founders of the discipline.

1. The **sociological imagination** is an awareness of the relationship between an individual and the wider society. It is based on the ability to view our own society as an outsider might, rather than from the perspective of our limited experiences and cultural biases.

2. In contrast to other **social sciences**, sociology emphasizes the influence that groups can have on people's behavior and attitudes and the ways in which people shape society.

3. Knowledge that relies on common sense is not always reliable. Sociologists must test and analyze each piece of information they use.

4. Sociologists employ **theories** to examine relationships between observations or data that may seem completely unrelated.

Thinking Critically

1. What aspects of the social and work environment in a fast-food restaurant would be of particular interest to a sociologist? How would the sociological imagination help in analyzing the topic?

2. Can you think of any explanation, other than lack of community, for the high suicide rate in Las Vegas? Does that explanation agree with Durkheim's theory?

3. Think about the sociologists profiled in this module, Mills and Durkheim. Whose work seems most relevant to today's social problems? Why did you choose that thinker, and which social problems were you thinking of?

Key Terms

Natural science

Science

Social science

Sociological imagination

Sociology

Theory

People have always been curious about sociological matters—how we get along with others, what we do for a living, whom we select as our leaders. Philosophers and religious authorities of ancient and medieval societies made countless observations about human behavior. They did not test or verify those observations scientifically; nevertheless, their observations often became the foundation for moral codes. Several of these early social philosophers correctly predicted that a systematic study of human behavior would emerge one day. Beginning in the 19th century, European theorists made pioneering contributions to the development of a science of hu-man behavior.

Early Thinkers

Auguste Comte

The 19th century was an unsettling time in France. The French monarchy had been deposed in the revolution of 1789, and Napoleon had suffered defeat in his effort to conquer Europe. Amid this chaos, philosophers considered how society might be improved. Auguste Comte (1798–1857), credited with being the most influential of the philosophers of the early 1800s, believed

Harriet Martineau, an early pioneer of sociology who studied social behavior both in her native England and in the United States, proposed some of the methods still used by sociologists.

that a theoretical science of society and a systematic investigation of behavior were needed to improve society. He coined the term *sociology* to apply to the science of human behavior.

Writing in the 1800s, Comte feared that the excesses of the French Revolution had permanently impaired France's stability. Yet he hoped that the systematic study of social behavior would eventually lead to more rational human interactions. In Comte's hierarchy of the sciences, sociology was at the top. He called it the "queen," and its practitioners "scientist-priests." This French theorist did not simply give sociology its name; he presented a rather ambitious challenge to the fledgling discipline.

Harriet Martineau

Scholars learned of Comte's works largely through translations by the English sociologist Harriet Martineau (1802–1876). But Martineau was a pathbreaker in her own right: she offered insightful observations of the customs and social practices of both her native Britain and the United States. Martineau's book *Society in America* ([1837] 1962) examined religion, politics, child rearing, and immigration in the young nation. It gave special attention to social class distinctions and to such factors as gender and race. Martineau ([1838] 1989) also wrote the first book on sociological methods.

Martineau's writings emphasized the impact that the economy, law, trade, health, and population could have on social problems. She spoke out in favor of the rights of women, the emancipation of slaves, and religious tolerance. Later in life, deafness did not keep her from being an activist. In Martineau's ([1837] 1962) view, intellectuals and scholars should not simply offer observations of social conditions; they should *act* on their convictions in a manner that will benefit society. That is why Martineau conducted research on the nature of female employment and pointed to the need for further investigation of the issue (Deegan 2003; Hill and Hoecker-Drysdale 2001).

Herbert Spencer

Another important early contributor to the discipline of sociology was Herbert Spencer (1820–1903). A relatively prosperous Victorian Englishman, Spencer (unlike Martineau) did not feel compelled to correct or improve society; instead, he merely hoped to understand it better. Drawing on Charles Darwin's study *On the Origin of Species,* Spencer applied the concept of evolution of the species to societies in order to explain how they change, or evolve, over time. Similarly, he adapted Darwin's evolutionary view of the "survival of the fittest" by arguing that it is "natural" that some people are rich while others are poor.

FIGURE 2-1 Contributors to Sociology

	Émile Durkheim 1858–1917	Max Weber 1864–1920	Karl Marx 1818–1883	W. E. B. DuBois 1868–1963
Academic training	Philosophy	Law, economics, history, philosophy	Philosophy, law	Sociology
Key works	1893—*The Division of Labor in Society* 1897—*Suicide: A Study in Sociology* 1912—*Elementary Forms of Religious Life*	1904–1905—*The Protestant Ethic and the Spirit of Capitalism* 1921—*Economy and Society*	1848—*The Communist Manifesto* 1867—*Das Kapital*	1899—*The Philadelphia Negro* 1903—*The Negro Church* 1903—*Souls of Black Folk*

Spencer's approach to societal change was extremely popular in his lifetime. Unlike Comte, Spencer suggested that since societies are bound to change eventually, one need not be highly critical of present social arrangements or work actively for social change. This viewpoint appealed to many influential people in England and the United States who had a vested interest in the status quo and were suspicious of social thinkers who endorsed change.

Émile Durkheim

Émile Durkheim made many pioneering contributions to sociology, including his important theoretical work on suicide. The son of a rabbi, Durkheim (1858–1917) was educated in both France and Germany. He established an impressive academic reputation and was appointed one of the first professors of sociology in France. Above all, Durkheim will be remembered for his insistence that behavior must be understood within a larger social context, not just in individualistic terms.

To give one example of this emphasis, Durkheim ([1912] 2001) developed a fundamental thesis to help explain all forms of society. Through intensive study of the Arunta, an Australian tribe, he focused on the functions that religion performed and underscored the role of group life in defining what we consider to be religion. Durkheim concluded that like other forms of group behavior, religion reinforces a group's solidarity.

Another of Durkheim's main interests was the consequences of work in modern societies. In his view, the growing division of labor in industrial societies, as workers became much more specialized in their tasks, led to what he called "anomie." **Anomie** refers to the loss of direction felt in a society when social control of individual behavior has become ineffective. Often, the state of anomie occurs during a time of profound social change, when people have lost their sense of purpose or direction. In a period of

anomie, people are so confused and unable to cope with the new social environment that they may resort to suicide.

Durkheim was concerned about the dangers that alienation, loneliness, and isolation might pose for modern industrial societies. He shared Comte's belief that sociology should provide direction for social change. As a result, he advocated the creation of new social groups—mediators between the individual's family and the state—that would provide a sense of belonging for members of huge, impersonal societies. Unions would be an example of such groups.

Like many other sociologists, Durkheim did not limit his interests to one aspect of social behavior. Later in this book we will consider his thinking on crime and punishment, religion, and the workplace. Few sociologists have had such a dramatic impact on so many different areas within the discipline.

Max Weber

Another important early theorist was Max Weber (pronounced VAY-ber). Born in Germany, Weber (1864–1920) studied legal and economic history, but gradually developed an interest in sociology. Eventually, he became a professor at various German universities. Weber taught his students that they should employ **verstehen** (pronounced fair-SHTAY-en), the German word for "understanding" or "insight," in their intellectual work. He pointed out that we cannot analyze our social behavior by the same type of objective criteria we use to measure weight or temperature. To fully comprehend behavior, we must learn the subjective meanings people attach to their actions—how they themselves view and explain their behavior.

For example, suppose that a sociologist was studying the social ranking of individuals in a fraternity. Weber would expect the researcher to employ *verstehen* to determine the significance of the fraternity's social hierarchy for its members. The researcher might examine the effects of athleticism or grades or social skills or seniority on standing within the fraternity. He or she would seek to learn how the fraternity members relate to other members of higher or lower status. While investigating these questions, the researcher would take into account people's emotions, thoughts, beliefs, and attitudes (L. Coser 1977).

We also owe credit to Weber for a key conceptual tool: the ideal type. An **ideal type** is a construct or model for evaluating specific cases. In his works, Weber identified various characteristics of bureaucracy as an ideal type (discussed in detail in Module 19). In presenting this model of bureaucracy, Weber was not describing any particular organization, nor was he using the term *ideal* in a way that suggested a positive evaluation. Instead, his purpose was to provide a useful standard for measuring how bureaucratic an actual organization is (Gerth and Mills 1958). Later in this book, we will use the concept of *ideal type* to study the family, religion, authority, and economic systems, as well as to analyze bureaucracy.

Although their professional careers coincided, Émile Durkheim and Max Weber never met and probably were unaware of each other's existence, let alone ideas. Such was not true of the work of Karl Marx. Durkheim's thinking about the impact of the division of labor in industrial societies was related to Marx's writings, while Weber's concern for a value-free, objective sociology was a direct response to Marx's deeply held convictions. Thus, it is not surprising that Karl Marx is viewed as a major figure in the development of sociology, as well as several other social sciences (Figure 2-1).

Karl Marx

Karl Marx (1818–1883) shared with Durkheim and Weber a dual interest in abstract philosophical issues and the concrete reality of everyday life. Unlike them, however, Marx was so critical of existing institutions that a conventional academic career was impossible. He spent most of his life in exile from his native Germany.

Marx's personal life was a difficult struggle. When a paper he had written was suppressed, he fled to France. In Paris, he met Friedrich Engels (1820–1895), with whom he formed a lifelong friendship. The two lived at a time when European and North American economic life was increasingly dominated by the factory rather than the farm.

While in London in 1847, Marx and Engels attended secret meetings of an illegal coalition of labor unions known as the Communist League. The following year they prepared a platform called *The Communist Manifesto,* in which they argued that the masses of people with no resources other than their labor (whom they referred to as the *proletariat*) should unite to fight for the overthrow of capitalist societies. In the words of Marx and Engels:

> The history of all hitherto existing society is the history of class struggles. . . . The proletarians have nothing to lose but their chains. They have a world to win. WORKING MEN OF ALL COUNTRIES UNITE! (L. Feuer 1989:7, 41)

After completing *The Communist Manifesto,* Marx returned to Germany, only to be expelled. He then moved to England, where he continued to write books and essays. Marx lived there in extreme poverty; he pawned most of his possessions, and several of his children died of malnutrition and disease. Marx clearly was an outsider in British society, a fact that may well have influenced his view of Western cultures.

In Marx's analysis, society was fundamentally divided between two classes that clashed in pursuit of their own interests. When he examined the industrial societies of his time, such as Germany, England, and the United States, he saw the factory as the center of conflict between the exploiters (the owners of the means of production) and the exploited (the workers). Marx viewed these relationships in systematic terms; that is, he believed that a system of economic, social, and political relationships maintained the power and dominance of the owners over the workers. Consequently, Marx and Engels argued that the working class should overthrow the existing class system. Marx's influence on contemporary thinking has been dramatic. His writings inspired those who would later lead communist revolutions in Russia, China, Cuba, Vietnam, and elsewhere.

Even apart from the political revolutions that his work fostered, Marx's significance is profound. Marx emphasized the *group* identifications and associations that influence an *individual's* place in society. This area of study is the major focus of contemporary sociology. Throughout this textbook, we will consider how membership in a particular gender classification, age group, racial group, or economic class affects a person's attitudes and behavior. In an important sense, we can trace this way of understanding society back to the pioneering work of Karl Marx.

W. E. B. DuBois

Marx's work encouraged sociologists to view society through the eyes of those segments of the population that rarely influence decision making. In the United States, some early Black sociologists, including W. E. B. DuBois (1868–1963), conducted research that they hoped would assist in the struggle for a racially egalitarian society. DuBois (pronounced doo-BOYSS) believed that knowledge was essential in combating prejudice and achieving tolerance and justice. Sociologists, he contended, needed to draw on scientific principles to study social problems such as those experienced by Blacks in the United States. To separate opinion from fact, he advocated basic research on the lives of Blacks. Through his in-depth studies of urban life, both White and Black, in cities such as Philadelphia and Atlanta, DuBois ([1899] 1995) made a major contribution to sociology.

Like Durkheim and Weber, DuBois saw the importance of religion to society. However, he tended to focus on religion at the community level and the role of the church in the lives of its members ([1903] 2003). DuBois had little patience with theorists such as Herbert Spencer, who seemed content with the status quo. He believed that the granting of full political rights to Blacks was essential to their social and economic progress.

Because many of his ideas challenged the status quo, DuBois did not find a receptive audience within either the government or the academic world. As a result, he became increasingly involved with organizations whose members questioned the established social order. In 1909 he helped to found the National Association for the Advancement of Colored People, better known today as the NAACP (Wortham 2008).

DuBois's insights have been lasting. In 1897 he coined the term **double consciousness** to refer to the division of an

In a photograph taken around 1930, social reformer Jane Addams reads to children at the Mary Crane Nursery. Addams was an early pioneer both in sociology and in the settlement house movement.

individual's identity into two or more social realities. He used the term to describe the experience of being Black in White America. Today, an African American holds the most powerful office in the nation, President of the United States. Yet for millions of African Americans, the reality of being Black in the United States typically is not one of power ([1903] 1961).

Twentieth-Century Developments

Sociology today builds on the firm foundation developed by Émile Durkheim, Max Weber, Karl Marx, and W. E. B. DuBois. However, the field certainly has not remained stagnant over the past hundred years. While Europeans have continued to make contributions to the discipline, sociologists from throughout the world and especially the United States have advanced sociological theory and research. Their new insights have helped us to better understand the workings of society.

Charles Horton Cooley

Charles Horton Cooley (1864–1929) was typical of the sociologists who came to prominence in the early 1900s. Born in Ann Arbor, Michigan, Cooley received his graduate training in economics but later became a sociology professor at the University of Michigan. Like other early sociologists, he had become interested in this new discipline while pursuing a related area of study.

Cooley shared the desire of Durkheim, Weber, and Marx to learn more about society. But to do so effectively, he preferred to use the sociological perspective to look first at smaller units—intimate, face-to-face groups such as families, gangs, and friendship networks. He saw these groups as the seedbeds of society, in the sense that they shape people's ideals, beliefs, values, and social nature. Cooley's work increased our understanding of groups of relatively small size.

Jane Addams

In the early 1900s, many leading sociologists in the United States saw themselves as social reformers dedicated to systematically studying and then improving a corrupt society. They were genuinely concerned about the lives of immigrants in the nation's growing cities, whether those immigrants came from Europe or from the rural American South. Early female sociologists, in particular, often took active roles in poor urban areas as leaders of community centers known as *settlement houses*. For example, Jane Addams (1860–1935), a member of the American Sociological Society, cofounded the famous Chicago settlement, Hull House.

Addams and other pioneering female sociologists commonly combined intellectual inquiry, social service work, and political activism—all with the goal of assisting the underprivileged and creating a more egalitarian society. For example, working with the Black journalist and educator Ida Wells-Barnett, Addams successfully prevented racial segregation in the Chicago public schools. Addams's efforts to establish a juvenile court system and a women's trade union reveal the practical focus of her work (Addams 1910, 1930; Deegan 1991; Lengermann and Niebrugge-Brantley 1998).

By the middle of the 20th century, however, the focus of the discipline had shifted. Sociologists for the most part restricted themselves to theorizing and gathering information; the aim of transforming society was left to social workers and activists. This shift away from social reform was accompanied by a growing commitment to scientific methods of research and to value-free interpretation of data. Not all sociologists were happy with this emphasis. A new organization, the Society for the Study of Social Problems, was created in 1950 to deal more directly with social inequality and other social problems.

Robert Merton

Sociologist Robert Merton (1910–2003) made an important contribution to the discipline by successfully combining theory and research. Born to Slavic immigrant parents in Philadelphia, Merton won a scholarship to Temple University. He continued his studies at Harvard, where he acquired his lifelong interest in sociology. Merton's teaching career was based at Columbia University.

Merton (1968) produced a theory that is one of the most frequently cited explanations of deviant behavior. He noted different ways in which people attempt to achieve success in life. In his view, some may deviate from the socially approved goal of accumulating material goods or the socially accepted means of achieving that goal. For example, in Merton's classification scheme, *innovators* are people who accept the goal of pursuing material wealth but use illegal means to do so, including robbery, burglary, and extortion. Although Merton based his explanation of crime on individual behavior that has been influenced by society's approved goals and means, it has wider applications. His theory helps to account for the high crime rates among the nation's poor, who may see no hope of advancing themselves through traditional roads to success. Module 24 discusses Merton's theory in greater detail.

Merton also emphasized that sociology should strive to bring together the *macro-level* and *micro-level* approaches to the study of society. **Macrosociology** concentrates on large-scale phenomena or entire civilizations. Émile Durkheim's cross-cultural study of suicide is an example of macro-level research. More recently, macrosociologists have examined international crime rates (see Module 25), and the stereotype of Asian Americans as a "model minority" (see Module 33). In contrast, **microsociology** stresses the study of small groups, often through experimental means. Sociological research on the micro level has included studies of how divorced men and women disengage from significant social roles (see Module 10); of how conformity can influence the expression of prejudiced attitudes (see Module 24); and of how a teacher's expectations can affect a student's academic performance (see Module 42).

Pierre Bourdieu

Increasingly, scholars in the United States have been drawing on the insights of sociologists in other countries. The ideas of the late French sociologist Pierre Bourdieu (1930–2002) have found a broad following in North America and elsewhere. As a young man, Bourdieu did fieldwork in Algeria during its struggle for independence from France. Today, scholars study Bourdieu's research techniques as well as his conclusions.

Bourdieu wrote about how capital in its many forms sustains individuals and families from one generation to the next. To Bourdieu, *capital* included not just material goods, but cultural and social assets. **Cultural capital** refers to noneconomic goods, such as family background and education, which are reflected in a knowledge of language and the arts. Not necessarily book knowledge, cultural capital refers to the kind of education that is valued by the socially elite. Though a knowledge of Chinese cuisine is culture, for example, it is not the prestigious kind of culture that is valued by the elite. In the United States, immigrants—especially those who arrived in large numbers and settled in ethnic enclaves—have generally taken two or three generations to develop the same level of cultural capital enjoyed by more established groups. In comparison, **social capital** refers to the collective benefit of social networks, which are built on reciprocal trust. Much has been written about the importance of family and friendship networks in providing people with an opportunity to advance. In his emphasis on cultural and social capital, Bourdieu's work extends the insights of early social thinkers such as Marx and Weber (Bourdieu and Passerson 1990; Field 2008).

Today sociology reflects the diverse contributions of earlier theorists. As sociologists approach such topics as divorce, drug addiction, and religious cults, they can draw on the theoretical insights of the discipline's pioneers. A careful reader can hear Comte, Durkheim, Weber, Marx, DuBois, Cooley, Addams, and many others speaking through the pages of current research. Sociology has also broadened beyond the intellectual confines of North America and Europe. Contributions to the discipline now come from sociologists studying and researching human behavior in other parts of the world. In describing the work of these sociologists, it is helpful to examine a number of influential *theoretical perspectives,* also known as *approaches* or *views.*

MODULE 2 | Recap and Review

Summary

The thinkers who founded the discipline of sociology and developed it in the 19th and 20th centuries were reacting to the social world in which they lived.

1. Nineteenth-century thinkers who contributed sociological insights included Auguste Comte, a French philosopher; Harriet Martineau, an English sociologist; and Herbert Spencer, an English scholar.

2. Other important figures in the development of sociology were Émile Durkheim, who pioneered work on suicide; Max Weber, who taught the need for insight in intellectual work; Karl Marx, who emphasized the importance of the economy and social conflict; and W. E. B. DuBois, who advocated for the usefulness of basic research in combating prejudice and fostering racial tolerance and justice.

3. In the 20th century, the discipline of sociology was indebted to the U.S. sociologists Charles Horton Cooley and Robert Merton, as well as to the French sociologist Pierre Bourdieu.

4. **Macrosociology** concentrates on large-scale phenomena or entire civilizations; **microsociology** stresses the study of small groups.

Thinking Critically

1. Consider the work of early sociologists such as Comte and Martineau. What social problems were they reacting to? To what extent have those problems been rectified today?

2. How is 19th-century industrialization related to the development of sociological thought?

3. What are some examples of social and cultural capital that you possess?

Key Terms

Anomie

Cultural capital

Double consciousness

Ideal type

Macrosociology

Microsociology

Social capital

Verstehen

What Is the Scientific Method?

Like all of us, sociologists are interested in the central questions of our time. Is the family falling apart? Why is there so much crime in the United States? Is the world falling behind in its ability to feed a growing population? Such issues concern most people, whether or not they have academic training. However, unlike the typical citizen, the sociologist has a commitment to use the **scientific method** in studying society. The scientific method is a systematic, organized series of steps that ensures maximum objectivity and consistency in researching a problem.

Many of us will never actually conduct scientific research. Why, then, is it important that we understand the scientific method? The answer is that it plays a major role in the workings of our society. Residents of the United States are constantly bombarded with "facts" or "data." A television news report informs us that "one in every two marriages in this country now ends in divorce," yet Module 41 will show that this assertion is based on misleading statistics. Almost daily, advertisers cite supposedly scientific studies to prove that their products are superior. Such claims may be accurate or exaggerated. We can better evaluate such information—and will not be fooled so easily—if we are familiar with the standards of scientific research. These standards are quite stringent, and they demand as strict adherence as possible.

The scientific method requires precise preparation in developing useful research. Otherwise, the research data collected may not prove accurate. Sociologists and other researchers follow five basic steps in the scientific method: (1) defining the problem, (2) reviewing the literature, (3) formulating the hypothesis, (4) selecting the research design and then collecting and analyzing data, and (5) developing the conclusion (see Figure 5-1). We'll use an actual example to illustrate the workings of the scientific method.

Defining the Problem

Does it "pay" to go to college? Some people make great sacrifices and work hard to get a college education. Parents borrow money for their children's tuition. Students work part-time jobs or even take full-time positions while attending evening or weekend classes. Does it pay off? Are there monetary returns for getting that degree?

The first step in any research project is to state as clearly as possible what you hope to investigate—that is, *define the problem.* In this instance, we are interested in knowing how schooling relates to income. We want to find out the earnings of people with different levels of formal schooling.

FIGURE 5-1 **The Scientific Method**

The scientific method allows sociologists to objectively and logically evaluate the data they collect. Their findings can suggest ideas for further sociological research.

Early on, any social science researcher must develop an operational definition of each concept being studied. An **operational definition** is an explanation of an abstract concept that is specific enough to allow a researcher to assess the concept. For example, a sociologist interested in status might use membership in exclusive social clubs as an operational definition of status. Someone studying prejudice might consider a person's unwillingness to hire or work with members of minority groups as an operational definition of prejudice. In our example, we need to develop two operational definitions—education and earnings—in order to study whether it pays to get an advanced educational degree. We'll define *education* as the number of years of schooling a person has achieved and *earnings* as the income a person reports having received in the past year.

Initially, we will take a functionalist perspective (although we may end up incorporating other perspectives). We will argue that opportunities for more earning power are related to level of schooling and that schools prepare students for employment.

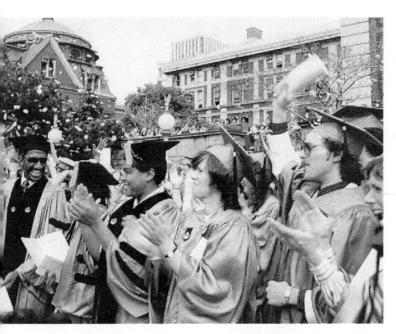

It seems reasonable to assume that these Columbia University graduates will earn more income than high school graduates. But how would you go about testing that hypothesis?

Reviewing the Literature

By conducting a *review of the literature*—relevant scholarly studies and information—researchers refine the problem under study, clarify possible techniques to be used in collecting data, and eliminate or reduce avoidable mistakes. In our example, we would examine information about the salaries for different occupations. We would see if jobs that require more academic training are better rewarded. It would also be appropriate to review studies on the relationship between education and income.

The review of the literature would soon tell us that many factors besides years of schooling influence earning potential. For example, we would learn that the children of rich parents are more likely to go to college than those of poor parents so we might consider the possibility that rich parents may later help their children to secure better-paying jobs.

We might also look at macro-level data, such as state-by-state comparisons of income and educational levels. In one macro-level study based on census data, researchers found that in states whose residents have a relatively high level of education, household income levels are high as well (Figure 5-2). This finding suggests that schooling may well be related to income, though it does not speak to the micro-level relationship we are interested in. That is, we want to know whether *individuals* who are well educated are also well paid.

Formulating the Hypothesis

After reviewing earlier research and drawing on the contributions of sociological theorists, the researchers may then *formulate the hypothesis*. A **hypothesis** is a speculative statement about the relationship between two or more factors known as variables. Income, religion, occupation, and gender can all serve as variables in a study. We can define a **variable** as a measurable trait or characteristic that is subject to change under different conditions.

Researchers who formulate a hypothesis generally must suggest how one aspect of human behavior influences or affects another. The variable hypothesized to cause or influence another is called the **independent variable.** The other variable is termed the **dependent variable** because its action *depends* on the influence of the independent variable. In other words, the researcher believes that the independent variable predicts or causes change in the dependent variable. For example, a researcher in sociology might anticipate that the availability of affordable housing (the independent variable, x) affects the level of homelessness in a community (the dependent variable, y).

Our hypothesis is that the higher one's educational degree, the more money one will earn. The independent variable that is to be measured is the level of education. The variable that is thought to depend on it—income—must also be measured.

Identifying independent and dependent variables is a critical step in clarifying cause-and-effect relationships. As shown in Figure 5-3, **causal logic** involves the relationship between a condition or variable and a particular consequence, with one event leading to the other. For instance, being less integrated into society may be directly related to, or produce a greater likelihood of, suicide. Similarly, the time students spend reviewing material for a quiz may be directly related to, or produce a greater likelihood of, getting a high score on the quiz.

A **correlation** exists when a change in one variable coincides with a change in the other. Correlations are an indication that causality *may* be present; they do not necessarily indicate causation. For example, data indicate that people who prefer to watch televised news programs are less knowledgeable than those who read newspapers and newsmagazines. This correlation between people's relative knowledge and their choice of news media seems to make sense, because it agrees with the common belief that television dumbs down information. But the correlation between the two variables is actually caused by a third variable, people's relative ability to comprehend large amounts of information. People with poor reading skills are much more likely than others to get their news from television, while those who are more educated or skilled turn more often to the print media. Though television viewing is *correlated* with lower news comprehension, then, it does not *cause* it. Sociologists seek to identify the *causal* link between variables; the suspected causal link is generally described in the hypothesis (Neuman 2009).

Collecting and Analyzing Data

How do you test a hypothesis to determine if it is supported or refuted? You need to collect information, using one of the research designs described in Module 6. The research design guides the researcher in collecting and analyzing data.

FIGURE 5-2 **Educational Level and Household Income in the United States**

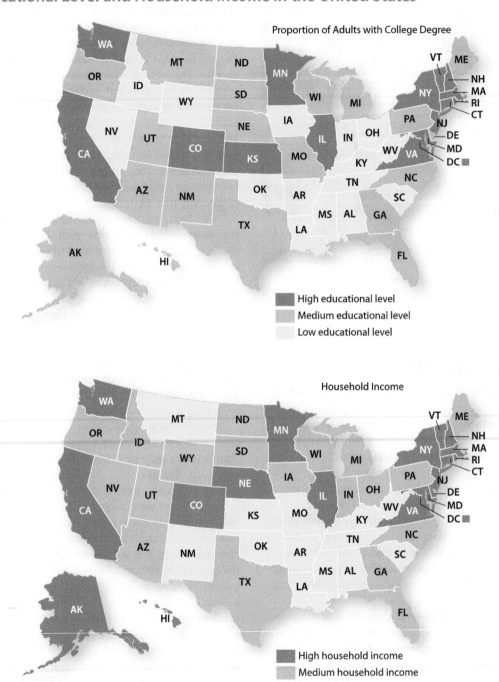

Proportion of Adults with College Degree

High educational level
Medium educational level
Low educational level

Household Income

High household income
Medium household income
Low household income

Notes: Cutoffs for high/medium and medium/low educational levels in 2008 were 29.6 percent and 24.6 percent of the population with a college degree, respectively; median for the entire nation was 27.7 percent. Cutoffs for high/medium and medium/low household income levels in 2008 were $55,200 and $45,500, respectively; national median household income was $52,029 in 2008.
Sources: American Community Survey 2009: Table R1502; Semega 2009.

In general, states with high educational levels (top) also have high household incomes (bottom).

Selecting the Sample

In most studies, social scientists must carefully select what is known as a sample. A **sample** is a selection from a larger population that is statistically representative of that population. There are many kinds of samples, but the one social scientists use most frequently is the random sample. In a **random sample,** every member of an entire population being studied has the same chance of being selected. Thus, if researchers want to examine

FIGURE 5-3 Causal Logic

Independent variable	Dependent variable
x ⟶	y
Level of educational degree ⟶	Level of income
Degree of lack of integration into society ⟶	Likelihood of suicide
Availability of affordable housing ⟶	Level of homelessness
Parents' church attendance ⟶	Children's church attendance
Time spent preparing for quiz ⟶	Performance on quiz
Parents' income ⟶	Likelihood of children's enrolling in college

In *causal logic* an independent variable (often designated by the symbol *x*) influences a dependent variable (often designated as *y*); thus, *x* leads to *y*. For example, parents who attend church regularly (*x*) are more likely to have children who are churchgoers (*y*). Notice that the first two pairs of variables are taken from studies already described in this textbook.

Think about It

Identify two or three dependent variables that might be influenced by this independent variable: number of alcoholic drinks ingested.

the opinions of people listed in a city directory (a book that, unlike the telephone directory, lists all households), they might use a computer to randomly select names from the directory. The results would constitute a random sample. The advantage of using specialized sampling techniques is that sociologists do not need to question everyone in a population (Igo 2007).

In some cases, the subjects researchers want to study are hard to identify, either because their activities are clandestine or because lists of such people are not readily available. How do researchers create a sample of illegal drug users, for instance, or of women whose husbands are at least 10 years younger than they are? In such cases, researchers employ what are called *snowball* or *convenience samples*—that is, they recruit participants through word of mouth or by posting notices on the Internet. With the help of special statistical techniques, researchers can draw conclusions from such nonrandom samples.

It is all too easy to confuse the careful scientific techniques used in representative sampling with the many *nonscientific* polls that receive much more media attention. For example, television viewers and radio listeners are often encouraged to e-mail their views on headline news or political contests. Such polls reflect nothing more than the views of those who happened to see the television program (or hear the radio broadcast) and took the time, perhaps at some cost, to register their opinions. These data do not necessarily reflect (and indeed may distort) the views of the broader population. Not everyone has access to a television or radio, time to watch or listen to a program, or the means and/ or inclination to send e-mail. Similar problems are raised by the *mail-back questionnaires* found in many magazines and by *mall intercepts*, in which shoppers are asked about some issue. Even when these techniques include answers from tens of thousands of people, they will be far less accurate than a carefully selected representative sample of 1,500 respondents.

For the purposes of our research example, we will use information collected in the Current Population Survey conducted by the Bureau of the Census. Each year the Census Bureau surveys approximately 54,000 households across the United States. Technicians at the bureau then use the data to estimate the nation's entire population.

Ensuring Validity and Reliability

The scientific method requires that research results be both valid and reliable. **Validity** refers to the degree to which a measure or scale truly reflects the phenomenon under study. A valid measure of income depends on the gathering of accurate data. Various studies show that people are reasonably accurate in reporting how much money they earned in the most recent year. If a question is written unclearly, however, the resulting data might not be accurate. For example, respondents to an unclear question about income might report their parents' or spouse's income instead of their own. **Reliability** refers to the extent to which a measure produces consistent results. Some people may not disclose accurate information, but most do. In the Current Population Survey, only 7.8 percent of the respondents refused to give their income or indicated they did not know what their income was. That means more than 92 percent of the respondents gave their income, which we can assume is reasonably accurate (given their other responses about occupation and years in the labor force).

● Developing the Conclusion

Scientific studies, including those conducted by sociologists, do not aim to answer all the questions that can be raised about a particular subject. Therefore, the conclusion of a research study represents both an end and a beginning. It terminates a specific phase of the investigation but should also generate ideas for future study.

Supporting Hypotheses

In our example, we find that the data support our hypothesis: people with more formal schooling *do* earn more money than others.

trend|spotting

Every 10 years, as required by the Constitution, the U.S. government conducts a census to determine how many congressional representatives each state is allowed. Besides determining the states' political power, these data are used for a myriad of other purposes, from distributing federal aid to education to researching the market for breakfast cereal.

Despite concerns about government intrusion into people's private lives, U.S. citizens are relatively compliant with the head count. About two-thirds of households fill out and return the form or answer face-to-face questions from a census worker. Other industrial countries have much less success than the United States. Because of strong concerns about privacy, for example, the Netherlands has not had a door-to-door census since 1971.

With detailed knowledge of two out of every three households in the United States, census workers can use statistical techniques to estimate data for the other third. Still, officials have long recognized that the count is more likely to miss certain groups of people than others. This tendency, called *undercounting,* applies especially to low-income people, non-English speakers, and the homeless. Those who have good reason to avoid census workers, such as illegal immigrants and families who crowd together in inadequate housing, also swell the ranks of the undercounted.

Recently, however, concern has been growing about *overcounting,* or the tendency to count some people twice. College students who live at school rather than at home with their parents, "snowbirds" (retirees who move to warmer climes during the winter), active military personnel, and children whose parents share their custody all are likely to be overcounted.

Census officials estimate that the 2000 Census undercounted 10.2 million people and overcounted 11.6 million. In a nation of over 300 million people, a population count that is off by a net figure of a million or so may not seem much of a problem. However, the error biases the count toward or against particular racial and socioeconomic groups. Whites, homeowners, and the educated are more likely than others to show up twice in the census. Blacks, Hispanics, and renters are more likely not to show up. Given the growing importance of accuracy in the nation's population count, this problem looms large for those who must interpret the 2010 Census.

Those with a high school diploma earn more than those who failed to complete high school, but those with an associate's degree earn more than high school graduates. The relationship continues through more advanced levels of schooling, so that those with graduate degrees earn the most.

The relationship is not perfect, however. Some people who drop out of high school end up with high incomes, whereas some with advanced degrees earn modest incomes, as shown in Figure 5-4. A successful entrepreneur, for example, might not have much formal schooling, while a holder of a doctorate may choose to work for a low-paying nonprofit institution. Sociologists are interested in both the general pattern that emerges from their data and exceptions to the pattern.

Sociological studies do not always generate data that support the original hypothesis. Many times, a hypothesis is refuted, and researchers must reformulate their conclusions. Unexpected results may also lead sociologists to reexamine their methodology and make changes in the research design.

Controlling for Other Factors

A **control variable** is a factor that is held constant to test the relative impact of an independent variable. For example, if researchers wanted to know how adults in the United States feel about restrictions on smoking in public places, they would probably attempt to use a respondent's smoking behavior as a control variable. That is, how do smokers versus nonsmokers feel about smoking in public places? The researchers would compile separate statistics on how smokers and nonsmokers feel about antismoking regulations.

Our study of the influence of education on income suggests that not everyone enjoys equal educational opportunities, a disparity that is one of the causes of social inequality. Since education affects a person's income, we may wish to call on the conflict perspective to explore this topic further. What impact does a person's race or gender have? Is a woman with a college degree likely to earn as much as a man with similar schooling? Later in this textbook we will consider these other factors and variables. That is, we will examine the impact that education has on income while controlling for variables such as gender and race.

High school diploma or less

Associate's degree or more

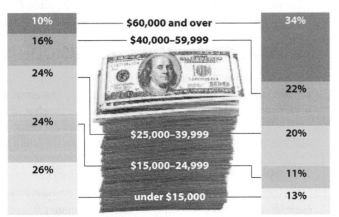

High school diploma or less		Associate's degree or more
10%	$60,000 and over	34%
16%	$40,000–59,999	
24%		22%
24%	$25,000–39,999	20%
26%	$15,000–24,999	11%
	under $15,000	13%

FIGURE 5-4 Impact of a College Education on Income

Fifty percent of people with a high school diploma or less (left) earn under $25,000 a year, while only 26 percent earn $40,000 or more. In contrast, 56 percent of those with an associate's degree or higher (right) earn $40,000 or more, while only 24 percent earn less than $25,000.

Source: Author's analysis of DeNavas-Walt et al. 2009, Detailed Table PINC-03.

Think about It

What kinds of knowledge and skills do people with an associate's degree or higher possess, compared to those with a high school education or less? Why would employers value those kinds of knowledge and skills?

In Summary: The Scientific Method

Let us briefly summarize the process of the scientific method through a review of the example. We *defined a problem* (the question of whether it pays to get a higher educational degree). We *reviewed the literature* (other studies of the relationship between education and income) and *formulated a hypothesis* (the higher one's educational degree, the more money one will earn). We *collected and analyzed the data,* making sure the sample was representative and the data were valid and reliable. Finally, we *developed the conclusion:* the data do support our hypothesis about the influence of education on income.

MODULE 5 | Recap and Review

Summary

Sociologists are committed to the use of the **scientific method** in their research efforts. In this module we examine the basic principles of the scientific method.

1. There are five basic steps in the scientific method: define the problem, review the literature, formulate a hypothesis, collect and analyze data, and develop the conclusion.
2. Whenever researchers wish to study abstract concepts, such as intelligence or prejudice, they must develop workable **operational definitions.**
3. A **hypothesis** states a possible relationship between two or more **variables.**
4. By using a **sample,** sociologists avoid having to test everyone in a population.
5. According to the scientific method, research results must possess both **validity** and **reliability.**

Thinking Critically

1. What might be the effects of a college education on society as a whole? Think of some potential effects on the family, government, and the economy.
2. Suppose that two researchers used different operational definitions for the same term. Could both researchers' results be reliable and valid? Explain your answer.

Key Terms

Causal logic

Control variable

Correlation

Dependent variable

Hypothesis

Independent variable

Operational definition

Random sample

Reliability

Sample

Scientific method

Validity

Variable

What Is Culture?

Culture is the totality of learned, socially transmitted customs, knowledge, material objects, and behavior. It includes the ideas, values, and artifacts (for example, DVDs, comic books, and birth control devices) of groups of people. Patriotic attachment to the flag of the United States is an aspect of culture, as is a national passion for the tango in Argentina.

Sometimes people refer to a particular person as "very cultured" or to a city as having "lots of culture." That use of the term *culture* is different from our use in this textbook. In sociological terms, culture does not refer solely to the fine arts and refined intellectual taste. It consists of *all* objects and ideas within a society, including slang words, ice-cream cones, and rock music. Sociologists consider both a portrait by Rembrandt and the work of graffiti spray painters to be aspects of culture. A tribe that cultivates soil by hand has just as much culture as a people that relies on computer-operated machinery. Each people has a distinctive culture with its own characteristic ways of gathering and preparing food, constructing homes, structuring the family, and promoting standards of right and wrong.

The fact that you share a similar culture with others helps to define the group or society to which you belong. A fairly large number of people are said to constitute a **society** when they live in the same territory, are relatively independent of people outside their area, and participate in a common culture. Metropolitan Los Angeles is more populous than at least 150 nations, yet sociologists do not consider it a society in its own right. Rather, they see it as part of—and dependent on—the larger society of the United States.

A society is the largest form of human group. It consists of people who share a common heritage and culture. Members of the society learn this culture and transmit it from one generation to the next. They even preserve their distinctive culture through literature, art, video recordings, and other means of expression.

Sociologists have long recognized the many ways in which culture influences human behavior. Through what has been termed a tool kit of habits, skills, and styles, people of a common culture construct their acquisition of knowledge, their interactions with kinfolk, their entrance into the job market—in short, the way in which they live. If it were not for the social transmission of culture, each generation would have to reinvent television, not to mention the wheel (Swidler 1986).

Dance, like many other aspects of culture, can be expressed in many different ways. On the left, pop star Christina Aguilera executes the latest moves on tour. On the right, traditional Irish American step dancers perform in a street parade.

Having a common culture also simplifies many day-to-day interactions. For example, when you buy an airline ticket, you know you don't have to bring along hundreds of dollars in cash. You can pay with a credit card. When you are part of a society, you take for granted many small (as well as more important) cultural patterns. You assume that theaters will provide seats for the audience, that physicians will not disclose confidential information, and that parents will be careful when crossing the street with young children. All these assumptions reflect basic values, beliefs, and customs of the culture of the United States.

Today, when text, sound, and video can be transmitted around the world instantaneously, some aspects of culture transcend national borders. The German philosopher Theodor Adorno and others have spoken of the worldwide **culture industry** that standardizes the goods and services demanded by consumers. Adorno contends that globally, the primary effect of popular culture is to limit people's choices. Yet others have shown that the culture industry's influence does not always permeate international borders. Sometimes the culture industry is embraced; at other times, soundly rejected (Adorno [1971] 1991:98–106; Horkheimer and Adorno [1944] 2002).

Cultural Universals

All societies have developed certain common practices and beliefs, known as **cultural universals.** Many cultural universals are, in fact, adaptations to meet essential human needs, such as the need for food, shelter, and clothing. Anthropologist George Murdock (1945:124) compiled a list of cultural universals, including athletic sports, cooking, dancing, visiting, personal names, marriage, medicine, religious ritual, funeral ceremonies, sexual restrictions, and trade.

The cultural practices Murdock listed may be universal, but the manner in which they are expressed varies from culture to culture. For example, one society may let its members choose their marriage partners; another may encourage marriages arranged by the parents.

Not only does the expression of cultural universals vary from one society to another; within a society, it may also change dramatically over time. Each generation, and each year for that matter, most human cultures change and expand.

Ethnocentrism

Many everyday statements reflect our attitude that our culture is best. We use terms such as *underdeveloped, backward,* and *primitive* to refer to other societies. What "we" believe is a religion; what "they" believe is superstition and mythology.

It is tempting to evaluate the practices of other cultures on the basis of our perspectives. Sociologist William Graham Sumner (1906) coined the term **ethnocentrism** to refer to the tendency to assume that one's culture and way of life represent the norm or are superior to all others. The ethnocentric person sees his or her group as the center or defining point of culture and view all other cultures as deviations from what is "normal." Westerners who think cattle are to be used for food might look down on India's Hindu religion and culture, which view the cow as sacred. Or people in one culture may dismiss as unthinkable the mate selection or child-rearing practices of another culture. In sum, our view of the world is dramatically influenced by the society in which we were raised.

Ethnocentric value judgments have complicated U.S. efforts at democratic reform of the Iraqi government. Before the 2003 war in Iraq, U.S. planners had assumed that Iraqis would adapt to a new form of government in the same way the Germans and Japanese did following World War II. But in the Iraqi culture, unlike the German and Japanese cultures, loyalty to the family and the extended clan comes before patriotism and the common good. In a country in which almost half of all people, even those in the cities, marry a first or second cousin, citizens are predisposed to favor their kin in government and business dealings. Why trust a stranger from outside the family? What Westerners would criticize as nepotism, then, is actually an acceptable, even admirable, practice to Iraqis (J. Tierney 2003).

Conflict theorists point out that ethnocentric value judgments serve to devalue groups and to deny equal opportunities. Functionalists, on the other hand, point out that ethnocentrism serves to maintain a sense of solidarity by promoting group pride. Denigrating other nations and cultures can enhance our patriotic feelings and belief that our way of life is superior. Yet this type of social stability is established at the expense of other peoples. In extreme cases, ethnocentrism can lead to the destruction of an entire culture. The Sociology in the Global Community box describes several instances of what social scientists have termed *cultural genocide.*

Ethnocentrism is hardly limited to citizens of the United States. Visitors from many African cultures are surprised at the disrespect that children in the United States show their parents. People from India may be repelled by our practice of living in the same household with dogs and cats. Many Islamic fundamentalists in the Arab world and Asia view the United States as corrupt, decadent, and doomed to destruction. All these people may feel comforted by membership in cultures that in their view are superior to ours.

Culture and the Dominant Ideology

Functionalist and conflict theorists agree that culture and society are mutually supportive, but for different reasons. Functionalists maintain that social stability requires a consensus and the support of society's members; strong central values and common norms provide that support. This view of culture became popular in sociology beginning in the 1950s. It was borrowed from British anthropologists who saw cultural traits as a stabilizing element in a culture. From a functionalist perspective, a cultural trait or practice will persist if it performs functions that society seems to need or contributes to overall social stability and consensus.

Conflict theorists agree that a common culture may exist, but they argue that it serves to maintain the privileges of certain groups. Moreover, while protecting their self-interest, powerful groups may keep others in a subservient position. The term **dominant ideology** describes the set of cultural beliefs and practices that helps to maintain powerful social, economic, and political interests. This concept was first used by Hungarian Marxist Georg

Sociology in the Global Community

Cultural Genocide

Usually, the term **genocide** refers to the deliberate, systematic killing of an entire people or nation. However, social scientists have long recognized another form of genocide, called *cultural genocide,* in which a nation's culture is eliminated even though the people live on.

Formally defined, **cultural genocide** refers to the systematic destruction of a group's culture. Social scientists have used the term to describe one nation's efforts to suppress another nation's language. Japan's attempt to eliminate the Korean people's language, history, and even names during its occupation of Korea in the early 20th century is one example. However, the term also applies to government efforts to eliminate indigenous people's traditions. Australia, Canada, New Zealand, and the United States illustrate this second form of cultural genocide.

> Agents of the U.S. government took American Indian children from their parents' homes and sent them to be raised in families far from their native culture.

In the United States, government officials encouraged White families to "adopt" indigenous children and raise them in the dominant culture. Agents of the U.S. government took American Indian children from their parents' homes and sent them to be raised in families far from their native culture. Sometimes the children were removed with their parents' permission, but often they were taken against their parents' will. Government officials assumed that the supposed benefit of familiarizing the children with the dominant culture would outweigh and ultimately excuse the personal and cultural losses the children experienced.

Inevitably, the forced removal of generations of American Indian children from their families led to the near extinction of their culture. Only in 1968, following political pressure by Native Americans, did Congress call a halt to the program. Under the Indian Child Welfare Act (ICWA), even if a family agrees to a child's removal from the home, the tribe must also agree. In placing children for adoption and foster care, social workers must give priority first to the child's extended family, then to members of the child's tribe, and finally to all American Indian families.

In Australia, too, thousands of Aboriginal children were forcibly removed from their families so they could be raised by Whites. From 1910 to 1970, the government program affected 10 to 30 percent of all Aboriginal children. Only in 2008 did the Australian government express regret for the removal to members of the "Stolen Generations." Today, the Australian government is committed to improving the living conditions and future prospects of all Aboriginals.

LET'S DISCUSS

1. Can you imagine being taken from your parents' home by a government agent and moved to a different family with a different culture? How would you react?

2. What might be the long-term consequences of American Indian children's removal from their families, besides the destruction of their culture?

Sources: Cantzler 2008; National Indian Child Welfare Association 2010; R. Schaefer 2008a.

Lukacs (1923) and Italian Marxist Antonio Gramsci (1929), but it did not gain an audience in the United States until the early 1970s. In Karl Marx's view, a capitalist society has a dominant ideology that serves the interests of the ruling class.

From a conflict perspective, the dominant ideology has major social significance. Not only do a society's most powerful groups and institutions control wealth and property; even more important, they control the means of producing beliefs about reality through religion, education, and the media. Feminists would also argue that if all a society's most important institutions tell women they should be subservient to men, that dominant ideology will help to control women and keep them in a subordinate position.

A growing number of social scientists believe that it is not easy to identify a core culture in the United States. For support, they point to the lack of consensus on national values, the diffusion of cultural traits, and diversity within our culture. Yet there is no way of denying that certain expressions of values have greater influence than others, even in as complex a society as the United States.

Cultural Relativism

While ethnocentrism means evaluating foreign cultures using the familiar culture of the observer as a standard of correct behavior, **cultural relativism** means viewing people's behavior from the perspective of their culture. It places a priority on understanding other cultures, rather than dismissing them as "strange" or "exotic." Unlike ethnocentrists, cultural relativists employ the kind of value neutrality in scientific study that Max Weber saw as so important.

Cultural relativism stresses that different social contexts give rise to different norms and values. Thus, we must examine

FIGURE 9-1 **Countries with High Child Marriage Rates**

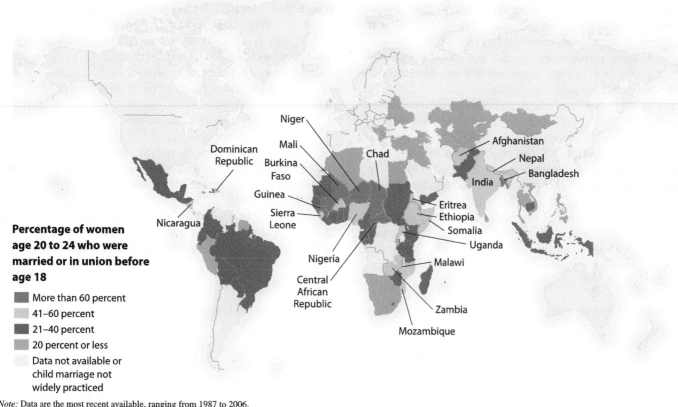

Percentage of women age 20 to 24 who were married or in union before age 18

- More than 60 percent
- 41–60 percent
- 21–40 percent
- 20 percent or less
- Data not available or child marriage not widely practiced

Note: Data are the most recent available, ranging from 1987 to 2006.
Source: UNICEF 2010.

In 21 countries, 40 percent or more of the women under 18 are married.

practices such as polygamy, bullfighting, and monarchy within the particular contexts of the cultures in which they are found. Although cultural relativism does not suggest that we must unquestioningly accept every cultural variation, it does require a serious and unbiased effort to evaluate norms, values, and customs in light of their distinctive culture.

Consider the practice of children marrying adults. Most people in North America cannot fathom the idea of a 12-year-old girl marrying. The custom, which is illegal in the United States, is common in West Africa and South Asia. Should the United States respect such marriages? The apparent answer is no. In 2006 the U.S. government spent $623 million to discourage the practice in many of the countries with the highest child-marriage rates (Figure 9-1).

From the perspective of cultural relativism, we might ask whether one society should spend its resources to dictate the norms of another. However, federal officials have defended the government's actions. They contend that child marriage deprives girls of education, threatens their health, and weakens public health efforts to combat HIV/AIDS (Jain and Kurz 2007; B. Slavin 2007).

Sociobiology and Culture

While sociology emphasizes diversity and change in the expression of culture, another school of thought, sociobiology, stresses the universal aspects of culture. **Sociobiology** is the systematic study of how biology affects human social behavior. Sociobiologists assert that many of the cultural traits humans display, such as the almost universal expectation that women will be nurturers and men will be providers, are not learned but are rooted in our genetic makeup.

Sociobiology is founded on the naturalist Charles Darwin's (1859) theory of evolution. In traveling the world, Darwin had noted small variations in species—in the shape of a bird's beak, for example—from one location to another. He theorized that over hundreds of generations, random variations in genetic makeup had helped certain members of a species to survive in a particular environment. A bird with a differently shaped beak might have been better at gathering seeds than other birds, for instance. In reproducing, these lucky individuals had passed on their advantageous genes to succeeding generations. Eventually, given their advantage in survival, individuals with the variation began to outnumber other members of the species. The species was slowly adapting to its environment. Darwin called this process of adaptation to the environment through random genetic variation *natural selection.*

Sociobiologists apply Darwin's principle of natural selection to the study of social behavior. They assume that particular forms of behavior become genetically linked to a species if they contribute to its fitness to survive (van den Berghe 1978). In its extreme form, sociobiology suggests that *all* behavior is the result of genetic or biological factors and that social interactions play no role in shaping people's conduct.

Sociobiologists do not seek to describe individual behavior on the level of "Why is Fred more aggressive than Jim?" Rather, they focus on how human nature is affected by the genetic composition of a *group* of people who share certain characteristics (such as men or women, or members of isolated tribal bands). In general, sociobiologists have stressed the basic genetic heritage that *all* humans share and have shown little interest in speculating about alleged differences between racial groups or nationalities. A few researchers have tried to trace specific behaviors, like criminal activity, to certain genetic markers, but those markers are not deterministic. Family cohesiveness, peer group behavior,

and other social factors can override genetic influences on behavior (Guo et al. 2008; E. Wilson 1975, 1978).

Some researchers insist that intellectual interest in sociobiology will only deflect serious study of the more significant influence on human behavior, the social environment. Yet Lois Wladis Hoffman (1985), in her presidential address to the Society for the Psychological Study of Social Issues, argued that sociobiology poses a valuable challenge to social scientists to better document their research. Interactionists, for example, could show how social behavior is not programmed by human biology, but instead adjusts continually to the attitudes and responses of others.

Certainly most social scientists would agree that there is a biological basis for social behavior. But there is less support for the extreme positions taken by certain advocates of sociobiology. Like interactionists, conflict theorists and functionalists believe that people's behavior rather than their genetic structure defines social reality. Conflict theorists fear that the sociobiological approach could be used as an argument against efforts to assist disadvantaged people, such as schoolchildren who are not competing successfully (Freese 2008; Machalek and Marten 2010; E. Wilson 2000).

MODULE 9 | Recap and Review

Summary

Culture is the totality of learned, socially transmitted customs, knowledge, material objects, and behavior. This module examines the social practices common to all cultures.

1. A shared culture helps to define the group or **society** to which we belong.

2. Anthropologist George Murdock compiled a list of **cultural universals,** or common practices found in every culture, including marriage, sports, cooking, medicine, and sexual restrictions.

3. People who assume their own culture is superior to other cultures engage in **ethnocentricism.** In contrast, **cultural relativism** is the practice of viewing other people's behavior from the perspective of their own culture.

4. The **dominant ideology** of a culture is the set of cultural beliefs and practices that help to maintain powerful social, economic, and political interests.

Thinking Critically

1. Select three cultural universals from George Murdock's list and analyze them from a functionalist perspective. Why are these practices found in every culture? What functions do they serve?

2. Do you think the United States has a dominant ideology? If so, how would you describe it? Whose interests does it serve?

Key Terms

Cultural genocide

Cultural relativism

Cultural universal

Culture

Culture industry

Dominant ideology

Ethnocentrism

Genocide

Society

Sociobiology

11 Cultural Variation

Each culture has a unique character. Inuit tribes in northern Canada, wrapped in furs and dieting on whale blubber, have little in common with farmers in Southeast Asia, who dress for the heat and subsist mainly on the rice they grow in their paddies. Cultures adapt to meet specific sets of circumstances, such as climate, level of technology, population, and geography. Thus, despite the presence of cultural universals such as courtship and religion, great diversity exists among the world's many cultures. Moreover, even *within* a single nation, certain segments of the populace develop cultural patterns that differ from the patterns of the dominant society.

Subcultures

Rodeo riders, residents of a retirement community, workers on an offshore oil rig—all are examples of what sociologists refer to as *subcultures*. A **subculture** is a segment of society that shares a distinctive pattern of customs, rules, and traditions that differs from the pattern of the larger society. In a sense, a subculture can be thought of as a culture existing within a larger, dominant culture. The existence of many subcultures is characteristic of complex societies such as the United States.

Members of a subculture participate in the dominant culture while at the same time engaging in unique and distinctive forms of behavior. Frequently, a subculture will develop an **argot,** or specialized language, that distinguishes it from the wider society. Athletes who play *parkour,* an extreme sport that combines forward running with fence leaping and the vaulting of walls, water barriers, and even moving cars, speak an argot they devised especially to describe their feats. Parkour runners talk about doing *King Kong vaults*—diving arms first over a wall or grocery cart and landing in a standing position. They may follow this maneuver with a *tic tac*—kicking off a wall to overcome some kind of obstacle (Wilkinson 2007).

Such argot allows insiders—the members of the subculture—to understand words with special meanings. It also establishes patterns of communication that outsiders can't understand. Sociologists associated with the interactionist perspective emphasize that language and symbols offer a powerful way for a subculture to feel cohesive and maintain its identity.

In India, a new subculture has developed among employees at the international call centers established by multinational corporations. To serve customers in the United States and Europe, the young men and women who work there must be fluent speakers of English. But the corporations that employ them demand more than proficiency in a foreign language; they expect their Indian employees to adopt Western values and work habits, including the grueling pace U.S. workers take for granted. In return they offer perks such as Western-style dinners, dances, and coveted consumer goods. Significantly, they allow employees to take the day off only on U.S. holidays, like Labor Day and Thanksgiving—not on Indian holidays like Diwali, the Hindu festival of lights. While most Indian families are home celebrating, call center employees see only each other; when they have the day off, no one else is free to socialize with them. As a result, these employees have formed a tight-knit subculture based on hard work and a taste for Western luxury goods and leisure-time pursuits.

Increasingly, call center workers are the object of criticism from Indians who live a more conventional lifestyle centered on family and holiday traditions. In response to such negative public opinion, the government of the Indian state where call centers are located has banned schools from teaching English rather than Kannada, the local language. Beginning in 2008, some 300,000 students were affected by the ban (Chu 2007; Kalita 2006).

Another shared characteristic among some employees at Indian call centers is their contempt for the callers they serve. In performing their monotonous, repetitive job day after day, hundreds of thousands of these workers have come to see the faceless Americans they deal with as slow, often rude customers. As described in the recent Indian bestseller *One Night @ the Call Centre,* new trainees quickly learn the "35 = 10 rule," meaning that a 35-year-old American's IQ is the same as a 10-year-old Indian's. Such shared understandings underpin this emerging subculture (Bhagat 2007; Gentleman 2006).

Functionalist and conflict theorists agree that variation exists within cultures. Functionalists view subcultures as variations of particular social environments and as evidence that differences can exist within a common culture. However, conflict theorists suggest that variations often reflect the inequality of social arrangements within a society. A conflict theorist would view the challenges to dominant social norms by African American activists, the feminist movement, and the disability rights movement as reflections of inequity based on race, gender, and disability status. Conflict theorists also argue that subcultures sometimes emerge when the dominant society unsuccessfully tries to suppress a practice, such as the use of illegal drugs.

Employees of an international call center in India socialize after their shift has ended. Call center employees, whose odd working hours isolate them from others, tend to form tight-knit subcultures.

more humanistic values, such as sharing, love, and coexistence with the environment. As a political force, this subculture opposed the United States' involvement in the war in Vietnam and encouraged draft resistance (Flacks 1971; Roszak 1969).

When a subculture conspicuously and deliberately opposes certain aspects of the larger culture, it is known as a **counterculture.** Countercultures typically thrive among the young, who have the least investment in the existing culture. In most cases, a 20-year-old can adjust to new cultural standards more easily than someone who has spent 60 years following the patterns of the dominant culture (Zellner 1995).

In the wake of the terrorist attacks of September 11, 2001, people around the country learned of the existence of terrorist groups operating as a counterculture within the United States. This was a situation that generations have lived with in Northern Ireland, Israel and the Palestinian territory, and many other parts of the world. But terrorist cells are not necessarily fueled only by outsiders. Frequently people become disenchanted with the policies of their own country, and a few take very violent steps.

Culture Shock

Anyone who feels disoriented, uncertain, out of place, or even fearful when immersed in an unfamiliar culture may be experiencing **culture shock.** For example, a resident of the United States who visits certain areas in China and wants local meat for dinner may be stunned to learn that the specialty is dog meat. Similarly, someone from a strict Islamic culture may be shocked by the comparatively provocative dress styles and open displays of affection common in the United States and various European cultures.

All of us, to some extent, take for granted the cultural practices of our society. As a result, it can be surprising and even disturbing to realize that other cultures do not follow our way of life. The fact is, customs that seem strange to us may be considered normal and proper in other cultures, which may see our customs as odd.

"IT'S ENDLESS. WE JOIN A COUNTER-CULTURE; IT BECOMES THE CULTURE. WE JOIN ANOTHER COUNTER-CULTURE; IT BECOMES THE CULTURE..."

Cultures change. Fashions we once regarded as unacceptable—such as men wearing earrings and people wearing jeans in the workplace—or associated with fringe groups—such as men and women with tattoos—are now widely accepted. These countercultural practices have been absorbed by mainstream culture.

Countercultures

By the end of the 1960s, an extensive subculture had emerged in the United States, composed of young people turned off by a society they believed was too materialistic and technological. This group included primarily political radicals and hippies who had dropped out of mainstream social institutions. These young men and women rejected the pressure to accumulate cars, homes, and an endless array of material goods. Instead, they expressed a desire to live in a culture based on

use your **sociological imagination**

You arrive in a developing African country as a Peace Corps volunteer. What aspects of a very different culture do you think would be the hardest to adjust to? What might the citizens of that country find shocking about your culture?

Summary

Each human culture has unique characteristics that evolve to meet specific circumstances of climate, geography, technological development, and population.

1. A **subculture** is a small culture that exists within a larger, dominant culture. **Countercultures** are subcultures that deliberately oppose aspects of the larger culture.

2. A person who becomes immersed in an unfamiliar culture may experience **culture shock.**

Thinking Critically

1. To what subcultures do you belong? How do they function in relation to the larger society?

2. Why do people experience culture shock? What does this phenomenon reveal about the role of culture and of everyday customs?

Key Terms

Argot

Counterculture

Culture shock

Subculture

Language

Language is one of the major elements of culture that underlie cultural variations. It is also an important component of cultural capital. Recall from Module 2 that Pierre Bourdieu used the term *cultural capital* to describe noneconomic assets, such as family background and past educational investments, which are reflected in a person's knowledge of language and the arts.

Members of a society generally share a common language, which facilitates day-to-day exchanges with others. When you ask a hardware store clerk for a flashlight, you don't need to draw a picture of the instrument. You share the same cultural term for a small, portable, battery-operated light. However, if you were in England and needed this item, you would have to ask for an electric torch. Of course, even within the same society, a term can have a number of different meanings. In the United States, *pot* signifies both a container that is used for cooking and an intoxicating drug. In this section we will examine the cultural influence of language, which includes both the written and spoken word and nonverbal communication.

Language: Written and Spoken

Seven thousand languages are spoken in the world today—many more than the number of countries. Within a nation's political boundaries, the number of languages spoken may range from only one (as in North Korea) to several hundred (as in Papua New Guinea, with 820). For the speakers of each one, whether they number 2,000 or 200 million, language is fundamental to their shared culture (Raymond Gordon 2005).

The English language, for example, makes extensive use of words dealing with war. We speak of "conquering" space, "fighting" the "battle" of the budget, "waging war" on drugs, making a "killing" on the stock market, and "bombing" an examination; something monumental or great is "the bomb." An observer from an entirely different and warless culture could gauge the importance that war and the military have had in our lives simply by recognizing the prominence that militaristic terms have in our language. As another example, in the Old West, words such as *gelding, stallion, mare, piebald,* and *sorrel* were all commonly used to describe one animal—the horse. Even if we knew little of that period in history, we could conclude from the list of terms that horses were important to the culture. Similarly, the Sami people of northern Norway and Sweden have a rich diversity of terms for snow, ice, and reindeer (Haviland et al. 2008; Magga 2006).

Language is, in fact, the foundation of every culture. **Language** is an abstract system of word meanings and symbols for all aspects of culture. It includes speech, written characters, numerals, symbols, and nonverbal gestures and expressions. Because language is the foundation of every culture, the ability to speak other languages is crucial to intercultural relations. Throughout the Cold War era, beginning in the 1950s and continuing well into the 1970s, the U.S. government encouraged the study of Russian by developing special language schools for diplomats and military advisers who dealt with the Soviet Union. And following September 11, 2001, the nation recognized how few skilled translators it had for Arabic and other languages spoken in Muslim countries. Language quickly became a key, not only to tracking potential terrorists, but to building diplomatic

trend|spotting

Linguistic Isolation

In 2006, a severe winter storm hit the northwest United States, knocking out electrical power in many communities. Residents turned on their generators, some without heeding warnings about the risk of carbon monoxide poisoning. Although local media ran public service announcements about the need for adequate ventilation of the generators, six people died and several others fell ill from exposure to carbon monoxide. Investigators later determined that the victims had been unable to understand the English-only warnings. In response to the discovery, the *Seattle Times* took the unprecedented step of publishing the front-page story in six languages: English, Vietnamese, Chinese, Spanish, Russian, and Somali.

Although most immigrants can communicate effectively in English, language does isolate a small percentage of them. Social scientists use the term *linguistic isolation* to refer to households in which all members age 14 and older speak a non-English language and at the same time do not speak English very well. They have found that the proportion of the U.S. population that is linguistically isolated has been increasing steadily, from 3.2 percent in 2000 to 8.6 percent in 2008.

Studies show that those who are linguistically isolated are cut off from many public services. For example, public health professionals find that even after controlling for education and income, members of linguistically isolated households are less likely than others to receive adequate health care, or even to participate in basic health screening. And as the 2006 power outage in the Northwest showed, in some cases linguistic isolation can be deadly.

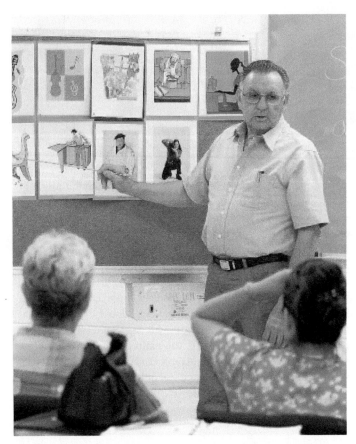

A native speaker trains instructors from the Oneida Nation of New York in the Berlitz method of language teaching. Many Native American tribes are taking steps to recover their seldom-used languages, realizing that language is the essential foundation of any culture. Their efforts are helping to reverse the cultural genocide they endured in the past.

Their effort to change the Navajo language, not easy in itself, is complicated by the Navajo belief that to talk about the disease is to bring it on one's people (Fonseca 2008).

Similarly, feminists have noted that gender-related language can reflect—although in itself it does not determine—the traditional acceptance of men and women in certain occupations. Each time we use a term such as *mailman, policeman,* or *fireman,* we are implying (especially to young children) that these occupations can be filled only by males. Yet many women work as *mail carriers, police officers,* and *firefighters*—a fact that is being increasingly recognized and legitimized through the use of such nonsexist language.

Language can also transmit stereotypes related to race. Look up the meanings of the adjective *black* in dictionaries published in the United States. You will find *dismal, gloomy or forbidding, destitute of moral light or goodness, atrocious, evil, threatening, clouded with anger.* In contrast, dictionaries list *pure* and *innocent* among the meanings of the adjective *white.* Through such patterns of language, our culture reinforces positive associations with the term (and skin color) *white* and negative associations with *black.* Is it surprising, then, that a list meant to prevent people from working in a profession is called a *blacklist,* while a lie that we think of as somewhat acceptable is called a *white lie?*

Language can shape how we see, taste, smell, feel, and hear. It also influences the way we think about the people, ideas, and objects around us. Language communicates a culture's most important norms, values, and sanctions. That's why the decline of an old language or the introduction of a new one is such a sensitive issue in many parts of the world (see the Social Policy section at the end of this module).

bridges with Muslim countries willing to help in the war against terrorism.

Language does more than simply describe reality; it also serves to *shape* the reality of a culture. For example, most people in the United States cannot easily make the verbal distinctions concerning snow and ice that are possible in the Sami culture. As a result, they are less likely to notice such differences.

The **Sapir-Whorf hypothesis,** named for two linguists, describes the role of language in shaping our interpretation of reality. According to Sapir and Whorf, because people can conceptualize the world only through language, language *precedes* thought. Thus, the word symbols and grammar of a language organize the world for us. The Sapir-Whorf hypothesis also holds that language is not a given. Rather, it is culturally determined, and it encourages a distinctive interpretation of reality by focusing our attention on certain phenomena (Sapir 1929).

For decades, the Navajo have referred to cancer as *lood doo na'dziihii.* Now, through a project funded by the National Cancer Institute, the tribal college is seeking to change the phrase. Why? Literally, the phrase means "the sore that does not heal," and health educators are concerned that tribal members who have been diagnosed with cancer view it as a death sentence.

Nonverbal Communication

If you don't like the way a meeting is going, you might suddenly sit back, fold your arms, and turn down the corners of your mouth. When you see a friend in tears, you may give a quick hug. After winning a big game, you probably high-five your teammates. These are all examples of *nonverbal communication,* the use of gestures, facial expressions, and other visual images to communicate.

We are not born with these expressions. We learn them, just as we learn other forms of language, from people who share our same culture. This statement is as true for the basic expressions of happiness and sadness as it is for more complex emotions, such as shame or distress (Fridlund et al. 1987).

Like other forms of language, nonverbal communication is not the same in all cultures. For example, sociological research done at the micro level documents that people from various cultures differ in the degree to which they touch others during the course of normal social interactions. Even experienced travelers are sometimes caught off guard by these differences. In Saudi Arabia, a middle-aged man may want to hold hands with a partner after closing a business deal. In Egypt, men walk hand in hand in the street; in cafés, they fall asleep while lounging in each other's arms. These gestures, which would shock an American businessman, are considered compliments in those cultures.

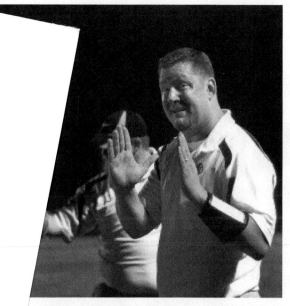

...al communication, a football coach discusses a play with his ...pions and the pride of the Alabama School for the Deaf, have

They also have a collective idea of what is good and desirable in life—or not. In this section we will learn to distinguish between the closely related concepts of norms and values.

Norms

Norms are the established standards of behavior maintained by a society. For a norm to become significant, it must be widely shared and understood. For example, in movie theaters in the United States, we typically expect that people will be quiet while the film is shown. Of course, the application of this norm can vary, depending on the particular film and type of audience. People who are viewing a serious artistic film will be more likely to insist on the norm of silence than those who are watching a slapstick comedy or horror movie.

...other form of nonverbal ...one culture to the next. In ...sidered rude (Passero 2002;

...ion is the use of symbols to ...ols are the gestures, objects, and words ... human communication. The thumbs-up gesture, a gold ... ...ker, and the smiley face in an e-mail are all symbols. Often deceptively simple, many symbols are rich in meaning and may not convey the same meaning in all social contexts. Around someone's neck, for example, a cross can symbolize religious reverence; over a grave site, a belief in everlasting life; or set in flames, racial hatred.

Some symbols or gestures, such as the basic emotional expressions—a smile, a look of horror—may be close to universal. Not long ago, a team of linguists, social scientists, and physical scientists collaborated on a system for communicating with those who live thousands of years from now, long after people have ceased to speak our languages. The challenge was to create a series of signs and explanations that would warn future generations of the dangers posed by the Waste Isolation Pilot Plant (WIPP), a nuclear waste repository in New Mexico. For the next few centuries, warning signs engraved in English, Spanish, Russian, French, Chinese, Arabic, and Navajo will alert those in the area to the presence of the underground dump, which will remain highly radioactive for at least 10,000 years. But the signs also include pictographs that researchers hope will be understandable to people who live millennia from now, no matter what their language (Figure 12-1; Department of Energy 2004; Piller 2006).

Norms and Values

"Wash your hands before dinner." "Thou shalt not kill." "Respect your elders." All societies have ways of encouraging and enforcing what they view as appropriate behavior while discouraging and punishing what they consider to be inappropriate behavior.

One persistent social norm in contemporary society is that of heterosexuality. Children are socialized to accept this norm from a very young age. Overwhelmingly, parents describe adult romantic relationships to their children exclusively as heterosexual relationships. That is not necessarily because they consider same-sex relationships unacceptable, but more likely because they see heterosexuality as the norm in marital partnerships. According to a national survey of mothers of 3- to 6-year-olds, one in five mothers teaches her young children that homosexuality is wrong. The same survey showed that parenting reflects

FIGURE 12-1 **A Timeless Alert**

The symbols on this subsurface marker at the Waste Isolation Pilot Plant in New Mexico are an attempt to communicate the presence of hazardous waste to people who may live 10,000 years from now. Would these symbols convince you not to dig? Might future generations misinterpret them?

the dominant ideology, in which homosexuality is treated as a rare exception. Most parents assume that their children are heterosexual; only one in four had even considered whether his or her child might grow up to be gay or lesbian (K. Martin 2009).

Types of Norms Sociologists distinguish between norms in two ways. First, norms are classified as either formal or informal. **Formal norms** generally have been written down and specify strict punishments for violators. In the United States, we often formalize norms into laws, which are very precise in defining proper and improper behavior. Sociologist Donald Black (1995) has termed **law** "governmental social control," meaning that laws are formal norms enforced by the state. Laws are just one example of formal norms. The requirements for a college major and the rules of a card game are also considered formal norms.

In contrast, **informal norms** are generally understood but not precisely recorded. Standards of proper dress are a common example of informal norms. Our society has no specific punishment or sanction for a person who comes to school, say, wearing a monkey suit. Making fun of the nonconforming student is usually the most likely response.

Norms are also classified by their relative importance to society. When classified in this way, they are known as *mores* and *folkways*. **Mores** (pronounced "MOR-ays") are norms deemed highly necessary to the welfare of a society, often because they embody the most cherished principles of a people. Each society demands obedience to its mores; violation can lead to severe penalties. Thus, the United States has strong mores against murder, treason, and child abuse, which have been institutionalized into formal norms.

Folkways are norms governing everyday behavior. Folkways play an important role in shaping the daily behavior of members of a culture. Society is less likely to formalize folkways than mores, and their violation raises comparatively little concern. For example, walking up a down escalator in a department store challenges our standards of appropriate behavior, but it will not result in a fine or a jail sentence.

In many societies around the world, folkways exist to reinforce patterns of male dominance. Various folkways reveal men's hierarchical position above women within the traditional Buddhist areas of Southeast Asia. In the sleeping cars of trains, women do not sleep in upper berths above men. Hospitals that house men on the first floor do not place women patients on the second floor. Even on clotheslines, folkways dictate male dominance: women's attire is hung lower than that of men (Bulle 1987).

In Iraq, a female member of the U.S. Army searches a covered Muslim woman. The searches, which are necessary to prevent terrorist attacks, violate a Muslim norm that forbids touching by strangers.

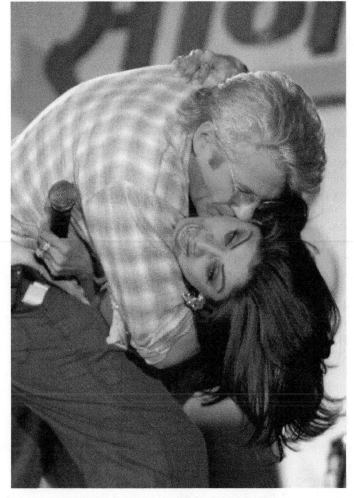

When is a kiss more than a kiss? In India, public displays of affection are decidedly not the norm, even among movie stars. When Richard Gere swept actress Shilpa Shethy into his arms at an AIDS awareness event, protests erupted, and some outraged onlookers demanded that he be sanctioned.

💡 use your **sociological imagination**

You are a high school principal. What norms would you want to govern the students' behavior? How might those norms differ from norms appropriate for college students?

Acceptance of Norms People do not follow norms, whether mores or folkways, in all situations. In some cases, they can evade a norm because they know it is weakly enforced. It is illegal for U.S. teenagers to drink alcoholic beverages, yet drinking by minors is common throughout the nation. (In fact, teenage alcoholism is a serious social problem.)

In some instances, behavior that appears to violate society's norms may actually represent adherence to the norms of a particular group. Teenage drinkers are conforming to the standards of their peer group when they violate norms that condemn underage drinking. Similarly, business executives who use shady accounting techniques may be responding to a corporate culture that demands the maximization of profits at any cost, including the deception of investors and government regulatory agencies.

Norms are violated in some instances because one norm conflicts with another. For example, suppose that you live in an apartment building and one night hear the screams of the woman next door, who is being beaten by her husband. If you decide to intervene by ringing their doorbell or calling the police, you are violating the norm of minding your own business, while at the same time following the norm of assisting a victim of violence.

Even if norms do not conflict, there are always exceptions to any norm. The same action, under different circumstances, can cause one to be viewed as either a hero or a villain. Secretly taping telephone conversations is normally considered illegal and abhorrent. However, it can be done with a court order to obtain valid evidence for a criminal trial. We would heap praise on a government agent who used such methods to convict an organized crime figure. In our culture, we tolerate killing another human being in self-defense, and we actually reward killing in warfare.

Acceptance of norms is subject to change as the political, economic, and social conditions of a culture are transformed. Until the 1960s, for example, formal norms throughout much of the United States prohibited the marriage of people from different racial groups. Over the past half century, however, such legal prohibitions were cast aside. The process of change can be seen today in the increasing acceptance of single parents and growing support for the legalization of marriage between same-sex couples (see Module 42).

When circumstances require the sudden violation of long-standing cultural norms, the change can upset an entire population. In Iraq, where Muslim custom strictly forbids touching by strangers for men and especially for women, the war that began in 2003 has brought numerous daily violations of the norm. Outside important mosques, government offices, and other facilities likely to be targeted by terrorists, visitors must now be patted down and have their bags searched by Iraqi security guards. To reduce the discomfort caused by the procedure, women are searched by female guards and men by male guards. Despite that concession, and the fact that many Iraqis admit or even insist on the need for such measures, people still wince at the invasion of their personal privacy. In reaction to the searches, Iraqi women have begun to limit the contents of the bags they carry or simply to leave them at home (Rubin 2003).

Sanctions

Suppose a football coach sends a 12th player onto the field. Imagine a college graduate showing up in shorts for a job interview at a large bank. Or consider a driver who neglects to put any money into a parking meter. These people have violated widely shared and understood norms. So what happens? In each of these situations, the person will receive sanctions if his or her behavior is detected.

Sanctions are penalties and rewards for conduct concerning a social norm. Note that the concept of *reward* is included in this definition. Conformity to a norm can lead to positive sanctions such as a pay raise, a medal, a word of gratitude, or a pat on the

Table **12-1** Norms and Sanctions

Norms	Sanctions	
	Positive	Negative
Formal	Salary bonus	Demotion
	Testimonial dinner	Firing from a job
	Medal	Jail sentence
	Diploma	Expulsion
Informal	Smile	Frown
	Compliment	Humiliation
	Cheers	Bullying

back. Negative sanctions include fines, threats, imprisonment, and stares of contempt.

Table 12-1 summarizes the relationship between norms and sanctions. As you can see, the sanctions that are associated with formal norms (which are written down and codified) tend to be formal as well. If a college coach sends too many players onto the field, the team will be penalized 15 yards. The driver who fails to put money in the parking meter will receive a ticket and have to pay a fine. But sanctions for violations of informal norms can vary. The college graduate who goes to the bank interview in shorts will probably lose any chance of getting the job; on the other hand, he or she might be so brilliant that bank officials will overlook the unconventional attire.

The entire fabric of norms and sanctions in a culture reflects that culture's values and priorities. The most cherished values will be most heavily sanctioned; matters regarded as less critical will carry light and informal sanctions.

Values

Though we each have a personal set of values—which may include caring or fitness or success in business—we also share a general set of values as members of a society. Cultural **values** are these collective conceptions of what is considered good, desirable, and proper—or bad, undesirable, and improper—in a culture. They indicate what people in a given culture prefer as well as what they find important and morally right (or wrong). Values may be specific, such as honoring one's parents and owning a home, or they may be more general, such as health, love, and democracy. Of course, the members of a society do not uniformly share its values. Angry political debates and billboards promoting conflicting causes tell us that much.

Values influence people's behavior and serve as criteria for evaluating the actions of others. The values, norms, and sanctions of a culture are often directly related. For example, if a culture places a high value on the institution of marriage, it may have norms (and strict sanctions) that prohibit the act of adultery or make divorce difficult. If a culture views private property as a basic value, it will probably have stiff laws against theft and vandalism.

The values of a culture may change, but most remain relatively stable during any one person's lifetime. Socially shared, intensely felt values are a fundamental part of our lives in the United States. Sociologist Robin Williams (1970) has offered a list of basic values. It includes achievement, efficiency, material comfort, nationalism, equality, and the supremacy of science and reason over faith. Obviously, not all 309 million people in this country agree on all these values, but such a list serves as a starting point in defining the national character.

Each year more than 219,864 entering college students at 297 of the nation's four-year colleges fill out a questionnaire about their attitudes. Because this survey focuses on an array of issues, beliefs, and life goals, it is commonly cited as a barometer of the nation's values. The respondents are asked what values are personally important to them. Over the past 40 years, the value of "being very well-off financially" has shown the strongest gain in popularity; the proportion of first-year college students who endorse this value as "essential" or "very important" rose from 44 percent in 1967 to 78.1 percent in 2009 (Figure 12-2). In contrast, the value that has shown the most striking decline in endorsement by students is "developing a meaningful philosophy of life." While this value was the most popular in the 1967 survey, endorsed by more than 80 percent

FIGURE 12-2 **Life Goals of First-Year College Students in the United States, 1966–2009**

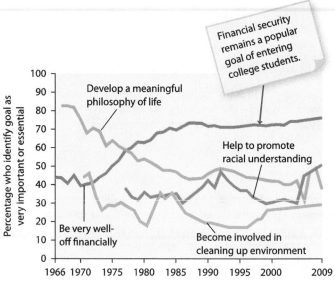

Sources: UCLA Higher Education Research Institute, as reported in Astin et al. 1994; Pryor et al. 2007, 2009.

Think about It

Why do you think values have shifted among college students in the past few decades? Which of these values is important to you?

of the respondents, it had fallen to seventh place on the list by 2009, when it was endorsed by 48.0 percent of students entering college.

During the 1980s and 1990s, support for values having to do with money, power, and status grew. At the same time, support for certain values having to do with social awareness and altruism, such as "helping others," declined. According to the 2009 nationwide survey, only 42.1 percent of first-year college students stated that "influencing social values" was an "essential" or "very important" goal. The proportion of students for whom "helping to promote racial understanding" was an essential or very important goal reached a record high of 42 percent in 1992, then fell to 33.1 in 2009—a decline from 2008, the year the nation elected Barack Obama president. Like other aspects of culture, such as language and norms, a nation's values are not necessarily fixed.

FIGURE 12-3 **Torture Values by Country**

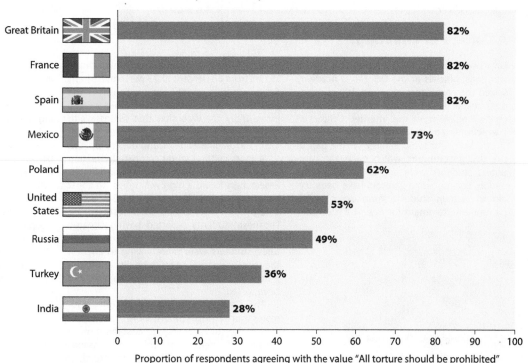

Source: World Public Opinion 2008.

Whether the slogan is "Plant a Tree" or "Think Green," students have been exposed to values associated with environmentalism. How many of them accept those values? Poll results over the past 40 years show fluctuations, with a high of nearly 46 percent of students indicating a desire to become involved in cleaning up the environment. Beginning in the 1980s, student support for embracing this objective dropped to around 20 percent or even lower (see Figure 12-2). Even with recent attention to global warming, the proportion remains level at only 26.9 percent of first-year students in 2009.

Recently, cheating has become a hot issue on college campuses. Professors who take advantage of computerized services that can identify plagiarism, such as the search engine Google, have been shocked to learn that many of the papers their students hand in are plagiarized in whole or in part. The Sociology on Campus box examines the shift in values that underlies this decline in academic integrity.

Another value that has begun to change recently, not just among students but among the public in general, is the right to privacy. Americans have always valued their privacy and resented government intrusions into their personal lives. In the aftermath of the terrorist attacks of September 11, 2001, however, many citizens called for greater protection against the threat of terrorism. In response, the U.S. government broadened its surveillance powers and increased its ability to monitor people's behavior without court approval. In 2001, shortly after the attacks, Congress passed the Patriot Act, which empowers the FBI to access individuals' medical, library, student, and phone records without informing them or obtaining a search warrant.

Antiterrorism campaigns, especially efforts to acquire information from suspected terrorists, have fueled debate about yet another value, freedom from torture. In the past few years, the use of torture to obtain information has become controversial around the world. As Figure 12-3 shows, public opinion regarding the use of torture varies dramatically from one country to another.

Global Culture War

For almost a generation, public attention in the United States has focused on **culture war,** or the polarization of society over controversial cultural elements. Originally, in the 1990s, the term referred to political debates over heated issues such as abortion, religious expression, gun control, and sexual orientation. Soon, however, it took on a global meaning—especially after 9/11, as Americans wondered, "Why do they hate us?" Through 2000, global studies of public opinion had reported favorable views of the United States in countries as diverse as Morocco and Germany. But by 2003, in the wake of the U.S. invasion of Iraq, foreign opinion of the United States had become quite negative (J. Hunter 1991; Kohut et al. 2005, 2007).

In the past 20 years, extensive efforts have been made to compare values in different nations, recognizing the challenges in interpreting value concepts in a similar manner across cultures. Psychologist Shalom Schwartz has measured values in

A Culture of Cheating?

On November 21, 2002, after issuing several warnings, officials at the U.S. Naval Academy seized the computers of almost 100 midshipmen suspected of downloading movies and music illegally from the Internet. Officers at the school may have taken the unusually strong action to avoid liability on the part of the U.S. government, which owns the computers students were using. But across the nation, college administrators have been trying to restrain students from downloading pirated entertainment for free. The practice is

> More than proctoring of exams or reliance on search engines to identify plagiarism, educating students about the need for academic honesty seems to reduce the incidence of cheating.

so widespread, it has been slowing down the high-powered computer networks colleges and universities depend on for research and admissions.

Illegal downloading is just one aspect of the growing problem of copyright violation, both on campus and off. Now that college students can use personal computers to surf the Internet, most do their research online. Apparently, the temptation to cut and paste passages from Web site postings and pass them off as one's own is irresistible to many. Surveys done by the Center for Academic Integrity show that from 1999 to 2005, the percentage of students who approved of this type of plagiarism rose from 10 percent to 41 percent. At the same time, the percentage who considered cutting and pasting

from the Internet to be a serious form of cheating fell from 68 percent to 23 percent. Perhaps the worst form of Internet plagiarism is the purchase of entire papers from other writers. Increasingly, the Web sites that sell essays to students are based in other countries, including India, Ukraine, Nigeria, and the Philippines.

A cross-cultural study compared cheating by students in Lebanon and the United States. Researchers found a high willingness to cheat among students in both countries: 54 percent of the U.S. students and 80 percent of the Lebanese students reported having cheated in some way during the past year. In both cultures, students were more willing to cheat if they perceived their peers to be dishonest and if they thought their cheating was unlikely to be reported.

The Center for Academic Integrity estimates that at most schools, more than 75 percent of the students engage in some form of cheating. Students not only cut passages from the Internet and paste them into their papers without citing the source; they share questions and answers on exams, collaborate on assignments they are supposed to do independently, and even falsify the results of their laboratory experiments. Worse, many

professors have become inured to the problem and have ceased to report it.

To address what they consider an alarming trend, many schools are rewriting or adopting new academic honor codes. This renewed emphasis on honor and integrity underscores the influence of cultural values on social behavior. Observers contend that the increase in student cheating reflects widely publicized instances of cheating in public life, which have served to create an alternative set of values in which the end justifies the means. When young people see sports heroes, authors, entertainers, and corporate executives exposed for cheating in one form or another, the message seems to be "Cheating is OK, as long as you don't get caught." More than proctoring of exams or reliance on search engines to identify plagiarism, then, educating students about the need for academic honesty seems to reduce the incidence of cheating. "The feeling of being treated as an adult and responding in kind," says Professor Donald McCabe of Rutgers University, "it's clearly there for many students. They don't want to violate that trust."

LET'S DISCUSS

1. Do you know anyone who has engaged in Internet plagiarism? What about cheating on tests or falsifying laboratory results? If so, how did the person justify these forms of dishonesty?

2. Even if cheaters aren't caught, what negative effects does their academic dishonesty have on them? What effects does it have on students who are honest? Could an entire college or university suffer from students' dishonesty?

Sources: Argetsinger and Krim 2002; Bartlett 2009; Center for Academic Integrity 2006; McCabe et al. 2008; R. Thomas 2003; Zernike 2002.

more than 60 countries. Around the world, certain values are widely shared, including benevolence, which is defined as "forgiveness and loyalty." In contrast, power, defined as "control or dominance over people and resources," is a value that is endorsed much less often (Hitlin and Piliavin 2004; S. Schwartz and Bardi 2001).

Despite this evidence of shared values, some scholars have interpreted the terrorism, genocide, wars, and military occupations of

the early 21st century as a "clash of civilizations." According to this thesis, cultural and religious identities, rather than national or political loyalties, are becoming the prime source of international conflict. Critics of this thesis point out that conflict over values is nothing new; only our ability to create havoc and violence has grown. Furthermore, speaking of a clash of "civilizations" disguises the sharp divisions that exist within large groups. Christianity, for example, runs the gamut from Quaker-style pacifism to

Table **12-2** Sociological Perspectives on Culture

	Functionalist Perspective	Conflict Perspective	Feminist Perspective	Interactionist Perspective
Cultural Variation	Subcultures serve the interests of subgroups; ethnocentrism reinforces group solidarity	Countercultures question the dominant social order; ethnocentrism devalues groups	Cultural relativism respects variations in the way men and women are viewed in different societies	Customs and traditions are transmitted through intergroup contact and through the media
Norms	Reinforce societal standards	Reinforce patterns of dominance	Reinforce roles of men and women	Are maintained through face-to-face interaction
Values	Are collective conceptions of what is good	May perpetuate social inequality	May perpetuate men's dominance	Are defined and redefined through social interaction
Culture and Society	Culture reflects a society's strong central values	Culture reflects a society's dominant ideology	Culture reflects society's view of men and women	A society's core culture is perpetuated through daily social interactions

certain elements of the Ku Klux Klan's ideology (Berman 2003; Huntington 1993; Said 2001).

Table 12-2 summarizes major sociological perspectives on culture. How one views a culture—whether from an ethnocentric viewpoint or through the lens of cultural relativism—has important consequences in the area of social policy. Should a nation accommodate non-native-language speakers by sponsoring bilingual programs, for example? We'll take a close look at this controversial issue in the Social Policy section below.

social policy and Culture

Bilingualism

Looking at the Issue

All over the world, nations face the challenge of how to deal with minorities who speak a different language from that of mainstream culture. Because languages know no political boundaries, minority languages are common. In India, for example, Hindi is the most widely spoken language, while English is used widely for official purposes. Yet 18 other languages are officially recognized in this nation of about 1 billion people.

Throughout the world, then, schools must deal with incoming students who speak many different languages. **Bilingualism** refers to the use of two languages in a particular setting, such as the workplace or schoolroom, treating each language as equally legitimate. Thus, a teacher of bilingual education may instruct children in their native language while gradually introducing them to the language of the host society. If the curriculum is also bicultural, children will learn about the mores and folkways of both the dominant culture and the subculture.

To what degree should schools in the United States present the curriculum in a language other than English? This issue has prompted a great deal of debate among educators and policymakers. According to the Bureau of the Census, 59 million U.S. residents over age five—that's about 19 percent of the population—spoke a language other than English as their primary language at home in 2008 (Figure 12-4). Indeed, 32 other languages are each spoken by at least 200,000 U.S. residents (Shin and Bruno 2003).

Do bilingual programs help the children of these families to learn English? It is difficult to reach firm conclusions because bilingual programs in general vary so widely in their quality and approach. They differ in the length of the transition to English and in how long they allow students to remain in bilingual classrooms. Moreover, results have been mixed. In the years since California effectively dismantled its bilingual education program, reading and math scores of students with limited English proficiency rose dramatically, especially in the lower grades. Yet a major overview of 17 studies, done at Johns Hopkins University, found that students who are offered lessons in both English and their home languages make better progress than similar students who are taught only in English (R. Slavin and Cheung 2003).

Applying Sociology

For a long time, people in the United States demanded conformity to a single language. This demand coincided with the functionalist view that language serves to unify members of a

(continued)

FIGURE 12-4 **Percentage of People Who Speak a Language Other Than English at Home, by State**

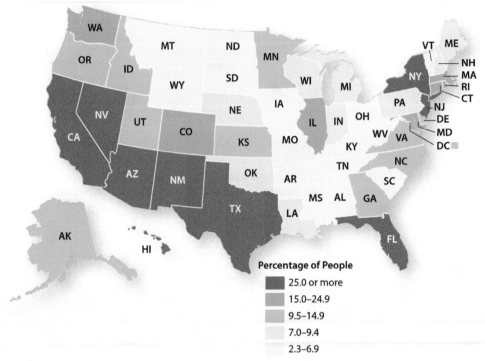

Percentage of People

- 25.0 or more
- 15.0–24.9
- 9.5–14.9
- 7.0–9.4
- 2.3–6.9

Note: Data drawn from the 2008 American Community Survey of people five years and over. National average was 19.7 percent.
Source: American Community Survey 2009: Table R1601.

The perspective of conflict theory also helps us to understand some of the attacks on bilingual programs. Many of them stem from an ethnocentric point of view, which holds that any deviation from the majority is bad. This attitude tends to be expressed by those who wish to stamp out foreign influence wherever it occurs, especially in our schools. It does not take into account that success in bilingual education may actually have beneficial results, such as decreasing the number of high school dropouts and increasing the number of Hispanics in colleges and universities.

Initiating Policy

Bilingualism has policy implications largely in two areas: efforts to maintain language purity and programs to enhance bilingual education. Nations vary dramatically in their tolerance for a variety of languages. China continues to tighten its cultural control over Tibet by extending instruction of Mandarin, a Chinese dialect, from high school into the elementary schools, which will now be bilingual along with Tibetan. In contrast, nearby Singapore establishes English as the medium of instruction but allows students to take their mother tongue as a second language, be it Chinese, Malay, or Tamil.

In many nations, language dominance is a regional issue—for example, in Miami or along the Tex-Mex border, where Spanish speaking is prevalent. A particularly virulent bilingual hot spot is Québec, the French-speaking province of Canada. The Québécois, as they are known, represent 83 percent of the province's population, but only 25 percent of Canada's total population. A law implemented in 1978 mandated education in French for all Québec's children except those whose parents or siblings had learned English elsewhere in Canada. While special laws like this one have advanced French in the province, dissatisfied

society. Immigrant children from Europe and Asia—including young Italians, Jews, Poles, Chinese, and Japanese—were expected to learn English once they entered school. In some cases, immigrant children were actually forbidden to speak their native languages on school grounds. Little respect was granted to immigrants' cultural traditions; a young person would often be teased about his or her "funny" name, accent, or style of dress.

Recent decades have seen challenges to this pattern of forced obedience to the dominant ideology. Beginning in the 1960s, active movements for Black pride and ethnic pride insisted that people regard the traditions of all racial and ethnic subcultures as legitimate and important. Conflict theorists explain this development as a case of subordinated language minorities seeking opportunities for self-expression. Partly as a result of these challenges, people began to view bilingualism as an asset. It seemed to provide a sensitive way of assisting millions of non-English-speaking people in the United States to *learn* English in order to function more effectively within the society.

Québécois have tried to form their own separate country. In 1995, the people of Québec indicated their preference of remaining united with Canada by only the narrowest of margins (50.5 percent). Language and language-related cultural areas both unify and divide this nation of 33 million people (*The Economist* 2005b; R. Schaefer 2010).

Policymakers in the United States have been somewhat ambivalent in dealing with the issue of bilingualism. In 1965, the Elementary and Secondary Education Act (ESEA) provided for bilingual, bicultural education. In the 1970s, the federal government took an active role in establishing the proper form for bilingual programs. However, more recently, federal policy has been less supportive of bilingualism, and local school districts have been forced to provide an increased share of funding for their bilingual programs. Yet bilingual programs are an expense that many communities and states are unwilling to pay for and are quick to cut back. In 1998, voters in California approved a proposition that all but eliminated bilingual education: it requires instruction in English for 1.4 million children who are not fluent in the language.

In the United States, repeated efforts have been made to introduce a constitutional amendment declaring English as the nation's official language. In 2006, the issue arose once again during debates over two extremely controversial congressional proposals—a House bill that would have criminalized the presence of illegal immigrants in the United States and expanded the penalties for aiding them, and a Senate bill that offered some illegal immigrants a path to citizenship. In an attempt to reach a compromise between the two sides, legislative leaders introduced a proposal to make English the national language. As they described it, the legislation would not completely outlaw bilingual or multilingual government services. As of 2010, 30 states had declared English their official language—an action that is now more symbolic than legislative in its significance.

Public concern over a potential decline in the use of English appears to be overblown. In reality, most immigrants and their offspring quickly become fluent in English and abandon

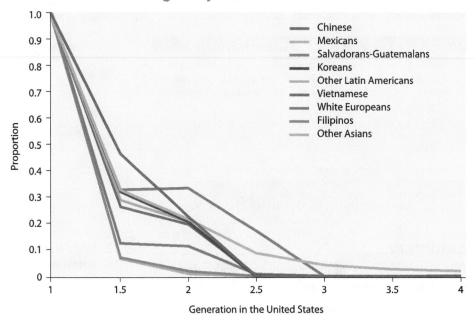

FIGURE 12-5 **Proportion of Immigrant Group Members in Southern California Who Speak the Mother Tongue, by Generation**

Legend:
- Chinese
- Mexicans
- Salvadorans-Guatemalans
- Koreans
- Other Latin Americans
- Vietnamese
- White Europeans
- Filipinos
- Other Asians

Y-axis: Proportion (0 to 1.0)
X-axis: Generation in the United States (1 to 4)

Note: Based on a survey of 5,703 people in Metropolitan Los Angeles and San Diego from 2000 to 2004. Generation 1.5 includes those who came to the United States before age 15. Generation 2 includes those who were born in the United States to at least one foreign-born parent. Generation 3 includes those who were born in the United States to U.S.-born parents, but had one or more foreign-born grandparents.
Source: Rumbaut et al. 2006:456.

their mother tongue. Figure 12-5 presents data from Southern California, a region with a high proportion of immigrants. It shows a steady, rapid move toward English, particularly in the first generation. Despite the presence of a large Latin enclave in the region, even Spanish-speaking immigrants quickly become speakers of English.

Nevertheless, many people are impatient with those immigrants who continue to use their mother tongue. The release in 2006 of *"Nuestro Himno,"* the Spanish-language version of the "Star-Spangled Banner," produced a strong public reaction: 69 percent of those who were surveyed on the topic said the anthem should be sung only in English. In reaction against the Spanish version, at least one congressman defiantly sang the national anthem in English—with incorrect lyrics. And the proprietor of a restaurant in Philadelphia posted signs advising patrons that he would accept orders for his famous steak sandwiches only in English. Throughout the year, passions ran high as policymakers debated how much support to afford people who speak other languages (J. Carroll 2006; U.S. English 2010).

(continued)

In the end, the immigrant's experience, whether in the United States or Australia, is not only about learning a new language. It is about learning a whole new culture—a new totality of socially transmitted customs, knowledge, material objects, and behavior (Viramontes 2007).

TAKE THE ISSUE WITH YOU

1. Have you attended a school with a number of students for whom English is a second language? If so, did the school set up a special bilingual program? Was it effective? What is your opinion of such programs?

2. The ultimate goal of both English-only and bilingual programs is for foreign-born students to become proficient in English. Why should the type of program students attend matter so much to so many people? List all the reasons you can think of for supporting or opposing such programs. What do you see as the primary reason?

3. Besides bilingualism, can you think of another issue that has become controversial recently because of a clash of cultures? If so, analyze the issue from a sociological point of view.

MODULE 12 | Recap and Review

Summary

This module discusses the major elements that all cultures share: **language, norms,** and **values.**

1. **Language** includes speech, written characters, numerals, and **symbols,** as well as gestures and other forms of nonverbal communication. Language both describes culture and shapes it.

2. Sociologists distinguish between **norms** in two ways, classifying them as **formal** or **informal** and as **mores** or **folkways.**

3. The formal norms of a culture will carry the heaviest **sanctions;** informal norms will carry light sanctions.

4. The social policy of **bilingualism** calls for the use of two or more languages, treating each as equally legitimate. It is supported by those who want to ease the transition of non-native-language speakers into a host society, but opposed by those who adhere to a single cultural tradition and language.

Thinking Critically

1. Do you agree with Sapir and Whorf's hypothesis that language precedes thought? What kind of evidence might you cite to refute their hypothesis? Could language shape our interpretation of reality without preceding thought?

2. In the United States, is the norm of heterosexuality a formal norm or an informal norm? Would you categorize it with mores or folkways? Explain your reasoning.

3. Do you believe that the world is experiencing a clash of civilizations rather than of nations, as some scholars assert? Why or why not?

Key Terms

Bilingualism

Culture war

Folkway

Formal norm

Informal norm

Language

Law

Mores

Norm

Sanction

Sapir-Whorf hypothesis

Symbol

Value

Sociologists are interested in the process of **socialization,** through which people learn the attitudes, values, and behaviors appropriate for members of their culture. Socialization occurs through human interactions that begin in infancy and continue throughout life. We learn a great deal from those people who are most important in our lives—immediate family members, best friends, and teachers. But we also learn from people we see on the street, on television, on the Internet, and in films and magazines. From a microsociological perspective, socialization helps us discover how to behave "properly" and what to expect from others if we follow (or challenge) society's norms and values. From a macrosociological perspective, socialization provides for the transmission of a culture from one generation to the next and thereby for the long-term continuance of society.

Socialization also shapes our self-images. For example, in the United States, a person who is viewed as "too heavy" or "too short" does not conform to the ideal cultural standard of physical attractiveness. This kind of unfavorable evaluation can significantly influence the person's self-esteem. In this sense, socialization experiences can help shape our personalities. In everyday speech, the term **personality** refers to a person's typical patterns of attitudes, needs, characteristics, and behavior.

How much of a person's personality is shaped by culture, as opposed to inborn traits? In other words, what makes us who we are? Is it the genes we are born with, or the environment in which we grow up? Researchers have traditionally clashed over the relative importance of biological inheritance and environmental factors in human development—a conflict called the *nature versus nurture* (or *heredity versus environment*) debate. Today, most social scientists have moved beyond this debate, acknowledging instead the *interaction* of these variables in shaping human development. We can best appreciate how heredity and environmental factors interact and influence the socialization process if we first examine situations in which one factor operates almost entirely without the other (Homans 1979).

Social Environment: The Impact of Isolation

In the 1994 movie *Nell,* Jodie Foster played a young woman hidden from birth by her mother in a backwoods cabin. Raised without normal human contact, Nell crouches like an animal, screams wildly, and speaks or sings in a language all her own. This movie was drawn from the actual account of an emaciated 16-year-old boy who appeared mysteriously in 1828 in the town square of Nuremberg, Germany (Lipson 1994).

Isabelle and Genie: Two Cases

Some viewers may have found the story of Nell difficult to believe, but the painful childhood of Isabelle was all too real. For the first six years of her life, Isabelle lived in almost total seclusion in a darkened room. She had little contact with other people, with the exception of her mother, who could neither speak nor hear. Isabelle's mother's parents had been so deeply ashamed of Isabelle's illegitimate birth that they kept her hidden away from the world. Ohio authorities finally discovered the child in 1938, when Isabelle's mother escaped from her parents' home, taking her daughter with her.

When she was discovered at age six, Isabelle could not speak; she could merely make various croaking sounds. Her only communications with her mother were simple gestures. Isabelle had been largely deprived of the typical interactions and socialization experiences of childhood. Since she had seen few people, she showed a strong fear of strangers and reacted almost like a wild animal when confronted with an unfamiliar person. As she became accustomed to seeing certain individuals, her reaction changed to one of extreme apathy. At first, observers believed that Isabelle was deaf, but she soon began to react to nearby sounds. On tests of maturity, she scored at the level of an infant rather than a six-year-old.

Specialists developed a systematic training program to help Isabelle adapt to human relationships and socialization. After a few days of training, she made her first attempt to verbalize. Although she started slowly, Isabelle quickly passed through six years of development. In a little over two months she was speaking in complete sentences. Nine months later she could identify both words and sentences. Before Isabelle reached age 9, she was ready to attend school with other children. By age 14 she was in sixth grade, doing well in school, and emotionally well adjusted.

Yet without an opportunity to experience socialization in her first six years, Isabelle had been hardly human in the social sense when she was first discovered. Her inability to communicate at the time of her discovery—despite her physical and cognitive potential to learn—and her remarkable progress over the next few years underscore the impact of socialization on human development (K. Davis 1940, 1947).

FIGURE 13-1 Genie's Sketch

This sketch was made in 1975 by Genie—a girl who had been isolated for most of her 14 years, until she was discovered by authorities in 1970. In her drawing, her linguist friend (on the left) plays the piano while Genie listens. Genie was 18 when she drew this picture.
Source: Curtiss 1977:274.

Unfortunately, other children who have been locked away or severely neglected have not fared so well as Isabelle. In many instances, the consequences of social isolation have proved much more damaging. For example, in 1970 a 14-year-old Californian named Genie was discovered in a room where she had been confined since age 20 months. During her years of isolation, no family member had spoken to her, nor could she hear anything other than swearing. Since there was no television or radio in her home, she had never heard the sounds of normal human speech. One year after beginning extensive therapy, Genie's grammar resembled that of a typical 18-month-old. Though she made further advances with continued therapy, she never achieved full language ability. Today Genie, now in her mid-50s, lives in a home for developmentally disabled adults. Figure 13-1 shows a sketch Genie made of her teacher five years after she was discovered (Curtiss 1977, 1985; Rymer 1993).

Isabelle's and Genie's experiences are important to researchers because there are only a few cases of children reared in total isolation. Unfortunately, however, there are many cases of children raised in extremely neglectful social circumstances. In the 1990s, public attention focused on infants and young children from orphanages in the formerly communist countries of Eastern Europe. In Romanian orphanages, babies once lay in their cribs for 18 to 20 hours a day, curled against their feeding bottles and receiving little adult care. Such minimal attention continued for the first five years of their lives. Many of them were fearful of human contact and prone to unpredictable anti-social behavior.

This situation came to light as families in North America and Europe began adopting thousands of the children. The adjustment problems for about 20 percent of them were often so dramatic that the adopting families suffered guilty fears of being ill-fit adoptive parents. Many of them have asked for assistance in dealing with the children. Slowly, efforts are being made to introduce the deprived youngsters to feelings of attachment that they have never experienced before (Groza et al. 1999; Craig Smith 2006).

Increasingly, researchers are emphasizing the importance of the earliest socialization experiences for children who grow up in more normal environments. We now know that it is not enough to care for an infant's physical needs; parents must also concern themselves with children's social development. If, for example, children are discouraged from having friends even as toddlers, they will miss out on social interactions with peers that are critical for emotional growth.

Primate Studies

Studies of animals raised in isolation also support the importance of socialization in development. Harry Harlow (1971), a researcher at the primate laboratory of the University of Wisconsin, conducted tests with rhesus monkeys that had been raised away from their mothers and away from contact with other monkeys. As was the case with Isabelle, the rhesus monkeys raised in isolation were fearful and easily frightened. They did not mate, and the females who were artificially inseminated became abusive mothers. Apparently, isolation had had a damaging effect on the monkeys.

A creative aspect of Harlow's experimentation was his use of "artificial mothers." In one such experiment, Harlow presented monkeys raised in isolation with two substitute mothers—one cloth-covered replica and one covered with wire that had the ability to offer milk. Monkey after monkey went to the wire mother for the life-giving milk, yet spent much more time clinging to the more motherlike cloth model. It appears that the infant monkeys developed greater social attachments from their need for warmth, comfort, and intimacy than from their need for milk.

While the isolation studies just discussed may seem to suggest that heredity can be dismissed as a factor in the social development of humans and animals, studies of twins provide insight into a fascinating interplay between hereditary and environmental factors.

 use your **sociological imagination**

What events in your life have had a strong influence on who you are?

trend|spotting

The Influence of Heredity

Identical twins Oskar Stohr and Jack Yufe were separated soon after their birth and raised on different continents, in very different cultural settings. Oskar was reared as a strict Catholic by his maternal grandmother in the Sudetenland of Czechoslovakia. As a member of the Hitler Youth movement in Nazi Germany, he learned to hate Jews. In contrast, his brother Jack was reared in Trinidad by the twins' Jewish father. Jack joined an Israeli kibbutz (a collective settlement) at age 17 and later served in the Israeli army. When the twins were reunited in middle age, however, some startling similarities emerged: They both wore wire-rimmed glasses and mustaches. They both liked spicy foods and sweet liqueurs, were absent-minded, flushed the toilet before using it, stored rubber bands on their wrists, and dipped buttered toast in their coffee (Holden 1980).

The twins also differed in many important respects: Jack was a workaholic; Oskar enjoyed leisure-time activities. Oskar was a traditionalist who was domineering toward women; Jack was a political liberal who was much more accepting of feminism. Finally, Jack was extremely proud of being Jewish, while Oskar never mentioned his Jewish heritage (Holden 1987).

Oskar and Jack are prime examples of the interplay of heredity and environment. For a number of years, the Minnesota Twin Family Study has been following pairs of identical twins reared apart to determine what similarities, if any, they show in personality traits, behavior, and intelligence. Preliminary results from the available twin studies indicate that *both* genetic factors *and* socialization experiences are influential in human development. Certain characteristics, such as temperaments, voice patterns, and nervous habits, appear to be strikingly similar even in twins reared apart, suggesting that these qualities may be linked to hereditary causes. However, identical twins reared apart differ far more in their attitudes, values, chosen mates, and even drinking habits; these qualities, it would seem, are influenced by environmental factors. In examining clusters of personality traits among such twins, researchers have found marked similarities in their tendency toward leadership or dominance, but significant differences in their need for intimacy, comfort, and assistance.

Researchers have also been impressed with the similar scores on intelligence tests of twins reared apart in *roughly similar* social

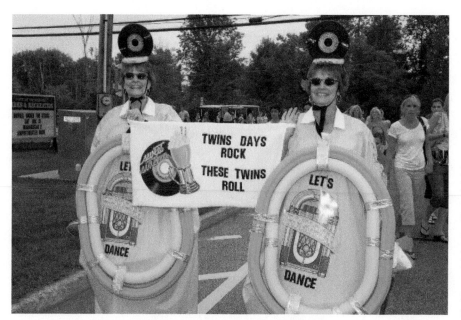

Despite the striking physical resemblance between these identical twins, there are undoubtedly many differences. Research points to some behavioral similarities between twins, but little beyond the likenesses found among nontwin siblings.

on intelligence tests—a finding that supports the impact of socialization on human development (Joseph 2004; Kronstadt 2008a; McGue and Bouchard 1998; Minnesota Center for Twin and Family Research 2010).

We need to be cautious in reviewing studies of twin pairs and other relevant research. Widely broadcast findings have often been based on preliminary analysis of extremely small samples. For example, one study (not involving twin pairs) was frequently cited as confirming genetic links with behavior. Yet the researchers had to retract their conclusions after they increased the sample and reclassified two of the original cases. After those changes, the initial findings were no longer valid.

Critics add that studies of twin pairs have not provided satisfactory information concerning the extent to which separated identical twins may have had contact with each other, even though they were raised apart. Such interactions—especially if they were extensive—could call into question the validity of the twin studies. As this debate continues, we can certainly anticipate numerous efforts to replicate the research and clarify the interplay between heredity and environmental factors in human development (Horgan 1993; Plomin 1989).

settings. Most of the identical twins register scores even closer than those that would be expected if the same person took a test twice. At the same time, however, identical twins brought up in *dramatically different* social environments score quite differently

MODULE 13 | Recap and Review

Summary

Socialization is the process through which people learn the attitudes, values, and actions appropriate for members of a particular culture.

1. Socialization affects the overall cultural practices of a society; it also shapes the images we hold of ourselves.

2. Heredity and environmental factors interact in influencing the socialization process.

Thinking Critically

1. What might be some ethical concerns regarding research on the influences of heredity and environment?

2. What are some social policy implications of research on the effects of early socialization experiences?

Key Terms

Personality
Socialization

As we have seen, the culture of the United States is defined by rather gradual movements from one stage of socialization to the next. The continuing and lifelong socialization process involves many different social forces that influence our lives and alter our self-images.

The family is the most important agent of socialization in the United States, especially for children. In this module, we'll also discuss six other agents of socialization: the school, the peer group, the mass media and technology, the workplace, religion, and the state. We'll explore the role of religion in socializing young people into society's norms and values more fully in Module 45.

Family

The lifelong process of learning begins shortly after birth. Since newborns can hear, see, smell, taste, and feel heat, cold, and pain, they are constantly orienting themselves to the surrounding world. Human beings, especially family members, constitute an important part of their social environment. People minister to the baby's needs by feeding, cleaning, carrying, and comforting the baby.

All families engage in socialization, but the way that Amish families encourage their children to accept their community's subculture is particularly striking. The Research Today box describes their tolerance for the period of rebellion known as *rum springa,* during which Amish children flirt with the adolescent subculture of mainstream American society.

Cultural Influences

As both Charles Horton Cooley and George Herbert Mead noted, the development of the self is a critical aspect of the early years of one's life. How children develop this sense of self can vary from one society to another, however. For example, most parents in the United States do not send six-year-olds to school unsupervised. But that is the norm in Japan, where parents push their children to commute to school on their own from an early age. In cities like Tokyo, first graders must learn to negotiate buses, subways, and long walks. To ensure their safety, parents carefully lay out rules: never talk to strangers; check with a station attendant if you get off at the wrong stop; if you miss your stop stay on to the end of the line, then call; take stairs, not escalators; don't fall asleep. Some parents equip the children with cell phones or pagers. One parent acknowledges that she worries, "but after they are six, children are supposed to start being independent from the mother. If you're still taking your child to school after the first

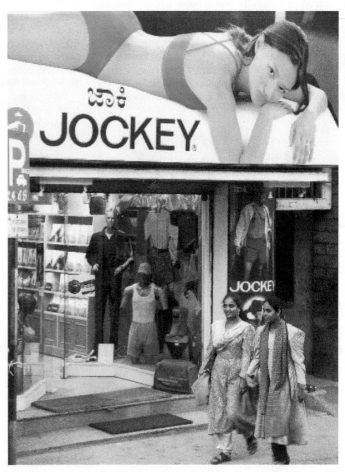

On a busy commercial street in Bangalore, India, pedestrians dressed in traditional garb stroll past a shop and billboard advertising Western fashions. Socialization comes from cultural influences as well as from family and friends. In today's globalized world, Western media expose children to cultural values that their parents and other authorities may not embrace.

month, everyone looks at you funny" (Tolbert 2000:17).

As we consider the family's role in socialization, we need to remember that children do not play a passive role. They are active agents, influencing and altering the families, schools, and communities of which they are a part.

The Impact of Race and Gender

In the United States, social development includes exposure to cultural assumptions regarding gender and race. Black parents, for example, have learned that children as young as age two can absorb negative messages about Blacks in children's books,

Rum Springa: **Raising Children Amish Style**

All families face challenges raising their children, but what if your parents expected you not to dance, listen to music, watch television, or access the Internet? This is the challenge faced by Amish teens and their parents, who embrace a lifestyle of the mid-1800s. Amish youths— boys in particular—often rebel against their parents' strict morals by getting drunk, behaving disrespectfully, and indulging in "worldly" activities, such as buying a car. At times even the girls may become involved, to their families' dismay. As one scholar puts it, "The rowdiness of Amish youth is an embarrassment to church leaders and a stigma in the larger community" (Kraybill 2001, 138).

> All families face challenges raising their children, but what if your parents expected you not to dance, listen to music, watch television, or access the Internet?

Yet the strong pull of mainstream American culture has led Amish parents to routinize, almost to accept, some of their children's worldly activities. They expect adolescents to test their subculture's boundaries during a period of discovery called *rum springa,* a German term meaning "running around." A common occurrence during which young people attend barn dances and break social norms that forbid drinking, smoking, and driving cars, *rum springa* is definitely not supported by the Amish religion.

A typical *rum springa* begins when Amish boys signal the Amish girls to come out with a flashlight:

> Once the young ladies hit the cars, and the cars have pulled away from the homestead,

appearances and behaviors begin to change. While riding along, each Amish girl performs at least one of many actions that have been forbidden to her throughout her childhood: lights up a cigarette, grabs a beer, switches on the rock and rap music on the car radio or CD player, converses loudly and in a flirtatious manner with members of the opposite sex (Shachtman 2006:6).

[Shortly the car full of adolescents makes its way to a truck stop.] When the girls emerge from the bathrooms, only two of the eight still look Amish; the other six have been transformed. They wear jeans, T-shirts, and other mainstream American teenage outfits, some revealing their navels. Hair coverings have been removed, and a few have also let down their hair, uncut since childhood. "Ready to party" one lady avows. "Cruisin' and boozin'," another responds. The counter clerk, an older woman . . . seems unabashed by the changes in attire (Shachtman 2006:7).

Parents often react to these escapades by looking the other way, sometimes literally. If they hear radio music coming from the barn, or a motorcycle driving onto their property in the middle of the night, they don't retaliate by punishing their offspring. Instead, they pretend not to notice, secure in the knowledge that Amish children almost always return to the community's traditional values. Indeed, despite the flirtation with popular culture and modern technology that is common during the *rum springa,* the vast majority of Amish youths do return to the Amish community and become baptized. Scholars report that 85 to 90 percent of Amish children accept the faith as young adults.

To mainstream Americans, this little known and understood subculture recently became a source of entertainment. In 2004, UPN aired a 10-week reality program called *Amish in the City.* In the series, five Amish youths allegedly on *rum springa* moved in with six worldly wise young adults in Los Angeles. On behalf of the Amish community, some critics called the series exploitative, a sign of how vulnerable the Amish are. No similar series would be developed on the rebellion of Muslim or Orthodox Jewish youths, they charged.

LET'S DISCUSS

1. Do you or anyone you know come from a subculture that rejects mainstream American culture? If so, describe the community's norms and values. How do they resemble and how do they differ from Amish norms and values?

2. Why do you think so many Amish youths return to their families' way of life after rebelling against it?

Sources: Kraybill 2001; Shachtman 2006; Stevick 2007; Weinraub 2004.

---

toys, and television shows—all of which are designed primarily for White consumers. At the same time, Black children are exposed more often than others to the inner-city youth gang culture. Because most Blacks, even those who are middle class, live near very poor neighborhoods, children such as Charisse (see the chapter-opening excerpt) are susceptible to these influences, despite their parents' strong family values (Linn and Poussaint 1999; Pattillo-McCoy 1999).

The term **gender role** refers to expectations regarding the proper behavior, attitudes, and activities of males and females. For example, we traditionally think of "toughness" as masculine—and desirable only in men—while we view "tenderness" as feminine. As we will see in Module 34, other cultures do not necessarily assign these qualities to each gender in the way that, our culture does. The existence of gender roles does not imply that, inevitably, males and females will assume certain roles, nor does it imply that those roles are quite distinct from one another. Rather, gender roles emphasize the fact that males and females are not genetically predetermined to occupy certain roles.

As the primary agents of childhood socialization, parents play a critical role in guiding children into those gender roles deemed appropriate in a society. Other adults, older siblings, the mass media, and religious and educational institutions also have a noticeable impact on a child's socialization into feminine and masculine norms. A culture or subculture may require that one sex or the other take primary responsibility for the socialization of children, economic support of the family, or religious or intellectual leadership. In some societies, girls are socialized mainly by their mothers and boys by their fathers—an arrangement that may prevent girls from learning critical survival skills. In South Asia, fathers teach their sons to swim to prepare them for a life as fishermen; girls typically do not learn to swim. When a deadly tsunami hit the coast of South Asia in 2004, many more men survived than women.

Interactionists remind us that socialization concerning not only masculinity and femininity but also marriage and parenthood begins in childhood as a part of family life. Children observe their parents as they express affection, deal with finances, quarrel, complain about in-laws, and so forth. Their learning represents an informal process of anticipatory socialization in which they develop a tentative model of what being married and being a parent are like. (We will explore socialization for marriage and parenthood more fully in Module 40.)

School

Where did you learn the national anthem? Who taught you about the heroes of the American Revolution? Where were you first tested on your knowledge of your culture? Like the family, schools have an explicit mandate to socialize people in the United States—especially children—into the norms and values of our culture.

As conflict theorists Samuel Bowles and Herbert Gintis (1976) have observed, schools in this country foster competition through built-in systems of reward and punishment, such as grades and evaluations by teachers. Consequently, a child who is experiencing difficulty trying to learn a new skill can sometimes come to feel stupid and unsuccessful. However, as the self matures, children become capable of increasingly realistic assessments of their intellectual, physical, and social abilities.

Functionalists point out that schools, as agents of socialization, fulfill the function of teaching children the values and customs of the larger society. Conflict theorists agree, but add that schools can reinforce the divisive aspects of society, especially those of social class. For example, higher education in the United States is costly despite the existence of financial aid programs. Students from affluent backgrounds therefore have an advantage in gaining access to universities and professional training. At the same time, less affluent young people may never receive the preparation that would qualify them for the best-paying and most prestigious jobs. The contrast between the functionalist and conflict views of education will be discussed in more detail in Module 43.

Table **15-1** **High School Popularity**

| What makes high school girls popular? | | What makes high school boys popular? | |
According to college men:	According to college women:	According to college men:	According to college women:
1. Physical attractiveness	1. Grades/intelligence	1. Participation in sports	1. Participation in sports
2. Grades/intelligence	2. Participation in sports	2. Grades/intelligence	2. Grades/intelligence
3. Participation in sports	3. General sociability	3. Popularity with girls	3. General sociability
4. General sociability	4. Physical attractiveness	4. General sociability	4. Physical attractiveness
5. Popularity with boys	5. Clothes	5. Car	5. School clubs/government

Note: Students at the following universities were asked in which ways adolescents in their high schools had gained prestige with their peers: Cornell University, Louisiana State University, Southeastern Louisiana University, State University of New York at Albany, State University of New York at Stony Brook, University of Georgia, and University of New Hampshire.

Source: Suitor et al. 2001:445.

In other cultures as well, schools serve socialization functions. Until the overthrow of Saddam Hussein in 2003, the sixth-grade textbooks used in Iraqi schools concentrated almost entirely on the military and its values of loyalty, honor, and sacrifice.

A young girl from Michigan displays Razanne, a modestly dressed doll made especially for Muslim children. Because girls learn about themselves and their social roles by playing with dolls, having a doll that represents their own heritage is important to them.

Children were taught that their enemies were Iran, the United States, Israel and its supporters, and NATO, the European military alliance. Within months of the regime's fall, the curriculum had been rewritten to remove indoctrination on behalf of Hussein, his army, and his Baath Socialist Party (Marr 2003).

Peer Group

Ask 13-year-olds who matters most in their lives and they are likely to answer "friends." As a child grows older, the family becomes somewhat less important in social development. Instead, peer groups increasingly assume the role of Mead's significant others. Within the peer group, young people associate with others who are approximately their age, and who often enjoy a similar social status (Giordano 2003).

We can see how important peer groups are to young people when their social lives are strained by war or disaster. In Baghdad, the overthrow of Saddam Hussein has profoundly changed teenagers' worlds, casting doubt on their future. Some young people have lost relatives or friends; others have become involved with fundamentalist groups or fled with their families to safer countries. Those youths who are left behind can suffer intense loneliness and boredom. Confined to their homes by crime and terrorism, those fortunate enough to have computers turn to Internet chat rooms or immerse themselves in their studies. Through e-mail, they struggle to maintain old friendships interrupted by wartime dislocation (Sanders 2004).

Gender differences are noteworthy among adolescents. Boys and girls are socialized by their parents, peers, and the media to identify many of the same paths to popularity, but to different degrees. Table 15-1 compares male and female college students' reports of how girls and boys they knew became popular in high school. The two groups named many of the same paths to popularity but gave them a different order of importance. While neither men nor women named sexual activity, drug use, or alcohol use as one of the top five paths, college men were much more likely than women to mention those behaviors as a means to becoming popular, for both boys and girls.

Mass Media and Technology

In the past 80 years, media innovations—radio, motion pictures, recorded music, television, and the Internet—have become important agents of socialization. Television, and increasingly the Internet, are critical forces in the socialization of children in the United States. One national survey indicates that 68 percent of U.S. children have a television in their bedroom, and nearly 50 percent of all youths ages 8 to 18 use the Internet every day (see Figure 15-1).

These media, however, are not always a negative socializing influence. Television programs and even commercials can introduce young people to unfamiliar lifestyles and cultures. Not only do children in the United States learn about life in "faraway lands," but inner-city children learn about the lives of farm children, and vice versa. The same thing happens in other countries.

Sociologists and other social scientists have begun to consider the impact of technology on socialization. They are particularly interested in the online friendship networks, like Facebook. Does this way of communicating resemble face-to-face interaction, or does it represent a new form of social interaction? The Research Today box explores the significance of this social phenomenon.

Not just in industrial nations, but in Africa and other developing areas, people have been socialized into relying on new communications technologies. Not long ago, if Zadhe Iyombe wanted to talk to his mother, he had to make an eight-day trip from the capital city of Kinshasa up the Congo River by boat to the rural town where he was born. Now both he and his mother have access to a cell phone, and they send text messages to each other daily. Iyombe and his mother are not atypical. Although cell phones aren't cheap, 1.4 billion owners in developing countries have come to consider them a necessity. Today, there are more cell phones in developing nations than in industrial nations—the first time in history that developing nations have outpaced the developed world in the adoption of a telecommunications technology (K. Sullivan 2006).

Workplace

Learning to behave appropriately in an occupation is a fundamental aspect of human socialization. In the United States, working full-time confirms adult status; it indicates that one has passed out of adolescence. In a sense, socialization into an occupation can represent both a harsh reality ("I have to work in order to buy food and pay the rent") and the realization of an ambition ("I've always wanted to be an airline pilot") (W. Moore 1968:862).

It used to be that going to work began with the end of our formal schooling, but that is no longer the case, at least not in the United States. More and more young people work today, and not just for a parent or relative. Adolescents generally seek jobs in order to make spending money; 80 percent of high school seniors say that little or none of what they earn goes to family expenses. These teens rarely look on their employment as a means of exploring vocational interests or getting on-the-job training.

Some observers feel that the increasing number of teenagers who are working earlier in life and for longer hours are finding the workplace almost as important an agent of socialization as school. In fact, a number of educators complain that student time at work is adversely affecting schoolwork. The level of teenage employment in the United States is the highest among industrial countries, which may provide one explanation for why U.S. high school students lag behind those in other countries on international achievement tests.

Socialization in the workplace changes when it involves a more permanent shift from an after-school job to full-time employment. Occupational socialization can be most intense during the transition from school to job, but it continues throughout one's work history. Technological advances may alter the requirements of the position and necessitate some degree of resocialization. Today, men and women change occupations, employers, or places of work many times during

FIGURE 15-1 **The New Normal: Internet at Home**

Percentage of 8- to 18-year-olds with

A computer at home
- 73%
- 86%
- 93%

Internet access at home
- 47%
- 74%
- 84%

High-speed/wireless Internet access at home
- 31%
- 59%

A computer in their bedroom
- 21%
- 31%
- 36%

Internet access in their bedroom
- 10%
- 20%
- 33%

Their own laptop
- 12%
- 29%

1999   2004   2009

Source: Rideout et al. 2010:21.

their adult years. Occupational socialization continues, then, throughout a person's years in the labor market.

College students today recognize that occupational socialization is not socialization into one lifetime occupation. They anticipate going through a number of jobs. The Bureau of Labor Statistics (2008) has found that from ages 18 to 42, the typical person has held 11 jobs. This high rate of turnover in employment applies to both men and women, and to those with a college degree as well as those with a high school diploma.

 # Research Today

Online Socializing: A New Agent of Socialization

Membership in the online social networks Facebook, Friendster, and MySpace has grown exponentially in recent years. At first, young adults monopolized these social networks. Indeed, Facebook was created in 2004 as a way for students on a single campus to become acquainted with one another before actually

> Online networks—especially those that indicate how many "friends" an individual has—can also be seen in terms of social capital.

meeting. Now there are well over 150 million profiles online, more than 70 percent of them from outside the United States. Sociologists are interested in these new social networks not because of the sophisticated technology that supports them, but because of their social significance. Much like face-to-face encounters with schoolmates or fellow workers, online social encounters serve as an agent of socialization. They affect both the development of the self and the identification of significant others, especially among youths, for whom online social networks are a particularly dominant agent of socialization.

Even in the brief history of online networking, sociologists can see social trends. For example, older people are now creating profiles on these sites. As Figure A shows, there is still a clear

correlation between age and online profiles: in a national survey of community college students, younger people were much more likely than older people to be online. However, the fastest-growing age groups are now those over 30, including those who are much older. As a result, online socializing is becoming much less age-specific—more like socializing in the real world. Moreover, this new agent of socialization can continue to influence people throughout the life course. Twitter is largely the exception to this trend; it is still a very age-specific method of social interaction, as Figure B shows.

Online networks—especially those that indicate how many "friends" an individual has—can also be seen in terms of social capital. In fact, "friending" is one, if not *the*, main activity on some online sites. Often the number of friends a person socializes with becomes the subject of boasting. By extension, individuals may use these sites to search for "friends" who may prove helpful to them in future endeavors. Becoming aware of new opportunities, either social or economic, through friends is a significant benefit of social capital.

Researchers have looked at the relationship between the display of friends online and the number of real-world friends people socialize with, and have proposed two competing hypotheses. According to the social enhancement hypothesis ("the rich get richer"), those who are popular offline further increase

FIGURE A **Staying Connected: Community College Students**

Ages 18–24
Ages 25 and above

Use social-networking tools: 95% (18–24), 68% (25 and above)
Multiple times a day: 64% (18–24), 41% (25 and above)
Multiple times a day for schoolwork: 18% (18–24), 10% (25 and above)

Note: Question asked was "How often do you use social networking tools, such as instant messaging, text messaging, MySpace and/or Facebook, Twitter, etc., for any purpose? (This does not include e-mail.)"
Source: Center for Community College Student Engagement 2009:8.

FIGURE B **Who Tweets?**

All online adults: 19%
Men: 17%
Women: 21%
18–29: 33%
30–49: 22%
50–64: 9%
65 and above: 4%

Age

Note: Data collected in September 2009 and limited to adult respondents because of ethical guidelines governing survey research. Includes other update services in addition to Twitter.
Source: Fox et al. 2009:4.

their popularity through online networking sites. According to the social compensation hypothesis ("the poor get richer"), however, social network users try to increase their popularity online to compensate for inadequate popularity offline. The social compensation hypothesis, if correct, would be an example of impression management. Research to date supports elements of both hypotheses; neither hypothesis fully defines the participants in online networking sites.

Another means of social networking, Twitter, emerged recently. A way of tracking people online, Twitter allows members to receive very brief instant messages from friends and acquaintances, who may signal their whereabouts or remark on what they are doing or seeing. This form of networking is even more passive than the original social networking sites. Once a member agrees to accept a tweet from someone, the alerts keep coming.

Viewed from a societal perspective, socializing online can have both positive and negative functions. For members of some marginalized populations, it is a way to socialize with like-minded people. For example, Muslims in Great Britain connect with friends online to learn how to navigate through a society in which they form a distinct minority. For other people, such as members of the Nazis in Germany and the Mafia in Italy, online networking is a way to proclaim allegiance to socially objectionable organizations. Governments agents frown on such online organizing, seeing it as dysfunctional, and periodically monitor these sites to see whether any laws have been violated.

LET'S DISCUSS

1. Do you list your "friends" on an online social networking site? If so, what is your motivation for doing so? How much social capital do you think your list represents?

2. Do you think the advantages of online social networking outweigh the disadvantages?

Sources: Donadio 2009; N. Ellison et al. 2007; Facebook 2009; Gentile 2009; Hundley and Ramirez 2008; Lenhart 2009; Miyata and Kobayashi 2008; Zywica and Danowski 2008.

Religion and the State

Increasingly, social scientists are recognizing the importance of both religion and government ("the state") as agents of socialization, because of their impact on the life course. Traditionally, family members have served as the primary caregivers in our culture, but in the 20th century, the family's protective function was steadily transferred to outside agencies such as hospitals, mental health clinics, and child care centers. Many of these agencies are run by groups affiliated with certain religions or by the state.

Both organized religion and government have impacted the life course by reinstituting some of the rites of passage once observed in agricultural communities and early industrial societies.

For example, religious organizations stipulate certain traditional rites that may bring together all the members of an extended family, even if they never meet for any other reason. And government regulations stipulate the ages at which a person may drive a car, drink alcohol, vote in elections, marry without parental permission, work overtime, and retire. These regulations do not constitute strict rites of passage: most 18-year-olds choose not to vote, and most people choose their age of retirement without reference to government dictates.

In the Social Policy section at the end of this module, we will see that government is under pressure to become a provider of child care, which would give it a new and direct role in the socialization of infants and young children.

In Israel, Aisheh and Eliza run a nursery for 29 Israeli and Palestinian children, ages four to six. Aisheh, who is Palestinian, speaks to the children in Arabic. Eliza, who is Jewish, speaks to them in Hebrew. The result: a bilingual, binational classroom that supports both Arab and Jewish culture—a first for Israel.

This unusual educational setting underscores the importance of early childhood socialization outside the home. Child care programs are not just babysitting services; they have an enormous influence on the development of young children—an influence that has been growing with the movement of more and more women into the paid labor force. The rise in single-parent families, increased job opportunities for women, and the need for additional family income have all propelled mothers of young children into the working world. Who should care for the children of working mothers during working hours?

Looking at the Issue

Preschoolers typically are not cared for by their parents. Seventy-three percent of employed mothers depend on others to care for their children, and 30 percent of mothers who aren't employed have regular care arrangements. In fact, children under age five are more likely to be cared for on a daily basis by their grandparents than by their parents. Over a third of them are cared for by non-relatives in nursery schools, Head Start programs, day care centers, family day care, and other arrangements (Bureau of the Census 2008c).

Researchers have found that high-quality child care centers do not adversely affect the socialization of children; in fact, good day care benefits children. The value of preschool programs was documented in a series of studies conducted in the United States. Researchers found no significant differences in infants who had received extensive nonmaternal care compared with those who had been cared for solely by their mothers. They also reported that more and more infants in the United States are being placed in child care outside the home, and that, overall, the quality of those arrangements is better than has been found in previous studies. It is difficult, however, to generalize about child care, since there is so much variability among day care providers, and even among government policies from one state to another (Loeb et al. 2004; Ludwig and Sawhill 2007; NICHD 2007).

Few people in the United States or elsewhere can afford the luxury of having a parent stay at home, or of paying for high-quality live-in child care. For millions of mothers and fathers, finding the right kind of child care is a challenge both to parenting and to the pocketbook. At present, the federal government supports child care through subsidized programs, which target low-income families, and income tax credits, which benefit families with more moderate incomes. The annual expenditure to assist low-income parents is about $12 billion; the expenditure to support more affluent parents is $58 billion (Cushing-Daniels and Zedlewski 2008).

Applying Sociology

Studies that assess the quality of child care outside the home reflect the micro level of analysis and the interest of interactionists in the impact of face-to-face interaction. These studies also explore macro-level implications for the functioning of social institutions like the family. But some of the issues surrounding day care have also been of interest to those who take the conflict perspective.

Children play at the Communicare day care center in Perth, Australia. The Australian government subsidizes children's attendance at day care and after-school programs from birth to age 12.

In the United States, high-quality day care is not equally available to all families. Parents in wealthy communities have an easier time finding day care than those in poor or working-class communities. Finding *affordable* child care is also a problem. Viewed from a conflict perspective, child care costs are an especially serious burden for lower-class families. The poorest families spend 25 percent of their income for preschool child care, while families who are *not* poor pay only 6 percent or less of their income.

Feminist theorists echo the concern of conflict theorists that high-quality child care receives little government support because it is regarded as "merely a way to let women work." Nearly all child care workers (97 percent) are women; many find themselves in low-status, minimum-wage jobs. Typically, food servers, messengers, and gas station attendants make more money than the 1.2 million child care workers in the United States, who averaged $9.43 per hour in 2008. Not surprisingly, turnover among employees in child care centers runs at 25 to 40 percent per year (Bureau of the Census 2009a:Table 596; NACCRRA 2010).

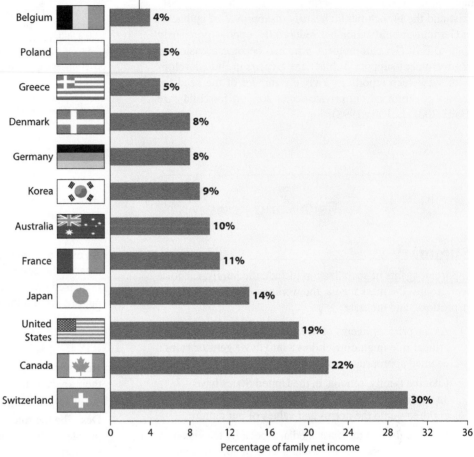

FIGURE 15-2 **Child Care Costs in Industrial Nations**

Note: Out-of-pocket expenses for two children in full-time care, less cash benefits and tax concessions.
Source: Organisation for Economic Co-operation and Development (OECD) 2007b:3.

Initiating Policy

Policies regarding child care outside the home vary throughout the world. As Figure 15-2 shows, the cost of child care as a proportion of one's income can vary dramatically, but at least it is available in industrial nations. Most developing nations do not have the economic base to provide subsidized child care. Thus, working mothers rely largely on relatives or take their children to work. In the comparatively wealthy industrialized countries of western Europe, government provides child care as a basic service, at little or no expense to parents. But even those countries with tax-subsidized programs occasionally fall short of the need for high-quality child care.

When policymakers decide that child care is desirable, they must determine the degree to which taxpayers should subsidize it. In Sweden and Denmark, one-half to two-thirds of preschoolers were in government-subsidized child care full-time in 2003. In the United States, annual fees for full-time child care of a four-year-old range from an average of $3,900 in Mississippi to an average of $11,678 in Massachusetts (Immervoll and Barber 2005; NACCRRA 2010).

We have a long way to go in making high-quality child care more affordable and accessible, not just in the United States but throughout the world. In an attempt to reduce

(continued)

government spending, France is considering cutting back the budgets of subsidized nurseries, even though waiting lists exist and the French public heartily disapproves of cutbacks. In Germany, reunification has reduced the options previously open to East German mothers, who had become accustomed to government-supported child care. Experts in child development view such reports as a vivid reminder of the need for greater government and private-sector support for child care (Hank 2001; L. King 1998).

MODULE 15 | Recap and Review

Summary

Important agents of socialization include the family, schools, peer groups, the mass media, the workplace, religious institutions, and the state.

1. As the primary agents of socialization, parents play a critical role in guiding children into those **gender roles** deemed appropriate in a society.

2. Like the family, schools in the United States have an explicit mandate to socialize people—especially children—into the norms and values of our culture.

3. Peer groups and the mass media, especially television and the Internet, are important agents of socialization for adolescents.

4. Socialization in the workplace begins with part-time employment while we are in school and continues as we work full-time and change jobs throughout our lives.

5. Religion and the state shape the socialization process by regulating the life course and influencing our views of appropriate behaviors at particular ages.

6. As more and more mothers of young children have entered the labor market, the demand for child care has increased dramatically, posing policy questions for many nations around the world.

Thinking Critically

1. How would functionalist and conflict theorists differ in their analysis of socialization by the mass media?

2. What sanctions limit participation in social networking? Describe the rules you have observed that limit the way people access and use online social networks. What are the purposes of such sanctions?

Key Term

Gender role

The prison experiment described in *The Lucifer Effect* took on new relevance during the Iraq War, in the wake of shocking revelations of prisoner abuse at the U.S.-run Abu Ghraib military facility. Graphic photos showed U.S. soldiers humiliating naked Iraqi prisoners and threatening to attack them with police dogs. The structure of the wartime prison, coupled with intense pressure on military intelligence officers to get information about terrorist plots, contributed to the breakdown in the guards' behavior. But the guards' depraved behavior could have been predicted on the basis of Zimbardo's research.

The two concepts of social interaction and social structure are central to sociology. **Social interaction,** the ways people respond to one another, and **social structure,** the way society is organized into predictable relationships, work together. Both concepts are closely related to socialization (see Module 13), the process through which people learn the attitudes, values, and behaviors appropriate to their society. When the students in Zimbardo's experiment entered the mock prison, they began a process of resocialization. In that process, they adjusted to a new social structure and learned new rules for social interaction.

Social Interaction and Reality

When someone in a crowd shoves you, do you automatically push back? Or do you consider the circumstances of the incident and the attitude of the instigator before you react? Chances are you do the latter. According to sociologist Herbert Blumer (1969:79), the distinctive characteristic of social interaction among people is that "human beings interpret or 'define' each other's actions instead of merely reacting to each other's actions." In other words, our response to someone's behavior is based on the *meaning* we attach to his or her actions. Reality is shaped by our perceptions, evaluations, and definitions.

These meanings typically reflect the norms and values of the dominant culture and our socialization experiences within that culture. As interactionists emphasize, the meanings that we attach to people's behavior are shaped by our interactions with them and with the larger society.

Social reality is literally constructed from our social interactions (Berger and Luckmann 1966).

How do we define our social reality? Consider something as simple as how we regard tattoos. At one time, most of us in the United States considered tattoos weird or kooky. We associated them with fringe countercultural groups, such as punk rockers, biker gangs, and skinheads. Among many people, a tattoo elicited an automatic negative response. Now, however, so many people have tattoos—including society's trendsetters and major sports figures—and the ritual of getting a tattoo has become so legitimized, that mainstream culture regards tattoos differently. At this point, as a result of increased social interaction with tattooed people, tattoos look perfectly at home to us in a number of settings.

The nature of social interaction and what constitutes reality varies across cultures. In Western societies, with their emphasis on romantic love, couples see marriage as a relationship as well as a social status. From Valentine's Day flowers to more informal, everyday gestures, professions of love are an expected part of marriage. In Japan, however, marriage is considered more a social status than a relationship. Although many or most Japanese couples undoubtedly do love each other, saying "I love you" does not come easily to them, especially not to husbands. Nor do most husbands call their wives by name (they prefer "Mother") or look them in the eyes. In 2006, in an effort to change these restrictive customs, some Japanese men formed the Devoted Husband Organization, which has been sponsoring a new holiday, Beloved Wives Day. Recently, the group organized an event called Shout Your Love from the Middle of a Cabbage Patch Day. Dozens of men stood in a cabbage patch north of Tokyo and shouted, "I love you!" to their wives, some of whom had never heard their husbands say those words (Kambayashi 2008).

The ability to define social reality reflects a group's power within a society. In fact, one of the most crucial aspects of the relationship between dominant and subordinate groups is the ability of the dominant or majority group to define a society's values. Sociologist William I. Thomas (1923), an early critic of theories of racial and gender differences, recognized that the "definition of the situation" could mold the thinking and personality of the individual. Writing from an interactionist perspective, Thomas observed that people respond not only to the objective features of a person or situation but also to the *meaning* that person or situation has for them. For example, in Philip Zimbardo's mock prison experiment, student "guards" and "prisoners" accepted the definition of the situation (including the traditional roles and behavior associated with being a guard or prisoner) and acted accordingly.

As we have seen throughout the past 60 years—first in the civil rights movement of the 1950s and 1960s and since then among such groups as women, the elderly, gays and lesbians, and people with disabilities—an important aspect of the process of social change involves redefining or reconstructing social reality. Members of subordinate groups challenge traditional definitions and begin to perceive and experience reality in a new way. An example of this challenge can be seen in the career of world champion boxer Muhammad Ali.

Ali began his career working for a White male syndicate, which sponsored his early matches when he was known as Cassius Clay. Soon, however, the young boxer rebelled against those who would keep him or his race down. He broke the old stereotypes of the self-effacing Black athlete, insisting on his political views (including refusing to serve in the Vietnam War), his religion (Black Muslim), and his name (Muhammad Ali). Not only did Ali change the world of sports; he also helped change the world of race relations. Viewed from a sociological perspective, then, Ali was redefining social reality by rebelling against the racist thinking and terminology that restricted him and other African Americans.

Elements of Social Structure

All social interaction takes place within a social structure, including those interactions that redefine social reality. For purposes of study, we can break down any social structure into five elements: statuses, social roles, groups, social networks, and social institutions. These elements make up social structure just as a foundation, walls, and ceilings make up a building's structure. The elements of social structure are developed through the lifelong process of socialization described in Module 14.

Statuses

We normally think of a person's *status* as having to do with influence, wealth, and fame. However, sociologists use the term **status** to refer to any of the full range of socially defined positions within a large group or society, from the lowest to the highest. Within our society, a person can occupy the status of president of the United States, fruit picker, son or daughter, violinist, teenager, resident of Minneapolis, dental technician, or neighbor. A person can hold a number of statuses at the same time.

Ascribed and Achieved Status Sociologists view some statuses as *ascribed* and others as *achieved* (Figure 16-1). An **ascribed status** is assigned to a person by society without regard for the person's unique talents or characteristics. Generally, the

FIGURE 16-1 **Social Statuses**

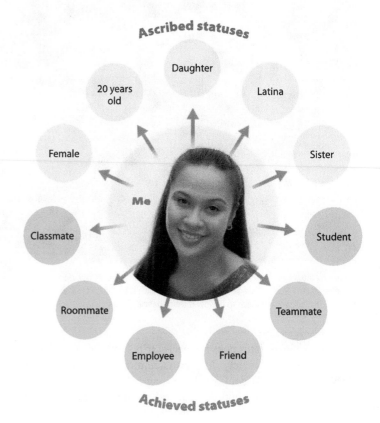

Think about It

The young woman in this figure—"me"—occupies many positions in society, each of which involves distinct statuses. How would you define your statuses? Which have the most influence in your life?

assignment takes place at birth; thus, a person's racial background, gender, and age are all considered ascribed statuses. Though these characteristics are biological in origin, they are significant mainly because of the *social* meanings they have in our culture. Conflict theorists are especially interested in ascribed statuses, since they often confer privileges or reflect a person's membership in a subordinate group. The social meanings of race, ethnicity, and gender will be analyzed more fully in Modules 32 and 34.

In most cases, we can do little to change an ascribed status, but we can attempt to change the traditional constraints associated with it. For example, the Gray Panthers—an activist political group founded in 1971 to work for the rights of older people—have tried to modify society's negative and confining stereotypes of the elderly. As a result of their work and that of other groups supporting older citizens, the ascribed status of "senior citizen" is no longer as difficult for millions of older people.

Ascribed status may intersect with a person's achieved status. As this doorman greets a resident, the worker's achieved status as a low-wage worker combines with his ethnic status as an African American, an identity that many in this society consider to be lower than that of Whites.

An ascribed status does not necessarily have the same social meaning in every society. In a cross-cultural study, sociologist Gary Huang (1988) confirmed the long-held view that respect for the elderly is an important cultural norm in China. In many cases, the prefix "old" is used respectfully: calling someone "old teacher" or "old person" is like calling a judge in the United States "your honor." Huang points out that positive age-seniority language distinctions are uncommon in the United States; consequently, we view the term *old man* as more of an insult than a celebration of seniority and wisdom.

Unlike ascribed statuses, an **achieved status** comes to us largely through our own efforts. Both "computer programmer" and "prison guard" are achieved statuses, as are "lawyer," "pianist," "sorority member," "convict," and "social worker." We must do something to acquire an achieved status—go to school, learn a skill, establish a friendship, invent a new product. But as we will see in the next section, our ascribed status heavily influences our achieved status. Being male, for example, would decrease the likelihood that we would consider child care as a career.

Master Status   Each person holds many different and sometimes conflicting statuses; some may connote higher social position and some, lower position. How, then, do others view one's overall social position? According to sociologist Everett Hughes (1945), societies deal with inconsistencies by agreeing that certain statuses are more important than others. A **master status** is a status that dominates others and thereby determines a person's general position in society. For example, Arthur Ashe, who died of AIDS in 1993, had a remarkable career as a tennis star, but at the end of his life, his status as a well-known personality with AIDS may have outweighed his statuses as a retired athlete, author, and political activist. Throughout the world,

many people with disabilities find that their status as disabled receives undue weight, overshadowing their actual ability to perform successfully in meaningful employment.

Our society gives such importance to race and gender that they often dominate our lives. These ascribed statuses frequently influence our achieved status. The Black activist Malcolm X (1925–1965), an eloquent and controversial advocate of Black power and Black pride during the early 1960s, recalled that his feelings and perspectives changed dramatically while in eighth grade. When his English teacher, a White man, advised him that his goal of becoming a lawyer was "no realistic goal for a nigger" and encouraged him instead to become a carpenter, Malcolm X ([1964] 1999:37) found that being a Black man (ascribed status) was an obstacle to his dream of becoming a lawyer (achieved status). In the United States, the ascribed statuses of race and gender can function as master statuses that have an important impact on one's potential to achieve a desired professional and social status.

Social Roles

What Are Social Roles?   Throughout our lives, we acquire what sociologists call social roles. A **social role** is a set of expectations for people who occupy a given social position or status. Thus, in the United States, we expect that cab drivers will know how to get around a city, that receptionists will be reliable in handling phone messages, and that police officers will take action if they see a citizen being threatened. With each distinctive social status—whether ascribed or achieved—come particular role expectations. However, actual performance varies from individual to individual. One secretary may assume extensive administrative responsibilities, while another may focus on clerical duties. Similarly, in Philip Zimbardo's mock prison experiment, some students were brutal and sadistic guards; others were not.

Roles are a significant component of social structure. Viewed from a functionalist perspective, roles contribute to a society's stability by enabling members to anticipate the behavior of others and to pattern their actions accordingly. Yet social roles can also be dysfunctional if they restrict people's interactions and relationships. If we view a person *only* as a "police officer" or "supervisor," it will be difficult to relate to him or her as a friend or neighbor.

Role Conflict   Imagine the delicate situation of a woman who has worked for a decade on an assembly line in an electrical plant, and has recently been named supervisor of her unit. How is this woman expected to relate to her longtime friends and co-workers? Should she still go out to lunch with them, as she has done almost daily for years? Is it her responsibility to recommend the firing of an old friend who cannot keep up with the demands of the assembly line?

Role conflict occurs when incompatible expectations arise from two or more social positions held by the same person. Fulfillment of the roles associated with one status may directly violate the roles linked to a second status. In the example just given, the newly promoted supervisor will most likely experience a sharp conflict between her social and occupational roles. Such role conflicts call for important ethical choices. The new supervisor will have to make a difficult decision about how much allegiance she owes her friend and how much she owes her employers, who have given her supervisory responsibilities.

Another type of role conflict occurs when individuals move into occupations that are not common among people with their ascribed status. Male preschool teachers and female police officers experience this type of role conflict. In the latter case, female officers must strive to reconcile their workplace role in law enforcement with the societal view of a woman's role, which does not embrace many skills needed in police work. And while female police officers encounter sexual harassment, as women do throughout the labor force, they must also deal with the "code of silence," an informal norm that precludes their implicating fellow officers in wrongdoing (Fletcher 1995; S. Martin 1994).

According to sociologist Helen Rose Fuchs Ebaugh, role exit is a four-stage process. Is this transexual in the first or the fourth stage of changing genders?

 use your **sociological imagination**

If you were a male nurse, what aspects of role conflict might you experience? Now imagine you are a professional boxer and a woman. What conflicting role expectations might that involve? In both cases, how well do you think you would handle role conflict?

Role Strain Role conflict describes the situation of a person dealing with the challenge of occupying two social positions simultaneously. However, even a single position can cause problems. Sociologists use the term **role strain** to describe the difficulty that arises when the same social position imposes conflicting demands and expectations.

People who belong to minority cultures may experience role strain while working in the mainstream culture. Criminologist Larry Gould (2002) interviewed officers of the Navajo Nation Police Department about their relations with conventional law enforcement officials, such as sheriffs and FBI agents. Besides enforcing the law, Navajo Nation officers practice an alternative form of justice known as Peacemaking, in which they seek reconciliation between the parties to a crime. The officers expressed great confidence in Peacemaking, but worried that if they did not make arrests, other law enforcement officials would think they were too soft, or "just taking care of their own." Regardless of the strength of their ties to traditional Navajo ways, all felt the strain of being considered "too Navajo" or "not Navajo enough."

Role Exit Often, when we think of assuming a social role, we focus on the preparation and anticipatory socialization a person undergoes for that role. Such is true if a person is about to become an attorney, a chef, a spouse, or a parent. Yet until recently, social scientists have given little attention to the adjustments involved in *leaving* social roles.

Sociologist Helen Rose Fuchs Ebaugh (1988) developed the term **role exit** to describe the process of disengagement from a role that is central to one's self-identity in order to establish a new role and identity. Drawing on interviews with 185 people— among them ex-convicts, divorced men and women, recovering alcoholics, ex-nuns, former doctors, retirees, and transexuals— Ebaugh (herself an ex-nun) studied the process of voluntarily exiting from significant social roles.

Ebaugh has offered a four-stage model of role exit. The first stage begins with *doubt*. The person experiences frustration, burnout, or simply unhappiness with an accustomed status and the roles associated with the social position. The second stage involves a *search for alternatives*. A person who is unhappy with his or her career may take a leave of absence; an unhappily married couple may begin what they see as a temporary separation.

The third stage of role exit is the *action stage* or *departure*. Ebaugh found that the vast majority of her respondents could identify a clear turning point that made them feel it was essential to take final action and leave their jobs, end their marriages, or engage in another type of role exit. Twenty percent of respondents saw their role exit as a gradual, evolutionary process that had no single turning point.

The last stage of role exit involves the *creation of a new identity*. Many of you participated in a role exit when you made the transition from high school to college. You left behind the role of offspring living at home and took on the role of a somewhat independent college student living with peers in a dorm. Sociologist Ira Silver (1996) has studied the central role that material objects play in this transition. The objects students choose to leave at home (like stuffed animals and dolls) are associated with their prior identities. They may remain deeply attached to those objects, but do not want them to be seen as part of their new identities at college. The objects they bring with them symbolize how they now see themselves and how they wish to be perceived. iPods and wall posters, for example, are calculated to say, "This is me."

Groups

In sociological terms, a **group** is any number of people with similar norms, values, and expectations who interact with one another on a regular basis. The members of a women's basketball team, a hospital's business office, a synagogue, or a symphony orchestra constitute a group. However, the residents of a suburb would not be considered a group, since they rarely interact with one another at one time.

Groups play a vital part in a society's social structure. Much of our social interaction takes place within groups and is influenced by their norms and sanctions. Being a teenager or a retired person takes on special meanings when we interact within groups designed for people with that particular status. The expectations associated with many social roles, including those accompanying the statuses of brother, sister, and student, become more clearly defined in the context of a group.

Social Institutions

The mass media, the government, the economy, the family, and the health care system are all examples of social institutions found in our society. **Social institutions** are organized patterns of beliefs and behavior centered on basic social needs, such as replacing personnel (the family) and preserving order (the government).

A close look at social institutions gives sociologists insight into the structure of a society. Consider religion, for example. The institution of religion adapts to the segment of society that it serves. Church work has very different meanings for ministers who serve a skid row area and those who serve a suburban middle-class community. Religious leaders assigned to a skid row mission will focus on tending to the ill and providing food and shelter. In contrast, clergy in affluent suburbs will be occupied with counseling those considering marriage and divorce, arranging youth activities, and overseeing cultural events (R. Schaefer 2008b).

Functionalist View One way to understand social institutions is to see how they fulfill essential functions. Anthropologist David F. Aberle and his colleagues (1950) and sociologists Raymond Mack and Calvin Bradford (1979) have identified five major tasks, or functional prerequisites, that a society or relatively permanent group must accomplish if it is to survive:

1. *Replacing personnel.* Any group or society must replace personnel when they die, leave, or become incapacitated. This task is accomplished through such means as immigration, annexation of neighboring groups, acquisition of slaves, or sexual reproduction. The Shakers, a religious sect that came to the United States in 1774, are a conspicuous example of a group that has *failed* to replace personnel. Their religious beliefs commit the Shakers to celibacy; to survive, the group must recruit new members. At first, the Shakers proved quite successful in attracting members, reaching a peak of about 6,000 members in the United States during the 1840s. As of 2010, however, the only Shaker community left in this country was a farm in Maine with three members—one man and two women (R. Schaefer and Zellner 2011).

2. *Teaching new recruits.* No group or society can survive if many of its members reject the group's established behavior and responsibilities. Thus, finding or producing new members is not sufficient; the group or society must also encourage recruits to learn and accept its values and customs. Such learning can take place formally, within schools (where learning is a manifest function), or informally, through interaction in peer groups (where learning is a latent function).

3. *Producing and distributing goods and services.* Any relatively permanent group or society must provide and distribute desired goods and services to its members. Each society establishes a set of rules for the allocation of financial and other resources. The group must satisfy the needs of most members to some extent, or it will risk the possibility of discontent and ultimately disorder.

4. *Preserving order.* Throughout the world, indigenous and aboriginal peoples have struggled to protect themselves from outside invaders, with varying degrees of success. Failure to preserve order and defend against conquest leads to the death, not only of a people, but of a culture.

5. *Providing and maintaining a sense of purpose.* People must feel motivated to continue as members of a group or society in order to fulfill the first four requirements. On January 20, 2009, in the midst of what would prove the worst economic crisis since the Great Depression, some 2 million Americans crowded the National Mall to witness the inauguration of President Barack Obama, the first African American to be elected to the nation's highest office. The celebration, an expression of both patriotism and Black pride, convinced people of all races that change was possible and better times lay ahead. Faced with huge layoffs and massive home foreclosures, Americans heard the new president's call to serve their nation. Patriotism and

racial pride, then, can help people to develop and maintain a sense of purpose. For others, tribal identities, religious values, or personal moral codes are especially meaningful. Whatever the motivator, in any society there remains one common and critical reality: if an individual does not have a sense of purpose, he or she has little reason to contribute to a society's survival.

This list of functional prerequisites does not specify *how* a society and its corresponding social institutions will perform each task. For example, one society may protect itself from external attack by amassing a frightening arsenal of weaponry, while another may make determined efforts to remain neutral in world politics and to promote cooperative relationships with its neighbors. No matter what its particular strategy, any society or relatively permanent group must attempt to satisfy all these functional prerequisites for survival. If it fails on even one condition, the society runs the risk of extinction.

Conflict View Conflict theorists do not agree with the functionalist approach to social institutions. Although proponents of both perspectives agree that social institutions are organized to meet basic social needs, conflict theorists object to the idea that the outcome is necessarily efficient and desirable.

From a conflict perspective, the present organization of social institutions is no accident. Major institutions, such as education, help to maintain the privileges of the most powerful individuals and groups within a society, while contributing to the powerlessness of others. To give one example, public schools in the United States are financed largely through property taxes. This arrangement allows more affluent areas to provide their children with better-equipped schools and better-paid teachers than low-income areas can afford. As a result, children from prosperous communities are better prepared to compete academically than children from impoverished communities. The structure of the nation's educational system permits and even promotes such unequal treatment of schoolchildren.

Conflict theorists argue that social institutions such as education have an inherently conservative nature. Without question, it has been difficult to implement educational reforms that promote equal opportunity—whether bilingual education, school desegregation, or mainstreaming of students with disabilities. From a functionalist perspective, social change can be dysfunctional, since it often leads to instability. However, from a conflict view, why should we preserve the existing social structure if it is unfair and discriminatory?

Social institutions also operate in gendered and racist environments, as conflict theorists, as well as feminists and interactionists, have pointed out. In schools, offices, and government institutions, assumptions about what people can do reflect the sexism and racism of the larger society. For instance, many people assume that women cannot make tough decisions—even those in the top echelons of corporate management. Others assume that all Black students at elite colleges represent affirmative action admissions. Inequality based on gender, economic status, race, and ethnicity thrives in such an environment—to

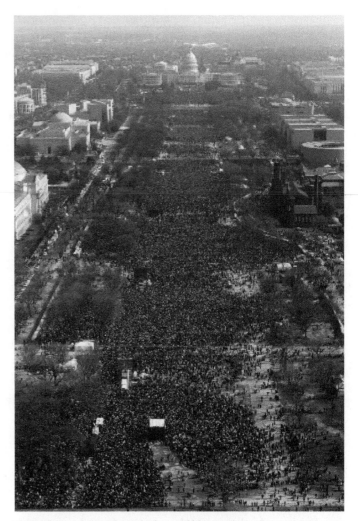

Waving flags and dressed in red, white, and blue, nearly 2 million Americans came together to celebrate the inauguration of President Barack Obama, the nation's first African American president, in January 2009. In the midst of a deepening economic and financial crisis, Obama's election brought hope to Americans of all races, helping them to maintain a sense of purpose in the face of adversity.

which we might add discrimination based on age, physical disability, and sexual orientation. The truth of this assertion can be seen in routine decisions by employers on how to advertise jobs, as well as whether to provide fringe benefits such as child care and parental leave.

Interactionist View Social institutions affect our everyday behavior, whether we are driving down the street or waiting in a long shopping line. Sociologist Mitchell Duneier (1994a,b) studied the social behavior of the word processors, all women, who work in the service center of a large Chicago law firm. Duneier was interested in the informal social norms that emerged in this work environment and the rich social network these female employees created.

The Network Center, as it is called, is a single, windowless room in a large office building where the law firm occupies seven floors. The center is staffed by two shifts of word

Perspective	Role of Social Institutions	Focus
Functionalist	Meeting basic social needs	Essential functions
Conflict	Meeting basic social needs	Maintenance of privileges and inequality
Interactionist	Fostering everyday behavior	Influence of the roles and statuses we accept

processors, who work either from 4:00 p.m. to midnight or from midnight to 8:00 a.m. Each word processor works in a cubicle with just enough room for her keyboard, terminal, printer, and telephone. Work assignments for the word processors are placed in a central basket and then completed according to precise procedures.

At first glance, we might think that these women labor with little social contact, apart from limited breaks and occasional conversations with their supervisor. However, drawing on the interactionist perspective, Duneier learned that despite working in a large office, these women find private moments to talk (often in the halls or outside the washroom) and share a critical view of the law firm's attorneys and day-shift secretaries. Indeed, the word processors routinely suggest that their assignments represent work that the "lazy" secretaries should have completed during the normal workday. Duneier (1994b) tells of one word processor who resented the lawyers' superior attitude and pointedly refused to recognize or speak with any attorney who would not address her by name.

Interactionist theorists emphasize that our social behavior is conditioned by the roles and statuses we accept, the groups to which we belong, and the institutions within which we function. For example, the social roles associated with being a judge occur within the larger context of the criminal justice system. The status of judge stands in relation to other statuses, such as attorney, plaintiff, defendant, and witness, as well as to the social institution of government. Although courts and jails have great symbolic importance, the judicial system derives its continued significance from the roles people carry out in social interactions (Berger and Luckmann 1966).

Table 16-1 summarizes the three major sociological perspectives on social institutions.

Social Networks

Groups do not merely serve to define other elements of the social structure, such as roles and statuses; they also link the individual with the larger society. We all belong to a number of different groups, and through our acquaintances make connections with people in different social circles. These connections are known as a **social network**—a series of social relationships that links a person directly to others, and through them indirectly to still more people.

Social networks can center on virtually any activity, from sharing job information to exchanging news and gossip, or even sharing sex. In the mid-1990s, sociologists Peter Bearman, James Moody, and Katherine Stovel (2004) studied romantic relationships at a high school with about 1,000 students. They found that about 61 percent of the girls had been sexually active over the past 18 months. Among the sexually active respondents, the researchers counted only 63 steady couples, or pairs with no other partners. A much larger group of 288 students—almost a third of the sample—was involved in a free-flowing network of relationships.

This research on high schoolers' sexual activity, an example of applied sociology, has clear implications for public health. The Research Today box describes a similar but longer-term study that used network analysis to inform government efforts to discourage smoking.

Involvement in social networks—commonly known as *networking*—is especially valuable in finding employment. Albert Einstein was successful in finding a job only when a classmate's father put him in touch with his future employer. These kinds of contacts—even those that are weak and distant—can be crucial in establishing social networks and facilitating the transmission of information.

In the workplace, networking pays off more for men than for women because of the traditional presence of men in leadership positions. One survey of executives found that 63 percent of the men used networking to find new jobs, compared to 41 percent of the women. Women were more likely than men to rely on classified advertisements to find jobs. Still, women at all levels of the paid labor force are beginning to make effective use of social networks. Now that job advertisements have largely migrated to the Internet, new research is needed on whether gender differences persist in in-person and online networking (Flynn 2008; Henly 1999).

Social Networks and Smoking

Over the past two generations, the incidence of smoking in the United States has decreased significantly. Scholars have been trying to determine the reasons for this shift in behavior. Certainly the health benefits of quitting must have influenced many people. But smoking is an addictive behavior that is difficult to stop. Could something more than potential health benefits lie behind its steep decline?

To find out, researchers repeatedly assessed the smoking habits of 12,067 subjects of a long-term survey of heart health. From the beginning, they examined the role of social networks in respondents' smoking. Not surprisingly, they found that social networks typically linked those who either smoked or did not smoke. The two groups rarely mixed.

Over the three decades since this survey began, researchers saw marked changes in respondents' smoking behavior. Although the size of their family and friendship clusters remained the same, in many clusters, members totally abandoned smoking. This finding suggests that whole groups of friends and family were quitting together.

> In many clusters, members totally abandoned smoking. This finding suggests that whole groups of friends and family were quitting together.

The accompanying figure shows the same social network at the beginning and end of the study's 30-year span. As might be expected, group membership and the links that connected members changed over time. More remarkable was the decline or outright disappearance of smoking in some clusters. The remaining smokers, especially heavy smokers,

A Network of Smokers and Nonsmokers, 1971 and 2000
● **Smoker**   ● **Nonsmoker**   —— **Social connection**

1971   2000

Details of social groups

Larger circles denote heavier smokers

Source: R. Stein 2008 based on Christakis and Fowler 2008.

were marginalized—that is, their ties to other members of the network declined.

Social pressure to quit smoking seems to underlie these changes. Notably, friends but not neighbors of those who quit were influenced by a person's decision to stop smoking. Among friends, smoking cessation by one person decreased the chances that the other would continue to smoke by 36 percent. Among siblings, the risk of the other person continuing to smoke fell by 25 percent, and among spouses, by 67 percent. Among co-workers at small firms, the drop in the chances of one smoking after the other stopped was 34 percent.

This study shows that social networks influence the way people behave. In this case, they strengthened their members' willpower to quit smoking. The practical, or applied, implication of the research is that public health programs that promote smoking cessation should target friendship groups or couples rather than individuals. Because this insight may also prove useful in other areas of public health, researchers are now planning to investigate the relationship between social networks and obesity, drinking, and drug abuse.

LET'S DISCUSS

1. In your experience, do smokers and nonsmokers tend to cluster in separate groups? Have you ever tried to quit smoking, and if so, did your cluster of friends and family help or hinder you?

2. Besides public health campaigns, what other applications can you think of for social network research?

Sources: Christakis and Fowler 2008, 2009; Kolata 2008; K. Smith and Christakis 2008; R. Stein 2008.

During the recent economic downturn, electronic social networks have served a new purpose, encouraging the jobless. Web sites and chat rooms that cannot locate jobs for those who have been thrown out of work concentrate instead on helping them to stick together, support one another, and maintain a positive attitude. For the unemployed, online conversations with friends or even strangers in the same predicament can be an invaluable morale booster (Scherer 2010b).

Virtual Worlds

Today, with recent advances in technology, people can maintain their social networks electronically; they don't need face-to-face contacts. Whether through text-messaging, handheld devices, or social networking sites like Facebook, a significant amount of networking occurs online. Adolescents can now interact freely with distant friends, even under close scrutiny by parents or teachers. Without leaving their cubicles,

Virtual worlds have just begun to test our imaginations. On the left, a group of avatars interacts in the Second Life® world, a Web-based three-dimensional virtual world that included about 18 million networked players as of January 2010. On the right, in the blockbuster film *Avatar*, the Na'vi people interact in the screen-based virtual world of Pandora.

employees with a taste for adventure can escape their work environments. In Module 15 we considered the impact of online social networks on the process of socialization. Facebook and MySpace are only the first stage in the creation of alternative forms of reality through new technology. A whole new society, the Second Life® world, has sprung up in virtual space.

Virtual life can and does migrate into real life. In 2007, college housing officials became worried when freshmen and their parents began checking out the Facebook profiles of prospective roommates. Soon, colleges were fielding requests for new roommates before students even arrived on campus. Concerns went far beyond tastes in music; the reservations expressed most often by parents included a potential roommate's race, religion, and sexual orientation (Collura 2007).

Online socialization may not necessarily reinforce people's prejudices, however. Researchers at Pennsylvania State University argue that participating in the Second Life virtual world opens us up to people from different cultural and linguistic backgrounds. In their view, online friendships among avatars may enhance cross-cultural encounters and friendships in the first life—that is, the real world (Diehl and Prins 2008).

Virtual networks can also help to preserve real-world networks interrupted by war and other dislocations. In 2003, the deployment of U.S. troops in the Middle East increased many people's reliance on e-mail. Today, digital photos and sound files accompany e-mail messages between soldiers and their families and friends. GIs can even view siblings' graduations or children's birthday parties live, via Webcams. And U.S. soldiers and Iraqi citizens have been posting their opinions of the war in Iraq in online journals called Web logs, or blogs. Though critics are skeptical of the identity of some of the authors, these postings have become yet another source of news about the war (Faith 2005; O'Connor 2004; Sisson 2007).

MODULE 16 | Recap and Review

Summary

Social interaction refers to the ways in which people respond to one another. **Social structure** refers to the way in which a society is organized into predictable relationships. This module examines the five basic elements of social structure: **statuses, social roles, groups, social networks,** and **social institutions.**

1. People shape their social reality based on what they learn through **social interactions.** Social change comes from redefining or reconstructing social reality.

2. An **ascribed status** is generally assigned to a person at birth, whereas an **achieved status** is attained largely through one's own effort. Some ascribed statuses, such as race and gender, can function as **master statuses** that affect one's potential to achieve a certain professional or social status.

3. With each distinctive status—whether ascribed or achieved—comes a particular **social role,** the set of expectations for people who occupy that status.

4. Much of our social behavior takes place in **groups.**

5. **Social institutions** fulfill essential functions, such as replacing personnel, training new recruits, and preserving order. The mass media, the government, the economy, the family, and the health care system are all examples of social institutions.

6. **Social networks** form linkages between individuals and groups and can center on virtually any activity. Virtual worlds are another important realm in which social interaction takes place and social networks form.

Thinking Critically

1. Think back over the events of the past few days. Identify two occasions on which different people defined the same social reality differently.

2. Describe a specific master status and explain how it was established. Is it a negative status? If so, how would a person overcome it?

3. Describe some specific ways in which participation in virtual worlds is changing the nature of social groups.

Key Terms

Achieved status

Ascribed status

Group

Master status

Role conflict

Role exit

Role strain

Social institution

Social interaction

Social network

Social role

Social structure

Status

Understanding Groups

Most of us use the term *group* loosely to describe any collection of individuals, whether three strangers sharing an elevator or hundreds attending a rock concert. However, in sociological terms a group is any number of people with similar norms, values, and expectations who interact with one another on a regular basis. College sororities and fraternities, dance companies, tenants' associations, and chess clubs are all considered groups. The important point is that members of a group share some sense of belonging. This characteristic distinguishes groups from mere *aggregates* of people, such as passengers who happen to be together on an airplane flight, or from *categories* of people, such as those who share a common feature (such as being retired) but otherwise do not act together.

Consider the case of a college singing group. It has agreed-on values and social norms. All members want to improve their singing skills and schedule lots of performances. In addition, like many groups, the singing ensemble has both a formal and an informal structure. The members meet regularly to rehearse; they choose leaders to run the rehearsals and manage their affairs. At the same time, some group members may take on unofficial leadership roles by coaching new members in singing techniques and performing skills.

Types of Groups

Sociologists have made a number of useful distinctions between types of groups—primary and secondary groups, in-groups and out-groups, and reference groups.

Primary and Secondary Groups

Charles Horton Cooley (1902) coined the term **primary group** to refer to a small group characterized by intimate, face-to-face association and cooperation. The members of a street gang constitute a primary group; so do members of a family living in the same household, as do a group of "sisters" in a college sorority.

Primary groups play a pivotal role both in the socialization process (see Module 13) and in the development of roles and statuses (see Module 16). Indeed, primary groups can be instrumental in a person's day-to-day existence. When we find ourselves identifying closely with a group, it is probably a primary group.

We also participate in many groups that are not characterized by close bonds of friendship, such as large college classes and business associations. The term **secondary group** refers to a formal, impersonal group in which there is little social intimacy or mutual understanding (Table 18-1). Secondary groups often emerge in the workplace among those who share special understandings about their occupation. The distinction between primary and secondary groups is not always clear-cut, however. Some social clubs may become so large and impersonal that they no longer function as primary groups.

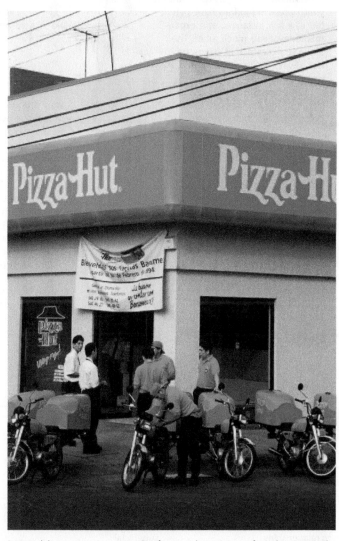

A pizza delivery crew is an example of a *secondary group*—a formal, impersonal group in which there is little social intimacy or mutual understanding. While waiting for the next delivery, members of this crew will become well enough acquainted to distinguish those who see the job as temporary from those who view it as permanent. They will learn who looks forward to deliveries in perceived high-risk areas and who does not. They may even spend time together after work, joking or boasting about their exploits on the job, but their friendships typically will not develop beyond that point.

The Drinking Rape Victim: Jury Decision Making

She was heavily intoxicated. He had drunk a few beers. They had sex. She said she was raped. He said it was consensual. The jury deliberated, and the verdict was. . . .

This is not an actual case, but an experiment in group decision making. Few small groups have received as much attention from sociologists over the past decade and a half as juries. Scholars have used several research methods to investigate juries' decision making: interviews with jury members after they have reached a verdict; observation of jurors as they sit through and react to courtroom events; observation of actual jury deliberations, which presiding judges have permitted in a few instances; and experiments involving mock juries. The findings indicate that jurors do not always make decisions the way they are supposed to.

For example, a jury's decision making may occur even before the first ballot is taken. Despite judges' instructions to the contrary, many jurors form tentative verdicts early in the trial. Studies suggest that jurors who have reached an initial judgment of "guilty" or "not guilty" give disproportionate weight to testimony that reinforces their impressions, while they tend to discount testimony that undermines them.

How do jurors form impressions in rape cases, especially those that involve intoxication? To find out, legal scholars Emily Finch and Vanessa

> Finch and Munro found that although mock jurors generally disapproved of a man's taking advantage of a woman who was drunk, they did not always return a guilty verdict.

Munro simulated a rape trial in which intoxication was an issue. The two researchers varied the story to see what the effect might be on the verdict: in one version the alleged victim was drunk; in another she was drugged by a third person; in another she was drugged by the defendant. Finch and Munro found that although mock jurors generally disapproved of a man's taking advantage of a woman who was drunk, they did not always return a guilty verdict. In these cases, the source of the intoxication often influenced the verdict. Even if the physical effect on the victim was the same, jurors were much less troubled by alcohol intoxication than by drug intoxication. Liquor and sex had come to be almost normalized in their view, to the extent that they were much less likely to convict the defendant when the

victim had been drinking than when she had been using drugs.

Today, research on juries is expanding to deal with generational changes in the experience of being a juror. Some jurors arrive at court expecting to see the kind of sophisticated DNA analysis or investigative methods featured on televised crime shows, such as *CSI*. Improved methods of documenting crime scenes, including the use of computer-generated re-creations, mean that today's jurors are more likely than past jurors to be exposed to images of graphic violence and gore. Mental health professionals and social scientists have documented that the trauma jurors sometimes suffer from such exposure can trigger classic symptoms of stress, including depression, anxiety, weight loss, sleep loss, and disruptions in close social relationships. As with membership in other small groups, serving on a jury can be an intense experience—especially during a long, combative criminal trial with a focus on violence and bloodshed.

LET'S DISCUSS

1. Have you ever served on a jury? If so, were you aware of jurors who made up their minds early in the trial, despite the judge's instructions? Did you experience stress from being exposed to graphic images of violence and bloodshed?

2. Is a jury a typical group? Why or why not?

Sources: S. Diamond and Rose 2005; Finch and Munro 2005, 2007, 2008.

Table **18-1** Comparison of Primary and Secondary Groups

summing up

Primary Group	Secondary Group
Generally small	Usually large
Relatively long period of interaction	Relatively short duration, often temporary
Intimate, face-to-face association	Little social intimacy or mutual understanding
Some emotional depth to relationships	Relationships generally superficial
Cooperative, friendly	More formal and impersonal

A significant amount of sociological research has been done on people's behavior in groups. The Research Today box describes the findings on one well-known but short-lived group, the jury.

In-Groups and Out-Groups

A group can hold special meaning for members because of its relationship to other groups. For example, people in one group sometimes feel antagonistic toward or threatened by another group, especially if that group is perceived as being different either culturally or racially. To identify these "we" and "they" feelings, sociologists use two terms first employed by William Graham Sumner (1906): *in-group* and *out-group*.

An **in-group** can be defined as any group or category to which people feel they belong. Simply put, it comprises everyone who is regarded as "we" or "us." The in-group may be as narrow as a teenage clique or as broad as an entire society. The very existence of an in-group implies that there is an out-group that is viewed as "they" or "them." An **out-group** is a group or category to which people feel they do *not* belong.

In-group members typically feel distinct and superior, seeing themselves as better than people in the out-group. Proper

"So long, Bill. This is my club. You can't come in."

An exclusive social club is an in-group whose members consider themselves superior to others.

behavior for the in-group is simultaneously viewed as unacceptable behavior for the out-group. This double standard enhances the sense of superiority. Sociologist Robert Merton (1968) described this process as the conversion of "in-group virtues" into "out-group vices." We can see this differential standard operating in worldwide discussions of terrorism. When a group or a nation takes aggressive actions, it usually justifies them as necessary, even if civilians are hurt or killed. Opponents are quick to label such actions with the emotion-laden term of *terrorist* and appeal to the world community for condemnation. Yet these same people may themselves retaliate with actions that hurt civilians, which the first group will then condemn.

Conflict between in-groups and out-groups can turn violent on a personal as well as a political level. In 1999 two disaffected students at Columbine High School in Littleton, Colorado, launched an attack on the school that left 15 students and teachers dead, including themselves. The gunmen, members of an out-group that other students referred to as the Trenchcoat Mafia, apparently resented taunting by an in-group referred to as the Jocks. Similar episodes have occurred in schools across the nation, where rejected adolescents, overwhelmed by personal and family problems, peer group pressure, academic responsibilities, or media images of violence, have struck out against more popular classmates.

 use your **sociological imagination**

Try putting yourself in the shoes of an out-group member. What does your in-group look like from that perspective?

Reference Groups

Both primary groups and in-groups can dramatically influence the way an individual thinks and behaves. Sociologists call any group that individuals use as a standard for evaluating themselves and their behavior a **reference group.** For example, a high school student who aspires to join a social circle of hip-hop music devotees will pattern his or her behavior after that of the group. The student will begin dressing like these peers, listening to the same downloads and DVDs, and hanging out at the same stores and clubs.

Reference groups have two basic purposes. They serve a normative function by setting and enforcing standards of conduct and belief. The high school student who wants the approval of the hip-hop crowd will have to follow the group's dictates, at least to some extent. Reference groups also perform a comparison function by serving as a standard against which people can measure themselves and others. An actor will evaluate himself or herself against a reference group composed of others in the acting profession (Merton and Kitt 1950).

Reference groups may help the process of anticipatory socialization. For example, a college student majoring in finance may read the *Wall Street Journal,* study the annual reports of corporations, and listen to midday stock market news on the radio. Such a student is using financial experts as a reference group to which he or she aspires.

Often, two or more reference groups influence us at the same time. Our family members, neighbors, and co-workers all shape different aspects of our self-evaluation. In addition, reference group attachments change during the life cycle. A corporate executive who quits the rat race at age 45 to become a social

At a powwow, a drum circle breathes spirit into an ancient tribal tradition. These accomplished ceremonial musicians may serve as a reference group for onlookers who want to know more about drumming.

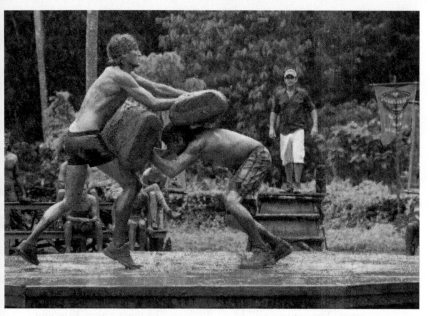

Can you outwit, outplay, outlast your competition? Maybe a coalition can help. In *Survivor: Heroes vs. Villains,* coalition building continued to be one of the keys to success in the long-running television series, now in its 20th season.

worker will find new reference groups to use as standards for evaluation. We shift reference groups as we take on different statuses during our lives.

Coalitions

As groups grow larger, coalitions begin to develop. A **coalition** is a temporary or permanent alliance geared toward a common goal. Coalitions can be broad-based or narrow and can take on many different objectives. Sociologist William Julius Wilson (1999)

has described community-based organizations in Texas that include Whites and Latinos, working class and affluent, who have banded together to work for improved sidewalks, better drainage systems, and comprehensive street paving. Out of this type of coalition building, Wilson hopes, will emerge better interracial understanding.

Some coalitions are intentionally short-lived. For example, short-term coalition building is a key to success in popular TV programs like *Survivor.* In the program's first season, *Survivor: Borneo,* broadcast in 2000, the four members of the "Tagi alliance" banded together to vote fellow castaways off the island. The political world is also the scene of many temporary coalitions. For example, in 1997 big tobacco companies joined with antismoking groups to draw up a settlement for reimbursing states for tobacco-related medical costs. Soon after the settlement was announced the coalition members returned to their decades-long fight against each other (Pear 1997).

 use your **sociological imagination**

Do coalitions always work toward positive goals? Imagine a coalition that was formed to achieve a socially undesirable goal. Who are the members, and why did they band together?

MODULE 18 | Recap and Review

Summary

Much of our social behavior takes place in **groups.**

1. When we find ourselves identifying closely with a group, it is probably a **primary group.** A **secondary group** is more formal and impersonal.

2. People tend to see the world in terms of **in-groups** and **out-groups,** a perception often fostered by the very groups to which they belong.

3. **Reference groups** set and enforce standards of conduct and serve as a source of comparison for people's evaluations of themselves and others.

4. Interactionist researchers have noted that groups allow **coalitions** to form and serve as links to social networks and their vast resources.

Thinking Critically

1. Describe an example of coalition building you have experienced or read about (perhaps in the political

realm). Was the coalition effective? What problems had to be overcome?

2. Think of a primary and secondary group to which you belong. Under what circumstances might the primary group become a secondary group, or the secondary group become a primary group?

Key Terms

Coalition

In-group

Out-group

Primary group

Reference group

Secondary group

For sociologists, the term *deviance* does not mean perversion or depravity. **Deviance** is exhibiting behavior that violates the standards of conduct or expectations of a group or society. In the United States, alcoholics, compulsive gamblers, and the mentally ill would all be classified as deviants. Being late for class is categorized as a deviant act; the same is true of wearing jeans to a formal wedding. On the basis of the sociological definition, we are all deviant from time to time. Each of us violates common social norms in certain situations (Best 2004).

Is being overweight an example of deviance? In the United States and many other cultures, unrealistic standards of appearance and body image place a huge strain on people—especially women and girls—based on how they look. Journalist Naomi Wolf (1992) has used the term *beauty myth* to refer to an exaggerated ideal of beauty, beyond the reach of all but a few females, which has unfortunate consequences. In order to shed their "deviant" image and conform to unrealistic societal norms, many women and girls become consumed with adjusting their appearances. Yet what is deviant in one culture may be celebrated in another.

In 2009 baseball fans were shocked by the revelation that, like several other baseball greats, superstar Alex Rodriguez had used banned substances and lied about it.

Think about It

If your friends or teammates violate a social norm, is their behavior still deviant?

Deviance involves the violation of group norms, which may or may not be formalized into law. It is a comprehensive concept that includes not only criminal behavior but also many actions that are not subject to prosecution. The public official who takes a bribe has defied social norms, but so has the high school student who refuses to sit in an assigned seat or cuts class. Of course, deviation from norms is not always negative, let alone criminal. A member of an exclusive social club who speaks out against a traditional policy of not admitting women, Blacks, and Jews is deviating from the club's norms. So is a police officer who blows the whistle on corruption or brutality within the department.

From a sociological perspective, deviance is hardly objective or set in stone. Rather, it is subject to social definition within a particular society and at a particular time. For that reason, what is considered deviant can shift from one social era to another. In most instances, those individuals and groups with the greatest status and power define what is acceptable and what is deviant. For example, despite serious medical warnings against the dangers of tobacco, made since 1964, cigarette smoking continued to be accepted for decades—in good part because of the power of tobacco farmers and cigarette manufacturers. Only after a long campaign led by public health and anticancer activists did cigarette smoking become more of a deviant activity. Today, many state and local laws limit where people can smoke.

Deviance and Social Stigma

A person can acquire a deviant identity in many ways. Because of physical or behavioral characteristics, some people are unwillingly cast in negative social roles. Once assigned a deviant role, they have trouble presenting a positive image to others and may even experience lowered self-esteem. Whole groups of people—for instance, "short people" or "redheads"—may be labeled in this way. The interactionist Erving Goffman coined the term **stigma** to describe the labels society uses to devalue members of certain social groups (Goffman 1963; Heckert and Best 1997).

Prevailing expectations about beauty and body shape may prevent people who are regarded as ugly or obese from advancing as rapidly as their abilities permit. Both overweight and anorexic people are assumed to be weak in character, slaves to their appetites or to media images. Because they do not conform to the beauty myth, they may be viewed as "disfigured" or "strange" in appearance, bearers of what Goffman calls a "spoiled identity." However, what constitutes disfigurement is a matter of interpretation. Of the 1 million cosmetic procedures done every year in the United States alone, many are performed on women who would be defined objectively as having a normal appearance. And while feminist sociologists have accurately noted that the beauty myth makes many women feel uncomfortable with themselves, men too lack confidence in their appearance. The number of males who choose to undergo cosmetic procedures has risen sharply in recent years; men now account for 20 percent of such surgeries (American Academy of Cosmetic Surgery 2008).

Often people are stigmatized for deviant behaviors they may no longer engage in. The labels "compulsive gambler," "ex-convict," "recovering alcoholic," and "ex–mental patient" can stick to a person for life. Goffman draws a useful distinction between a prestige symbol that draws attention to a positive aspect of one's identity, such as a wedding band or a badge, and a stigma symbol that discredits or debases one's identity, such as a conviction for child molestation. While stigma symbols may not always be obvious, they can become a matter of public knowledge. Starting in 1994, many states required convicted sex offenders to register with local police departments. Some communities publish the names and addresses, and in some instances even the pictures, of convicted sex offenders on the Web.

A person need not be guilty of a crime to be stigmatized. Homeless people often have trouble getting a job, because employers are wary of applicants who cannot give a home address.

Deviant or normal? Television personality and recording artist Heidi Montag shocked fans in 2010 by revealing that she had undergone 10 plastic surgery procedures in a single day. Montag had already undergone breast augmentation, collagen lip injections, and rhinoplasty. Would you consider her behavior deviant?

Moreover, hiding one's homelessness is difficult, since agencies generally use the telephone to contact applicants about job openings. If a homeless person has access to a telephone at a shelter, the staff generally answers the phone by announcing the name of the institution—a sure way to discourage prospective employers. Even if a homeless person surmounts these obstacles and manages to get a job, she or he is often fired when the employer learns of the situation. Regardless of a person's positive attributes, employers regard the spoiled identity of homelessness as sufficient reason to dismiss an employee.

While some types of deviance will stigmatize a person, other types do not carry a significant penalty. Examples of socially tolerated forms of deviance can be found in the world of high technology.

Deviance and Technology

Technological innovations such as pagers and voice mail can redefine social interactions and the standards of behavior related to them. When the Internet was first made available to the general public, no norms or regulations governed its use. Because online communication offers a high degree of anonymity, uncivil behavior—speaking harshly of others or monopolizing chat room space—quickly became common. Online bulletin boards designed to carry items of community interest became littered with commercial advertisements. Such deviant acts are beginning to provoke calls for the establishment of formal rules for online behavior. For example, policymakers have debated whether to regulate the content of Web sites featuring hate speech and pornography.

Some deviant uses of technology are criminal, though not all participants see it that way. The pirating of software, motion pictures, and music has become a big business. At conventions and swap meets, pirated copies of DVDs are sold openly. Some of the products are obviously counterfeit, but many come

Readily available technology now allows quick and easy transmission of sexually oriented messages ("sexting"), not just between individuals, but on into cyberspace.

in sophisticated packaging, complete with warranty cards. The vendors say they merely want to be compensated for their time and the cost of materials, or that the software they have copied is in the public domain.

Similarly, the downloading of music from the Internet, which is typically protected by copyright, is widely accepted. But file sharing, like the pirating of DVDs, has grown to the point that it is threatening the profits of copyright owners. Napster, the renegade Web site that allowed thousands of people to download from a wide selection of music files for free, has been shut down, the victim of a court challenge by the music industry. Nevertheless, its fleeting success has encouraged imitators, many of them college students who run file-sharing programs from their dorm rooms. The music industry is fighting back by urging law enforcement agents to track the pirates down and prosecute them.

Though most of these black market activities are clearly illegal, many consumers and small-time pirates are proud of their behavior. They may even think themselves smart for figuring out a way to avoid the "unfair" prices charged by "big corporations." Few people see the pirating of a new software program or a first-run movie as a threat to the public good, as they would see embezzling from a bank. Similarly, most businesspeople who "borrow" software from another department, even though they lack a site license, do not think they are doing anything wrong. No social stigma attaches to their illegal behavior.

Deviance, then, is a complex concept. Sometimes it is trivial, sometimes profoundly harmful. Sometimes it is accepted by society and sometimes soundly rejected. What accounts for deviant behavior and people's reaction to it? In the next section we will examine five theoretical explanations for deviance.

Sociological Perspectives on Deviance

Why do people violate social norms? We have seen that deviant acts are subject to both informal and formal social control. The nonconforming or disobedient person may face disapproval, loss of friends, fines, or even imprisonment. Why, then, does deviance occur?

Early explanations for behavior that deviated from societal expectations blamed supernatural causes or genetic factors (such as "bad blood" or evolutionary throwbacks to primitive ancestors). By the 1800s, substantial research efforts were being made to identify biological factors that lead to deviance, and especially to criminal activity. Though such research was discredited in the 20th century, contemporary studies, primarily by biochemists, have sought to isolate genetic factors that suggest a likelihood of certain personality traits. Although criminality (much less deviance) is hardly a personality characteristic, researchers have focused on traits that might lead to crime, such as aggression. Of course, aggression can also lead to success in the corporate world, in professional sports, or in other walks of life.

The contemporary study of the possible biological roots of criminality is but one aspect of the larger debate over sociobiology. In general, sociologists reject any emphasis on the genetic roots of crime and deviance. The limitations of current knowledge, the possibility of reinforcing racist and sexist assumptions, and the disturbing implications for the rehabilitation of criminals have led sociologists to draw largely on other approaches to explain deviance (Sagarin and Sanchez 1988).

Functionalist Perspective

According to functionalists, deviance is a common part of human existence, with positive as well as negative consequences for social stability. Deviance helps to define the limits of proper behavior. Children who see one parent scold the other for belching at the dinner table learn about approved conduct. The same is true of the driver who receives a speeding ticket, the department store cashier who is fired for yelling at a customer, and the college student who is penalized for handing in papers weeks overdue.

Durkheim's Legacy Émile Durkheim ([1895] 1964) focused his sociological investigations mainly on criminal acts, yet his conclusions have implications for all types of deviant behavior. In Durkheim's view, the punishments established within a culture (including both formal and informal mechanisms of social control) help to define acceptable behavior and thus contribute to stability. If improper acts were not sanctioned, people might stretch their standards of what constitutes appropriate conduct.

Kai Erikson (1966) illustrated the boundary-maintenance function of deviance in his study of the Puritans of 17th-century New England. By today's standards, the Puritans placed tremendous emphasis on conventional morals. Their persecution and execution of women as witches represented a continuing attempt to define and redefine the boundaries of their community. In effect, their changing social norms created crime waves, as people whose behavior was previously acceptable suddenly faced punishment for being deviant (R. Schaefer 2011).

Durkheim ([1897] 1951) introduced the term **anomie** into sociological literature to describe the loss of direction felt in a society when social control of individual behavior has become ineffective. Anomie is a state of normlessness that typically occurs during a period of profound social change and disorder, such as a time of economic collapse. People become more aggressive or depressed, which results in higher rates of violent crime and suicide. Since there is much less agreement on what constitutes proper behavior during times of revolution, sudden prosperity, or economic depression, conformity and obedience become less significant as social forces. It also becomes much more difficult to state exactly what constitutes deviance.

Merton's Theory of Deviance What do a mugger and a teacher have in common? Each is "working" to obtain money that can then be exchanged for desired goods. As this example illustrates, behavior that violates accepted norms (such as mugging) may

Research Today

Does Crime Pay?

A driver violates the speed limit to get to a job interview on time. A financially strapped parent shoplifts goods that her family needs. These people may feel justified in violating the law because they do so to meet a reasonable objective. In Robert Merton's terms, they are *innovators*—people who violate social norms to achieve a commonly shared societal goal. Although their actions are criminal and potentially hurtful to others, from their own short-term perspective, their actions are functional.

Carried to its logical conclusion, innovation can and does become a career for some people. Yet from a purely economic point of view, even considering the fact that crime may pay is controversial, because doing so may seem to tolerate or encourage rule violation. Nothing is more controversial than the suggestion that gang-run drug deals are profitable and produce "good jobs." Although some people may see drug dealers as a cross between MBA-educated professionals and streetwise entrepreneurs, society in general does not admire these innovators.

Sociologist Sudhir Venkatesh collected detailed data on the illegal drug trade during his observation research on a Chicago street gang. Working with economist Steven Levitt, coauthor of the best seller *Freakonomics,* to analyze the business of selling crack cocaine, he found that less than 5 percent of even the gang leaders earned $100,000 per year. The rest of

> Less than 5 percent of even the gang leaders earned $100,000 per year. The rest of the leaders and virtually all the rank and file earned less than the minimum wage.

the leaders and virtually all the rank and file earned less than the minimum wage. In fact, most were unpaid workers seeking to move up in the gang hierarchy. (Thus the title of a chapter in Levitt's book, "Why Do Drug Dealers Still Live with Their Moms?") As Levitt notes, the drug gang is like most corporations: the top 2 percent of workers take home most of the money.

Why, from a sociological *and* an economic perspective, do these nonprofitable practices persist, especially considering that one in every four members of drug-oriented street gangs are eventually killed? One reason, of course, is the public's almost insatiable demand for illegal drugs. And from the drug peddler's perspective, few legitimate jobs are available to young adults in poverty-stricken areas, urban or rural. Functionally, these youths are contributing to their household incomes by dealing drugs.

In an interesting footnote to Venkatesh's observation research, the sociologist revealed that he shared in the gang's poor earnings. In fact, his cut of the meager take led members to increase the amount of money they demanded from residents for "protection." "I felt awful when I found out that my work was unwittingly hurting people," he reflected. "All of a sudden I was finding out that information was a commodity, and if I wanted something from them, they wanted something from me" (Venkatesh 2008b:45).

Scholars see a need for further research on Merton's concept of innovation. Why, for example, do some disadvantaged groups have lower rates of reported crime than others? Why do many people who are caught in adverse circumstances reject criminal activity as a viable alternative? Merton's theory of deviance does not easily answer such questions.

LET'S DISCUSS

1. Do you know anyone who has stolen out of need? If so, did the person feel justified in stealing, or did he or she feel guilty? How long did the theft continue?

2. Economically, profit is the difference between revenues and costs. What are the costs of the illegal drug trade, both economic and social? Is this economic activity profitable for society?

Sources: Clinard and Miller 1998; Kingsbury 2008; S. Levitt and Dubner 2006; Venkatesh 2000, 2008a, 2008b.

---

be performed with the same basic objectives in mind as those of people who pursue more conventional lifestyles.

On the basis of this kind of analysis, sociologist Robert Merton (1968) adapted Durkheim's notion of anomie to explain why people accept or reject the goals of a society, the socially approved means of fulfilling their aspirations, or both. Merton maintained that one important cultural goal in the United States is success, measured largely in terms of money. In addition to providing this goal for people, our society offers specific instructions on how to pursue success—go to school, work hard, do not quit, take advantage of opportunities, and so forth.

What happens to individuals in a society with a heavy emphasis on wealth as a basic symbol of success? Merton reasoned that people adapt in certain ways, either by conforming to or by deviating from such cultural expectations. His **ano-**

mie theory of deviance posits five basic forms of adaptation (Table 24-1).

Conformity to social norms, the most common adaptation in Merton's typology, is the opposite of deviance. It involves acceptance of both the overall societal goal ("become affluent") and the approved means ("work hard"). In Merton's view, there must be some consensus regarding accepted cultural goals and the legitimate means for attaining them. Without such a consensus, societies could exist only as collectives of people rather than as unified cultures, and might experience continual chaos.

The other four types of behavior represented in Table 24-1 all involve some departure from conformity. The "innovator" accepts the goals of society but pursues them with means that are regarded as improper. For instance, a safecracker may steal money to buy consumer goods and expensive vacations.

Table 24-1 Modes of Individual Adaptation

Mode	Institutionalized Means (hard work)	Societal Goal (acquisition of wealth)
Nondeviant		
Conformity	Accept	Accept
Deviant		
Innovation	Reject	Accept
Ritualism	Accept	Reject
Retreatism	Reject	Reject
Rebellion	Replace with new means	Replace with new goals

Source: Adapted from Merton 1968:194.

In Merton's typology, the "ritualist" has abandoned the goal of material success and become compulsively committed to the institutional means. Work becomes simply a way of life rather than a means to the goal of success. An example would be the bureaucratic official who blindly applies rules and regulations without remembering the larger goals of the organization. Certainly that would be true of a welfare caseworker who refuses to assist a homeless family because their last apartment was in another district.

The "retreatist," as described by Merton, has basically retreated (or withdrawn) from both the goals and the means of society. In the United States, drug addicts and vagrants are typically portrayed as retreatists. Concern has been growing that adolescents who are addicted to alcohol will become retreatists at an early age.

The final adaptation identified by Merton reflects people's attempts to create a *new* social structure. The "rebel" feels alienated from the dominant means and goals and may seek a dramatically different social order. Members of a revolutionary political organization, such as a militia group, can be categorized as rebels according to Merton's model. Although this theory of deviance is popular, it has not been applied systematically to real-world crime. The Research Today box examines scholars' efforts to confirm the theory's validity.

Merton made a key contribution to the sociological understanding of deviance by pointing out that deviants such as innovators and ritualists share a great deal with conforming people. The convicted felon may hold many of the same aspirations as people with no criminal background. The theory helps us to understand deviance as a socially created behavior rather than as the result of momentary pathological impulses.

Interactionist Perspective

The functionalist approach to deviance explains why rule violations continue to happen despite pressure to conform and obey. However, functionalists do not indicate how a given person comes to commit a deviant act or why on some occasions crimes do or do not occur. The emphasis on everyday behavior that is the focus of the interactionist perspective offers two explanations of crime—cultural transmission and routine activities theory.

Cultural Transmission In the course of studying graffiti writing by gangs in Los Angeles, sociologist Susan A. Phillips (1999) discovered that the writers learned from one another. In fact, Phillips was surprised by how stable their focus was over time. She also noted how other ethnic groups built on the models of the African American and Chicano gangs, superimposing Cambodian, Chinese, or Vietnamese symbols.

Humans *learn* how to behave in social situations, whether properly or improperly. There is no natural, innate manner in which people interact with one another. These simple ideas are not disputed today, but such was not the case when sociologist Edwin Sutherland (1883–1950) first advanced the idea that an individual undergoes the same basic socialization process in learning conforming and deviant acts.

Sutherland's ideas have been the dominating force in criminology. He drew on the **cultural transmission** school, which emphasizes that one learns criminal behavior by interacting with others. Such learning includes not only the techniques of lawbreaking (for example, how to break into a car quickly and quietly) but also the motives, drives, and rationalizations of the criminal. The cultural transmission approach can also be used to explain the behavior of those who habitually abuse alcohol or drugs.

Sutherland maintained that, through interactions with a primary group and significant others, people acquire definitions of proper and improper behavior. He used the term **differential association** to describe the process through which exposure to attitudes *favorable* to criminal acts leads to the violation of rules. Research suggests that this view of differential association also applies to noncriminal deviant acts, such as smoking, truancy, and early sexual behavior.

To what extent will a given person engage in activity that is regarded as proper or improper? For each individual, it will depend on the frequency, duration, and importance of two types of social interaction—those experiences that promote acceptance of social norms and those that endorse deviant behavior. People are more likely to engage in norm-defying behavior if they are part of a group or subculture that stresses deviant values, such as a street gang.

Sutherland offers the example of a boy who is sociable, outgoing, and athletic and who lives in an area with a high rate of delinquency. The youth is very likely to come into contact with peers who commit acts of vandalism, fail to attend school, and so forth, and may come to adopt such behavior. However, an introverted boy who lives in the same neighborhood may stay away from his peers and avoid delinquency. In another community, an outgoing and athletic boy may join a Little League baseball team or a scout troop because of his interactions with peers. Thus, Sutherland views improper behavior as the result of the types of groups to which one belongs and the kinds of friendships one has.

According to critics, however, the cultural transmission approach may explain the deviant behavior of juvenile delinquents or graffiti artists, but it fails to explain the conduct of the first-time impulsive shoplifter or the impoverished person who steals

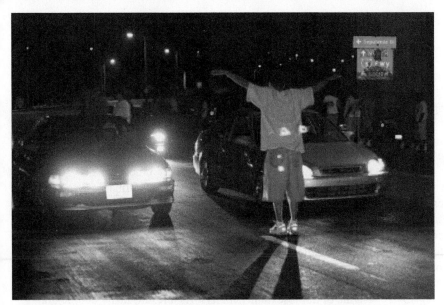

Under cover of darkness, drag racers await the start signal on a deserted Los Angeles street. Sutherland's concepts of differential association and cultural transmission would both apply to the practice of drag racing on city streets.

out of necessity. While it is not a precise statement of the process through which one becomes a criminal, differential association theory does direct our attention to the paramount role of social interaction in increasing a person's motivation to engage in deviant behavior (Harding 2009; Sutherland et al. 1992).

Social Disorganization Theory The social relationships that exist in a community or neighborhood affect people's behavior. Philip Zimbardo (2007a:24–25), author of the mock prison experiment described in the opening excerpt in Chapter 5, once did an experiment that demonstrated the power of communal relationships. He abandoned a car in each of two different neighborhoods, leaving its hood up and removing its hub caps. In one neighborhood, people started to strip the car for parts before Zimbardo had finished setting up a remote video camera to record their behavior. In the other neighborhood, weeks passed without the car being touched, except for a pedestrian who stopped to close the hood during a rainstorm.

What accounts for the strikingly different outcomes of Zimbardo's experiment in the two communities? According to **social disorganization theory,** increases in crime and deviance can be attributed to the absence or breakdown of communal relationships and social institutions, such as the family, school, church, and local government. This theory was developed at the University of Chicago in the early 1900s to describe the apparent disorganization that occurred as cities expanded with rapid immigration and migration from rural areas. Using the latest survey techniques, Clifford Shaw and Henry McKay literally mapped the distribution of social problems in Chicago. They found high rates of social problems in neighborhoods where buildings had deteriorated and the population had declined. Interestingly, the patterns persisted over time, despite changes in the neighborhoods' ethnic and racial composition.

This theory is not without its critics. To some, social disorganization theory seems to "blame the victim," leaving larger societal forces, such as the lack of jobs or high-quality schools, unaccountable. Critics also argue that even troubled

neighborhoods have viable, healthy organizations, which persist despite the problems that surround them.

More recently, social disorganization theorists have taken to emphasizing the effect of social networks on communal bonds. These researchers acknowledge that communities are not isolated islands. Residents' bonds may be enhanced or weakened by their ties to groups outside the immediate community (Jensen 2005; Sampson and Graves 1989; Shaw and McKay 1942).

Labeling Theory

The Saints and the Roughnecks were groups of high school males who were continually engaged in excessive drinking, reckless driving, truancy, petty theft, and vandalism. There the similarity ended. None of the Saints was ever arrested, but every Roughneck was frequently in trouble with police and townspeople. Why the disparity in their treatment? On the basis of observation research in their high school, sociologist William Chambliss (1973) concluded that social class played an important role in the varying fortunes of the two groups.

The Saints hid behind a facade of respectability. They came from "good families," were active in school organizations, planned on attending college, and received good grades. People generally viewed their delinquent acts as a few isolated cases of sowing wild oats. The Roughnecks had no such aura of respectability. They drove around town in beat-up cars, were generally unsuccessful in school, and aroused suspicion no matter what they did.

We can understand such discrepancies by using an approach to deviance known as **labeling theory.** Unlike Sutherland's work, labeling theory does not focus on why some individuals come to commit deviant acts. Instead, it attempts to explain why certain people (such as the Roughnecks) are *viewed* as deviants, delinquents, bad kids, losers, and criminals, while others whose behavior is similar (such as the Saints) are not seen in such harsh terms. Reflecting the contribution of interactionist theorists, labeling theory emphasizes how a person comes to be labeled as deviant or to accept that label. Sociologist Howard Becker (1963:9; 1964), who popularized this approach, summed it up with this statement: "Deviant behavior is behavior that people so label."

Labeling theory is also called the **societal-reaction approach,** reminding us that it is the *response* to an act, not the behavior itself, that determines deviance. For example, studies have shown that some school personnel and therapists expand educational programs designed for learning-disabled students to include those with behavioral problems. Consequently, a "troublemaker" can be improperly labeled as "learning-disabled," and vice versa.

Labeling and Agents of Social Control Traditionally, research on deviance has focused on people who violate social norms. In contrast, labeling theory focuses on police, probation officers, psychiatrists, judges, teachers, employers, school officials, and other regulators of social control. These agents, it is argued, play a significant role in creating the deviant identity by designating certain people (and not others) as deviant. An important aspect of labeling theory is the recognition that some individuals or groups have the power to *define* labels and *apply* them to others. This view ties into the conflict perspective's emphasis on the social significance of power.

In recent years the practice of *racial profiling,* in which people are identified as criminal suspects purely on the basis of their race, has come under public scrutiny. Studies confirm the public's suspicions that, in some jurisdictions, police officers are much more likely to stop Black males than White males for routine traffic violations, in the expectation of finding drugs or guns in their cars. Civil rights activists refer to these cases sarcastically as DWB (Driving While Black) violations. Beginning in 2001, profiling took a new turn as people who appeared to be Arab or Muslim came under special scrutiny. (Racial profiling will be examined in more detail in Module 32).

The labeling approach does not fully explain why certain people accept a label and others manage to reject it. In fact, this perspective may exaggerate the ease with which societal judgments can alter our self-images. Labeling theorists do suggest, however, that the power one has relative to others is important in determining a person's ability to resist an undesirable label. Competing approaches (including that of Sutherland) fail to explain why some deviants continue to be viewed as conformists rather than as violators of rules. According to Howard Becker (1973), labeling theory was not conceived as the *sole* explanation for deviance; its proponents merely hoped to focus more attention on the undeniably important actions of those people who are officially in charge of defining deviance (N. Davis 1975; compare with F. Cullen and Cullen 1978).

The popularity of labeling theory is reflected in the emergence of a related perspective, called social constructionism. According to the **social constructionist perspective,** deviance is the product of the culture we live in. Social constructionists focus specifically on the decision-making process that creates the deviant identity. They point out that "child abductors," "deadbeat dads," "spree killers," and "date rapists" have always been with us, but at times have become *the* major social concern of policymakers because of intensive media coverage (Liska and Messner 1999; E. R. Wright et al. 2000).

How do certain behaviors come to be viewed as a problem? Cigarette smoking, which was once regarded as a polite, gentlemanly activity, is now considered a serious health hazard, not only to the smoker but to others nearby who don't smoke. Recently, people have become concerned about the danger, especially to children, posed by *thirdhand smoke*—smoke-related chemicals that cling to clothes and linger in rooms, cars, even elevators (Winickoff et al. 2009).

Labeling and Sexual Deviance Labels have been applied to many types of deviance. Certainly one of the most visible examples has to do with human sexuality and gender. What is deviant sexual behavior? What is criminal sexual behavior? Labeling theory focuses on the process through which these behaviors come to be considered deviant.

The definition of deviant sexual behavior has varied significantly both over time and from culture to culture. Until 1973, the American Psychiatric Association considered homosexuality a "sociopathic personality disorder," which in effect meant that homosexuals should seek therapy. Two years later, however, the association removed homosexuality from its list of mental illnesses. Today, the organization publicly proclaims that "being gay is just as healthy as being straight." In Goffman's term mental health professionals have removed the stigma from this form of sexual expression. As a result, in the United States and many other countries, consensual sex between same-sex adults is no longer a crime (American Psychological Association 2008; International Gay and Lesbian Human Rights Commission 2010).

Despite the change in health professionals' attitudes, the stigma of homosexuality lingers. As a result, many people prefer the more positive terms *gay* and *lesbian.* Others, in defiance of the stigma, have proudly adopted the pejorative term *queer* in a deliberate reaction to the ridicule they have borne because of their sexual orientation. Still others maintain that constructing one's sexual orientation as either homosexual or heterosexual is too limiting. Indeed, such either/or language ignores those who are *bisexual,* or sexually attracted to both sexes.

Another group whose sexual orientation does not fit into the usual categories is *transgendered persons,* or those people whose current gender identity does not match their physical identity at birth. Some transgendered persons see themselves as both male and female. Others, called *transexuals,* may take hormones or undergo surgery in an effort to draw physically closer to their chosen gender identity. Transgendered persons are sometimes confused with *transvestites,* or cross-dressers who wear the clothing of the opposite sex. Transvestites are typically men, either gay or heterosexual, who choose to wear women's clothing.

The use of all these terms even in a positive or nonjudgmental way is problematic, since they imply that human sexuality can be confined in neat, mutually exclusive categories. Moreover, the destigmatization of these labels tends to reflect the influence of the socially privileged—that is, the affluent—who have the resources to overcome the stigma. In contrast, the traditional Native American concept of the *two spirit,* a personality that blends the masculine and the feminine, has been largely ridiculed or ignored (Gilley 2006; Wentling et al. 2008).

What does constitute sexual deviance, then? The answer to this question seems to change with each generation. Today, U.S. laws allow married women to accuse their husbands of rape, when a generation ago such an offense was not recognized. Similarly, *pedophilia*—an adult having sex with a minor—is generally regarded with disgust today, even when it is consensual. Yet in many countries, fringe groups now speak positively of "intergenerational sex," arguing that "childhood" is not a biological given (Hendershott 2002).

Though this and some other aspects of sexual expression are still against the law, the meaning of the labels is beginning to blur. Similarly, child pornography is both illegal and abhorrent to most people, yet many fashion advertisements

The true story of Brandon Teena, presented in the 1999 motion picture *Boys Don't Cry*, illustrates the complexity of human sexuality. The transgendered teen from Nebraska, played by Hilary Swank (right), was born female but preferred life as a male.

in mainstream magazines seem to verge on it. And while sex work and sex trafficking seem wrong to most of us, society tolerates and even regulates many aspects of those activities (Barton 2006).

 use your **sociological imagination**

You are a teacher. What labels, freely used in education, might you attach to your students?

In the 1930s, the Federal Bureau of Narcotics launched a campaign to portray marijuana as a dangerous drug rather than a pleasure-inducing substance. From a conflict perspective, those in power often use such tactics to coerce others into adopting a different point of view.

Conflict Theory

Conflict theorists point out that people with power protect their interests and define deviance to suit their needs. Sociologist Richard Quinney (1974, 1979, 1980) is a leading exponent of the view that the criminal justice system serves the interests of the powerful. Crime, according to Quinney (1970), is a definition of conduct created by authorized agents of social control—such as legislators and law enforcement officers—in a politically organized society. He and other conflict theorists argue that lawmaking is often an attempt by the powerful to coerce others into their morality (see also Spitzer 1975).

This theory helps to explain why our society has laws against gambling, drug use, and prostitution, many of which are violated on a massive scale. (We will examine these "victimless crimes" in Module 25.) According to conflict theorists, criminal law does not represent a consistent application of societal values, but instead reflects competing values and interests. Thus, the U.S. criminal code outlaws marijuana because of its alleged harm to users, yet cigarettes and alcohol—both of which can be harmful to users—are sold legally almost everywhere.

In fact, conflict theorists contend that the entire criminal justice system in the United States treats suspects differently based on their racial, ethnic, or social-class background. In many cases, officials in the system use their own discretion to make biased decisions about whether to press charges or drop them, whether to set bail and how much, whether to offer parole or deny it. Researchers have found that this kind of **differential justice**—differences in the way social control is exercised over different groups—puts African Americans and Latinos at a disadvantage in the justice system, both as juveniles and as adults. On average, White offenders receive shorter sentences than comparable Latino and African American offenders, even when prior arrest records and the relative severity of the crime are taken into consideration (R. Brewer and Heitzeg 2008; Quinney 1974; Sandefur 2008; Schlesinger 2010).

Differential justice is not limited to the United States. In 2007, the people of India were alarmed to learn that a series of killings in the slums of New Delhi had never been investigated by police. Only after 17 bodies of recently murdered children were found in a sewer drain on the edge of a slum were police moved to act. For many onlookers, it was just the latest example

Table **24-2**   Sociological Perspectives on Deviance

Approach	Theoretical Perspective	Proponents	Emphasis
Anomie	Functionalist	Émile Durkheim Robert Merton	Adaptation to societal norms
Cultural transmission/ Differential association	Interactionist	Edwin Sutherland	Patterns learned through others
Social disorganization	Interactionist	Clifford Shaw Henry McKay	Communal relationships
Labeling/Social constructionist	Interactionist	Howard Becker	Societal response to acts
Conflict	Conflict	Richard Quinney	Dominance by authorized agents Discretionary justice
Feminist	Conflict/Feminist	Freda Adler Meda Chesney-Lind	Role of gender Women as victims and perpetrators

of the two-tier justice system found in India and many other countries throughout the world (Gentleman 2007a).

Such dramatic differences in social treatment may lead to heightened violence and crime. People who view themselves as the victims of unfair treatment may strike out, not against the powerful so much as against fellow victims. In studying crime in rural Mexico, Andrés Villarreal (2004) found that crime rates were high in the areas where land distribution was most inequitable. In areas where land was distributed more equally, communities appeared to suffer less violence and to enjoy greater social cohesion.

The perspective advanced by conflict and labeling theorists forms quite a contrast to the functionalist approach to deviance. Functionalists see standards of deviant behavior as merely reflecting cultural norms; conflict and labeling theorists point out that the most powerful groups in a society can shape laws and standards and determine who is (or is not) prosecuted as a criminal. These groups would be unlikely to apply the label "deviant" to the corporate executive whose decisions lead to large-scale environmental pollution. In the opinion of conflict theorists, agents of social control and other powerful groups can impose their own self-serving definitions of deviance on the general public.

Feminist Perspective

Feminist criminologists such as Freda Adler and Meda Chesney-Lind have suggested that many of the existing approaches to deviance and crime were developed with only men in mind. For example, in the United States, for many years any husband who forced his wife to have sexual intercourse—without her consent and against her will—was not legally considered to have committed rape. The law defined rape as pertaining only to sexual relations between people who were not married to each other, reflecting the overwhelmingly male composition of state legislatures at the time.

It took repeated protests by feminist organizations to get changes in the criminal law defining rape. Beginning in 1993, husbands in all 50 states could be prosecuted under most circumstances for the rape of their wives. There remain alarming exceptions in no fewer than 30 states, however. For example, the husband is exempt when he does not need to use force because his wife is asleep, unconscious, or mentally or physically impaired. These interpretations still rest on the notion that the marriage contract entitles a husband to sex (Bergen 2006).

When it comes to crime and to deviance in general, society tends to treat women in a stereotypical fashion. For example, consider how women who have many and frequent sexual partners are more likely to be viewed with scorn than men who are promiscuous. Cultural views and attitudes toward women influence how they are perceived and labeled. The feminist perspective also emphasizes that deviance, including crime, tends to flow from economic relationships. Traditionally, men have had greater earning power than their wives. As a result, wives may be reluctant to report acts of abuse to the authorities, and lose what may be their primary or even sole source of income. In the workplace, men have exercised greater power than women in pricing, accounting, and product control, giving them greater opportunity to engage in such crimes as embezzlement and fraud. But as women have taken more active and powerful roles both in the household and in business, these gender differences in deviance and crime have narrowed (F. Adler 1975; F. Adler et al. 2007; Irwin and Chesney-Lind 2008).

In the future, feminist scholarship can be expected to grow dramatically. Particularly on topics such as white-collar crime, drinking behavior, drug abuse, and differential sentencing rates between the genders, as well as on the fundamental question of how to define deviance, feminist scholars will have much to say.

We have seen that over the past century, sociologists have taken many different approaches in studying deviance, arousing some controversy in the process. Table 24-2 summarizes the various theoretical approaches to this topic.

Summary

Deviant behavior is behavior that violates social norms. A very wide range of behavior may be classified as deviant, and everyone violates social norms in some situations.

1. Some forms of **deviance** carry a negative social **stigma,** while other forms are more or less accepted.

2. From a functionalist point of view, deviance and its consequences help to define the limits of proper behavior.

3. Some interactionists maintain that people learn criminal behavior by interacting with others (**cultural transmission**). To them, deviance results from exposure to attitudes that are favorable to criminal acts (**differential association**).

4. Other interactionists attribute increases in crime and deviance to the absence or breakdown of communal relationships and social institutions, such as the family, school, church, and local government (**social disorganization theory**).

5. An important aspect of **labeling theory** is the recognition that some people are viewed as deviant, while others who engage in the same behavior are not.

6. From the conflict perspective, laws and punishments are a reflection of the interests of the powerful.

7. The feminist perspective emphasizes cultural attitudes and differential economic relationships to help explain gender differences in deviance and crime.

Thinking Critically

1. Do some research on a culture you are unfamiliar with. Do any of the customs seem deviant to you? Which of your own customs might seem deviant to members of that culture?

2. Using examples drawn from work or college life, illustrate each of Merton's five modes of individual adaptation.

3. Explain the presence of both criminals and law-abiding citizens in an inner-city neighborhood in terms of the interactionist perspective.

Key Terms

Anomie

Anomie theory of deviance

Cultural transmission

Deviance

Differential association

Differential justice

Labeling theory

Social constructionist perspective

Social disorganization theory

Societal-reaction approach

Stigma

Crime is a violation of criminal law for which some governmental authority applies formal penalties. It represents a deviation from formal social norms administered by the state. Laws divide crimes into various categories, depending on the severity of the offense, the age of the offender, the potential punishment, and the court that holds jurisdiction over the case.

Crime is on everyone's mind. Until recently, college campuses were viewed as safe havens from crime. But as the Sociology on Campus box shows, at today's colleges and universities, crime goes well beyond cheating and senior class pranks.

The term **index crimes** refers to the eight types of crime that are tabulated each year by the Federal Bureau of Investigation (FBI). This category of criminal behavior generally consists of those serious offenses that people think of when they express concern about the nation's crime problem. Index crimes include murder, rape, robbery, and assault—all of which are violent crimes committed against people—as well as the property crimes of burglary, theft, motor vehicle theft, and arson.

Types of Crime

Rather than relying solely on legal categories, sociologists classify crimes in terms of how they are committed and how society views the offenses. In this section, we will examine five types of crime differentiated by sociologists: victimless crimes, professional crime, organized crime, white-collar and technology-based crime, and transnational crime.

Victimless Crimes

When we think of crime, we tend to think of acts that endanger people's economic or personal well-being against their will (or without their direct knowledge). In contrast, sociologists use the term **victimless crime** to describe the willing exchange among adults of widely desired, but illegal, goods and services, such as prostitution (Schur 1965, 1985).

Some activists are working to decriminalize many of these illegal practices. Supporters of decriminalization are troubled by the attempt to legislate a moral code for adults. In their view, prostitution, drug abuse, gambling, and other victimless crimes are impossible to prevent. The already overburdened criminal justice system should instead devote its resources to street crimes and other offenses with obvious victims.

Despite widespread use of the term *victimless crime,* however, many people object to the notion that there is no victim other than the offender in such crimes. Excessive drinking, compulsive gambling, and illegal drug use contribute to an enormous amount of personal and property damage. A person with a drinking problem may become abusive to a spouse or children; a compulsive gambler or drug user may steal to pursue his or her obsession. And feminist sociologists contend that prostitution, as well as the more disturbing aspects of pornography, reinforce the misconception that women are "toys" who can be treated as objects rather than people. According to critics of decriminalization, society must not give tacit approval to conduct that has such harmful consequences (Melissa Farley and Malarek 2008).

The controversy over decriminalization reminds us of the important insights of labeling and conflict theorists presented earlier. Underlying this debate are two questions: Who has the power to label gambling, prostitution, and public drunkenness as "crimes"? and Who has the power to label such behaviors as "victimless"? The answer is generally the state legislatures, and in some cases, the police and the courts.

Again, we can see that criminal law is not simply a universal standard of behavior agreed on by all members of society. Rather, it reflects a struggle among competing individuals and groups to gain government support for their moral and social values. For example, organizations such as Mothers Against Drunk Driving (MADD) and Students Against Drunk Driving (SADD) have been successful in recent years in modifying public attitudes toward drunkenness. Rather than being viewed as a victimless crime, drunkenness is increasingly associated with the potential dangers of driving while under the influence of alcohol. As a result, the mass media are giving greater (and more critical) attention to people found guilty of drunk driving, and many states have instituted severe fines and jail terms for a wide variety of alcohol-related offenses.

Professional Crime

Although the adage "Crime doesn't pay" is familiar, many people do make a career of illegal activities. A **professional criminal,** or *career criminal,* is a person who pursues crime as a day-to-day occupation, developing skilled techniques and enjoying a certain degree of status among other criminals. Some professional criminals specialize in burglary, safecracking, hijacking of cargo, pickpocketing, and shoplifting. Such people have acquired skills that reduce the likelihood of arrest, conviction,

Sociology on Campus

Campus Crime

According to a national survey released in 2008, 72 percent of college students consider campus safety "very important" in selecting a college. A generation earlier, would campus crime have been uppermost in the minds of prospective students?

Research on crime in college has focused on interpersonal violence ("date rape," as it is sometimes trivialized) and the way in which colleges handle such incidents. In 2007, two very different events brought campus crime to national attention. First, there was the April 16, 2007, rampage at Virginia Tech. In its aftermath, observers questioned whether campus officials should have notified students and employees of the first shootings, at a dormitory, during the two hours that passed before the gunman's second attack in a classroom building. The federal law known as the Clery Act, passed in 1990, requires timely warnings of campus crime, but how they should be delivered and how specific they should be (for example, whether the names of alleged assailants should be revealed) is unclear.

The second incident, the death of a girl in her dormitory room at Eastern Michigan University, led to the resignation of the university's

> The federal law known as the Clery Act, passed in 1990, requires timely warnings of campus crime, but how they should be delivered and how specific they should be is unclear.

president. For two months, officials had assured her parents that she died a natural death. Later, her family learned that she had been raped and murdered, and that her body had been missing for three days.

These and other, less publicized, incidents have prompted colleges to become more forthcoming about campus crime and to provide better security. However, the growing trend toward living (and partying) off campus poses a challenge to their efforts. Student safety at internship sites and study-abroad programs is even more difficult to ensure.

Making judgments about campus crime based on the reports mandated by the Clery Act is difficult. Because these documents include only reported incidents, they may or may not be accurate. The latest data from the University of California, which has over 20,000 students, for example, show that the total number of forcible sex offenses per year ranges from 2 to more than 62.

LET'S DISCUSS

1. Is crime a problem on your campus? If so, what kinds of crime? What have college officials done to discourage it?

2. Choose two theories of crime and apply them to crimes that have occurred on your campus. Which theory seems to fit better?

Sources: Department of Justice 2009; Interface Group Report (Virginia Tech) 2007; Lipka 2009; National Institute of Justice 2005; *New York Times* 2007, 2008; Security on Campus 2008.

---

and imprisonment. As a result, they may have long careers in their chosen professions.

Edwin Sutherland (1937) offered pioneering insights into the behavior of professional criminals by publishing an annotated account written by a professional thief. Unlike the person who engages in crime only once or twice, professional thieves make a business of stealing. They devote their entire working time to planning and executing crimes, and sometimes travel across the nation to pursue their "professional duties." Like people in regular occupations, professional thieves consult with their colleagues concerning the demands of work, becoming part of a subculture of similarly occupied individuals. They exchange information on places to burglarize, on outlets for unloading stolen goods, and on ways of securing bail bonds if arrested.

Organized Crime

A 1976 government report devotes three pages to defining the term *organized crime*. For our purposes, we will consider **organized crime** to be the work of a group that regulates relations among criminal enterprises involved in illegal activities, including prostitution, gambling, and the smuggling and sale of illegal drugs. Organized crime dominates the world of illegal business just as large corporations dominate the conventional business world. It allocates territory, sets prices for goods and services, and acts as an arbitrator in internal disputes. A secret, conspiratorial activity, it generally evades law enforcement. It takes over legitimate businesses, gains influence over labor unions, corrupts public officials, intimidates witnesses in criminal trials, and even "taxes" merchants in exchange for "protection" (National Advisory Commission on Criminal Justice 1976).

Organized crime serves as a means of upward mobility for groups of people struggling to escape poverty. Sociologist Daniel Bell (1953) used the term *ethnic succession* to describe the sequential passage of leadership from Irish Americans in the early part of the 20th century to Jewish Americans in the 1920s and then to Italian Americans in the early 1930s. Ethnic succession has become more complex, reflecting the diversity of the nation's latest immigrants. Colombian, Mexican, Russian, Chinese, Pakistani, and Nigerian immigrants are among those who have begun to play a significant role in organized crime activities (Chin 1996; Kleinknecht 1996).

There has always been a global element in organized crime. But law enforcement officials and policymakers now acknowledge the emergence of a form of organized crime that takes advantage of advances in electronic communications. *Transnational* organized crime includes drug and arms smuggling, money laundering, and trafficking in illegal immigrants and stolen goods; see the discussion on the next page (Lumpe 2003; Office of Justice Programs 1999).

White-Collar and Technology-Based Crime

Income tax evasion, stock manipulation, consumer fraud, bribery and extraction of kickbacks, embezzlement, and misrepresentation in advertising—these are all examples of **white-collar crime,** illegal acts committed in the course of business activities, often by affluent, "respectable" people. Edwin Sutherland (1949, 1983) likened these crimes to organized crime because they are often perpetrated through occupational roles.

A new type of white-collar crime has emerged in recent decades: computer crime. The use of high technology allows criminals to carry out embezzlement or electronic fraud, often leaving few traces, or to gain access to a company's inventory without leaving home. According to a study by the FBI and the National White Collar Crime Center, over 270,000 Internet crimes are reported every year, ranging from scams on online auction sites to identity theft (Internet Crime Complaint Center 2009).

When Charles Horton Cooley spoke of the self and Erving Goffman of impression management, surely neither scholar could have envisioned the insidious crime of identity theft. Each year about 14 percent of all adults find that their personal information has been misused for criminal purposes. Unfortunately, with our society's growing reliance on electronic financial transactions, assuming someone else's identity has become increasingly easy (Vamosi et al. 2010).

Identity theft does not necessarily require technology. A criminal can obtain someone's personal information by pickpocketing or by intercepting mail. However, the widespread exchange of information online has allowed criminals to access large amounts of personal information. Public awareness of the potential harm from identity theft took a giant leap in the aftermath of September 11, 2001, when investigations revealed that several hijackers had used fraudulent IDs to open bank accounts, rent apartments, and board planes. A law enacted in 2004 makes identity theft punishable by a mandatory prison sentence if it is linked to other crimes. Still, unauthorized disclosures of information, even if accidental, persist (Brubaker 2008).

Sutherland (1940) coined the term *white-collar crime* in 1939 to refer to acts by individuals, but the term has been broadened more recently to include offenses by businesses and corporations as well. *Corporate crime,* or any act by a corporation that is punishable by the government, takes many forms and includes individuals, organizations, and institutions among its victims. Corporations may engage in anticompetitive behavior, environmental pollution, medical fraud, tax fraud, stock fraud and manipulation, accounting fraud, the production of unsafe goods, bribery and corruption, and health and safety violations (J. Coleman 2006).

For many years, corporate wrongdoers got off lightly in court by documenting their long history of charitable contributions and agreeing to help law enforcement officials find other white-collar criminals. Unfortunately, that is still the case. The highly visible jailing of multimedia personality Martha Stewart in 2004, as well as recent disclosures of "Wall Street greed," may lead the casual observer to think that government is cracking down on white-collar crime. However, an independent analysis found that from 2000 through 2009, the number of white-collar crimes that were prosecuted increased only modestly (Transactional Records Access Clearinghouse 2009).

Even when a person is convicted of corporate crime, the verdict generally does not harm his or her reputation and career aspirations nearly so much as conviction for street crime would. Apparently, the label "white-collar criminal"

Our society's growing dependence on electronic transactions has greatly increased the white-collar crime of identity theft.

does not carry the stigma of the label "felon convicted of a violent crime." Conflict theorists don't find such differential treatment surprising. They argue that the criminal justice system largely disregards the crimes of the affluent, focusing on crimes committed by the poor. Generally, if an offender holds a position of status and influence, his or her crime is treated as less serious, and the sanction is much more lenient.

Transnational Crime

More and more, scholars and police officials are turning their attention to **transnational crime,** or crime that occurs across multiple national borders. In the past, international crime was often limited to the clandestine shipment of goods across the border between two countries. But increasingly, crime is no more restricted by such borders than is legal commerce. Rather than concentrating on specific countries, international crime now spans the globe.

Historically, probably the most dreadful example of transnational crime has been slavery. At first, governments did not regard slavery as a crime, but merely regulated it as they would the trade in goods. In the 20th century, transnational crime grew to embrace trafficking in endangered species, drugs, and stolen art and antiquities.

Transnational crime is not exclusive of some of the other types of crime we have discussed. For example, organized criminal networks are increasingly global. Technology definitely facilitates their illegal activities, such as trafficking in child pornography. Beginning in the 1990s, the United Nations began to categorize transnational crimes; Table 25-1 lists some of the more common types. In the Social Policy section of Module 30 we will con-

sider the crime of trafficking in human beings in the context of universal human rights.

Bilateral cooperation in the pursuit of border criminals such as smugglers has been common for many years. The first global effort to control international crime was the International Criminal Police Organization (Interpol), a cooperative network of European police forces founded to stem the movement of political revolutionaries across borders. While such efforts to fight transnational crime may seem lofty—an activity with which any government should cooperate—they are complicated by sensitive legal and security issues. Most nations that have signed protocols issued by the United Nations, including the United States, have expressed concern over potential encroachments on their national judicial systems, as well as concern over their national security. Thus, they have been reluctant to share certain types of intelligence data. The terrorist attacks of September 11, 2001, increased both the interest in combating transnational crime and sensitivity to the risks of sharing intelligence data (Deflem 2005; Felson and Kalaitzidis 2005).

 use your sociological imagination

As a newspaper editor, how might you treat stories on corporate or white-collar crime differently from those on violent crime?

Crime Statistics

Crime statistics are not as accurate as social scientists would like, especially since they deal with an issue of grave concern to the people of the United States. Unfortunately, they are frequently cited as if they were completely reliable. Such data do serve as an indicator of police activity, as well as an approximate indication of the level of certain crimes. Yet it would be a mistake to interpret these data as an exact representation of the incidence of crime.

Understanding Crime Statistics

Because reported crime is very high in the United States, the public regards crime as a major social problem. However, there has been a significant decline in violent crime nationwide following many years of increases. A number of explanations have been offered, including these:

- Community-oriented policing and crime prevention programs
- New gun control laws
- A massive increase in the prison population, which at least prevents inmates from committing crimes outside prison

It remains to be seen whether this pattern will continue, but even with current declines, reported crimes remain well above those of other nations. Yet reported rates in the United States are still the lowest in about 40 years. Feminist scholars draw our attention to one significant variation: the proportion of major crimes committed by women has increased. In a recent 10-year period

Table **25-1** **Types of Transnational Crime**

Bankruptcy and insurance fraud
Computer crime (treating computers as both a tool and a target of crime)
Corruption and bribery of public officials
Environmental crime
Hijacking of airplanes (skyjacking)
Illegal drug trade
Illegal money transfers (money laundering)
Illegal sales of firearms and ammunition
Infiltration of legal businesses
Intellectual property crime
Networking of criminal organizations
Sea piracy
Terrorism
Theft of art and cultural objects
Trafficking in body parts (includes illegal organ transplants)
Trafficking in human beings (includes sex trade)

Source: Compiled and updated by the author based on Mueller 2001 and United Nations Office on Drugs and Crime 2005.

Stephanie Vezzani wasn't sure what she wanted to major in when she entered the University of Akron, but she did know what she wanted to do with her life: she wanted a career as a crime fighter. Vezzani began as an accounting major, but switched to sociology when she discovered the department offered a special concentration in law enforcement.

Vezzani is now an agent with the U.S. Secret Service, whose twofold mission is to protect high-ranking officials and their families and to investigate financial crimes, including counterfeiting, identity theft, and computer-based attacks on the financial, banking, and telecommunications industries. She has tackled both aspects of the job. For her, a typical week would include working on a criminal investigation in a field office or traveling around the country with a government official in need of protection.

Vezzani finds that travel is one of the most exciting aspects of her job. Over the past six years she has visited Russia, Turkey, Jordan, Vietnam, and South Korea. She also attended the 2002 Winter Olympics in Salt Lake City, where she provided protection for the athletes living in the Olympic Village. Vezzani relishes meeting people from different cultures, and of course she loves the sights she gets to see. "The architecture in St. Petersburg, Russia, was amazing," she says.

Vezzani uses her training in sociology on a daily basis, as she interviews suspects, witnesses, and victims of crime. "It is critical in the field of law enforcement to have an understanding of people's relationships and the beliefs and value systems that contribute to their decision making," she explains. "Sociology has provided me the knowledge to speak to and listen to people with different values and cultures in order to complete my job at the highest level possible."

LET'S DISCUSS

1. Besides an awareness of different beliefs, values, and cultures, what else might sociology offer to those who serve in law enforcement?

2. Law enforcement is a relatively new career option for women. What special strengths do you think a woman might bring to police work?

(1999–2008), female arrests for major reported crimes increased 12 percent, while comparable male arrests declined 19 percent (Department of Justice 2009: Table 33; Sutch and Carter 2006).

Typically, the crime data used in the United States are based on the index crimes described earlier. The crime index, published annually by the FBI as part of the *Uniform Crime Reports,* includes statistics on murder, rape, robbery, assault, burglary, larceny-theft, motor vehicle theft, and arson (Table 25-2). Obviously, many serious offenses, such as white-collar crimes, are not included in this index (although they are recorded elsewhere). In addition, the crime index is disproportionately devoted to property crimes, whereas most citizens are more worried about violent crimes. Thus, a significant decrease in the number of rapes and robberies could be overshadowed by a slightly larger increase in the number of automobiles stolen, leading to the mistaken impression that *personal* safety is more at risk than before.

The most serious limitation of official crime statistics is that they include only those crimes actually *reported* to law enforcement agencies. Because members of racial and ethnic minority groups often distrust law enforcement agencies, they may not contact the police. Feminist sociologists and others have noted that many women do not report rape or spousal abuse out of fear they will be blamed for the crime.

Partly because of these deficiencies in official statistics, the National Crime Victimization Survey was initiated in 1972. The Bureau of Justice Statistics, in compiling this annual report, seeks information from law enforcement agencies, but also interviews members of over 76,000 households and asks if they were victims of a specific set of crimes during the preceding year. In general, those who administer **victimization surveys** question ordinary people, not police officers, to determine whether they have been victims of crime.

Unfortunately, like other crime data, victimization surveys have particular limitations. They require that victims understand what has happened to them and are willing to disclose such information to interviewers. Fraud, income tax evasion, and blackmail are examples of crimes that are unlikely to be reported in victimization studies. Nevertheless, 91 percent of all households have been willing to cooperate with investigators for the National Crime Victimization Survey. As Figure 25-1 shows, data from these surveys reveal a fluctuating crime rate, with significant declines in the 1980s and relatively low rates well into the 21st century. In 2009, reported crime continued to drop nationwide, declining 5.5 percent compared to the previous year. In the first quarter of 2010, most large cities continued to report declines.

What explains these declines? No single explanation suffices, but improvements in community-oriented policing, surveillance technologies, and the allocation of limited resources have helped to hold down crime rates, along with massive use of imprisonment and probation (Blumstein and Wallman 2006; *The Economist* 2009b; Perez 2010).

Table **25-2** **National Crime Rates and Percentage Change**

Crime Index Offenses in 2008	Number Reported	Rate per 100,000 Inhabitants	Percentage Change in Rate since 1999
Violent crime			
Murder	16,272	5	−6
Forcible rape	89,000	29	−11
Robbery	444,855	145	−3
Aggravated assault	834,885	275	−8
Total	1,382,012	455	−13
Property crime			
Burglary	2,222,196	731	−5
Larceny-theft	6,558,873	2,167	−15
Motor vehicle theft	956,846	315	−26
Total	9,767,915	3,213	−14

Notes: Arson was designated an index offense beginning in 1979; data on arson were still incomplete as of 2008. Because of rounding, the offenses may not add to totals.
Source: Department of Justice 2009: Tables 1, 1a.

International Crime Rates   If developing reliable crime data is difficult in the United States, making useful cross-national comparisons is even more difficult. Nevertheless, with some care, we can offer preliminary conclusions about how crime rates differ around the world.

During the 1980s and 1990s, violent crimes were much more common in the United States than in western Europe. Murders, rapes, and robberies were reported to the police at much higher rates in the United States. Yet the incidence of certain other types of crime appears to be higher elsewhere. For example, England, Italy, Australia, and New Zealand all have higher rates of car theft than the United States. Developing nations have significant rates of reported homicide due to civil unrest and political conflict among civilians (International Crime Victim Survey 2004; World Bank 2003).

Why are rates of violent crime so much higher in the United States than in Western Europe? Sociologist Elliot Currie (1985, 1998) has suggested that our society places greater emphasis on individual economic achievement than other societies. At the same time, many observers have noted that the culture of the United States has long tolerated, if not condoned, many forms of violence. Coupled with sharp disparities between poor and affluent citizens, significant unemployment, and substantial alcohol and drug abuse, these factors combine to produce a climate conducive to crime.

However, disturbing increases in violent crime are evident in other Western societies. For example, certain types of crime have skyrocketed in Russia since the overthrow of Communist Party rule (with its strict controls on guns and criminals) in 1991.

In 1998 there were fewer than 260 homicides in Moscow; now there are more than 1,000 homicides a year. Organized crime has filled the power vacuum in Moscow: one result is that gangland shoot-outs and premeditated "contract hits" have become more common. Some prominent reformist politicians have been targeted as well (Winslow and Zhang 2008a, 2008b).

In the United States, high rates of violent crime, especially in the cities, have long fueled calls for stricter controls on the purchase and use of firearms. We will take a close look at the contentious issue of gun control in the Social Policy section that follows.

FIGURE 25-1 **Victimization Rates, 1973–2007**

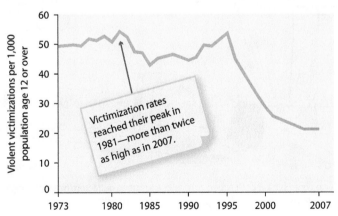

Sources: M. Rand 2008; Rennison 2002.

Two high school students present themselves at Kmart's national headquarters. They are not looking for jobs. Survivors of the mass murders at Columbine High School in 1999, they still have bullets lodged in their bodies—bullets their attackers bought at Kmart. In a symbolic protest, the two young people ask Kmart's representative if they may return the bullets.

This scene was shown in the 2004 Academy Award–winning documentary *Bowling for Columbine.* Producer-director Michael Moore was amazed when the day after he filmed the encounter, Kmart announced that the store would stop selling handgun ammunition.

Understanding the Issue

While reported crime has declined in recent years, the role of firearms in crime has remained fairly consistent. Over the past five years, two-thirds of all murders were committed with firearms. Although handgun owners frequently insist that they need to own firearms to protect themselves and their loved ones from violent crime, over the years, high-profile assassinations of public figures such as President John F. Kennedy, Senator Robert Kennedy, Dr. Martin Luther King Jr., and Beatle John Lennon have forced legislators to consider stricter gun control measures (Department of Justice 2009).

Gun control legislation began with the Brady Handgun Violence Prevention Act, named after White House press secretary Jim Brady, who was seriously wounded in the 1981 assassination attempt against President Ronald Reagan. John Hinckley, the would-be assassin, had given false information about himself at the pawnshop where he bought the gun he used to shoot Reagan and Brady. The Brady Act, which took effect in 1994, mandates that firearms dealers run criminal history background checks on people who wish to purchase handguns. Every year about 1 out of every 1,000 in a total of nearly 10 million firearms applications is rejected. Applications are most commonly denied because the person seeking to buy a firearm is a convicted felon or has had a restraining

Gun controls have both strong advocates and strong detractors. Not surprisingly, this division of opinion is reflected in cartoons that favor (left) and oppose (right) gun restrictions.

Think about It

Which cartoon delivers its message more effectively? How difficult is it for you to evaluate them objectively, given your own views?

order filed against him because of domestic violence (Bureau of Justice Statistics 2008; Hanes 2010).

Not satisfied with the restrictions in the Brady Act, gun control supporters claim that even stricter legislation is needed. But opponents charge that the Brady Act only hampers honest people, since those with criminal intent can turn to other sources for guns. Instead of passing further legislation, opponents suggest strengthening and enforcing existing criminal penalties for the illegal use of guns.

In 2008, in the landmark case *District of Columbia v. Heller,* the Supreme Court struck down a near-total ban on handguns in the nation's capitol by a 5–4 ruling. The verdict was lauded by those who favor gun rights but denounced by advocates of gun control. Gun rights groups are now testing the constitutionality of other restrictions on gun ownership. Gun control advocates are working to craft legislation that will be acceptable to the justices (Winkler 2009).

The battle over the freedom to bear arms versus government control of firearms ranges well beyond the federal courts and the District of Columbia. Figure 25-2 shows the range of state gun control laws, from the least to the most restrictive.

Applying Sociology

Guns and ammunition are big business in the United States, where the Second Amendment to the Constitution guarantees the "right of the people to keep and bear arms." Currently, about 42 percent of U.S. households have some type of firearm

FIGURE 25-2 **Restrictiveness of State Gun Laws**

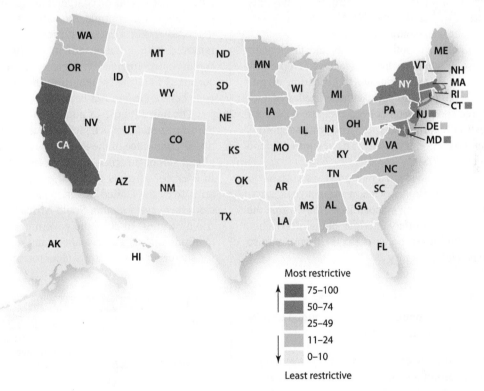

Most restrictive
- 75–100
- 50–74
- 25–49
- 11–24
- 0–10

Least restrictive

Note: Scored by the Brady Campaign to Prevent Gun Violence based on the relative strength of laws about background checks, assault weapons, gun possession in public places, and other measures affecting firearms.
Source: Brady Campaign 2010.

Think about It

How could you adjust the title and scale of this map to present the information from the point of view of preserving the freedom to bear arms?

(continued)

on the premises. Informal gun clubs of both a primary- and secondary-group nature flourish across the country. On a national basis, powerful formal organizations promote gun ownership. Clearly, owning a gun is not a deviant act in our society (Gallup 2009a).

Since the Brady Act went into effect, support for stricter gun control measures has declined. In 2009, 45 percent of people supported protecting gun owners' rights compared to only 34 percent in 1993. Similarly, 49 percent favored controlling gun ownership compared to 57 percent in 1993. The National Rifle Association (NRA) has been able to use its impressive power to block or dilute gun control efforts (Pew Research Center 2009).

Conflict theorists contend that powerful groups like the NRA can dominate the legislative process because of their ability to mobilize resources in opposition to the will of the majority. Founded in 1871, the NRA has nearly 4 million members; state rifle associations, with 4 to 5 million members, support many of the NRA's goals. In contrast, Handgun Control, a key organization in the gun control battle, has only 400,000 members. Compared to the NRA's formidable war chest, Handgun Control's resources are limited.

Interactionists note that both opponents and proponents of gun control use symbols to their advantage. Opponents typically point to the Constitution and the tradition of gun ownership. Proponents point to spectacular episodes of violence, such as spree shootings on college campuses, as proof of the need to restrict firearms sales. Yet gun rights supporters see the same events as proof that students need guns to defend themselves (Lio et al. 2008).

Interactionists have also studied how gun rights organizations like the National Rifle Association present their argument to their members. Among sympathizers, they frame the issue not so much as one of safety or crime, but of civil rights. They see the Constitution as the basis for their campaign to facilitate gun ownership (Gregory 2007).

Initiating Policy

Advocates for stricter gun control laws have identified a series of measures they would like to see enacted:

- Strengthen the tools law enforcement officers need to crack down on corrupt gun dealers and curb illegal gun trafficking.
- Extend Brady background checks to all gun sales.
- Stop large-volume gun sales that supply gun traffickers.

Because towns, states, and the federal government all have the authority to regulate the possession and sale of firearms, advocates have attempted to pass these measures at all levels of government (Brady Campaign 2009).

The proposed legal restrictions on gun ownership have met strong opposition from both the NRA and firearms manufacturers. The NRA has been particularly successful in defeating political candidates who favor stricter gun control, and in backing those who seek to weaken such restrictions. Except in a handful of states, office seekers rarely risk taking an antigun position. Alarmed by the NRA's rhetoric, many voters fear that gun control will restrict their ability to protect themselves, independent of law enforcement. Indeed, in light of growing concern over terrorism, the handgun debate has turned to legislation allowing airline pilots to carry guns in the cockpit.

Recently, public health advocates have weighed in on the issue, noting the 30,000 people in the United States who die every year through gun violence, whether by suicide, homicide, or accidental discharge. This group advocates making guns safer—for example, by adding an indicator that the gun is loaded and/or a latch that prevents a magazine from being removed with a bullet still in the firing chamber. A more sophisticated approach to increasing safety would be to "personalize" firearms by requiring the owner/user to activate a code before the gun can be used (G. Brown 2008a, 2008b).

The unlawful use of guns is an issue that is not limited to the United States; it is a global issue. In the 1990s the International Committee of the Red Cross expressed concern over the global glut of firearms—one gun for every 10 people on earth. In Mexico, officials are struggling to halt the flow of firearms from the United States, which are used in 1,000 homicides there *every month*. South Africa too has moved to clamp down on guns. In 2005 the government launched a campaign to eliminate "surplus" weapons and toughened the procedure for acquiring new firearms (Jonsson and Llana 2009; Kirsten 2008).

TAKE THE ISSUE WITH YOU

1. Do you see guns more as weapons that could jeopardize your safety or as protection against those who would harm you? What formal or informal sources of social control may have influenced you to form this attitude?
2. What are the statistics on crimes committed with a firearm in your state? How many people die or are injured by guns every year? How strict are restrictions on gun ownership?
3. Should weapons manufacturers be allowed to sell guns to anyone in the world who wants them? Why or why not?

Summary

Crime is deviation from formal social norms administered by the state.

1. Sociologists differentiate among **victimless crimes** (such as drug use and prostitution), crime committed by **professional criminals, organized crime, white-collar crime,** and **international crime.**

2. Crime statistics are among the least reliable social data, partly because so many crimes are not reported to law enforcement agencies. Rates of violent crime are higher in the United States than in other Western societies, although they have been dropping.

3. Illegal gun trafficking has become a major problem, not just in the United States but around the world. Yet gun control is extremely controversial, opposed by powerful interest groups whose members see it as an abridgement of their constitutional right to bear arms.

Thinking Critically

1. Why is it useful to sociologists to have victimization surveys in addition to reported crime data?

2. Apply at least two of the theories discussed in Module 24 to the problem of professional crime. Which theory seems to provide the best explanation?

Key Terms

Crime

Index crime

Organized crime

Professional criminal

Transnational crime

Victimization survey

Victimless crime

White-collar crime

We continually assess how wealthy people are by looking at the cars they drive, the houses they live in, the clothes they wear, and so on. Yet it is not so easy to locate an individual within our social hierarchies as it would be in slavery or caste systems of stratification. To determine someone's class position, sociologists generally rely on the objective method.

Measuring Social Class

In the **objective method** of measuring social class, class is viewed largely as a statistical category. Researchers assign individuals to social classes on the basis of criteria such as occupation, education, income, and place of residence. The key to the objective method is that the *researcher,* rather than the person being classified, identifies an individual's class position.

The first step in using this method is to decide what indicators or causal factors will be measured objectively, whether wealth, income, education, or occupation. The prestige ranking of occupations has proved to be a useful indicator of a person's class position. For one thing, it is much easier to determine accurately than income or wealth. The term **prestige** refers to the respect and admiration that an occupation holds in a society. "My daughter, the physicist" connotes something very different from "my daughter, the waitress." Prestige is independent of the particular individual who occupies a job, a characteristic that distinguishes it from esteem. **Esteem** refers to the reputation that a specific person has earned within an occupation. Therefore, one can say that the position of president of the United States has high prestige, even though it has been occupied by people with varying degrees of esteem. A hairdresser may have the esteem of his clients, but he lacks the prestige of a corporate executive.

Table 27-1 ranks the prestige of a number of well-known occupations. In a series of national surveys, sociologists assigned prestige rankings to about 500 occupations, ranging from surgeon to panhandler. The highest possible prestige score was 100; the lowest was 0. Surgeon, physician, lawyer, dentist, and college professor were the most highly regarded occupations. Sociologists have used such data to assign prestige rankings to virtually all jobs and have found a stability in rankings from 1925 to the present. Similar studies in other countries have also developed useful prestige rankings of occupations (Nakao and Treas 1994).

Gender and Occupational Prestige

For many years, studies of social class tended to neglect the occupations and incomes of *women* as determinants of social rank.

With more than half of all married women now working outside the home (see Module 35), this approach seems outmoded. How should we judge class or status in dual-career families—by the occupation regarded as having greater prestige, the average, or some other combination of the two? Sociologists—in particular, feminist sociologists in Great Britain—are drawing on new approaches to assess women's social class standing. One approach is to focus on the individual (rather than the family or household) as the basis for categorizing a woman's class position. Thus, a woman would be classified according to her own occupational status rather than that of her spouse (O'Donnell 1992).

Another feminist effort to measure the contribution of women to the economy reflects a more clearly political agenda. International Women Count Network, a global grassroots feminist organization, has sought to give a monetary value to women's unpaid work. Besides providing symbolic recognition of women's role in labor, this value would also be used to calculate pension and other benefits that are usually based on wages received. The United Nations has placed an $11 trillion price tag on unpaid labor by women, largely in child care, housework, and agriculture. Whatever the figure, the continued undercounting of many workers' contributions to a family and to an entire economy means that virtually all measures of stratification are in need of reform (United Nations Development Programme 1995; Wages for Housework Campaign 1999).

Multiple Measures

Another complication in measuring social class is that advances in statistical methods and computer technology have multiplied the factors used to define class under the objective method. No longer are sociologists limited to annual income and education in evaluating a person's class position. Today, studies use as criteria the value of homes, sources of income, assets, years in present occupations, neighborhoods, and considerations regarding dual careers. Adding these variables will not necessarily paint a different picture of class differentiation in the United States, but it does allow sociologists to measure class in a more complex and multidimensional way. When researchers use multiple measures, they typically speak of **socioeconomic status (SES),** a measure of social class that is based on income, education, and occupation. To determine the socioeconomic status of a young person, such as a college student under age 25, they use *parental* income, education, and occupation.

Whatever the technique used to measure class, the sociologist is interested in real and often dramatic differences in power, privilege, and opportunity in a society. The study of stratification

Table **27-1** Prestige Rankings of Occupations

Occupation	Score	Occupation	Score
Surgeon	87	Farm manager	48
Physician	86	Mail carrier	47
Lawyer	75	Secretary	46
Dentist	74	Insurance agent	45
College professor	74	Bank teller	43
Architect	73	Nurse's aide	42
Psychiatrist	72	Farmer	40
Clergy	69	Correctional officer	40
Pharmacist	68	Receptionist	39
Registered nurse	66	Carpenter	39
High school teacher	66	Barber	36
Accountant	65	Child care worker	35
Optician	65	Hotel clerk	32
Elementary school teacher	64	Bus driver	32
Banker	63	Auto body repairer	31
Veterinarian	62	Truck driver	30
Legislator	61	Salesworker (shoes)	28
Airline pilot	60	Garbage collector	28
Police officer or detective	60	Waiter and waitress	28
Prekindergarten teacher	55	Cook in a pizza shop	27
Librarian	54	Bartender	25
Firefighter	53	Farmworker	23
Social worker	52	Janitor	22
Dental hygienist	52	Newspaper vendor	19
Electrician	51	Prostitute	14
Funeral director	49	Panhandler	11

Note: 100 is the highest and 0 the lowest possible prestige score.
Source: J. Davis et al. 2009. See also Nakao and Treas 1994.

Think about It

> Can you name what you think are two more high-prestige occupations?
> Two more low-prestige occupations?

is a study of inequality. Nowhere is the truth of that statement more evident than in the distribution of income and wealth.

● Income and Wealth

By all measures, in the United States **income,** a term that refers to salaries and wages, is distributed unevenly. Nobel Prize–winning economist Paul Samuelson has described the situation in the following words: "If we made an income pyramid out of building blocks, with each layer portraying $500 of income, the peak would be far higher than Mount Everest, but most people would be within a few feet of the ground" (Samuelson and Nordhaus 2011:324).

Recent data support Samuelson's analogy. In 2008 the median household income in the United States was $50,303. In other words, half of all households had higher incomes that year and half had lower incomes. However, this fact does not fully convey the income disparities in our society. We can get some sense of income inequality by contrasting this median (middle) income with the mean arithmetic average, which in 2008 was $68,424. The mean is so much higher than the median because some people make a lot more money than others, which draws the mean up. Thus, the mean is a less useful statistic than the median for describing the average, or typical, income (DeNavas-Walt et al. 2009:29).

We can gain additional insight into income inequality in the United States by looking at the relative placement of households within the income distribution. One of the most common ways of doing so is to line up all income-earning households from low to high and then break them into quintiles, or fifths. Because there are approximately 117 million households in the United States, each quintile includes an equal number of about 23.4 million households. This method gives us a sense of the average income within each quintile, along with the percentage of the nation's total income earned in each quintile.

As Figure 27-1 shows, looking at the population in this way reveals a significant degree of income inequality. The mean income for households in the lowest quintile is $11,656; in the top quintile, it is $171,057. Those households in the top 5 percent—the ones most responsible for bringing up the arithmetic mean—average a staggering $294,709 in annual income. If we were to move up even higher in the income distribution, we would find that the top 0.01 percent of taxpayers—about 15,000 households—make incomes of at least $11.5 million a year. Collectively, they control 6 percent of the nation's total income (Sloan 2009:27).

There has been a modest redistribution of income in the United States over the past 80 years, but not always to the benefit of the poor or even the middle class. From 1929 through 1970, the government's economic and tax policies shifted some income to the poor. However, in the past four decades—especially in the 1980s and in the decade from 2001 through 2010—federal tax policies have favored the affluent. Moreover, while the salaries of highly skilled workers and professionals have continued to rise, the wages of less skilled workers have *decreased* when controlled for inflation.

As a result, the Census Bureau and other researchers report that regardless of the measure that is used, income inequality rose substantially from 1967 through the end of the century. Former Federal Reserve Board Chairman Alan Greenspan was referring to this significant increase in income inequality when

Women as Wage Earners

In 2010, for the first time, women outnumbered men in the U.S. workforce. The historic reversal was caused by long-term changes in women's roles that began four decades ago. In the 2008 recession, massive job losses among men tipped the balance.

This change in the trend reflects the growing importance of women as wage earners, although on average, women still work fewer hours than men. They also hold more part-time jobs than men, and they earn only 77 percent of what men make. And of course, men still dominate the higher-paying executive levels of the workforce.

Women's share of the once heavily male labor force has been growing for nearly a century. Big expansions occurred during the Great Depression, when payrolls were limited, and World War II, when millions of men left their jobs to join the service. In 2008, the boost to women's employment came from a severe economic slowdown that hit hard at male-dominated occupations, such as construction and manufacturing.

Although women's outnumbering of men in the labor force may be temporary—an artifact of the current recession—their transformation of the U.S. workplace is permanent. There are no signs of a countertrend to their participation in the workforce.

Careful economic analysis has shown that over the past 30 years, federal and state tax policies have tended to accentuate this trend toward income inequality. During one 25-year period, the top 1 percent of income earners *after taxes* saw their incomes rise 228 percent, compared to only 21 percent for households in the middle quintile. Little wonder that the middle class is shrinking (Billitteri 2009; Sherman 2007).

Finally, the impact of the recent recession is unlikely to be shared evenly among racial and ethnic groups.

FIGURE 27-1 **Mean Household Income by Quintile**

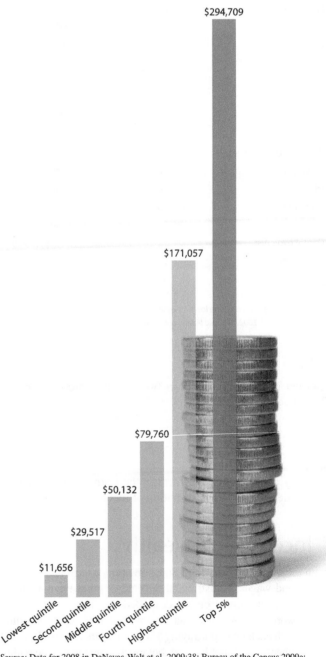

Source: Data for 2008 in DeNavas-Walt et al. 2009:38; Bureau of the Census 2009e: Table H-3.

he told Congress that the gap between the rich and the poor in the United States has become so wide that a democratic society must address it (Cushing-Daniels and Zedlewski 2008; Grier 2005; Neckerman and Torche 2007; Saez 2008).

Just how dramatic has this growth in inequality been? Consider the period between 1984 and 2008. In just 25 years, the following changes occurred in real household income (adjusted for inflation):

- For the lowest 20 percent of the population, income rose 9 percent.
- For the next lowest 20 percent of the population, income rose 10 percent.
- For the middle 20 percent of the population, income rose 13 percent.
- For the next highest 20 percent of the population, income rose 20 percent.
- For the top 20 percent of the population, income rose a whopping 40 percent.

The pattern is clear. Though everyone has done better, by far the biggest winners have been the affluent.

Has the recent economic slowdown reduced income inequality? Not really. A comparison of household incomes in 1999 (the peak before the 2001 recession) with the most recent income data shows that lower-income households' earnings have declined, while the higher-income households' earnings have held steady. By one measure, inequality between the top 10th and the bottom 10th of the income distribution has increased 9 percent (DeNavas-Walt et al. 2009:38–39).

FIGURE 27-2 **Distribution of Wealth in the United States**

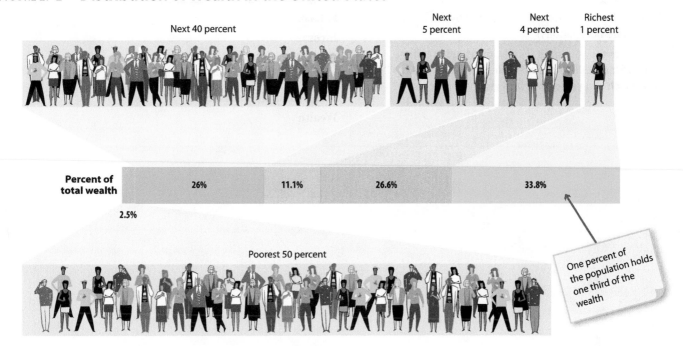

Source: Data for 2007, as reported in a 2009 Federal Reserve Bank study. See Kennickell 2009:35.

During the recession of 1999–2001, the median household wealth of Hispanic and Black Americans fell 27 percent. At the same time, White households' wealth grew 2 percent (D. Hamilton and Darity 2009).

Globalization is often blamed for this growing inequality, because it has forced less skilled workers to compete with lower-paid foreign-born workers. While that is true, research suggests that the number of displaced workers who are reemployed at similarly paid or even higher-paid jobs roughly equals the number of workers whose earnings drop (S. Zimmerman 2008a).

Americans often seem not to be seriously concerned about income and wealth inquality in the United States. In a comparison of opinions about social inequality in 27 different countries, respondents in the United States were less aware than those in other countries of the extent of inequality at the top of the income distribution. Americans would prefer to "level down" the top of the nation's earning distribution, but compared to

people in other countries, they are less concerned about reducing income differentials at the bottom of the distribution (Osberg and Smeeding 2006).

Wealth, an inclusive term encompassing all a person's material assets (including land, stocks, and other types of property), is distributed much more unevenly than income in the United States. A 2009 Federal Reserve Bank study showed that half the population controls 2.5 percent of the nation's wealth; the other half controls over 97 percent (Figure 27-2). Put another way, the wealth of the top 1 percent exceeds the collective wealth of the bottom 90 percent. Researchers have also found a dramatic disparity in wealth between African Americans and Whites. This disparity is evident even when educational backgrounds are held constant: the households of college-educated Whites have about three times as much wealth as the households of college-educated Blacks (Conley 2010; Kennickell 2009; Oliver and Shapiro 2006, 2008).

Summary

One consequence of social class in the United States is that both **income** and **wealth** are distributed unevenly.

1. Sociologists use the **objective method** of measuring social class, which uses criteria such as occupation,

education, and income. **Socioeconomic status (SES)** is an objective measure based on these criteria.

2. Regardless of the measure used, income inequality rose from the late 1960s to the end of the 20th century.

Thinking Critically

1. To what degree are students motivated by the prestige of their future occupations?

2. What does the pattern of income distribution in the United States tell you about your own future income? How much can you expect it to grow over the years?

Key Terms

Esteem

Income

Objective method

Prestige

Socioeconomic status (SES)

Wealth

28

Poverty and Social Mobility

Approximately one out of every nine people in the United States lives below the poverty line established by the federal government. In 2007, no fewer than 37.2 million people were living in poverty. The economic boom of the 1990s passed these people by. A Bureau of the Census report shows that one in five households has trouble meeting basic needs, from paying the utility bills to buying dinner (Bauman 1999; DeNavas-Walt et al. 2009).

One contributor to the United States' high poverty rate has been the large number of workers employed at minimum wage. The federal government has raised the minimum wage over the past half century from 75 cents in 1950 to $6.55 in 2008 and $7.25 in 2009. But in terms of its real value adjusted for inflation, the minimum wage has frequently failed to keep pace with the cost of living.

Moreover, raising the minimum wage does not remedy other difficulties that low-wage workers encounter. A 2009 survey of workers in various low-wage occupations, such as apparel manufacturing, child care (see Module 15), and discount retailing, showed that these workers lose about 15 percent of the pay that is due them through employers' wage violations. Typically, employers limit workers' wages by pressuring them not to file for workers' compensation after on-the-job injuries, requiring them to work off the clock, and paying the straight hourly wage rate for overtime hours. Women are far more likely than men to be cheated in this way (Bernhardt et al. 2009).

Sociologists have long had an interest in the impact of substandard work on society, beginning with the writings of Karl Marx, Émile Durkheim, and Max Weber. Their interest increased with the global economic decline that began in 2008, which trapped many people in jobs they did not want or left them unemployed. The Research Today box considers recent sociological work on *precarious work*.

In this section, we'll consider just how social scientists define *poverty*. We'll also take a closer look at the people who fall into that category—including the working poor.

Studying Poverty

The efforts of sociologists and other social scientists to better understand poverty are complicated by the difficulty of defining it. This problem is evident even in government programs that conceive of poverty in either absolute or relative terms. **Absolute poverty** refers to a minimum level of subsistence that no family should be expected to live below.

One commonly used measure of absolute poverty is the federal government's *poverty line,* a money income figure that is adjusted annually to reflect the consumption requirements of families based on their size and composition. The poverty line serves as an official definition of which people are poor. In 2008, for example, any family of four (two adults and two children) with a combined income of $21,834 or less fell below the poverty line. This definition determines which individuals and families will be eligible for certain government benefits (DeNavas-Walt et al. 2009:43).

Although by absolute standards, poverty has declined in the United States, it remains higher than in many other industrial nations. As Figure 28-1 shows, a comparatively high proportion of U.S. households are poor, meaning that they are unable to purchase basic consumer goods. If anything, this cross-national comparison understates the extent of poverty in the United States, since U.S. residents are likely to pay more for housing, health care, child care, and education than residents of other countries, where such expenses are often subsidized (Smeeding 2008).

In contrast, **relative poverty** is a floating standard of deprivation by which people at the bottom of a society, whatever their lifestyles, are judged to be disadvantaged *in comparison with the nation as a whole.* Therefore, even if the poor of 2005 are better off in absolute terms than the poor of the 1930s or 1960s, they are still seen as deserving of special assistance. The Sociology in the Global Community box explores the difference between relative poverty in Appalachia and relative affluence in the Congo.

Debate has been growing over the accuracy of the federal government's measure of poverty, which has remained largely unchanged since 1963. If noncash benefits such as Medicare, Medicaid, tax credits, food stamps, public housing, and health care and other employer-provided fringe benefits were included, the reported poverty rate would be lower. On the other hand, if out-of-pocket medical expenses and mandatory work expenses for transportation and child care were included, the poverty rate would be higher. Although the current poverty measure does consider family size, it does not consider a household's location, whether in a relatively expensive city like New York or in a less expensive rural area. Nor does it consider whether a householder pays rent or a mortgage installment, lives at home or with someone else. To address some of these shortcomings, in 2010 the federal government launched a second statistic called the Supplemental Poverty Measure (SPM), which will be used to estimate economic hardship. The SPM is a relative poverty measure that is based on a broad range of changing household resources and expenses. It will be calculated beginning in late

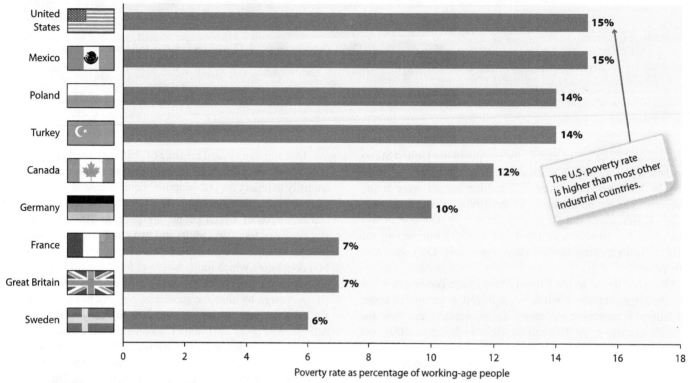

FIGURE 28-1   Poverty in Selected Countries

United States — 15%
Mexico — 15%
Poland — 14%
Turkey — 14%
Canada — 12%
Germany — 10%
France — 7%
Great Britain — 7%
Sweden — 6%

The U.S. poverty rate is higher than most other industrial countries.

Poverty rate as percentage of working-age people

Note: Data are averages for mid-2000s, as reported in 2009. Poverty threshold is 50 percent of a nation's median household income.
Source: Organisation for Economic Co-operation and Development 2009a.

Sociology in the Global Community

It's All Relative: Appalachian Poverty and Congolese Affluence

What does it mean to be well off? To be poor? To explore this question, the editors of the London-based publication *The Economist* compared the situations of two men living very different lives: an unemployed truck driver in the Appalachian Mountains and a physician in Congo.

Enos Banks makes his home in a forgotten pocket of rural poverty, described over 40 years ago in Michael Harrington's *The Other America*. Banks once worked for a coal-mining company, but a heart attack forced him to quit

> By U.S. standards, Kabamba's four-bedroom home, spacious compared to Banks's trailer, is overcrowded with 12 inhabitants.

his job. In his 60s, he lives in a trailer and gets by on a little more than $500 a month in supplemental security income (SSI). Because he owns a truck, he is not eligible for food stamps.

On the other side of the world, in the Democratic Republic of Congo, Mbwebwe Kabamba earns about $100 or $200 more per month than Enos Banks. Kabamba is a surgeon and head of the emergency room at a hospital in Kinshasa, the country's capital. His hospital salary is only $250 a month, but he supplements it by performing surgery on the side. In Congo, a similar income to that which impoverishes Enos Banks places Kabamba near the middle of his society's income distribution.

Though Kabamba may seem better off than Banks, especially given the Congo's lower cost of living, such is not the case. Kabamba supports a family of 12, while Banks supports only himself. By U.S. standards, Kabamba's four-bedroom home, spacious compared to Banks's trailer, is overcrowded with 12 inhabitants. And though Kabamba's home has a kitchen, it lacks running water, dependable electric service, and air-conditioning—services most Americans take for granted. Considered wealthy in his own country, Kabamba is worse off than a poor person in the United States.

Nevertheless, Banks's poverty is real; he occupies a position in the lowest quintile (see

Figure 27-1). In absolute terms defined by his own society, Kabamba is not poor, even though he is less well off than Enos Banks. Relative to most of the world's population, however, both men are doing well.

LET'S DISCUSS

1. Have you ever lived in or traveled to a foreign country where income and living standards were very different from those in the United States? If so, did the contrast give you a new perspective on poverty? What differences between the living standards in the two societies stand out in your mind?

2. If absolute measures of poverty, such as household income, are inconsistent from one country to the next, what other measures might give a clearer picture of people's relative well-being? Should the poverty level be the same everywhere in the world? Why or why not?

Sources: The Economist 2005f; Harrington 1962; Haub 2008.

Precarious Work

In 2008 Jim Marshall, age 39, lost his job in Detroit's faltering auto industry. Figuring that job prospects had to be better elsewhere, he moved to Florida. But by May 2009 Jim was homeless, living in a tent city just north of St. Petersburg. "My parents always taught me to work hard in school, graduate high school, go to college, get a degree and you'll do fine. You'll do better than your parents' generation," Marshall says. "I did all those things. . . . For a while, I did have that good life, but nowadays that's not the reality" (Bazar 2009:A2).

Jim's story is all too common. He is one of the millions of Americans who have been reduced to doing **precarious work**—employment that is poorly paid and, from the worker's perspective, insecure and unprotected. People who engage in precarious work often cannot support a household, and they are vulnerable to falling into poverty.

Even before economists recognized the economic downturn in 2009, there was ample statistical evidence that precarious work was increasing, despite the fact that the unemployment rate remained steady. In his presidential address to the ASA, Arne L. Kalleberg offered the following five social indicators:

1. *A decline in the average length of time workers remain with an employer.* This trend has been especially noticeable among older White men, who in the past were protected by employers.

2. *An increase in long-term unemployment.* The proportion of workers who remained unemployed after six months rose in the 2000s, when the number of manufacturing jobs shrank and fewer new jobs were created.

3. *A decrease in job security.* Given the increase in long-term unemployment and the decrease in average time spent with an employer, workers became increasingly insecure about their ability to replace a lost job.

> To meet cyclical fluctuations in supply and demand, employers have turned more and more to nontraditional labor sources. Today, virtually any job can be outsourced, including accounting, legal, and military services.

4. *An increase in outsourcing and temporary work.* To meet cyclical fluctuations in supply and demand, employers have turned more and more to nontraditional labor sources. Today, virtually any job can be outsourced, including accounting, legal, and military services.

5. *A shift in risk from employers to employees.* Few companies offer traditional pensions anymore. Employees are being asked to shoulder at least part of the cost and risk, not only of their retirement investments, but of their health insurance plans.

Although precarious work is becoming more common, people differ in their vulnerability to it. Members of racial and ethnic minorities are more likely than others to be engaged in precarious work. Immigrants, including those who are in the United States legally, are also more likely than others to be precariously employed. Around the world—in the United States, other industrial countries, and developing nations—women are much more likely than men to do precarious work.

What can be done to revitalize labor markets so that fewer workers end up doing substandard work—or at least, that those who do will suffer less from it? Denmark is one country that has tried to deal with the problem. Although the government there cannot make jobs more secure, it does provide significant assistance to the unemployed. Help finding a job, significant income compensation (90 percent of a worker's previous wage for one year, without conditions), and subsidized education and training are all available to Danish workers who have lost their jobs.

LET'S DISCUSS

1. Has the trend toward increasing reliance on precarious work touched your family or friends? Has anyone you know been unemployed longer than six months? If so, did that person or persons belong to one or more of the groups that are particularly vulnerable to precarious work?

2. Looking forward to your own career, can you think of a strategy for avoiding precarious work, frequent job loss, and long-term unemployment?

Sources: Bazar 2009; Fudge and Owens 2006; Kalleberg 2009; McDowell et al. 2009; Somavia 2008; Westergaard-Nielsen 2008.

2011, but will not replace the poverty line in determining a household's eligibility for benefits (Blank 2008; Department of Commerce 2010).

Who Are the Poor?

Not only does the category of the poor defy any simple definition; it counters the common stereotypes about "poor people." For example, many people in the United States believe that the vast majority of the poor are able to work but will not. Yet many poor adults do work outside the home, although only a small portion of them work full-time throughout the year. In 2008, about 27 percent of all poor working adults worked full-time, compared to 66 percent of all adults. Of those poor adults who do not work, most are ill or disabled, or are occupied in maintaining a home (DeNavas-Walt et al. 2009:14).

Though many of the poor live in urban slums, a majority live outside those poverty-stricken areas. Poverty is no stranger in rural areas, from Appalachia to hard-hit farming regions to Native American reservations. Table 28-1 provides additional statistical information regarding low-income people in the United States.

Table **28-1** Who Are the Poor in the United States?

Group	Percentage of the Population of the United States	Percentage of the Poor of the United States
Age		
Under 18 years old	25%	35%
18 to 64 years old	62	56
65 years and older	13	9
Race-Ethnicity		
Whites (non-Hispanic)	65	43
Blacks	13	24
Hispanics	16	28
Asians and Pacific Islanders	4	4
Family Composition		
Married couples with male householders	75	40
Female householders	18	51

Source: Data for 2008, as reported by the Bureau of the Census; DeNavas-Walt et al. 2009:14.

Feminization of Poverty

Since World War II, an increasing proportion of the poor people of the United States have been women, many of whom are divorced or never-married mothers. In 1959, female householders accounted for 26 percent of the nation's poor; by 2008, that figure had risen to 51 percent (see Table 28-1). This alarming trend, known as the **feminization of poverty,** is evident not just in the United States but around the world.

About half of all women living in poverty in the United States are in transition, coping with an economic crisis caused by the departure, disability, or death of a husband. The other half tend to be economically dependent either on the welfare system or on friends and relatives living nearby. A major factor in the feminization of poverty has been the increase in families with women as single heads of the household (see Module 40). Conflict theorists and other observers trace the higher rates of poverty among women to three distinct factors: the difficulty in finding affordable child care, sexual harassment, and sex discrimination in the labor market.

The Underclass

In 2008, 43 percent of poor people in the United States were living in central cities. These highly visible urban residents are the focus of most government efforts to alleviate poverty. Yet according to many observers, the plight of the urban poor is growing worse, owing to the devastating interplay of inadequate education and limited employment prospects. Traditional employment opportunities in the industrial sector are largely closed to the unskilled poor. Past and present discrimination heightens these problems for those

Even if this single parent works her way up the chain of command, supporting her family will still be difficult.

low-income urban residents who are Black or Hispanic (DeNavas-Walt et al. 2009:14).

Along with other social scientists, sociologist William Julius Wilson (1980, 1987, 1996) and his colleagues (2004) have used the term **underclass** to describe the long-term poor who lack training and skills. According to an analysis of Census 2000 data, 7.9 million people live in high-poverty neighborhoods. About 30 percent of the population in these neighborhoods is Black, 29 percent Hispanic, and 24 percent White. In central cities, about 49 percent of the underclass is Black, 29 percent Hispanic, 17 percent White, and 5 percent "other" (Jargowsky and Yang 2006; O'Hare and Curry-White 1992).

Conflict theorists, among others, have expressed alarm at the portion of the nation's population living on this lower rung of the stratification ladder, and at society's reluctance to address the lack of economic opportunities for these people. Often, portraits of the underclass seem to blame the victims for their plight, while ignoring the other factors that push people into poverty.

Analyses of the poor in general reveal that they are not a static social class. The overall composition of the poor changes continually, because some individuals and families near the top edge of poverty move above the poverty level after a year or two, while others slip below it. Still, hundreds of thousands of people remain in poverty for many years at a time. Blacks and Latinos are more likely than Whites to be persistently poor. Both Latinos and Blacks are less likely than Whites to leave the welfare rolls as a result of welfare reform, discussed in the Social Policy section of this module (Jäntii 2009).

Explaining Poverty

Why is it that poverty pervades a nation of such vast wealth? Sociologist Herbert Gans (1995), who has applied functionalist analysis to the existence of poverty, argues that various segments of society actually *benefit* from the existence of the poor. Gans has identified a number of social, economic, and political functions that the poor perform for society:

- The presence of poor people means that society's dirty work—physically dirty or dangerous, dead-end and underpaid, undignified and menial jobs—will be performed at low cost.
- Poverty creates jobs for occupations and professions that serve the poor. It creates both legal employment (public health experts, welfare caseworkers) and illegal jobs (drug dealers, numbers runners).

- The identification and punishment of the poor as deviants upholds the legitimacy of conventional social norms and mainstream values regarding hard work, thrift, and honesty.

- Within a relatively hierarchical society, the existence of poor people guarantees the higher status of the rich. As psychologist William Ryan (1976) noted, affluent people may justify inequality (and gain a measure of satisfaction) by *blaming the victims* of poverty for their disadvantaged condition.

- Because of their lack of political power, the poor often absorb the costs of social change. Under the policy of deinstitutionalization, mental patients released from long-term hospitals have been transferred primarily to low-income communities and neighborhoods. Similarly, halfway houses for rehabilitated drug abusers, rejected by more affluent communities, often end up in poorer neighborhoods.

In Gans's view, then, poverty and the poor actually satisfy positive functions for many nonpoor groups in the United States.

Life Chances

Max Weber saw class as being closely related to people's **life chances**—that is, their opportunities to provide themselves with material goods, positive living conditions, and favorable life experiences (Gerth and Mills 1958). Life chances are reflected in measures such as housing, education, and health. Occupying a higher social class in a society improves your life chances and brings greater access to social rewards. In contrast, people in the lower social classes are forced to devote a larger proportion of their limited resources to the necessities of life.

In times of danger, the affluent and powerful have a better chance of surviving than people of ordinary means. When the supposedly unsinkable British ocean liner *Titanic* hit an iceberg in 1912, it was not carrying enough lifeboats to accommodate all passengers. Plans had been made to evacuate only first- and second-class passengers. About 62 percent of the first-class passengers survived the disaster. Despite a rule that women and children would go first, about a third of those passengers were male. In contrast, only 25 percent of the third-class passengers survived. The first attempt to alert them to the need to abandon ship came well after other passengers had been notified (D. Butler 1998; Crouse 1999; Riding 1998).

Class position also affects people's vulnerability to natural disasters. When Hurricane Katrina hit the Gulf Coast of the United States in 2005, affluent and poor people alike became its victims. However, poor people who did not own automobiles (100,000 of them in New Orleans alone) were less able than others to evacuate in advance of the storm. The poor who survived its fury had no nest egg to draw on, and thus were more likely than others to accept relocation wherever social service agencies could place them—sometimes hundreds or thousands of miles from home. Those who were able to return are still dealing with the toxic debris left behind (Bullard and Wright 2009).

Class position affects people's vulnerability to natural disasters. Today, years after Hurricane Katrina forced the evacuation of New Orleans, many of the city's poor still have not returned home.

Some people have hoped that the Internet revolution would help to level the playing field by making information and markets uniformly available. Unfortunately, however, not everyone can get onto the information superhighway, so yet another aspect of social inequality has emerged—the **digital divide**. The poor, minorities, and those who live in rural communities and inner cities are not getting connected at home or at work. A recent government study found that despite falling computer prices, the Internet gap between the haves and have-nots has not narrowed. Although 74 percent of all people in the United States used the Internet in 2009, that group included 94 percent of people with incomes over $75,000 but 60 percent of people with incomes of less than $30,000. As wealthier people switch to high-speed Internet connections, they will be able to take advantage of even more sophisticated interactive services, and the digital divide will grow even wider (Pew Internet Project 2010).

Wealth, status, and power may not ensure happiness, but they certainly provide additional ways of coping with problems and disappointments. For this reason, the opportunity for advancement—for social mobility—is of special significance to those on the bottom of society. Most people want the rewards and privileges that are granted to high-ranking members of a culture. What can society do to increase their social mobility? One strategy is to offer financial aid to college students from low-income families, on the theory that education lifts people out of poverty. Yet such programs are not having as great an effect as their authors once hoped (the Sociology on Campus box).

 use your **sociological imagination**

Imagine a society in which there are no social classes—no differences in people's wealth, income, and life chances. What would such a society be like? Would it be stable, or would its social structure change over time?

Sociology on Campus

Social Class and Financial Aid

Today's young people have been dubbed Generation Y, but a more appropriate name for them could be Generation Debt. Every year, millions of prospective college students and their parents struggle through the intricate and time-consuming process of applying for financial aid. Originally, financial aid programs were intended to level the playing field—to allow qualified students from all walks of life to attend college, regardless of the cost. But have these programs fulfilled their promise?

In 2004, 40 percent of first-year students at major state universities came from families with incomes of more than $100,000 a year. In other words, close to half of all students

> Statistics that show the educational level in the United States rising overall obscure the widening gap between the advantaged and the less advantaged.

came from high-income families. This statistic should not be surprising, given the high cost of tuition, room, and board at state universities. For students from families with the lowest incomes, the cost can be prohibitive. Only 11 percent of children from the poorest families in the United States have earned college degrees, compared to 53 percent of children from families in the top fifth of the population. Those moderate-income students who do graduate, and even those who fail to complete their degrees, are often saddled with heavy postgraduate debt.

Community colleges, with their low tuition, are often regarded as a hedge against the high costs of higher education. Although these two-year commuter colleges may be cheaper than four-year residential schools, they are not inexpensive. In the academic year 2009–2010, the annual cost of attending community college was more than $14,000. For students at these schools, a greater proportion of their expenses goes to transportation and child care than for students who live on campus at four-year schools.

Besides the spiraling cost of an education, the widespread difficulty in paying for college stems from three trends. First, over the past few decades, colleges and universities have been moving away from making outright grants, such as scholarships, to deserving students, and toward low-interest student loans. Second, much of the assistance schools offer in the form of loans is not based strictly on need. Third, interest rates on federally guaranteed loans have risen steadily, increasing the burden of repayment.

These trends in financial aid for higher education are closely tied to trends in social inequality. As noted in Modules 27, over the past half century, rather than declining, inequality in income and wealth has actually increased. According to one analysis of U.S. economic trends over the past 30 years, this increase in wealth and income inequality has contributed to a modest increase in educational inequality, as measured by the number of years of formal schooling students achieve. In a variation on the truism that the rich tend to get richer while the poor get poorer, the rich are getting better educations and the poor are getting poorer educations. Statistics

that show the educational level in the United States rising overall obscure the widening gap between the advantaged and the less advantaged.

LET'S DISCUSS

1. How important is financial aid (grants, loans, work-study income) to you and your friends? Without these types of aid, would you be able to cover your college expenses?

2. Aside from a reduction in individual social mobility, what might be the long-term effects of the shortage of need-based financial aid? Relate your answer to the trend toward globalization.

Sources: Boushey 2005; Campbell et al. 2005; College Board 2009; Isaacs et al. 2008; Kamenetz 2006; Leonhardt 2004; Michals 2003; Trumbull 2006.

Social Mobility

In the movie *Maid in Manhattan*, Jennifer Lopez plays the lead in a modern-day Cinderella story, rising from the lowly status of chambermaid in a big-city hotel to a company supervisor and the girlfriend of a well-to-do politician. The ascent of a person from a poor background to a position of prestige, power, or financial reward is an example of social mobility. Formally defined, the term **social mobility** refers to the movement of individuals or groups from one position in a society's stratification system to another. But how significant—how frequent, how dramatic—is mobility in a class society such as the United States?

Open versus Closed Stratification Systems

Sociologists use the terms *open stratification system* and *closed stratification system* to indicate the degree of social mobility in a society. An **open system** implies that the position of each individual is influenced by his or her *achieved* status. Such a system encourages competition among members of society. The United States is moving toward this ideal type as the government attempts to reduce the barriers faced by women, racial and ethnic minorities, and people born in lower social classes. Even in the midst of the economic downturn of 2008–2009, nearly 80 percent of people in the United States felt they could get ahead (Economic Mobility Project 2009).

At the other extreme of social mobility is the **closed system,** which allows little or no possibility of individual social mobility. The slavery and caste systems of stratification are examples of closed systems. In such societies, social placement is based on *ascribed* statuses, such as race or family background, which cannot be changed.

Types of Social Mobility

An airline pilot who becomes a police officer moves from one social position to another of the same rank. Each occupation has the same prestige ranking: 60 on a scale ranging from a low of 0 to a high of 100 (see Table 27-1). Sociologists call this kind of movement **horizontal mobility.** However, if the pilot were to become a lawyer (prestige ranking of 75), he or she would experience **vertical mobility,** the movement of an individual from one social position to another of a different rank. Vertical mobility can also involve moving *downward* in a society's stratification system, as would be the case if the airline pilot became a bank teller (ranking of 43). Pitirim Sorokin ([1927] 1959) was the first sociologist to distinguish between horizontal and vertical mobility. Most sociological analysis, however, focuses on vertical rather than horizontal mobility.

One way of examining vertical social mobility is to contrast its two types, intergenerational and intragenerational mobility. **Intergenerational mobility** involves changes in the social position of children relative to their parents. Thus, a plumber whose father was a physician provides an example of downward intergenerational mobility. A film star whose parents were both factory workers illustrates upward intergenerational mobility. Because education contributes significantly to upward mobility, any barrier to the pursuit of advanced degrees can definitely limit intergenerational mobility (see the Sociology on Campus box; Isaacs 2007a; Isaacs et al. 2008; Sawhill and Morton 2007).

Figure 28-2 shows intergenerational mobility based on income. In 1978–1980, a national survey looked at the family income of 6,000 young people. Two decades later, in 1997–2003, researchers followed up on those young adults and their income. The results showed a strong stickiness in both the bottom and top quintiles, or fifths, of the income distribution. Just over 33 percent of those whose parents were in the bottom quintile and 37 percent of those who were in the top quintile remained in the same quintile as adults. Yet the study also showed mobility: almost 66 percent of those in the bottom quintile moved up, and over 60 percent of those at the top experienced downward mobility.

Among men born in the 1960s, this consistent intergenerational mobility resulted largely from economic growth. On average, these men earned more than their fathers did at the same age; their family incomes improved as well. However, the trend did not continue into the next generation. Currently, young men are earning less than their fathers did at the same age—about 12 percent less. Family incomes are slightly higher than in the

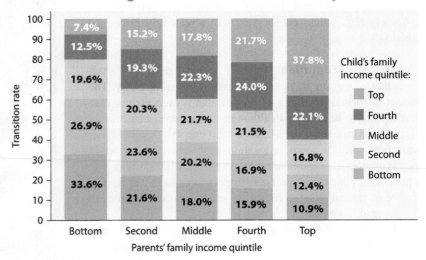

FIGURE 28-2 Intergenerational Income Mobility

Source: Mazumder 2008:10.

Over a 25-year period, adult children often end up in the same income bracket as their parents. About 7 percent of those who begin in the bottom quintile reach the top quintile as adults; their story is one of rags to riches. About 11 percent of those who start in the top quintile fall to the bottom.

last generation, but only because women have moved into the paid labor force to supplement their husbands' earnings. With so few women left to join the labor force, most families will need to increase their wages to raise their incomes further (Sawhill and Haskins 2009).

Intragenerational mobility involves changes in social position within a person's adult life. A woman who begins work as a teacher's aide and eventually becomes superintendent of the school district experiences upward intragenerational mobility. A man who becomes a taxicab driver after his accounting firm goes bankrupt undergoes downward intragenerational mobility.

Social Mobility in the United States

The belief in upward mobility is an important value in our society. Does that mean that the United States is indeed the land of opportunity? Not unless such ascriptive characteristics as race, gender, and family background have ceased to be significant in determining one's future prospects. We can see the impact of these factors in the occupational structure.

Occupational Mobility Two sociological studies conducted a decade apart offer insight into the degree of mobility in the nation's occupational structure (Blau and Duncan 1967; Featherman and Hauser 1978). Taken together, these investigations lead to several noteworthy conclusions. First, occupational mobility (both intergenerational and intragenerational) has been common among males. Approximately 60 to 70 percent of sons are employed in higher-ranked occupations than their fathers.

Second, although there is a great deal of mobility in the United States, much of it is minor. That is, people who reach an occupational level above or below that of their parents usually advance or fall back only one or two out of a possible eight occupational levels. Thus, the child of a laborer may become an artisan or a technician, but he or she is less likely to become a manager or professional. The odds against reaching the top are extremely high unless one begins from a relatively privileged position.

The Impact of Education Another conclusion of both studies is that education plays a critical role in social mobility. The impact of formal schooling on adult status is even greater than that of family background (although as we have seen, family background influences the likelihood that one will receive higher education). Furthermore, education represents an important means of intergenerational mobility. A person who was born into a poor family but who graduates from college has a one in five chance of entering the top fifth of all income earners as an adult (Isaacs et al. 2008).

The impact of education on mobility has diminished somewhat in the past decade, however. An undergraduate degree—a BA or a BS—serves less as a guarantee of upward mobility now than it did in the past, simply because more and more entrants into the job market hold such a degree. Moreover, intergenerational mobility is declining, since there is no longer such a stark difference between generations. In earlier decades, many high school–educated parents successfully sent their children to college, but today's college students are increasingly likely to have college-educated parents (Sawhill and Morton 2007).

The Impact of Race and Ethnicity Sociologists have long documented the fact that the class system is more rigid for African Americans than it is for members of other racial groups. African American men who have good jobs, for example, are less likely than White men to see their adult children attain the same status. The cumulative disadvantage of discrimination plays a significant role in the disparity between the two groups' experiences. Compared to White households, the relatively modest wealth of African American households means that adult African

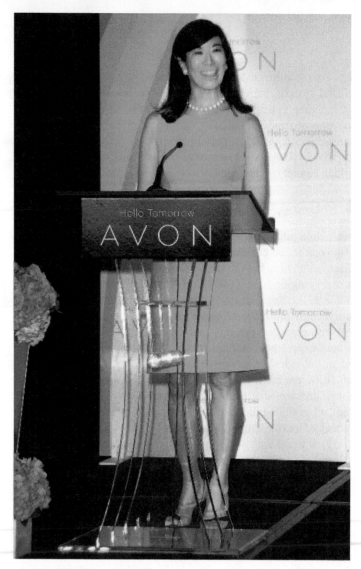

Andrea Jung, chairman and chief executive officer of Avon Corporation since 1999, is one of the few women in the United States who have risen to the top of the corporate hierarchy. In 2008, Jung was elected to Apple's board of directors. Despite the passage of equal opportunity laws, occupational barriers still limit most women's social mobility.

If this lawyer were the son of a car mechanic, his rise to the upper-middle class would illustrate intergenerational mobility. If he had begun as a paralegal and worked his way up the occupational ladder, his career would illustrate intragenerational mobility.

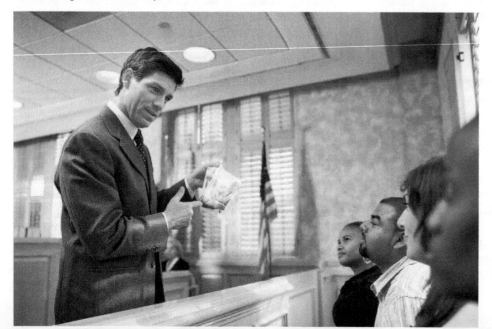

American children are less likely than adult White children to receive financial support from their parents. Indeed, young African American couples are much more likely than young White couples to be assisting their parents—a sacrifice that hampers their social mobility (Favreault 2008).

Not surprisingly, African Americans are more likely than Whites to experience downward intergenerational mobility, and less likely to move up the social ladder. A study of the income data for people born between 1955 and 1970 shows that four in five Black children who began in the top quintile experienced downward mobility, compared to just two in five White children. Similarly, three in five White children who began in the bottom two quintiles experienced upward social mobility, compared to one in four Black children (Sharkey 2009).

The African American middle class has grown over the past few decades, due to economic expansion and the benefits of the civil rights movement of the 1960s. Yet many of these middle-class households have little savings, a fact that puts them in danger during times of crisis. We noted earlier that recession hits Black and Latino households harder than White households. Studies have consistently shown that downward mobility is significantly higher for Blacks than it is for Whites (Conley 2010; Oliver and Shapiro 2006, 2008; Sernau 2001; W. Wilson 1996).

The Latino population is not doing much better. The typical Hispanic has less than 10 percent of the wealth that a White person has. A 2008 study suggests that in recent years, Latinos have even lost ground. Their continuing immigration accounts for part of the disparity: most of the new arrivals are destitute. But even the wealthiest 5 percent of Latino households have only a third as much net worth as the top 5 percent of White households (Kochhar 2008).

The Impact of Gender   Studies of mobility, even more than those of class, have traditionally ignored the significance of gender, but some research findings are now available that explore the relationship between gender and mobility.

Women's employment opportunities are much more limited than men's (as Module 35 will show). Moreover, according to recent research, women whose skills far exceed the jobs offered them are more likely than men to withdraw entirely from the paid labor force. Their withdrawal violates an assumption common to traditional mobility studies: that most people will aspire to upward mobility and seek to make the most of their opportunities.

In contrast to men, women have a rather large range of clerical occupations open to them. But the modest salary ranges and few prospects for advancement in many of these positions limit the possibility of upward mobility. Self-employment as shopkeepers, entrepreneurs, independent professionals, and the like—an important road to upward mobility for men—is more difficult for women, who find it harder to secure the necessary financing. Although sons commonly follow in the footsteps of their fathers, women are unlikely to move into their fathers' positions. Consequently, gender remains an important factor in shaping social mobility. Women in the United States (and in other parts of the world) are especially likely to be trapped in poverty, unable to rise out of their low-income status (Beller 2009; Heilman 2001).

On the positive side, though today's women lag behind men in employment, their earnings have increased faster than their mothers' did at a comparable age, so that their incomes are substantially higher. The one glaring exception to this trend is the daughters of low-income parents. Because these women typically care for children—many as single parents—and sometimes for other relatives as well, their mobility is severely restricted (Isaacs 2007b).

social policy and Stratification

Rethinking Welfare in North America and Europe

In Pasadena, Denise Sims-Bowles, who has been out of work for more than two years, has sent 273 resumes to prospective employers. A victim of the deep economic recession that followed the stock market crash of 2008, she has more than two decades of experience as a white-collar worker, yet she cannot find an opening. She is not alone. At the end of 2009, about 40 percent of the nation's unemployed had been out of work for half a year or more.

In Tokyo, Atsushi Nakanishi lives in a coffin-sized cubicle that he rented after he lost his job. He, too, is not alone. When the global economic crisis hit Japan in 2009, millions of workers lost their jobs; many became homeless. To contain political unrest, the government has opened emergency shelters to house jobless workers.

In Middlebury, Indiana, Scott and Kelly Nichols confront a hard reality. Scott, once a well-paid blue-collar worker, and Kelly, an office clerk, have been out of work since the recreational vehicle industry collapsed, hit by high gas prices and tight credit. Now, nine months later, the Nichols can no longer afford the rent. They will move in with Kelly's mother, in her basement (Scherer 2010a; Schwartzman 2009; Tabuchi 2010).

These are the faces of people living on the edge—including women with children who are seeking to make a go of it amid changing social policies. Governments in all parts of the world are searching for the right solution to welfare: How much subsidy should they provide? How much responsibility should fall on the shoulders of the poor?

Understanding the Issue

In the 1990s, an intense debate took place in the United States over the issue of welfare. Welfare programs were costly, and concern was widespread (however unfounded) that welfare payments discouraged recipients from seeking jobs. Both Democrats and Republicans vowed to "end welfare as we know it."

In late 1996, in a historic shift in federal policy, Congress passed the Personal Responsibility and Work Opportunity

(continued)

Reconciliation Act, ending the long-standing federal guarantee of assistance to every poor family that meets eligibility requirements. The law set a lifetime limit of five years of welfare benefits, and required all able-bodied adults to work after receiving two years of benefits (although hardship exceptions were allowed). The federal government would give block grants to the states to use as they wished in assisting poor and needy residents, and it would permit states to experiment with ways to move people off welfare (Seccombe 2011).

A decade later, however, the severe economic downturn of 2008–2009 forced many more people into this shrunken safety net. By 2009, over 16 percent of all personal income in the United States was coming from Social Security, food stamps, and unemployment insurance. That was the highest percentage since the government began compiling such data in 1929. In the 1960s, the proportion of income coming from these sources was less than 8 percent (Bureau of Economic Analysis 2009).

Despite this increase in dependency, reliance on the government safety net still falls far short of that in Europe, even after recent cutbacks there. Available data indicate that in Great Britain, 87 percent of health expenditures are paid for by the government; in Sweden, 82 percent; in Canada, 70 percent; but in the United States, only 46 percent. In fact, most industrialized nations devote higher proportions of their expenditures to housing, social security, welfare, health care, and unemployment compensation than the United States does. As U.S. economist Dean Baker declared recently, "The increase in social spending is still relatively modest given the severity of the downturn. We're not France" (Cauchon 2009; World Bank 2009:98–100).

Applying Sociology

Many sociologists tend to view the debate over welfare reform in industrialized nations from a conflict perspective: the "haves" in positions of policymaking listen to the interests of other "haves," while the cries of the "have-nots" are drowned out. Critics of welfare reform believe that the nation's economic problems are unfairly blamed on welfare spending and the poor. From a conflict perspective, this backlash against welfare recipients reflects deep fears and hostility toward the nation's urban, predominantly African American and Hispanic underclass.

Those who are critical of the backlash note that "welfare scapegoating" conveniently ignores the lucrative federal handouts that go to *affluent* individuals and families. For example, while federal housing aid to the poor was cut drastically in the 1980s, tax deductions for mortgage interest and property taxes more than doubled.

Conflict theorists have noted an oft-ignored aspect of the welfare system, administrative sanctions. The law allows administrators to end welfare payments if clients fail to complete job-readiness classes, community work, or job searches. A great deal of discretion is used in applying sanctions. According to a recent study, Black clients are more likely to be sanctioned than White clients (Schram et al. 2009).

Those who take a conflict perspective also urge policymakers and the general public to look closely at **corporate welfare**—the tax breaks, bailouts, direct payments, and grants that the government gives to corporations—rather than looking closely at the comparatively small allowances being given to welfare mothers and their children. Yet any suggestion to curtail such corporate welfare brings a strong response from special-interest groups that are much more powerful than any coalition on behalf of the poor. One example of corporate welfare is the huge federal bailouts of distressed financial

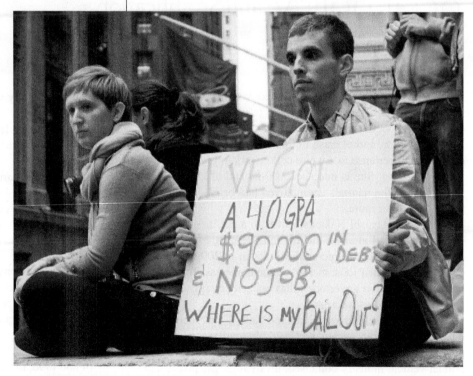

In the deep economic recession that began in 2008, recent college graduates faced the most difficult job market of all. This young man vents his anger against the billion-dollar corporate bailouts that were supposed to get people back to work.

institutions in fall 2008 and of bankrupt automobile companies in 2009. Although the layout of hundreds of billions of dollars was vital to the nation's economic recovery, the measure received relatively little scrutiny from Congress. Just a few months later, however, when legislation was proposed to extend the safety net for laid-off workers—unemployment compensation, food stamps, subsidized child care, assistance to the homeless, disability support, and infant nutrition—it met with loud demands for the monitoring of expenditures (DeParle 2009; Piven and Cloward 1996).

Initiating Policy

The government likes to highlight welfare reform success stories. Though many people who once depended on tax dollars are now working and paying taxes themselves, it is much too soon to see if "workfare" will be successful. The new jobs that were generated by the booming economy of the late 1990s were an unrealistic test of the system. Prospects have faded for the hard-core jobless—people who are difficult to train or are encumbered by drug or alcohol abuse, physical disabilities, or child care needs—since the boom passed and the economy moved into recession (Jencks et al. 2006; M. Turner et al. 2007).

True, fewer people remain on the rolls since welfare reform was enacted in August 1996. By September 2009 just over 1.7 million families were still on the rolls, down 65 percent from a high of 5.1 million in 1994. But while those families that have left the rolls are modestly better off now, most of their breadwinners continue to hold low-paying, unskilled jobs. For them, the economic downturn that was well in place by 2009 made finding work tougher than ever. Of those adults who remain on welfare, nearly 60 percent are not in school or in welfare-to-work programs, as the law requires them to be. This group tends to face the greatest challenges—substance abuse, mental illness, or a criminal record. Finally, while the welfare rolls have declined, the number of people who receive Medicaid and food stamps has increased by 50 percent since 2000 (Health and Human Services Department 2010b; Handler 2009; R. Wolf 2006).

European governments have encountered many of the same citizen demands as in North America: keep our taxes low, even if it means reducing services to the poor. However, nations in eastern and central Europe have faced a special challenge since the end of communism. Though governments in those nations traditionally provided an impressive array of social services, they differed from capitalist systems in several important respects. First, the communist system was premised on full employment, so there was no need to provide unemployment insurance; social services focused on the old and the disabled. Second, subsidies for housing and even utilities played an important role. With new competition from the West and tight budgets, some of these countries are beginning to realize that universal coverage is no longer affordable and must be replaced with targeted programs. Even Sweden, despite its long history of social welfare programs, is feeling the pinch. Yet by any standard, the European safety net is still significantly better than that of the United States (Petrášová 2006; Walker and Thurow 2009).

Both in North America and in Europe, people are beginning to turn to private means to support themselves. For instance, they are investing money for their later years rather than depending on government social security programs. That solution works only if you have a job and can save money, however. Increasingly, people are seeing the gap between themselves and the affluent grow, with fewer government programs available to assist them. Solutions are frequently left to the private sector, while government policy initiatives at the national level all but disappear.

TAKE THE ISSUE WITH YOU

1. Do you personally know anyone who has had to depend on public assistance, such as food stamps? If so, what were the circumstances? Would you yourself need government assistance under such circumstances?

2. Do you think welfare recipients should be required to work? If so, what kind of support should they receive? Should any exceptions be granted to the work requirement?

3. Why do you think western and northern European countries have more generous welfare programs than the United States?

MODULE 28 | Recap and Review

Summary

Poverty is difficult to explain or define, although its effects are obvious and pervasive.

1. Many of those who live in poverty are full-time workers who struggle to support their families at minimum-wage jobs. The long-term poor—those who lack the training

and skills to lift themselves out of poverty—form an **underclass.**

2. Functionalists find that the poor satisfy positive functions for many of the nonpoor in the United States.

3. One's **life chances**—opportunities for obtaining material goods, positive living conditions, and favorable life experiences—are related to one's social class. Occupying a high social position improves a person's life chances.

4. **Social mobility** is more likely to be found in an **open system** that emphasizes achieved status than in a **closed system** that emphasizes ascribed status. Race, gender, and family background are important factors in social mobility.

5. Today, many governments are struggling with the question of how much tax revenue to spend on welfare programs. The trend in the United States is to put welfare recipients to work.

Thinking Critically

1. How do you identify areas of poverty in your own community or one nearby? Do you consider residents' achieved or ascribed characteristics?

2. How do people's life chances affect society as a whole?

3. Which factor—occupation, education, race and ethnicity, or gender—do you expect will have the greatest impact on your own social mobility? Explain.

Key Terms

Absolute poverty

Closed system

Corporate welfare

Digital divide

Feminization of poverty

Horizontal mobility

Intergenerational mobility

Intragenerational mobility

Life chances

Open system

Precarious work

Relative poverty

Social mobility

Underclass

Vertical mobility

MODULE 31 | Minority, Racial, and Ethnic Groups

Sociologists frequently distinguish between racial and ethnic groups. The term **racial group** describes a group that is set apart from others because of physical differences that have taken on social significance. Whites, African Americans, and Asian Americans are all considered racial groups in the United States. While race does turn on physical differences, it is the culture of a particular society that constructs and attaches social significance to those differences, as we will see later. Unlike racial groups, an **ethnic group** is set apart from others primarily because of its national origin or distinctive cultural patterns. In the United States, Puerto Ricans, Jews, and Polish Americans are all categorized as ethnic groups (Table 31-1).

Minority Groups

A numerical minority is any group that makes up less than half of some larger population. The population of the United States includes thousands of numerical minorities, including television actors, green-eyed people, tax lawyers, and descendants of the Pilgrims who arrived on the *Mayflower*. However, these numerical minorities are not considered to be minorities in the sociological sense; in fact, the number of people in a group does not necessarily determine its status as a social minority (or a dominant group). When sociologists define a minority group, they are concerned primarily with the economic and political power, or powerlessness, of that group. A **minority group** is a subordinate group whose members have significantly less control or power over their lives than the members of a dominant or majority group have over theirs.

Sociologists have identified five basic properties of a minority group: unequal treatment, physical or cultural traits, ascribed status, solidarity, and in-group marriage (Wagley and Harris 1958):

1. Members of a minority group experience unequal treatment compared to members of a dominant group. For example, the management of an apartment complex may refuse to rent to African Americans, Hispanics, or Jews. Social inequality may be created or maintained by prejudice, discrimination, segregation, or even extermination.

2. Members of a minority group share physical or cultural characteristics that distinguish them from the dominant group. Each society arbitrarily decides which characteristics are most important in defining groups.

Table 31-1 Racial and Ethnic Groups in the United States, 2008

Classification	Number in Thousands	Percentage of Total Population
Racial Groups		
Whites (non-Hispanic)	198,943	65.4%
Blacks/African Americans	37,586	12.4
Native Americans, Alaskan Natives	2,443	0.8
Asian Americans	13,414	4.4
Chinese	3,078	1.0
Asian Indians	2,496	0.8
Filipinos	2,426	0.8
Vietnamese	1,432	0.5
Koreans	1,344	0.4
Japanese	710	0.2
Pacific Islanders and other	2,356	0.8
Ethnic Groups		
White ancestry (single or mixed, non-Hispanic)		
Germans	50,272	16.5
Irish	36,278	11.9
English	27,517	9.0
Italians	17,749	5.8
Poles	9,887	3.3
French	9,447	3.1
Scottish and Scotch-Irish	9,365	3.1
Jews	6,489	2.1
Hispanics (or Latinos)	46,891	15.4
Mexican Americans	30,739	10.1
Puerto Ricans	4,217	1.4
Cubans	1,617	0.5
Salvadorans	1,592	0.5
Dominicans	1,328	0.4
Other Hispanics	7,398	2.4
TOTAL (all groups)	**304,060**	

Note: Percentages do not total 100 and subtotals do not add up to totals in major categories because of overlap between groups (e.g., Polish American Jews or people of mixed ancestry, such as Irish and Italian).

Source: 2008 data from American Community Survey 2009:Tables B02003, B02005, B02006, B03001, B03002, C0207, and Bureau of the Census 2009a:Table 77.

3. Membership in a minority (or dominant) group is not voluntary; people are born into the group. Thus, race and ethnicity are considered *ascribed* statuses.

4. Minority group members have a strong sense of group solidarity. William Graham Sumner, writing in 1906, noted that people make distinctions between members of their own group (the *in-group*) and everyone else (the *out-group*). When a group is the object of long-term prejudice and discrimination, the feeling of "us versus them" can and often does become extremely intense.

5. Members of a minority group generally marry others from the same group. A member of a dominant group is often unwilling to marry into a supposedly inferior minority group. In addition, the minority group's sense of solidarity encourages marriage within the group and discourages marriage to outsiders.

Race

Many people think of race as a series of biological classifications. However, research shows that is not a meaningful way of differentiating people. Genetically, there are no systematic differences between the races that affect people's social behavior and abilities. Instead, sociologists use the term *racial group* to refer to those minorities (and the corresponding dominant groups) who are set apart from others by obvious physical differences. But what is an "obvious" physical difference? Each society labels those differences that people consider important, while ignoring other characteristics that could serve as a basis for social differentiation.

Social Construction of Race

Because race is a social construction, the process of defining races typically benefits those who have more power and privilege than others. In the United States, we see differences in both skin color and hair color. Yet people learn informally that differences in skin color have a dramatic social and political meaning, while differences in hair color do not.

When observing skin color, many people in the United States tend to lump others rather casually into the traditional categories of "Black," "White," and "Asian." More subtle differences in skin color often go unnoticed. In many nations of Central America and South America, in contrast, people recognize color gradients on a continuum from light to dark skin color. Brazil has approximately 40 color groupings, while in other countries people may be described as "Mestizo Hondurans," "Mulatto Colombians," or "African Panamanians." What we see as "obvious" differences, then, are subject to each society's social definitions.

The largest racial minorities in the United States are African Americans (or Blacks), Native Americans (or American Indians), and Asian Americans (Japanese Americans, Chinese Americans, and other Asian peoples). Figure 31-1 provides information about the population of racial and ethnic groups in the United States over the past five centuries. Given current population patterns, it is

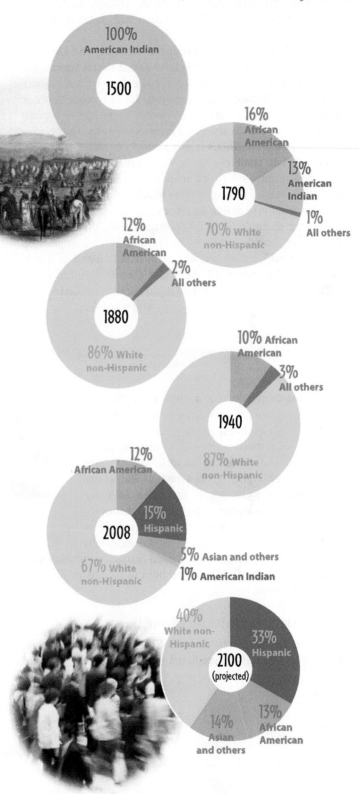

FIGURE 31-1 Racial and Ethnic Groups in the United States, 1500–2100 (Projected)

1500
100% American Indian

1790
16% African American
13% American Indian
1% All others
70% White non-Hispanic

1880
12% African American
2% All others
86% White non-Hispanic

1940
10% African American
3% All others
87% White non-Hispanic

2008
12% African American
15% Hispanic
5% Asian and others
1% American Indian
67% White non-Hispanic

2100 (projected)
40% White non-Hispanic
33% Hispanic
13% African American
14% Asian and others

Sources: Author's estimate; American Community Survey 2009; Bureau of the Census 2004a. Data for 2008 and 2100, African American and Asian and others, are for non-Hispanics.

The racial and ethnic composition of what is today the United States has been undergoing change not just for the past 50 years, but for the past 500. Five centuries ago the land was populated only by indigenous Native Americans.

clear that the nation's diversity will continue to increase. Half of all children now under age 5 belong to racial and ethnic minorities. As those children become students, workers, and parents, the transformation of the U.S. population will continue (Mather 2007).

Racial definitions are crystallized through what Michael Omi and Howard Winant (1994) have called **racial formation,** a sociohistorical process in which racial categories are created, inhabited, transformed, and destroyed. In this process, those who have power define groups of people according to a racist social structure. The creation of a reservation system for Native Americans in the late 1800s is one example of racial formation. Federal officials combined what were distinctive tribes into a single racial group, which we refer to today as Native Americans. The extent and frequency with which peoples are subject to racial formation is such that no one escapes it.

Another example of racial formation from the 1800s was known as the "one-drop rule." If a person had even a single drop of "Black blood," that person was defined and viewed as Black, even if he or she *appeared* to be White. Clearly, race had social significance, enough so that White legislators established official standards about who was "Black" and who was "White."

become the foremost problem of the 20th century. DuBois, born a free Black man in 1868, had witnessed prejudice and discrimination throughout the United States. His comment was prophetic. Today, over a century later, race and ethnicity still carry enormous weight in the United States (DuBois [1900] 1969).

The color line has blurred significantly since 1900, however. Interracial marriage is no longer forbidden by law and custom. Thus, Geetha Lakshmi-narayanan, a native of Ann Arbor, Michigan, is both White and Asian Indian. Often mistaken for a Filipina or Latina, she has grown accustomed to the blunt question, "What are you?" (Navarro 2005).

In the late 20th century, with immigration from Latin America rising, the fluid nature of racial formation became evident. Suddenly, people were speaking about the "Latin Americanization" of the United States, or about a biracial, Black/White society being replaced by a triracial one. In a 2008 Bureau of the Census estimate, over 6 million people in the United States (or about 2 percent of the population) reported that they were of two or more races. Half the people classified as multiracial were under age 18, suggesting that this segment of the population will

The one-drop rule was a vivid example of the *social construction of race*—the process by which people come to define a group as a race based in part on physical characteristics, but also on historical, cultural, and economic factors. For example, in the 1800s, immigrant groups such as Italian and Irish Americans were not at first seen as being "White," but as foreigners who were not necessarily trustworthy. The social construction of race is an ongoing process that is subject to debate, especially in a diverse society such as the United States, where each year increasing numbers of children are born to parents of different racial backgrounds.

Today, some children of mixed-race families identify themselves as biracial or multiracial, rejecting efforts to place them in a single racial category.

Recognition of Multiple Identities

In 1900, in an address to the Anti-Slavery Union in London, scholar W. E. B. DuBois predicted that "the color line" would

grow in the years to come. People who claimed both White and American Indian ancestry were the largest group of multiracial residents (American Community Survey 2009:Table BO2001; Bonilla-Silva 2004).

This statistical finding of millions of multiracial people obscures how individuals are often asked to handle their identity. For example, the enrollment forms for government programs typically include only a few broad racial-ethnic categories. This approach to racial categorization is part of a long history that dictates single-race identities. Still, many individuals, especially young adults, struggle against social pressure to choose a single identity, and instead openly embrace multiple heritages. Public figures, rather than hide their mixed ancestry, now flaunt it. Singer Mariah Carey celebrates her Irish American background, and President Barack Obama speaks of being born in Hawai'i to a Kenyan father and a White mother from Kansas. Tiger Woods, the world's best-known professional golfer, considers himself both Asian and African American.

A dominant or majority group has the power not only to define itself legally but to define a society's values. The interactionist William I. Thomas, observing how we assign social meanings, saw that the "definition of the situation" could mold the individual personality. To put it another way, people respond not only to the objective features of a situation or person but also to the *meaning* that situation or person has for them. Thus, we can create false images or stereotypes that become real in their consequences. **Stereotypes** are unreliable generalizations about all members of a group that do not recognize individual differences within the group.

The inauguration of President Barack Obama in 2009 was clearly historic. To put its significance in perspective, however, Obama's Senate seat was the only one held by a Black man when he left it to become president. More than half of White voters in the 2008 presidential election—57 percent—cast their ballots for candidates other than Obama.

use your **sociological imagination**

Using a TV remote control, how quickly do you think you could find a television show in which all the characters share your racial or ethnic background? What about a show in which all the characters share a different background from yours—how quickly could you find one?

Ethnicity

An ethnic group, unlike a racial group, is set apart from others because of its national origin or distinctive cultural patterns. Among the ethnic groups in the United States are peoples with a Spanish-speaking background, referred to collectively as *Latinos* or *Hispanics,* such as Puerto Ricans, Mexican Americans, Cuban Americans, and other Latin Americans. Other ethnic groups in this country include Jewish, Irish, Italian, and Norwegian Americans. Although these groupings are convenient, they serve to obscure differences *within* ethnic categories (as in the case of Hispanics), as well as to overlook the mixed ancestry of so many people in the United States.

The distinction between racial and ethnic minorities is not always clear-cut. Some members of racial minorities, such as Asian Americans, may have significant cultural differences from other racial groups. At the same time, certain ethnic minorities, such as Latinos, may have obvious physical differences that set them apart from other ethnic groups in the United States.

Despite categorization problems, sociologists continue to feel that the distinction between racial groups and ethnic groups

is socially significant. In most societies, including the United States, socially constructed physical differences tend to be more visible than ethnic differences. Partly as a result of this fact, stratification along racial lines is more resistant to change than stratification along ethnic lines. Over time, members of an ethnic minority can sometimes become indistinguishable from the majority—although the process may take generations and may never include all members of the group. In contrast, members of a racial minority find it much more difficult to blend in with the larger society and gain acceptance from the majority.

Prejudice and Discrimination

Looking at the United States in the 21st century, some people wonder aloud if race and ethnicity are still relevant to social stratification. After all, African Americans have served as secretary of state, secretary of defense, and chairman of the Joint Chiefs of Staff; the office of attorney general has been held by both an African American and a Hispanic. Most notably, an African American now serves as president. As historic as these leaders' achievements have been, however, in every case their elevation meant that they left behind a virtually all-White government department or assembly.

At the same time, college campuses across the United States have been the scene of bias-related incidents. Student-run newspapers and radio stations have ridiculed racial and ethnic minorities; threatening literature has been stuffed under the doors of minority students; graffiti endorsing the views of White supremacist organizations such as the Ku Klux Klan have been scrawled on university walls. In some cases, there have even been violent clashes between groups of White and Black students (Southern Poverty Law Center 2009). What causes such ugly incidents?

Prejudice

Prejudice is a negative attitude toward an entire category of people, often an ethnic or racial minority. If you resent your roommate because he or she is sloppy, you are not necessarily guilty of prejudice. However, if you immediately stereotype your roommate on the basis of such characteristics as race, ethnicity, or religion, that is a form of prejudice. Prejudice tends to perpetuate false definitions of individuals and groups.

Sometimes prejudice results from **ethnocentrism**—the tendency to assume that one's culture and way of life represent the norm or are superior to all others. Ethnocentric people judge other cultures by the standards of their group, which leads quite easily to prejudice against cultures they view as inferior.

One important and widespread ideology that reinforces prejudice is **racism,** the belief that one race is supreme and all others are innately inferior. When racism prevails in a society, members of subordinate groups generally experience prejudice, discrimination, and exploitation. In 1990, as concern mounted about racist attacks in the United States, Congress passed the Hate Crimes Statistics Act. A **hate crime** is a criminal offense committed because of the offender's bias against a race, religion, ethnic group, national origin, or sexual orientation. In 2008 alone, more than 7,700 hate crimes were reported to authorities. As Figure 31-2 shows, more than half those crimes involved racial bias. Most were carried out by one or more individuals.

Color-Blind Racism

Over the past three generations, nationwide surveys have consistently shown growing support among Whites for integration, interracial dating, and the election of minority group members to public office—including the presidency of the United States. How can this trend be explained, given the persistence of residential segregation and the commission of thousands of hate

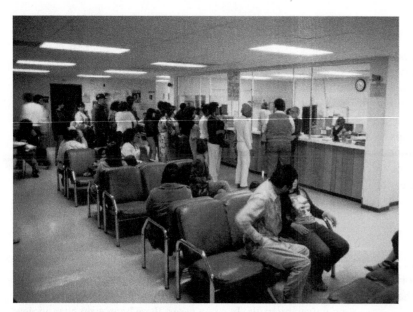

A government public assistance office does brisk business. People who oppose government welfare programs but support other forms of government assistance, such as financial aid to college students, may be exhibiting color-blind racism.

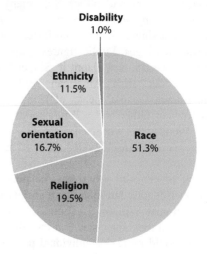

FIGURE 31-2 **Categorization of Reported Hate Crimes**

- Disability 1.0%
- Ethnicity 11.5%
- Sexual orientation 16.7%
- Race 51.3%
- Religion 19.5%

Source: Department of Justice 2009.

crimes every year? The answer, to some extent, is that prejudice and discriminatory attitudes are no longer expressed as freely as they once were. Often, they are couched in terms of equal opportunity.

Color-blind racism is the use of the principle of race neutrality to defend a racially unequal status quo. Proponents of race neutrality claim they believe that everyone should be treated equally. However, the way they apply the principle to government policy is anything but neutral. Proponents of this approach oppose affirmative action, public welfare assistance, and, to a large extent, government-funded health insurance, all of which they see largely as favors to minority groups. Yet they do not object to practices that privilege Whites, such as college admissions criteria that give preference to the relatives of alumni. Nor do they oppose tax breaks for homeowners, most of whom are White, or government financial aid to college students, who are also disproportionately White. Though race neutrality is not based on theories of racial superiority or inferiority, then, the idea that society should be color-blind only perpetuates racial inequality.

Color-blind racism has also been referred to as "covert racism." Although its proponents rarely speak of racism, other indicators of social status, such as social class or citizenship, tend to become proxies for race. Thus, many White people can convince themselves that they are not racist—nor do they know anyone who is—and yet remain prejudiced against "welfare mothers" and "immigrants." They can conclude, mistakenly, that racial tolerance, or even racial and ethnic equality, has been achieved.

Researchers who have surveyed White attitudes toward African Americans over the past several decades have reached two inescapable conclusions. First, people's attitudes do change. In periods of social upheaval, dramatic attitudinal shifts can occur within a single generation. Second, less racial progress was made in the late 20th and early 21st centuries than in the relatively brief period of the 1950s and 1960s. Today, economically disadvantaged groups such as African Americans and Latinos have become so closely associated with urban decay, homelessness, welfare, and crime that those problems are now viewed as racial issues, even if they are not labeled as such. The tendency to *blame the victims* of these social ills complicates their resolution (see Module 28), especially at a time when government's ability to address social problems is limited by recession, antitax initiatives, and concern over terrorism. In short, the color line is still in place, even if more and more people refuse to acknowledge its existence (Ansell 2008; Bonilla-Silva 2006; Coates 2008; M. King 2007:3–4; Quillian 2006; Winant 1994:106–108).

Discriminatory Behavior

Prejudice often leads to **discrimination,** the denial of opportunities and equal rights to individuals and groups because of prejudice or other arbitrary reasons. Say that a White corporate president with a prejudice against Asian Americans has to fill an executive position. The most qualified candidate for the job is a Vietnamese American. If the president refuses to hire this candidate and instead selects an inferior White candidate, he or she is engaging in an act of racial discrimination.

Prejudiced *attitudes* should not be equated with discriminatory *behavior.* Although the two are generally related, they are not identical; either condition can be present without the other. A prejudiced person does not always act on his or her biases. The White corporate president, for example, might choose—despite his or her stereotypes—to hire the Vietnamese American. That would be prejudice without discrimination. On the other hand, a White corporate president with a completely respectful view of Vietnamese Americans might refuse to hire them for executive posts out of fear that biased clients would take their business elsewhere. In that case, the president's action would constitute discrimination without prejudice.

A field experiment by Devah Pager, a doctoral candidate in sociology at the University of Wisconsin, documented racial discrimination in hiring. Pager sent four polite, well-dressed young men out to look for an entry-level job in Milwaukee, Wisconsin. All were 23-year-old college students, but they presented themselves as high school graduates with similar job histories. Two of the men were Black and two were White. One Black applicant and one White applicant claimed to have served 18 months in jail for a felony conviction—possession of cocaine with intent to distribute.

As one might expect, the four men's experiences with 350 potential employers were vastly different. Predictably, the White applicant with a purported prison record received

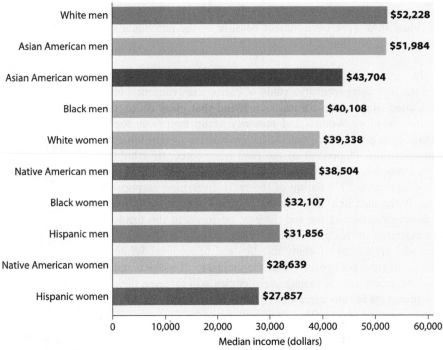

FIGURE 31-3 **U.S. Median Income by Race, Ethnicity, and Gender**

Note: Data released in 2009 for income earned in 2008. Median income is from all sources and is limited to year-round, full-time workers at least 25 years old. Data for White men and women are for non-Hispanics.
Source: DeNavas-Walt et al. 2009. For Native Americans, author's estimate based on Bureau of the Census data in Ogunwole 2006.

only half as many callbacks as the other White applicant—17 percent compared to 34 percent. But as dramatic as the effect of his criminal record was, the effect of his race was more significant. Despite his prison record, he received slightly more callbacks than the Black applicant *with no criminal record* (17 percent compared to 14 percent). Race, it seems, was more of a concern to potential employers than a criminal background.

The implications of this research are not limited to any one city, such as Milwaukee. Similar studies have confirmed discriminatory handling of job applications in Chicago; New York City; Long Island, New York; San Diego; and Washington, D.C. Over time, the cumulative effect of such differential behavior by employers contributes to significant differences in income. Figure 31-3 vividly illustrates the income inequality between White men and almost everyone else (Pager 2007; Pager et al. 2009).

Sometimes racial and ethnic discrimination is overt. Internet forums like Craigslist.org or Roommate.com feature classified ads that state "African Americans and Arabians tend to clash with me" or "Clean, Godly Christian men only." While antidiscrimination laws prevent such notices from being published in the newspapers, existing law has not caught up with online bigotry in hiring and renting (Liptak 2006).

Discrimination persists even for the most educated and qualified minority group members from the best family backgrounds. Despite their talents and experiences, they sometimes encounter attitudinal or organizational bias that prevents them from reaching their full potential. The term **glass ceiling** refers to an invisible barrier that blocks the promotion of a qualified individual in a work environment because of the individual's gender, race, or ethnicity (R. Schaefer 2011; Yamagata et al. 1997).

In early 1995, the federal Glass Ceiling Commission issued the first comprehensive study of barriers to promotion in the United States. The commission found that glass ceilings continue to block women and minority group men from top management positions in the nation's industries. While White men constitute 45 percent of the paid labor force, they hold down a much higher proportion of top positions. Even in *Fortune* magazine's 2002 listing of the most diversified corporations, White men held more than 80 percent of both the board of directors seats and the top 50 paid positions in the firms. The existence of this glass ceiling results principally from the fears and prejudices of many middle- and upper-level White male managers, who believe that the inclusion of women and minority group men in management circles will threaten their own prospects for advancement (Bureau of the Census 2008a; Department of Labor 1995a, 1995b; Hickman 2002).

 use your **sociological imagination**

How might online social networking maintain prejudice and discrimination?

The Privileges of the Dominant

One aspect of discrimination that is often overlooked is the privileges that dominant groups enjoy at the expense of others. For instance, we tend to focus more on the difficulty women have getting ahead at work and getting a hand at home than on the ease with which men manage to make their way in the world and avoid household chores. Similarly, we concentrate more on discrimination against racial and ethnic minorities than on the advantages members of the White majority enjoy. Indeed, most White people rarely think about their "Whiteness," taking their status for granted.

Sociologists and other social scientists are becoming increasingly interested in what it means to be "White," for White privilege is the other side of the proverbial coin of racial discrimination. In this context, **White privilege** refers to rights or immunities granted to people as a particular benefit or favor simply because they are White (Ferber and Kimmel 2008). This view of whiteness as a privilege echoes an observation by W. E. B. DuBois, that rather than wanting fair working conditions for all laborers, White workers had accepted the "public and psychological wage" of whiteness ([1935] 1962:700).

The feminist scholar Peggy McIntosh (1988) became interested in White privilege after noticing that most men would not acknowledge that there were privileges attached to being male—even if they would agree that being female had its disadvantages. Did White people suffer from a similar blind spot regarding their racial privilege? she wondered. Intrigued, McIntosh began to list all the ways in which she benefited from her Whiteness. She soon realized that the list of unspoken advantages was long and significant.

McIntosh found that as a White person, she rarely needed to step out of her comfort zone, no matter where she went. If she wished to, she could spend most of her time with people of her race. She could find a good place to live in a pleasant neighborhood, buy the foods she liked to eat from almost any grocery store, and get her hair styled in almost any salon. She could attend a public meeting without feeling that she did not belong, that she was different from everyone else.

McIntosh discovered, too, that her skin color opened doors for her. She could cash checks and use credit cards without suspicion, browse through stores without being shadowed by security guards. She could be seated without difficulty in a restaurant. If she asked to see the manager, she could assume he or she would be of her race. If she needed help from a doctor or a lawyer, she could get it.

McIntosh also realized that her Whiteness made the job of parenting easier. She did not need to worry about protecting her children from people who didn't like them. She could be sure that their schoolbooks would show pictures of people who looked like them, and that their history texts would describe White people's achievements. She knew that the television programs they watched would include White characters.

Finally, McIntosh had to admit that others did not constantly evaluate her in racial terms. When she appeared in public, she

trend|spotting

Members of the Board

Significant trends do not always involve dramatic shifts upward or downward. Sometimes, the *lack* of change can be socially significant. Such is the case with the elite individuals who meet in corporate boardrooms: collectively, their racial and ethnic makeup is not changing.

As a rule, the corporate board is and always has been White and male. Of the 1,219 individuals who currently sit on the boards of the *Fortune* 100 largest corporations, 1,031—that is, 85 percent—are White non-Hispanic males. In the most diverse companies, including PepsiCo, IBM, DuPont, and Hartland Financial Services, about 30 percent of the directors belong to minority groups—a proportion that matches that in the general population. No corporation's board exceeds the general population in diversity.

This static trend is significant. Not only do the directors of the nation's largest corporations interact with other economic elites, and in doing so influence major economic forces; they also serve as role models for those who hope to climb the corporate ladder. To the extent that their ranks do not include members of minority groups, their influence as role models will be limited to members of their own exclusive club: White males.

Prudence Hannis, *Liaison Officer, National Institute of Science Research, University of Québec*

Prudence Hannis is a First Nations (Native American) woman who serves as an official liaison between her people and Canadian researchers. In her position, she interacts with sociologists, anthropologists, political scientists, legal scholars, and researchers in health and medicine at several Canadian universities, all of whom wish to work with First Nations communities. Hannis is enthusiastic about her job, which gives her an opportunity to educate and sensitize would-be researchers who "never set foot in First Nations communities." In 10 years of work on behalf of the native peoples of Canada, Hannis has seen a dramatic change in their representation in Canadian research and policy. "We are everywhere in research efforts and policy consultation, but whether we are listened to is another matter," she notes.

Before taking her current position, Hannis served as a researcher and community activist with Québec Native Women. There she oversaw the women's health portfolio, organized seminars on sexual abuse for local communities, and produced a resource booklet on the subject. "The purpose of my job was to defend First Nations' women's concerns, to be their spokesperson when needed, to analyze critical situations for our sisters, and mostly, to determine ways in which women can empower themselves, their families, and their communities," she says.

Hannis has also worked for the Centre of Excellence on Women's Health, Consortium Université de Montréal, where she focused on First Nations women's health issues. A member of the Abenaki tribe, Hannis received her BA in sociology from the University of Québec at Montréal. She has found her background in the discipline to be invaluable. "Sociology is now, more than it has ever been, a part of my job," she says.

LET'S DISCUSS

1. What may be some of the challenges to improving the health of Native Americans in Canada?

2. In speaking of empowering First Nations women, what sociological perspective do you think Hannis is drawing on?

---

didn't need to worry that her clothing or behavior might reflect poorly on White people. If she was recognized for an achievement, it was seen as her achievement, not that of an entire race. And no one ever assumed that the personal opinions she voiced should be those of all White people. Because McIntosh blended in with the people around her, she wasn't always onstage.

These are not all the privileges White people take for granted as a result of their membership in the dominant racial group in the United States. As Devah Pager's study showed, White job seekers enjoy a tremendous advantage over equally well-qualified—even better-qualified—Blacks. Whiteness *does* carry privileges—to a much greater extent than most White people realize (Fitzgerald 2008; Picca and Feagin 2007).

use your sociological imagination

How often do you think people are privileged because of their race or ethnicity? How about yourself—how often are you privileged?

Institutional Discrimination

Discrimination is practiced not only by individuals in one-to-one encounters but also by institutions in their daily operations. Social scientists are particularly concerned with the ways in which structural factors such as employment, housing, health care, and government operations maintain the social significance of race and ethnicity. **Institutional discrimination** refers to the denial of opportunities and equal rights to individuals and groups

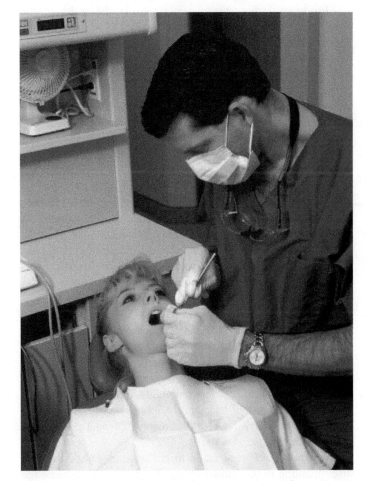

White people are accustomed to seeing other White people in professional positions and jobs with authority and prestige. Whiteness *does* have its privileges.

that results from the normal operations of a society. This kind of discrimination consistently affects certain racial and ethnic groups more than others.

The Commission on Civil Rights (1981:9–10) has identified various forms of institutional discrimination:

- Rules requiring that only English be spoken at a place of work, even when it is not a business necessity to restrict the use of other languages.

- Preferences shown by law and medical schools in the admission of children of wealthy and influential alumni, nearly all of whom are White.

- Restrictive employment-leave policies, coupled with prohibitions on part-time work, that make it difficult for the heads of single-parent families (most of whom are women) to obtain and keep jobs.

Before passage of the Civil Rights Act (1964), segregation of public accommodations was the norm throughout the South. Whites used the most up-to-date bathrooms, waiting rooms, and even drinking fountains, while Blacks ("Colored") were directed to older facilities in inferior condition. Such separate but unequal arrangements are a blatant example of institutional discrimination.

Institutional discrimination occurred in the wake of the September 11, 2001, terrorist attacks on the United States. In the heat of demands to prevent terrorist takeovers of commercial airplanes, Congress passed the Aviation and Transportation Security Act, which was intended to strengthen airport screening procedures. The law stipulated that all airport screeners must be U.S. citizens. Nationally, 28 percent of all airport screeners were legal residents but not citizens of the United States; as a group, they were disproportionately Latino, Black, and Asian. Many observers noted that other airport and airline workers, including pilots, cabin attendants, and even armed National Guardsmen stationed at airports, need not be citizens. Efforts are being made to test the constitutionality of the act. At the least, the debate over its fairness shows that even well-meant legal measures can have disastrous consequences for racial and ethnic minorities (H. Weinstein 2002).

In some cases, even seemingly neutral institutional standards can have discriminatory effects. African American students at a midwestern state university protested a policy under which fraternities and sororities that wished to use campus facilities for a dance were required to pay a $150 security deposit to cover possible damages. African American students complained that the policy had a discriminatory impact on minority student organizations. Campus police countered that the university's policy applied to all student groups interested in using the facilities. However, since the overwhelmingly White fraternities and sororities at the school had their own houses, which they used for dances, the policy indeed affected only African American and other minority organizations.

Attempts have been made to eradicate or compensate for discrimination in the United States. The 1960s saw the passage of many pioneering civil rights laws, including the landmark 1964 Civil Rights Act (which prohibits discrimination in public accommodations and publicly owned facilities on the basis of race, color, creed, national origin, and gender). In two important rulings in 1987, the Supreme Court held that federal prohibitions against racial discrimination protect members of all ethnic minorities—including Hispanics, Jews, and Arab Americans—even though they may be considered White.

For more than 40 years, affirmative action programs have been instituted to overcome past discrimination. **Affirmative action** refers to positive efforts to recruit minority group members or women for jobs, promotions, and educational opportunities. Many people resent these programs, arguing that advancing one group's cause merely shifts the discrimination to another group. By giving priority to African Americans in admissions, for example, schools may overlook more qualified White candidates. In many parts of the country and many sectors of the economy, affirmative action is being rolled back, even though it was never fully implemented. We will discuss affirmative action in more detail in Module 44.

Discriminatory practices continue to pervade nearly all areas of life in the United States today. In part, that is because various individuals and groups actually *benefit* from racial and ethnic discrimination in terms of money, status, and influence. Discrimination permits members of the majority to enhance their wealth, power, and prestige at the expense of others. Less qualified people get jobs and promotions simply because they are members of the dominant group. Such individuals and groups will not surrender these advantages easily. We'll turn now to a closer look at this functionalist analysis, as well as the conflict, labeling, and interactionist perspectives on race and ethnicity.

Summary

The social dimensions of race and ethnicity are important factors in shaping people's lives.

1. A **racial group** is set apart from others by physical differences; an **ethnic group** is set apart primarily by national origin or cultural patterns.

2. When sociologists define a **minority group,** they are concerned primarily with the economic and political power, or powerlessness, of the group.

3. The meaning people attach to the physical differences between races gives social significance to race, producing **stereotypes.**

4. **Prejudice** often but not always leads to **discrimination.** Sometimes, through **color-blind racism,** prejudiced people try to use the principle of racial neutrality to defend a racially unequal status quo.

5. **Institutional discrimination** results from the normal operations of a society.

Thinking Critically

1. Why does the social construction of race defy the traditional notion of race as a biological category?

2. Which would be more socially significant, the elimination of prejudice or the elimination of discrimination?

Key Terms

Affirmative action

Color-blind racism

Discrimination

Ethnic group

Ethnocentrism

Glass ceiling

Hate crime

Institutional discrimination

Minority group

Prejudice

Racial formation

Racial group

Racism

Stereotype

White privilege

Few societies have a more diverse population than the United States; the nation is truly a multiracial, multiethnic society. Of course, that has not always been the case. The population of what is now the United States has changed dramatically since the arrival of European settlers in the 1600s, as Figure 31-1 shows. Immigration, colonialism, and in the case of Blacks, slavery determined the racial and ethnic makeup of our present-day society.

Today, the largest racial minorities in the United States are African Americans, Native Americans, and Asian Americans. The largest ethnic groups are Latinos, Jews, and the various White ethnic groups. Figure 33-1 shows where the major racial and ethnic minorities are concentrated.

African Americans

"I am an invisible man," wrote Black author Ralph Ellison in his novel *Invisible Man* (1952:3). "I am a man of substance, of flesh and bone, fiber and liquids—and I might even be said to possess a mind. I am invisible, understand, simply because people refuse to see me."

Over five decades later, many African Americans still feel invisible. Despite their large numbers, they have long been treated as second-class citizens. Currently, by the standards of the federal government, more than 1 out of every 4 African Americans— as opposed to 1 out of every 11 White non-Hispanics—is poor (DeNavas-Walt et al. 2009:14).

Contemporary institutional discrimination and individual prejudice against African Americans are rooted in the history of slavery in the United States. Many other subordinate groups had little wealth and income, but as sociologist W. E. B. DuBois ([1909] 1970) and others have noted, enslaved African Americans were in an even more oppressive situation, because by law they could not own property and could not pass on the benefits of their labor to their children. Today, increasing numbers of African Americans and sympathetic Whites are calling for *slave reparations* to compensate for the injustices of forced servitude. Reparations could include official expressions of apology from governments such as the United States, ambitious programs to improve African Americans' economic status, or even direct payments to descendants of slaves (D. Williams and Collins 2004).

The end of the Civil War did not bring genuine freedom and equality for Blacks. The Southern states passed Jim Crow laws to enforce official segregation, and the Supreme Court upheld them as constitutional in 1896. In addition, Blacks faced the danger of lynching campaigns, often led by the Ku Klux Klan, during the late 1800s and early 1900s. From a conflict perspective, Whites maintained their dominance formally through legalized segregation and informally by means of vigilante terror and violence (Franklin and Higginbotham 2011).

During the 1960s, a vast civil rights movement emerged, with many competing factions and strategies for change. The Southern Christian Leadership Conference (SCLC), founded by Dr. Martin Luther King Jr., used nonviolent civil disobedience to oppose segregation. The National Association for the Advancement of Colored People (NAACP) favored use of the courts to press for equality for African Americans. But many younger Black leaders, most notably Malcolm X, turned toward an ideology of Black power. Proponents of **Black power** rejected the goal of assimilation into White middle-class society. They defended the beauty and dignity of Black and African cultures and supported the creation of Black-controlled political and economic institutions (Ture and Hamilton 1992).

Despite numerous courageous actions to achieve Black civil rights, Black and White citizens are still separate, still unequal. From birth to death, Blacks suffer in terms of their life chances. Life remains difficult for millions of poor Blacks, who must attempt to survive in ghetto areas shattered by high unemployment and abandoned housing. Today the median household income of Blacks is still 60 percent that of Whites, and the unemployment rate among Blacks is more than twice that of Whites.

Some African Americans—especially middle-class men and women—have made economic gains over the past 50 years. For example, data show that the number of African Americans in management increased nationally from 2.4 percent of the total in 1958 to 7.2 percent in 2008. Yet Blacks still represent only 7 percent or less of all physicians, engineers, scientists, lawyers, judges, and marketing managers.

In many respects, the civil rights movement of the 1960s left institutionalized discrimination against African Americans untouched. Consequently, in the 1970s and 1980s, Black leaders worked to mobilize African American political power as a force for social change. Between 1970 and 2007, the number of African American elected officials increased sixfold. Yet today, Blacks remain significantly *underrepresented,* despite the election of President Barack Obama. Their underrepresentation is especially distressing in view of sociologist W. E. B. DuBois's observation over a century ago that Blacks could not expect to achieve equal social and economic opportunity without first gaining political rights (Bureau of the Census 2009a:386; Joint Center 2010).

FIGURE 33-1 **The United States: The Image of Diversity**

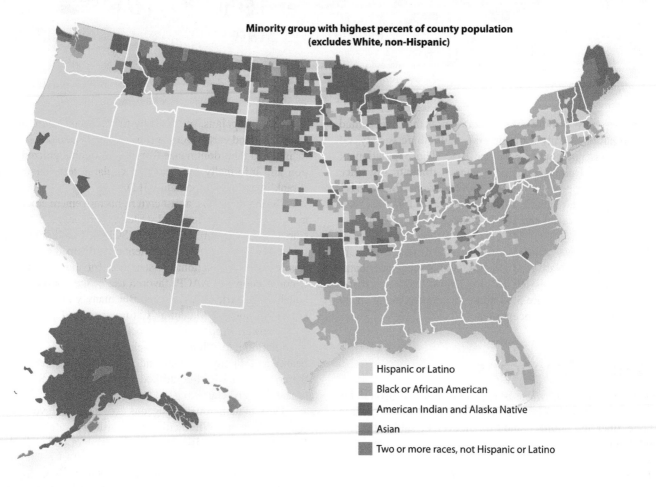

Minority group with highest percent of county population
(excludes White, non-Hispanic)

- Hispanic or Latino
- Black or African American
- American Indian and Alaska Native
- Asian
- Two or more races, not Hispanic or Latino

Source: C. Brewer and Suchan 2001:20.

Think about It

The United States is a diverse nation. Why, in many parts of the country, can't people see that diversity in their towns?

Native Americans

Today, about 2.4 million Native Americans represent a diverse array of cultures distinguishable by language, family organization, religion, and livelihood. The outsiders who came to the United States—European settlers—and their descendants came to know these native peoples' forefathers as "American Indians." By the time the Bureau of Indian Affairs (BIA) was organized as part of the War Department in 1824, Indian–White relations had already included more than two centuries of hostile actions that had led to the virtual elimination of native peoples (see Figure 31-1). During the 19th century, many bloody wars wiped out a significant part of the Indian population. By the end of the century, schools for Indians—operated by the BIA or by church missions—prohibited the practice of Native American cultures.

Yet at the same time, such schools did little to make the children effective members of White society.

Today, life remains difficult for members of the 554 tribal groups in the United States, whether they live in cities or on reservations. For example, one Native American teenager in six has attempted suicide—a rate four times higher than the rate for other teenagers. Traditionally, some Native Americans have chosen to assimilate and abandon all vestiges of their tribal cultures to escape certain forms of prejudice. However, by the 1990s, an increasing number of people in the United States were openly claiming a Native American identity. Since 1960, the federal government's count of Native Americans has tripled. According to the 2000 Census, the Native American population increased 26 percent during the 1990s. Demographers believe that more and more Native Americans who previously concealed their identity are no longer pretending to be White (Grieco and Cassidy 2001).

Native Americans have made some progress in redressing their mistreatment. In 2009 the federal government settled a 13-year-old lawsuit for the recovery of lease payments due on tribal lands used by the government for oil and gas exploration and grazing. Although the $3.4 billion settlement was large, it was long overdue—some of the government's debts dated back to 1887—and from the perspective of tribal leaders, it was too little, too late. The United States is not the only country that has tried to redress the government's past actions toward indigenous peoples (Sociology in the Global Community: The Aboriginal People of Australia).

The introduction of gambling on Indian reservations has transformed the lives of some Native Americans. Native Americans got into the gaming industry in 1988, when Congress passed the Indian Gambling Regulatory Act. The law stipulates that states must negotiate agreements with tribes interested in commercial gaming; they cannot prevent tribes from engaging in gambling operations, even if state law prohibits such ventures. The income from these lucrative operations is not evenly distributed, however. About two-thirds of recognized Indian tribes are not involved in gambling ventures. Those tribes that earn substantial revenues from gambling constitute a small fraction of Native Americans (Conner and Taggart 2009).

 use your **sociological imagination**

You are a Native American whose tribe is about to open a reservation-based casino. Will the casino further the assimilation of your people into mainstream society or encourage pluralism?

Asian Americans

Asian Americans are a diverse group, one of the fastest-growing segments of the U.S. population (up 84 percent between 1990 and 2008). Among the many groups of Americans of Asian descent are Vietnamese Americans, Chinese Americans, Japanese Americans, and Korean Americans (Figure 33-2).

Asian Americans are also economically diverse. There are rich and poor Japanese Americans, rich and poor Filipino Americans, and so forth. In fact, Southeast Asians living in the United States have the highest rate of welfare dependency of any racial or ethnic group. Though Asian Americans have substantially more schooling than other ethnic groups, their median income is only slightly higher than Whites' income, and their poverty rate is higher. In 2008, for every Asian American household with an annual income of $100,000 or more, there was another earning less than $35,000 a year (DeNavas-Walt et al. 2009:33).

The fact that as a group, Asian Americans work in the same occupations as Whites suggests that they have been successful—and many have. However, there are some differences between the two groups. Asian immigrants, like other minorities and immigrants before them, are found disproportionately in low-paying

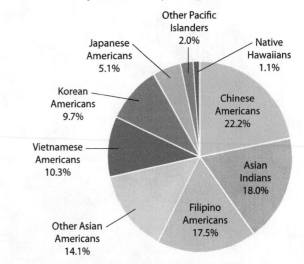

FIGURE 33-2 Asian American and Pacific Islander Population by Origin

Other Pacific Islanders 2.0%
Japanese Americans 5.1%
Native Hawaiians 1.1%
Korean Americans 9.7%
Chinese Americans 22.2%
Vietnamese Americans 10.3%
Asian Indians 18.0%
Other Asian Americans 14.1%
Filipino Americans 17.5%

Source: 2008 data from American Community Survey 2009:Tables B02006, B02007.

Think about It

Do Asian Americans really have a common identity?

service occupations. At the same time, better-educated Asian Americans are concentrated near the top in professional and managerial positions, although they rarely reach the pinnacle. Instead, they hit the glass ceiling, or try to "climb a broken ladder," as some put it.

Ironically, Asian Americans are often held up as a **model minority,** or **ideal minority,** supposedly because they have succeeded economically, socially, and educationally despite past prejudice and discrimination, and without resorting to confrontations with Whites. To some Whites, the existence of a model minority seems to reaffirm the notion that anyone can get ahead in the United States through talent and hard work. The implication is that those minorities that do not succeed are somehow responsible for their failure. Viewed from a conflict perspective, this attitude is yet another instance of *blaming the victims.* Moreover, the stereotype on which it is based is a false one (Bascara 2008; Choi and Lahey 2006).

Chinese Americans

Unlike African slaves and Native Americans, the Chinese were initially encouraged to immigrate to the United States. From 1850 to 1880, thousands of Chinese immigrated to this country, lured by job opportunities created by the discovery of gold. However, as employment possibilities decreased and competition for mining jobs grew, the Chinese became the target of a bitter campaign to limit their numbers and restrict their rights. Chinese laborers were exploited, then discarded.

In 1882, Congress enacted the Chinese Exclusion Act, which prevented Chinese immigration and even forbade Chinese

Despite their tourist appeal, Chinatowns offer their residents limited job opportunities in return for low wages and long hours.

mainstream U.S. culture, religious orthodoxy is often stronger among first-generation immigrants to the United States than it is in India. New immigrants try to practice their religion just as they did in India rather than join congregations already established by other immigrant groups.

Maintaining family traditions is a major challenge for Asian Indian immigrants to the United States. Family ties remain strong despite their immigration—so much so that many Asian Indians feel more connected to their relatives in India than Americans do to relatives nearby. These *Desi* (pronounced DAY-see, colloquial for people who trace their ancestry to South Asia, and especially India) are particularly concerned about the erosion of traditional family authority. Indian American children dress like their peers, go to fast-food restaurants, and even eat hamburgers, rejecting the vegetarian diet typical of both Hindus and many Asian Indian Muslims. Sons do not feel the extent of responsibility to the family that tradition dictates. Daughters, whose occupations and marriage partners the family could control in India, assert their right to choose their own careers, and even their husbands (Rangaswamy 2005).

in the United States to send for their families. As a result, the Chinese population declined steadily until after World War II. More recently, the descendants of the 19th-century immigrants have been joined by a new influx from Hong Kong and Taiwan. These groups may contrast sharply in their degree of assimilation, desire to live in Chinatowns, and feelings about this country's relations with the People's Republic of China.

Currently, over 3 million Chinese Americans live in the United States. Some Chinese Americans have entered lucrative occupations, yet many immigrants struggle to survive under living and working conditions that belie the model-minority stereotype. New York City's Chinatown district is filled with illegal sweatshops in which recent immigrants—many of them Chinese women—work for minimal wages. Even in legal factories in the garment industry, hours are long and rewards are limited. Half the households in Chinatown earn less than $20,000 per year. Outside of Chinatown, only 23 percent of Asian Americans fall into that low-income category. At the other end of the income distribution, barely 5 percent of Chinatown's residents earn more than $100,000 a year, compared to 25 percent of Asian Americans who live elsewhere in New York City (Logan et al. 2002; Wong 2006).

Asian Indians

After Chinese Americans, the second-largest Asian American group, immigrants from India and their descendants, numbers nearly 2.5 million. It is difficult to generalize about Asian Indian Americans because Asian Indians are such a diverse population. India, a country of more than 1.2 billion people that is fast becoming the most populous nation in the world, is multiethnic. In fact, the Indian government recognizes 18 official languages, each with its own cultural heritage. Perhaps because Asian Indian immigrants feel threatened by

Japanese Americans

Approximately 700,000 Japanese Americans live in the United States. As a people, they are relatively recent arrivals. In 1880, only 148 Japanese lived in the United States, but by 1920 there were more than 110,000. Japanese immigrants—called the *Issei*

Asian Americans rarely head the casts of motion pictures unless they feature the martial arts. One exception is Kal Penn, who starred in the successful Harold & Kumar movies. Born Kalpen Modi of Asian Indian immigrants to the United States, the former actor now prefers to use his birth name. In 2009 President Obama appointed Modi associate director of the Office of Public Engagement, where he served as a liaison with the Asian American and Pacific Islander communities.

Sociology in the Global Community

The Aboriginal People of Australia

The indigenous, or Aboriginal, people of Australia have inhabited their home continent continuously for at least 50,000 years. Today they make up about 2.4 percent of Australia's total population. Although their numbers are small, they are highly visible in Australian society.

The cultural practices of the Aboriginal people are quite diverse, given their many clans, language groups, and communities. Except for occasional connections between kin or trading partners, these groups have little social contact. When Europeans first arrived in Australia, the diversity of Aborigines was even greater: an estimated 600 to 700 different

> From 1910 to 1970, thousands of Aboriginal children were forcibly removed from their families so they could be raised by Whites and impressed into the dominant culture.

groups spoke 200 to 250 languages as distinct from each other as French is from German. The existence of many dialects, or variants of languages that were more or less understandable to others, increased the complexity.

Aboriginals' spirituality reflects the diversity not only of their languages and culture, but of the Australian terrain. From the Outback to the tropical rain forests, the Aboriginal

peoples see themselves as having arisen from the land itself, and as destined ultimately to return to the land. These beliefs, commonly referred to as Dreaming or Dreamtime, resemble what is known as cosmology or oral folklore in the West.

Like the American Indians, Australia's Aboriginal population declined dramatically following European settlement. New diseases, some of which were not life-threatening to Europeans, had a devastating effect on Aboriginal communities, which lacked immunity to them. Mistreatment under the British colonial regime, dispossession of their land, and the disruption and disintegration of their culture also overwhelmed the Aboriginal people. Decades of protests and legal efforts regarding their land rights have brought little change.

Historically, the Aboriginal people received little legal recognition from Europeans. Only in 1967 did the government of Australia extend citizenship and voting rights to the Aboriginals, along with access to welfare and unemployment benefits. Yet it would be misleading to view the Aboriginal people as passive victims, either in colonial days or in more recent times. They have worked actively to secure their rights.

As in the United States, Whites' low regard for the Aboriginal people became the basis for an effort to stamp out their culture. From 1910 to 1970, thousands of Aboriginal children were forcibly removed from their families so they could be raised by Whites and impressed into the dominant culture. Between 10 to 30 percent of all Aboriginal

children were affected by this program. Not until 2008 did the Australian government finally apologize to Aboriginals for "the Stolen Generations." The government has expressed its intention to improve the Aboriginal people's living conditions and their prospects for the future.

LET'S DISCUSS

1. Try to think of a situation in your culture in which the government might forcibly remove a child from his or her family. Do you know anyone who has had such an experience? If so, what were the repercussions?

2. What kind of reasoning do you think lay behind the Australian government's forced removal of Aboriginal children from their families? In sociological terms, what actually happened?

Sources: W. Anderson 2003; Attwood 2003; Australia 1997, 2008; R. Schaefer 2008a.

(pronounced EE-say), or first generation—were usually males seeking employment opportunities. Many Whites saw them (along with Chinese immigrants) as a "yellow peril" and subjected them to prejudice and discrimination.

In 1941, the attack on Hawai'i's Pearl Harbor by Japan had severe repercussions for Japanese Americans. The federal government decreed that all Japanese Americans on the West Coast must leave their homes and report to "evacuation camps." In effect, Japanese Americans became scapegoats for the anger that other people in the United States felt concerning Japan's role in World War II. By August 1943, in an unprecedented application of guilt by virtue of ancestry, 113,000 Japanese Americans had been forced into hastily built camps. In striking contrast, only a few German Americans and Italian Americans were sent to evacuation camps (Hosokawa 1969).

This mass detention was costly for Japanese Americans. The Federal Reserve Board estimates their total income and property losses at nearly half a billion dollars. Moreover, the psychological effect on these citizens—including the humiliation of being labeled "disloyal"—was immeasurable. Eventually, children born in the United States to the *Issei*, called *Nisei* (pronounced NEE-say), were allowed to enlist in the Army and serve in Europe in a segregated combat unit. Others resettled in the East and Midwest to work in factories.

In 1983, a federal commission recommended government payments to all surviving Japanese Americans who had been held in detention camps. The commission reported that the detention was motivated by "race prejudice, war hysteria, and a failure of political leadership." It added that "no documented acts of espionage, sabotage, or fifth-column activity were shown to have been

MODULE 33 Race and Ethnicity in the United States

committed" by Japanese Americans. In 1988, President Ronald Reagan signed the Civil Liberties Act, which required the federal government to issue individual apologies for all violations of Japanese Americans' constitutional rights, and established a $1.25 billion trust fund to pay reparations to the approximately 77,500 surviving Japanese Americans who had been interned (Department of Justice 2000).

Vietnamese Americans

Vietnamese Americans came to the United States primarily during and after the Vietnam War—especially after U.S. withdrawal from the conflict in 1975. Refugees from the communist government in Vietnam, assisted by local agencies, settled throughout the United States, tens of thousands of them in small towns. But over time, Vietnamese Americans have gravitated toward the larger urban areas, establishing Vietnamese restaurants and grocery stores in their ethnic enclaves there.

In 1995, the United States resumed normal diplomatic relations with Vietnam. Gradually, the *Viet Kieu,* or Vietnamese living abroad, began to return to their old country to visit, but usually not to take up permanent residence. Today, more than 35 years after the end of the Vietnam War, sharp differences of opinion remain among Vietnamese Americans, especially the older ones, concerning the war and the present government of Vietnam (Pfeifer 2008).

Korean Americans

At over 1.3 million, the population of Korean Americans now exceeds that of Japanese Americans. Yet Korean Americans are often overshadowed by other groups from Asia.

Today's Korean American community is the result of three waves of immigration. The initial wave arrived between 1903 and 1910, when Korean laborers migrated to Hawai'i. The second wave followed the end of the Korean War in 1953; most of those immigrants were wives of U.S. servicemen and war orphans. The third wave, continuing to the present, has reflected the admissions priorities set up in the 1965 Immigration Act. These well-educated immigrants arrive in the United States with professional skills. Yet because of language difficulties and discrimination, many must settle at least initially for positions of lower responsibility than those they held in Korea and must suffer through a period of disenchantment. Stress, loneliness, and family strife may accompany the pain of adjustment.

In the early 1990s, the apparent friction between Korean Americans and another subordinate racial group, African Americans, attracted nationwide attention. In New York City, Los Angeles, and Chicago, Korean American merchants confronted Blacks who were allegedly threatening them or robbing their stores. Black neighborhoods responded with hostility to what they perceived as the disrespect and arrogance of Korean American entrepreneurs. In South Central Los Angeles, the only shops in which to buy groceries, liquor, or gasoline were owned by Korean immigrants, who had largely replaced White businesspeople. African Americans were well aware of the dominant role that Korean Americans played in their local retail markets.

During the 1992 riots in South Central Los Angeles, small businesses owned by Koreans were a particular target. More than 1,800 Korean businesses were looted or burned during the riots (Kim 1999).

Conflict between the two groups was dramatized in Spike Lee's 1989 movie *Do the Right Thing.* The situation stemmed from Korean Americans' position as the latest immigrant group to cater to the needs of inner-city populations abandoned by those who have moved up the economic ladder. This type of friction is not new; generations of Jewish, Italian, and Arab merchants have encountered similar hostility from what to outsiders seems an unlikely source—another oppressed minority.

Arab Americans

Arab Americans are immigrants, and their descendants, who hail from the 22 nations of the Arab world. As defined by the League of Arab States, these are the nations of North Africa and what is popularly known as the Middle East, including Lebanon, Syria, Palestine, Morocco, Iraq, Saudi Arabia, and Somalia. Not all residents of those countries are Arab; for example, the Kurds, who live in northern Iraq, are not Arab. And some Arab Americans may have immigrated to the United States from non-Arab countries such as Great Britain or France, where their families have lived for generations.

The Arabic language is the single most unifying force among Arabs, although not all Arabs, and certainly not all Arab Americans, can read and speak Arabic. Moreover, the language has evolved over the centuries so that people in different parts of the Arab world speak different dialects. Still, the fact that the Koran (or Qur'an) was originally written in Arabic gives the language special importance to Muslims, just as the Torah's composition in Hebrew gives that language special significance to Jews.

Estimates of the size of the Arab American community differ widely. By some estimates, up to 3 million people of Arab ancestry reside in the United States. Among those who identify themselves as Arab Americans, the most common country of origin is Lebanon, followed by Syria, Egypt, and Palestine. In 2000, these four countries of origin accounted for two-thirds of all Arab Americans. Their rising numbers have led to the development of Arab retail centers in several cities, including Dearborn and Detroit, Michigan; Los Angeles; Chicago; New York City; and Washington, D.C.

As a group, Arab Americans are extremely diverse. Many families have lived in the United States for several generations; others are foreign born. Their points of origin range from the metropolis of Cairo, Egypt, to the rural villages of Morocco. Despite the stereotype, most Arab Americans are *not* Muslim (Figure 33-3). Nor can Arab Americans be characterized as having a specific family type, gender role, or occupational pattern (David 2004, 2008).

Despite this great diversity, profiling of potential terrorists at airports has put Arab and Muslim Americans under special surveillance. For years, a number of airlines and law enforcement

FIGURE 33-3 Arab American Religious Affiliations

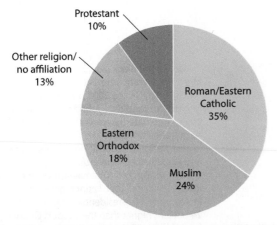

Protestant
10%

Other religion/
no affiliation
13%

Roman/Eastern
Catholic
35%

Eastern
Orthodox
18%

Muslim
24%

Notes: Roman/Eastern Catholic includes Roman Catholic, Maronite, and Mel kite (Greek Catholic); Eastern Orthodox includes Antiochian, Syrian, Greek, and Coptic; Muslim includes Sunni, Shi'a, and Druze.
Source: Arab American Institute 2010, based on 2002 Zogby International Survey.
Unlike Arabs in other parts of the world, most Arab Americans are Christian.

authorities have used appearance and ethnic-sounding names to identify and take aside Arab Americans and search their belongings. After the terrorist attacks of September 2001, criticism of this practice declined as concern for the public's safety mounted.

Latinos

Together, the various groups included under the general category *Latinos* represent the largest minority in the United States. There are more than 46 million Hispanics in this country, including 30 million Mexican Americans, more than 4 million Puerto Ricans, and smaller numbers of Cuban Americans and people of Central and South American origin (Figure 33-4). The latter group represents the fastest-growing and most diverse segment of the Hispanic community.

According to Census Bureau data, the Latino population now outnumbers the African American population in 6 of the 10 largest cities of the United States: Los Angeles, Houston, Phoenix, San Diego, Dallas, and San Antonio. Hispanics are now the majority of residents in cities such as Miami, Florida; El Paso, Texas; and Santa Ana, California. The rise in the Hispanic population of the United States—fueled by comparatively high birthrates and levels of immigration—has intensified debates over public policy issues such as bilingualism and immigration. Coincidentally, these discussions are taking place just as Latinos are beginning to flex their muscles as voters (Research Today: Latinos in the Voting Booth).

The various Latino groups share a heritage of Spanish language and culture, which can cause serious problems in their assimilation. An intelligent student whose first language is Spanish may be presumed slow or even unruly by English-speaking schoolchildren, and frequently by English-speaking teachers as well. The labeling of Latino children as underachievers, as learning disabled, or as emotionally disturbed can act as a self-fulfilling prophecy for some children. Bilingual education aims at easing the educational

difficulties experienced by Hispanic children and others whose first language is not English.

The educational difficulties of Latino students certainly contribute to Hispanics' generally low economic status. In 2008, about 17 percent of all Hispanic households earned less than $15,000, compared to 11 percent of White non-Hispanic households; and the poverty rate was 23.2 percent for Hispanics, compared to 8.6 percent for White non-Hispanics. Overall, Latinos are not as affluent as White non-Hispanics, but a middle class is beginning to emerge (DeNavas-Walt et al. 2009:14, 31, 34).

Mexican Americans

The largest Latino population is Mexican Americans, who can be further subdivided into those descended from residents of the territories annexed after the Mexican American War of 1848 and those who have immigrated from Mexico to the United States. The opportunity for a Mexican to earn in one hour what it would take an entire day to earn in Mexico has pushed millions of legal and illegal immigrants north.

Aside from the family, the most important social organization in the Mexican American (or Chicano) community is the church, specifically the Roman Catholic Church. This strong identification with the Catholic faith has reinforced the already formidable barriers between Mexican Americans and their predominantly White and Protestant neighbors in the Southwest. At the same time, the Catholic Church helps many immigrants to develop a sense of identity and assists their assimilation into the norms and values of the dominant culture of the United States. The complexity of the Mexican American community

FIGURE 33-4 Hispanic Population by Origin

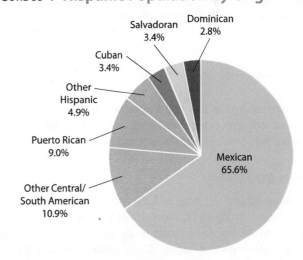

Salvadoran
3.4%

Dominican
2.8%

Cuban
3.4%

Other
Hispanic
4.9%

Puerto Rican
9.0%

Other Central/
South American
10.9%

Mexican
65.6%

Note: "Other Hispanic" includes Spanish Americans and Latinos identified as mixed ancestry as well as other Central and South Americans not otherwise indicated by specific country.
Source: American Community Survey 2009:Table B03001.

Think about It

Do Hispanic Americans really have a common identity?

Research Today

Latinos in the Voting Booth

Over the past 40 years, the two major political parties have slowly acknowledged Latinos as a force at the ballot box. The rapid growth of the Hispanic population, together with policies that facilitate voting by non-English speakers, underlie this shift. In 1975, Congress moved to recognize the multilingual background of the U.S. population. Federal law now requires bilingual or even multilingual ballots in voting districts where at least 10,000 people or 5 percent of the voting-age population do not speak English.

These voting reforms have not had the impact many advocates hoped, however, and turnout remains poor. Hispanics are interested in voting, but many are ineligible because they are not citizens. Thus, in the 2008 presidential election, Hispanics accounted for 15.4 percent of the total U.S. population but only 9.5 percent of the eligible electorate. Apathy is another hurdle to voter participation. Like African Americans, many Latinos resent the fact that political movers and shakers seem to recognize their existence only once every four years. Between major elections, they hear little except from Latino elected officials.

Although national surveys show that Latino policy concerns mirror those of the general electorate—the economy, education, health care, national security, the environment, and energy—there is one exception. Immigration policy usually ranks among Latinos' top five or six concerns. Latinos want

> Like African Americans, many Latinos resent the fact that political movers and shakers seem to recognize their existence only once every four years.

less restrictive immigration laws that will speed up the immigration and naturalization process. Non-Hispanics tend to see immigration as either an economic threat or a national security concern.

The potential for a stronger Latino political presence is great. In anticipation of a larger turnout, both political parties are now nominating more Hispanic candidates. As a rule, Democrats have been more successful than Republicans in attracting the Hispanic vote: a 2008 national survey showed registered Latino voters leaning toward Democratic candidates. The one exception to this preference is Cuban Americans, who have long supported the Republican Party because of its strong opposition to the communist government in Cuba. Even among Cuban Americans, however, Democrats made gains in the 2008 election.

Unlike the Black vote, which is overwhelmingly Democratic, the Latino vote is still very much in play. In the 2008 presidential election, Republican candidate John McCain and Democratic candidate Barack Obama made back-to-back appearances before the annual meeting of the National Association of Latino Elected and Appointed Officials. Ultimately, 67 percent of Latinos backed Obama—much the same level of support that Latinos gave Democrats in the past 10 presidential elections. That is 24 percent higher than the support Obama got from Whites (43 percent), but 28 percent lower than the support he got from Blacks (95 percent). Given the Hispanic community's rapidly growing population, together with stepped-up voter registration and increasing participation in elections, we can expect that, in the future, candidates from both parties will vie for their support.

LET'S DISCUSS

1. Do you vote in a community where polling places offer multilingual ballots? If so, do the names on the ballot mirror the community's multiethnic background?

2. If you were a campaign worker, how would you go about appealing to the Latino vote?

Sources: Connelly 2008; Kiely 2008; Lopez and Livingston 2009; Lopez and Minushkin 2008; Lopez and Taylor 2009; Padgett 2008; Suro and Escobar 2006.

---

is underscored by the fact that Protestant churches—especially those that endorse expressive, open worship—have attracted increasing numbers of Mexican Americans.

Puerto Ricans

The second-largest segment of Latinos in the United States is Puerto Ricans. Since 1917, residents of Puerto Rico have held the status of American citizens; many have migrated to New York and other eastern cities. Unfortunately, Puerto Ricans have experienced serious poverty both in the United States and on the island. Those who live in the continental United States earn barely half the family income of Whites. As a result, a reverse migration began in the 1970s, when more Puerto Ricans were leaving for the island than were coming to the mainland (Torres 2008).

Politically, Puerto Ricans in the United States have not been as successful as Mexican Americans in organizing for their rights. For many mainland Puerto Ricans—as for many residents of the island—the paramount political issue is the destiny of Puerto Rico itself: should it continue in its present commonwealth status, petition for admission to the United States as the 51st state, or attempt to become an independent nation? This question has divided Puerto Rico for decades and remains a central issue in Puerto Rican elections. In a 1998 referendum, voters supported a "none of the above" option, effectively favoring continuation of the commonwealth status over statehood or independence.

Cuban Americans

Cuban immigration to the United States dates back as far as 1831, but it began in earnest following Fidel Castro's assumption of power in the Cuban revolution (1959). The first wave of 200,000 Cubans included many professionals with relatively high levels of schooling; these men and women were largely welcomed as refugees from communist tyranny. However, more recent waves of immigrants have aroused growing concern, partly because they were less likely to be skilled professionals. Throughout these waves of immigration, Cuban Americans have been encouraged to locate around the United States. Nevertheless, many continue to settle in (or return to) metropolitan Miami, Florida, with its warm climate and proximity to Cuba.

The Cuban experience in the United States has been mixed. Some detractors worry about the vehement anticommunism of Cuban Americans and the apparent growth of an organized crime syndicate that engages in the drug trade and ganglike violence. Recently, Cuban Americans in Miami have expressed concern over what they view as the indifference of the city's Roman Catholic hierarchy. Like other Hispanics, Cuban Americans are underrepresented in leadership positions within the church. Also—despite many individual success stories—as a group, Cuban Americans in Miami remain behind Whites in income, rate of employment, and proportion of professionals (Masud-Piloto 2008).

Central and South Americans

Immigrants from Central and South America are a diverse population that has not been closely studied. Indeed, most government statistics treat members of this group collectively as "other," rarely differentiating among them by nationality. Yet people from Chile and Costa Rica have little in common other than their hemisphere of origin and the Spanish language—if that. The fact is, not all Central and South Americans speak Spanish. Immigrants from Brazil, for example, speak Portuguese; immigrants from French Guyana speak French; and immigrants from Suriname speak Dutch.

Racially, many of the nations of Central and South America follow a complex classification system that recognizes a multitude of color gradients. Experience with this multiracial system does not prepare immigrants to the United States for the stark Black–White racial divide that characterizes U.S. society. Beyond their diversity in color and language, immigrants from Central and South America are differentiated by social class distinctions, religious differences, urban or rural upbringings, and dialects. Some of them may come from indigenous populations, especially in Guatemala and Belize. If so, their social identity would be separate from any national allegiance.

In short, social relations among Central and South Americans, who collectively number nearly 7 million people, defy generalization. The same can be said about their relations with other Latinos and with non-Latinos. Central and South Americans do not form, nor should they be expected to form, a cohesive group. Nor do they easily form coalitions with Cuban Americans, Mexican Americans, or Puerto Ricans.

Jewish Americans

Jews constitute about 2 percent of the population of the United States. They play a prominent role in the worldwide Jewish community, because the United States has the world's largest concentration of Jews. Like the Japanese, many Jewish immigrants came to this country and became white-collar professionals in spite of prejudice and discrimination.

Anti-Semitism—that is, anti-Jewish prejudice—has often been vicious in the United States, although rarely so widespread and never so formalized as in Europe. In many cases, Jews have been used as scapegoats for other people's failures. Not surprisingly, Jews have not achieved equality in the United States. Despite high levels of education and professional training, they are still conspicuously absent from the top management of large corporations (except for the few firms founded by Jews). Nonetheless, a national survey in 2009 showed that one out of four people in the United States blame "the Jews" for the financial crisis. In addition, private social clubs and fraternal groups frequently continue to limit membership to Gentiles (non-Jews), a practice upheld by the Supreme Court in the 1964 case *Bell v. Maryland* (Malhotra and Margalit 2009).

The Anti-Defamation League (ADL) of B'nai B'rith funds an annual tally of reported anti-Semitic incidents. Although the number has fluctuated, in 2008 the tabulation reached the highest level in the 19 years the ADL has been recording them. In 2007 the total reported incidents of harassment, threats, vandalism, and assaults came to 1,352. Some incidents were inspired and

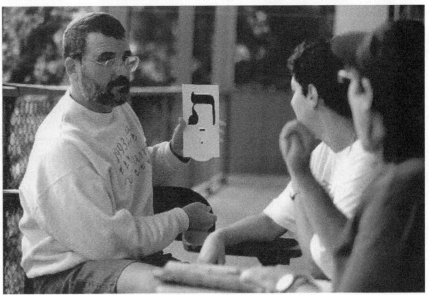

For practicing Jews, the Hebrew language is an important part of religious instruction. This teacher is showing flashcards of Hebrew alphabetic characters to deaf students.

carried out by neo-Nazi skinheads—groups of young people who champion racist and anti-Semitic ideologies. Such threatening behavior only intensifies the fears of many Jewish Americans, who remember the Holocaust—the extermination of 6 million Jews by the Nazi Third Reich during World War II (Anti-Defamation League 2009).

As is true for other minorities discussed in this module, Jewish Americans face the choice of maintaining ties to their long religious and cultural heritage or becoming as indistinguishable as possible from Gentiles. Many Jews have tended to assimilate, as is evident from the rise in marriages between Jews and Christians. In marriages that occurred in the 1970s, more than 70 percent of Jews married Jews or people who converted to Judaism. In marriages since 1996, that proportion has dropped to 53 percent. This trend means that today, American Jews are almost as likely to marry a Gentile as a Jew. For many, religion is a nonissue—neither parent practices religious rituals. Two-thirds of the children of these Jewish–Gentile marriages are not raised as Jews. Finally, in 2005, two-thirds of Jews felt that the biggest threat to Jewish life was anti-Semitism; only one-third named intermarriage as the biggest threat (American Jewish Committee 2005; Sanua 2007).

White Americans often express their ethnicity with special celebrations, such as this Greek Independence Day parade in New York City.

White Ethnics

A significant segment of the population of the United States is made up of White ethnics whose ancestors arrived from Europe within the past century. The nation's White ethnic population includes about 50 million people who claim at least partial German ancestry, 36 million Irish Americans, 18 million Italian Americans, and 10 million Polish Americans, as well as immigrants from other European nations. Some of these people continue to live in close-knit ethnic neighborhoods, while others have largely assimilated and left the "old ways" behind.

Many White ethnics today identify only sporadically with their heritage. **Symbolic ethnicity** refers to an emphasis on concerns such as ethnic food or political issues rather than on deeper ties to one's ethnic heritage. It is reflected in the occasional family trip to an ethnic bakery, the celebration of a ceremonial event such as St. Joseph's Day among Italian Americans, or concern about the future of Northern Ireland among Irish Americans. Such practices are another example of the social construction of race and ethnicity. Except in cases in which new immigration reinforces old traditions, symbolic ethnicity tends to decline with each passing generation (Alba 1990; Winter 2008).

Although the White ethnic identity may be a point of pride to those who share it, they do not necessarily celebrate it at the expense of disadvantaged minorities. It is all too easy to assume that race relations are a zero-sum game in which one group gains at the expense of the other. Rather, the histories of several White ethnic groups, such as the Irish and the Italians, show that once marginalized people can rise to positions of prestige and influence (Alba 2009).

That is not to say that White ethnics and racial minorities have not been antagonistic toward one another because of economic competition—an interpretation that agrees with the conflict approach to sociology. As Blacks, Latinos, and Native Americans emerge from the lower class, they must compete with working-class Whites for jobs, housing, and educational opportunities. In times of high unemployment or inflation, any such competition can easily generate intense intergroup conflict.

In many respects, the plight of White ethnics raises the same basic issues as that of other subordinate people in the United States. How ethnic can people be—how much can they deviate from an essentially White, Anglo-Saxon, Protestant norm—before society punishes them for their willingness to be different? Our society does seem to reward people for assimilating, yet as we have seen, assimilation is no easy process. In the years to come, more and more people will face the challenge of fitting in, not only in the United States but around the world, as the flow of immigrants from one country to another continues to increase. In the Social Policy section that follows, we focus on global immigration and its implications for the future.

Worldwide, immigration is at an all-time high. Each year, about 191 million people move from one country to another—a number that is roughly the equivalent of the total populations of Russia and Italy. A million of these immigrants enter the United States legally, to join the 12 percent of the U.S. population who are foreign born. Perhaps more significantly, one-fourth of the U.S. labor force is foreign born—the largest proportion in at least 120 years (Newburger and Gryn 2009).

Globally, these mass migrations have had a tremendous social impact. The constantly increasing numbers of immigrants and the pressure they put on job opportunities and welfare capabilities in the countries they enter raise troubling questions for many of the world's economic powers. Who should be allowed in? At what point should immigration be curtailed (United Nations 2009)?

Understanding the Issue

The migration of people is not uniform across time or space. At certain times, war or famine may precipitate large movements of people, either temporarily or permanently. Temporary dislocations occur when people wait until it is safe to return to their home areas. However, more and more migrants who cannot make an adequate living in their home nations are making permanent moves to developed nations. The major migration streams flow into North America, the oil-rich areas of the Middle East, and the industrial economies of western Europe and Asia. Currently, seven of the world's wealthiest nations (including Germany, France, the United Kingdom, and the United States) shelter about one-third of the world's migrant population, but less than one-fifth of the world's total population. As long as disparities in job opportunities exist among countries, there is little reason to expect this international trend to reverse.

One consequence of global immigration is the emergence of **transnationals**—immigrants who sustain multiple social relationships that link their societies of origin with the society of settlement. The industrial tycoons of the early 20th century, whose power outmatched that of many nation-states, were among the world's first transnationals. Today, millions of people, many of very modest means, move back and forth between countries much as commuters do between city and suburbs. More and more of these people have dual citizenship. Rather than being shaped by allegiance to one country, their identity is rooted in their struggle to survive—and in some instances prosper—by transcending international borders (Croucher 2004; Sassen 2005). We will take a closer look

at these citizens of the world in the Social Policy section of Module 57.

Countries that have long been a destination for immigrants, such as the United States, usually have policies regarding who has preference to enter. Often, clear racial and ethnic biases are built into these policies. In the 1920s, U.S. policy gave preference to people from western Europe, while making it difficult for residents of southern and eastern Europe, Asia, and Africa to enter the country. During the late 1930s and early 1940s, the federal government refused to lift or loosen restrictive immigration quotas in order to allow Jewish refugees to escape the terror of the Nazi regime. In line with this policy, the SS *St. Louis,* with more than 900 Jewish refugees on board, was denied permission to land in the United States in 1939. The ship was forced to sail back to Europe, where it is estimated that at least a few hundred of its passengers later died at the hands of the Nazis (Morse 1967; G. Thomas and Witts 1974).

Since the 1960s, U.S. policy has encouraged the immigration of relatives of U.S. residents as well as of people who have desirable skills. This change has significantly altered the pattern of sending nations. Previously, Europeans dominated, but for the past 40 years, immigrants have come primarily from Latin America and Asia. Thus, an ever-growing proportion of the U.S. population will be Asian or Hispanic (see Figure 33-5). To a large degree, fear and resentment of growing racial and ethnic diversity is a key factor in opposition to immigration. In many nations, people are concerned that the new arrivals do not reflect their own cultural and racial heritage.

Applying Sociology

Research suggests that immigrants adapt well to life in the United States, becoming an asset to the nation's economy. In some areas, heavy immigration may drain a local community's resources, but in other areas it revitalizes the local economy. Contrary to the notion that Latinos resist learning English, a national survey in 2007 showed that 77 percent of Hispanics believe immigrants should be required to learn English as a condition for remaining in the country (J. Carroll 2007a).

Despite people's fears, immigration performs many valuable functions. For the receiving society, it alleviates labor shortages, as it does in health care and technology in the United States. For the sending nation, migration can relieve an economy unable to support large numbers of people. Often

(continued)

FIGURE 33-5 Legal Migration to the United States, 1820–2010

| 1820s | 1840s | 1860s | 1880s | 1900s | 1920s | 1940s | 1960s | 1980s | 2000s |

0.1

0.6

1.7

2.6

2.3

2.8

3.7

Millions of immigrants

5.2

5.7

4.1

0.5

1.0

2.5

3.2

From Europe and Canada

6.2

4.2

From all other countries

8.8

9.7

10.2

Sources: Author's estimates for the period 2000–2010; Office of Immigration Statistics 2008:8–11.

overlooked is the large amount of money, called *remittances,* that immigrants send *back* to their home nations.

Immigration can be dysfunctional as well. Although studies generally show that it has a positive impact on the receiving nation's economy, areas that accept high concentrations of immigrants may find it difficult to meet short-term social service needs. And when migrants with skills or educational potential leave developing countries, their departure can be dysfunctional for those nations. No amount of payments sent

back home can make up for the loss of valuable human resources from poor nations (Borjas et al. 2006; Kochhar 2006; Sum et al. 2006).

Conflict theorists note how much of the debate over immigration is phrased in economic terms. But the debate intensifies when the arrivals are of a different racial and ethnic background from the host population. For example, Europeans often refer to "foreigners," but the term does not necessarily mean one of foreign birth. In Germany, "foreigners" refers to people of non-German ancestry, even if they were *born* in Germany; it does not refer to people of German ancestry born in another country, who may choose to return to their mother country. Fear and dislike of "new" ethnic groups divides countries throughout the world.

The feminist perspective pays special attention to the role that women play in global immigration. Immigrant women face all the challenges that immigrant men do, plus some additional ones. Typically, they bear the responsibility for obtaining services for their families, particularly their children. Because the men are likely to be consumed with work, the women are left to navigate through the bureaucratic tangle of schools, city services, and medical facilities, as well as the unfamiliar stores and markets they must visit to feed their families. Women who need special medical services or are victims of domestic violence are often reluctant to seek outside help. Yet they are more likely than the men to serve as the liaison between their households and community and religious associations. Also, because many new immigrants view the United States as a dangerous place to raise a family, women must be especially watchful over their children's lives (Hondagneu-Sotelo 2003).

Initiating Policy

The long border with Mexico provides ample opportunity for illegal immigration into the United States. Throughout the 1980s, the public perception that the United States had lost

U.S. employers' demand for low-paid labor fuels illegal immigration.

control of its borders grew. Feeling pressure for immigration control, Congress ended a decade of debate by approving the Immigration Reform and Control Act of 1986. The act marked a historic change in the nation's immigration policy. For the first time, the hiring of illegal aliens was outlawed, and employers caught violating the law became subject to fines and even prison sentences. Just as significant a change was the extension of amnesty and legal status to many illegal immigrants already living in the United States. More than 20 years later, however, the act appears to have had mixed results. Substantial numbers of illegal immigrants continue to enter the country each year, with an estimated 11 million present now at any given time—a marked increase since 2000 (D. Wood 2010).

In 2010, frustrated by the continuing flow of illegal immigrants across the Mexican border, Arizona enacted a law empowering police to detain without authorization people whom they reasonably suspect of being illegal immigrants and to verify their immigration status. Immediately, opponents charged that the new law would lead to racial profiling. Legal experts questioned whether state enforcement of immigration law was constitutional. Although implementation of the law has been problematic, it has highlighted the resolve of those seeking to tighten control of the nation's borders. It has also galvanized those seeking to reform the nation's immigration law.

Recently, immigrants have staged massive marches to pressure Congress to speed the naturalization process and develop ways for illegal immigrants to gain legal residency. Counterdemonstrations by those who oppose illegal immigration have called for more resources with which to detect and deport illegal immigrants and to strengthen the U.S.–Mexican border. Despite this widespread public dissatisfaction with the nation's immigration policy, little progress has been made. Congress has had difficulty reaching a bipartisan compromise that pleases both sides: both supporters of strict social control and those who would allow illegal immigrants to remain in the country legally, under some circumstances.

The entire world feels the overwhelming impact of globalization on immigration patterns. The European Union agreement of 1997 gave the governing commission authority to propose a Europe-wide policy on immigration. An EU policy that allows residents of one EU country to live and work in another EU country is expected to complicate efforts by sending nations, such as Turkey, to become members of the EU. Immigrants from Turkey's predominantly Muslim population are not welcome in many EU countries (Denny 2004).

In the wake of the attacks of September 11, 2001, on the World Trade Center and the Pentagon, immigration procedures were complicated by the need to detect potential terrorists. Illegal immigrants especially, but even legal immigrants, have felt increased scrutiny by government officials around the world. For would-be immigrants to many nations, the wait to receive the right to enter a country—even to join relatives—has increased substantially, as immigration officials scrutinize more closely what were once routine applications.

The intense debate over immigration reflects deep value conflicts in the cultures of many nations. One strand of our culture, for example, has traditionally emphasized egalitarian principles and a desire to help people in time of need. At the same time, hostility to potential immigrants and refugees—whether the Chinese in the 1880s, European Jews in the 1930s and 1940s, or Mexicans, Haitians, and Arabs today—reflects not only racial, ethnic, and religious prejudice, but a desire to maintain the dominant culture of the in-group by keeping out those viewed as outsiders.

TAKE THE ISSUE WITH YOU

1. Did you or your parents or grandparents immigrate to the United States from another nation? If so, when and where did your family come from, and why?

2. On balance, do the functions of immigration to the United States outweigh the dysfunctions?

3. Do you live, work, or study with recent immigrants to the United States? If so, are they well accepted in your community, or do they face prejudice and discrimination?

Summary

The U.S. population is highly diverse, both racially and ethnically.

1. Contemporary prejudice and discrimination against African Americans are rooted in the history of slavery in the United States.

2. Asian Americans are commonly viewed as a **model** or **ideal minority,** a false stereotype that is not necessarily beneficial to members of that group.

3. The various groups included under the general term *Latinos* represent the largest ethnic minority in the United States.

4. Worldwide, immigration is at an all-time high, fueling controversy not only in the United States but also in the European Union. A new kind of immigrant, the **transnational,** moves back and forth across international borders in search of a better job or education.

Thinking Critically

1. Summarize the major differences (a) among Asian Indian, Vietnamese, Chinese, Japanese, and Korean Americans, or (b) among Mexican Americans, Puerto Ricans, Cuban Americans, and Central and South Americans.

2. To what extent has U.S. society achieved pluralism? Give examples from your own experience to support your viewpoint.

Key Terms

Anti-Semitism

Black power

Model, or **ideal, minority**

Symbolic ethnicity

Transnationals

11 Stratification by Gender

MODULE **34** | **Social Construction of Gender**

MODULE **35** | **Women: The Oppressed Majority**

"YOUNG PEOPLE SOUGHT

Elvis's café [in Tehran, Iran] as refuge from the relentless ugliness that pervaded most public gathering places. Even in the rainy winter, people would crowd outside in the drizzle for an hour, smoking soggy cigarettes and waiting for a table. It was the only café in Tehran designed with innovative elegance and attracted young people starved for aesthetic beauty....

Elvis's coffeehouse inspired imitations all over the neighborhood and then the city. In early 2000, when Celine and I first began to haunt the tiny, modern nook, it was one of a kind. By the following summer of 2001, dozens of tastefully decorated cafés dotted the city.... In the Gandhi shopping complex, where it was located, at least six others sprang up, and the area became center stage in a café scene of shocking permissiveness. By that time, the dress code was so relaxed that everyone buzzed with tales of 'You'll never believe what I saw this girl wearing!'; the fashion spring was likened to a silent coup.

Girls dressed in every color imaginable—veils of bright emerald, violet, buttercup—and in short, coat-like tunics called *manteaus* (also known by the Farsi word *roopoosh*) that hugged their curves, Capri pants that exposed long stretches of calf, pedicured

> The throng of students and young professionals flirted brazenly, and the coquettish slipping of veils produced nothing less than social theater. The Tehran of the revolution was one of the most sexualized milieus I had ever encountered.

toes in delicate sandals. They sat at the tables outside, in mixed groups, alone with boyfriends, laughing and talking into the late evening, past eleven. For a few weeks, Tehran actually had something like nightlife in public, not just sequestered parties inside people's houses....

... The throng of students and young professionals flirted brazenly, and the coquettish slipping of veils produced nothing less than social theater. The Tehran of the revolution was one of the most sexualized milieus I had ever encountered....

... Made neurotic by the innate oppressiveness of restriction, Iranians were preoccupied with sex in the manner of dieters constantly thinking about food. The subject meant to be *unmentionable*—to which end women were forced to wear veils, sit in the back of the bus, and order hamburgers from the special 'women's line' at fast food joints—had somehow become the most mentioned of all. The constant exposure to covered flesh—whether it was covered hideously, artfully, or plainly—brought to mind, well, flesh.

The relaxing of the dress code encouraged this tendency, by breathing sexuality back into public space. Women walked down the street with their elbows, necks, and feet exposed, their figures outlined in form-fitting tunics. After two decades in exile, skin was finally back. And so imaginations flared, everyone eagerly thought about and talked about sex a lot, as though they were afraid if they didn't exploit the new permissiveness in dress and mood, they might wake up to find it had disappeared."

(Moaveni 2005a:69–70, 71)

Azadeh Moaveni, the author of *Lipstick Jihad*, was born in California after her parents fled the political turbulence of the Iranian revolution. In 1979, Islamic religious leaders overthrew the U.S.-backed monarchy that had ruled the country for decades. Almost overnight, the country was transformed from a relatively secular, Western-oriented society into a conservative Muslim state. Women were suddenly expected to cover themselves in dark robes. Young women, who had been required to attend school and serve in the armed forces, were now forbidden even to appear in public without a male escort.

Though Moaveni grew up in the United States, she was conversant with her Persian cultural heritage. After graduating from college, she lived in Iran for two years, where she covered the country's affairs as a news correspondent. There she found a different society from the one her parents had fled a generation before. The "lipstick jihad" is an allusion to the recent relaxation of the strict standards for women's dress and behavior—a change that Iranian women effected by personally defying government sanctions. (*Jihad* is the Arabic term for one's inner struggle against the forces of ungodliness [Moaveni 2005b].)

In her current role as *Time* magazine's correspondent from Tehran, Moaveni (2007, 2009) continues to observe women's lives inside Iran. She has noted a new trend in the formerly austere capital—an appetite for high-priced designer-label fashion accessories, particularly among the young. Today, *nouveau riche* Iranians are indulging in Western-style conspicuous consumption. Iranian housewives can be seen driving through the city in BMW SUVs, Burberry scarves showing beneath their full-length black *chadors* (coats).

How do gender roles differ from one culture to another? Are women in the United States still oppressed because of their gender? Have men's and women's positions in society changed? In these modules we will study these and other questions by looking first at how various cultures, including our own, assign women and men to particular social roles. Then we will consider sociological explanations for gender stratification. We will see that around the world, women constitute an oppressed majority of the population. We will close Module 35 with a Social Policy section on the controversy over a woman's right to abortion.

34 | Social Construction of Gender

How many airline passengers do you think are startled on hearing a female captain's voice from the cockpit? What do we make of a father who announces that he will be late for work because his son has a routine medical checkup? Consciously or unconsciously, we are likely to assume that flying a commercial plane is a *man's* job and that most parental duties are, in fact, a *woman's.* Gender is such a routine part of our everyday activities that we typically take notice only when someone deviates from conventional behavior and expectations.

Although a few people begin life with an unclear sexual identity, the overwhelming majority begin with a definite sex and quickly receive societal messages about how to behave. In fact, virtually all societies have established social distinctions between females and males that do not inevitably result from biological differences between the sexes (such as women's reproductive capabilities).

In studying gender, sociologists are interested in the gender-role socialization that leads females and males to behave differently. In Module 14, **gender roles** were defined as expectations regarding the proper behavior, attitudes, and activities of males and females. The application of dominant gender roles leads to many forms of differentiation between women and men. Both sexes are capable of learning to cook and sew, yet most Western societies determine that women should perform those tasks. Both men and women are capable of learning to weld and to fly airplanes, but those functions are generally assigned to men.

As we will see throughout this module, however, social behavior does not mirror the mutual exclusivity suggested by these gender roles. Nor are gender roles independent: in real life, the way men behave influences women's behavior, and the way women behave affects men's behavior. Thus, most people do not display strictly "masculine" or "feminine" qualities all the time. Indeed, such standards can be ambiguous. For instance, though men are supposed to be unemotional, they are allowed to become emotional when their favorite athletic team wins or loses a critical game. Yet our society still focuses on "masculine" and "feminine" qualities as if men and women must be evaluated in those terms. Despite recent inroads by women into male-dominated occupations, our construction of gender continues to define significantly different expectations for females and males (J. Howard and Hollander 1997; West and Zimmerman 1987).

Gender roles are evident not only in our work and behavior but in how we react to others. We are constantly "doing gender" without realizing it. If the father mentioned earlier sits in the doctor's office with his son in the middle of a workday, he will probably receive approving glances from the receptionist and from other patients. "Isn't he a wonderful father?" runs through

their minds. But if the boy's mother leaves *her* job and sits with the son in the doctor's office, she will not receive such silent applause.

We socially construct our behavior so as to create or exaggerate male/female differences. For example, men and women come in a variety of heights, sizes, and ages. Yet traditional norms regarding marriage and even casual dating tell us that in heterosexual couples, the man should be older, taller, and wiser than the woman. As we will see throughout this module, such social norms help to reinforce and legitimize patterns of male dominance.

Gender Roles in the United States

Gender-Role Socialization

Male babies get blue blankets; females get pink ones. Boys are expected to play with trucks, blocks, and toy soldiers; girls receive dolls and kitchen goods. Boys must be masculine—active, aggressive, tough, daring, and dominant—but girls must be feminine—soft, emotional, sweet, and submissive. These traditional gender-role patterns have been influential in the socialization of children in the United States.

An important element in traditional views of proper "masculine" and "feminine" behavior is **homophobia,** fear of and prejudice against homosexuality. Homophobia contributes significantly to rigid gender-role socialization, since many people stereotypically associate male homosexuality with femininity and lesbianism with masculinity. Consequently, men and women who deviate from traditional expectations about gender roles are often presumed to be gay. Despite the advances made by the gay liberation movement, the continuing stigma attached to homosexuality in our culture places pressure on all males (whether gay or not) to exhibit only narrow masculine behavior and on all females (whether lesbian or not) to exhibit only narrow feminine behavior (Seidman 1994; see also Lehne 1995).

It is *adults,* of course, who play a critical role in guiding children into those gender roles deemed appropriate in a society. Parents are normally the first and most crucial agents of socialization. But other adults, older siblings, the mass media, and religious and educational institutions also exert an important influence on gender-role socialization, in the United States and elsewhere.

It is not hard to test how rigid gender-role socialization can be. Just try transgressing some gender norm—say, by smoking a cigar in public if you are female, or by carrying a purse if you

Table **34-1** An Experiment in Gender Norm Violation by College Students

Norm Violations by Women	Norm Violations by Men
Send men flowers	Wear fingernail polish
Spit in public	Needlepoint in public
Use men's bathroom	Throw Tupperware party
Buy jock strap	Cry in public
Buy/chew tobacco	Have pedicure
Talk knowledgeably about cars	Apply to babysit
Open doors for men	Shave body hair

Source: Nielsen et al. 2000:287.

In an experiment testing gender-role stereotypes, sociology students were asked to behave in ways that might be regarded as violations of gender norms, and to keep notes on how others reacted. This is a sample of their choices of behavior over a seven-year period. Do you agree that these actions test the boundaries of conventional gender behavior?

In our society, men and women receive different messages about the ideal body image. For women, the Miss America pageant promotes a very slim, statuesque physique. For men, "action figures" like the G.I. Joe doll promote an exaggerated muscularity typical of professional wrestlers (Angier 1998; Byrd-Bredbenner and Murray 2003).

are male. That was exactly the assignment given to sociology students at the University of Colorado and Luther College in Iowa. Professors asked students to behave in ways that they thought violated the norms of how a man or woman should act. The students had no trouble coming up with gender-norm transgressions (Table 34-1), and they kept careful notes on others' reactions to their behavior, ranging from amusement to disgust (Nielsen et al. 2000).

Women's Gender Roles

How does a girl come to develop a feminine self-image, while a boy develops one that is masculine? In part, they do so by identifying with females and males in their families and neighborhoods and in the media. If a young girl regularly sees female television characters of all ages and body types, she is likely to grow up with a normal body image. And it will not hurt if the women she knows—her mother, sister, parents' friends, and neighbors—are comfortable with their body types, rather than constantly obsessed with their weight. In contrast, if this young girl sees only wafer-thin actresses and models on television, her self-image will be quite different. Even if she grows up to become a well-educated professional, she may secretly regret falling short of the media stereotype—a thin, sexy young woman in a bathing suit.

Television is far from alone in stereotyping women. Studies of children's books published in the United States in the 1940s, 1950s, and 1960s found that females were significantly underrepresented in central roles and illustrations. Virtually all female characters were portrayed as helpless, passive, incompetent, and in need of a strong male caretaker. Studies of picture books published from the 1970s through the present have found some improvement, but males still dominate the central roles. While

males are portrayed as a variety of characters, females tend to be shown mostly in traditional roles, such as mother, grandmother, or volunteer, even if they also hold nontraditional roles, such as working professional (Etaugh 2003).

The pervasiveness of these traditional gender roles extends even to education. The Sociology on Campus box considers the impact of the federal mandate called Title IX on gender equity in college athletics.

Traditional gender roles have restricted females more severely than males. This module shows how women have been confined to subordinate roles in the political and economic institutions of the United States. Yet it is also true that gender roles have restricted males.

Men's Gender Roles

Stay-at-home fathers? Until recent decades such an idea was unthinkable. Yet in a nationwide survey done in 2002, 69 percent of respondents said that if one parent stays home with the children,

Sociology on Campus

The Debate over Title IX

Few federal policies have had such a visible effect on education over the past 30 years as Title IX, which mandates gender equity in education in federally funded schools. Congressional amendments to the Education Act of 1972, together with guidelines for their implementation developed by the Department of Health, Education, and Welfare in 1974–1975, have brought significant changes for both men and women at all levels of schooling. Title IX eliminated sex-segregated classes, prohibited sex discrimination in admissions and financial aid, and mandated that girls receive more opportunities to play sports, in proportion to their enrollment and interest.

Under this landmark legislation, to receive federal funds, a school or college must pass one of three tests. First, the numbers of male and female athletes must be proportional to the numbers of men and women enrolled at the school. Second, lacking that, the school must show a continuing history of expanding opportunities for female athletes. Or third, the school must demonstrate that the level of female participation in sports meets female students' level of interest or ability.

Today, Title IX is still one of the more controversial attempts ever made by the federal government to promote equality for all citizens. Its consequences for the funding of college athletics programs are hotly debated, while its real and lasting effects on college admissions and employment are often forgotten. Critics charge that men's teams have suffered from proportional funding of

> Critics charge that men's teams have suffered from proportional funding of women's teams and athletic scholarships.

women's teams and athletic scholarships, since schools with tight athletic budgets can expand women's sports only at the expense of men's sports.

To a certain extent, non-revenue-producing men's sports such as wrestling and golf do appear to have suffered as women's teams have been added. But the high expense of some men's sports, particularly football, would be beyond many schools' means even without Title IX expenditures. And the gains for women have more than made up for the losses to men. In 1971, when there were few opportunities for women athletes on college campuses, 300,000 girls participated in high school sports. In 2004, more than three decades after Title IX opened college athletics to women, the figure was 2.6 million.

For minority women, however, the results have been less satisfactory. Most of the women's sports that have benefited from increases in scholarships over the past 20 years, like rowing, lacrosse,

and volleyball, traditionally have not attracted minority women. Twenty-five years ago, just 2 percent of female college athletes were African American. Today, the percentage is a disappointing 2.7 percent.

Sociologists note, too, that the social effects of sports on college campuses are not all positive. Michael A. Messner, professor of sociology at the University of Southern California, points to some troubling results of a survey by the Women's Sports Foundation. The study shows that teenage girls who play sports simply for fun have more positive body images than girls who don't play sports. But those who are "highly involved" in sports are more likely than other girls to take steroids and to become binge drinkers and risk takers. "Everyone has tacitly agreed, it seems, to view men's sports as the standard to which women should strive to have equal access," Messner writes. He is skeptical of a system that propels a lucky few college athletes to stardom each year while leaving the majority, many of them African American, without a career or an education. Certainly that was not the kind of equal opportunity legislators envisioned when they wrote Title IX.

LET'S DISCUSS

1. Has Title IX had an effect on you personally? If so, explain. On balance, do you think the increase in women's participation in sports has been good for society as a whole?

2. How might Title IX affect the way students and the public view gender roles?

Sources: Brady 2010; V. Gutierrez 2002; H. Mason 2003; Messner 2002; Pennington 2008; L. Smith 2007; Spencer 2008.

---

it makes no difference whether that parent is the mother or the father. Only 30 percent thought that the mother should be the one to stay home. But while people's conceptions of gender roles are obviously changing, the fact is that men who stay home to care for their children are still an unusual phenomenon. For every stay-at-home dad there are 38 stay-at-home moms (Jason Fields 2004:11–12; Robison 2002).

While attitudes toward parenting may be changing, studies show little change in the traditional male gender role. Men's roles are socially constructed in much the same way as women's are. Family, peers, and the media all influence how a boy or man comes to view his appropriate role in society. The male gender role, besides being antifeminine (no "sissy stuff"), includes proving one's masculinity at work and sports—often by using force in

dealing with others—as well as initiating and controlling all sexual relations.

Males who do not conform to the socially constructed gender role face constant criticism and even humiliation, both from children when they are boys and from adults as men. It can be agonizing to be treated as a "chicken" or a "sissy" as a youth—particularly if such remarks come from one's father or brothers. And grown men who pursue nontraditional occupations, such as preschool teaching or nursing, must constantly deal with others' misgivings and strange looks. In one study, interviewers found that such men frequently had to alter their behavior in order to minimize others' negative reactions. One 35-year-old nurse reported that he had to claim he was "a carpenter or something like that" when he "went clubbing," because women weren't interested in getting to know a male nurse. The subjects made similar accommodations in casual exchanges with other men (Cross and Bagilhole 2002:215).

At the same time, boys who successfully adapt to cultural standards of masculinity may grow up to be inexpressive men who cannot share their feelings with others. They remain forceful and tough, but as a result they are also closed and isolated. In fact, a small but growing body of scholarship suggests that for men as well as women, traditional gender roles may be disadvantageous. In many communities across the nation, girls seem to outdo boys in high school, grabbing a disproportionate share of the leadership positions, from valedictorian to class president to yearbook editor—everything, in short, except captain of the boys' athletic teams. Their advantage continues after high school. In the 1980s, girls in the United States became more likely than boys to go to college. By 2006, women accounted for over 57 percent of college students nationwide. And in 2002, for the first time, more women than men in the United States earned doctoral degrees (Bureau of the Census 2008a:174).

Aside from these disadvantages, many men find that traditional masculinity does not serve them well in the job market. The growth of a service economy over the past two generations has created a demand for skills, attitudes, and behaviors that are the antithesis of traditional masculinity. Increasingly, this sector is the place where low-skilled men must look for jobs. As a recent British study showed, many out-of-work men are reluctant to engage in the kind of sensitive, deferential behavior required by service sector jobs (D. Nixon 2009).

In the past 40 years, inspired in good part by the contemporary feminist movement (examined in Module 35), increasing numbers of men in the United States have criticized the restrictive aspects of the traditional male gender role. Some men have taken strong public positions in support of women's struggle for full equality and have even organized voluntary associations for the purpose. However, their actions have been countered by other men who feel they are unfairly penalized by laws related to alimony, child support and custody, family violence, and affirmative action (Kimmel 2008; National Organization for Men Against Sexism 2009).

Recent research on gender roles has shown that in fact there is no single, simple characterization of the male gender role. Australian sociologist R. W. Connell (1987, 2002, 2005) has spoken of **multiple masculinities,** meaning that men play a variety of gender roles, including a nurturing-caring role and an effeminate-gay role, in addition to their traditional gender role of dominating women. Nevertheless,

Conventional notions of femininity, masculinity, and gender roles do not begin to address the complexities of contemporary society. Consider transgendered persons, whose current gender identity no longer matches their physical identity at birth.

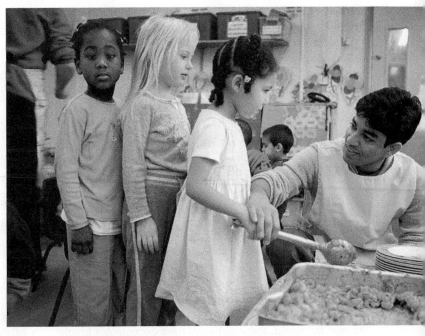

Gender roles serve to discourage men from entering certain low-paying female-dominated occupations, such as child care. Only 5 percent of day care workers are male.

society reinforces their traditional, dominating role more than any other role (Schrock and Schwalbe 2009).

One example of multiple masculinities is the difference between the roles of extremely advantaged men with high-status positions and those of working-class men, whose roles are not necessarily devalued, but afford fewer opportunities for advancement. For example, an analysis of the attack on the World Trade Center on September 11, 2001, contrasts the roles of men from different social classes. Consider the relatively modest status of first responders to the disaster compared with the high status of the affluent managerial professionals who worked at the trade center. Many of the first responders lost their lives rescuing the high-status men in upper-echelon positions in finance and investment banking. One can only imagine the firefighters climbing up the stairwells as the financiers made their way down (Langewiesche 2002).

Gender and Human Sexuality

As we saw in Module 24, society uses labels to condone or sanction specific sexual behaviors. Traditionally, those labels have derived from very definite gender-role distinctions, which are independent and do not overlap. Separating gender from sex is of course impossible. Yet it would be incorrect simply to equate males with stereotypically masculine expressions of sexuality, or females with stereotypically feminine expressions of sexuality.

Over time, social norms regarding sexual behavior have changed as gender roles have changed, becoming more ambiguous. Today, popularly coined words like *metrosexual* and *bromance* suggest that men should feel comfortable embracing traditionally feminine tastes or developing deep friendships with other men. Similarly, society is beginning to accept, not only same-sex couples, but individuals whose gender and identity do not fit a simple either/or pattern, such as bisexuals and transgendered people.

 use your **sociological imagination**

What evidence can you see of women's changing roles over the past few generations?

Cross-Cultural Perspective

To what extent do actual biological differences between the sexes contribute to the cultural differences associated with gender? This question brings us back to the debate over "nature versus nurture." In assessing the alleged and real differences between men and women, it is useful to examine cross-cultural data.

Around the world, anthropologists have documented highly diverse constructions of gender that do not always conform to our ideals of masculinity and femininity. Beginning with the pathbreaking work of Margaret Mead ([1935] 2001) and continuing through contemporary fieldwork, these scholars have shown that gender roles can vary greatly from one physical environment, economy, and political system to the next. Peggy Reeves Sanday's (2002, 2008) work in West Sumatra, Indonesia, for example, describes the 4-million-member Minangkabau society as one in which men and women are not competitors, but partners for the common good. This society is based on a nurturing approach to the environment, blended with Islamic religious ethics. Women control the land through inheritance; in the event of a divorce, the ex-husband leaves with only his clothes. The larger community may be governed by men, women, or both men and women working together. Sanday's findings, together with Mead's, confirm the influential role of culture and socialization in gender-role differentiation. There appear to be no innate or biologically determined gender roles for men and women.

In any society, gender stratification requires, not only individual socialization into traditional gender roles within the family, but the promotion and support of those traditional roles by other social institutions, such as religion and education. Moreover, even with all major institutions socializing the young into conventional gender roles, every society has women and men who resist and successfully oppose the stereotypes: strong women who become leaders or professionals, gentle men who care for children, and so forth. It seems clear that differences between the sexes are not dictated by biology. Indeed, the maintenance of traditional gender roles requires constant social controls—and those controls are not always effective.

We can see the social construction of gender roles in process in societies strained by war and social upheaval. By summer 2004, a year after the war in Iraq began, young girls in Baghdad seldom ventured out to the park or swimming pool. When they did, their parents made sure they were dressed conservatively, in loose clothing and perhaps a head scarf. The overthrow of Saddam Hussein's

Gender roles vary considerably from one country to another. After studying the Minangkabau women of West Sumatra, Indonesia, anthropologist Peggy Reeves Sanday concluded that they wield more authority than the supposedly emancipated women of North America and Europe.

secular regime had emboldened Islamic fundamentalists, who had begun visiting schools, urging young women to wear long sleeves and cover their heads. Though school officials resisted, many girls dropped out, some out of fear for their safety and others because of financial hardship. In the atmosphere of violence and lawlessness that followed the 2003 occupation, young women wondered what the future would hold for them, and whether they would ever have the opportunity to become educated professionals, as their mothers had (Sengupta 2004).

 use your **sociological imagination**

Has exposure to different cultures introduced you to different gender roles? If so, describe them.

Sociological Perspectives on Gender

Cross-cultural studies indicate that societies dominated by men are much more common than those in which women play the decisive role. Sociologists have turned to all the major theoretical perspectives to understand how and why these social distinctions are established. Each approach focuses on culture rather than biology as the primary determinant of gender differences. Yet, in other respects, advocates of these sociological perspectives disagree widely.

Functionalist View

Functionalists maintain that gender differentiation has contributed to overall social stability. Sociologists Talcott Parsons and Robert Bales (1955) argued that to function most effectively, the family requires adults who specialize in particular roles. They viewed the traditional gender roles as arising out of the need to establish a division of labor between marital partners.

Parsons and Bales contended that women take the expressive, emotionally supportive role and men the instrumental, practical role, with the two complementing each other. **Expressiveness** denotes concern for the maintenance of harmony and the internal emotional affairs of the family. **Instrumentality** refers to an emphasis on tasks, a focus on more distant goals, and a concern for the external relationship between one's family and other social institutions. According to this theory, women's interest in expressive goals frees men for instrumental tasks, and vice versa. Women become anchored in the family as wives, mothers, and household managers; men become anchored in the occupational world outside the home. Of course, Parsons and Bales offered this framework in the 1950s, when many more women were full-time homemakers than is true today. These theorists did not explicitly endorse traditional gender roles, but they implied that dividing tasks between spouses was functional for the family as a unit.

Given the typical socialization of women and men in the United States, the functionalist view is initially persuasive. However, it would lead us to expect girls and women who have no interest in children to become babysitters and mothers. Similarly, males who love spending time with children might be programmed into careers in the business world. Such differentiation might harm the individual who does not fit into prescribed roles, as well as deprive society of the contributions of many talented people who feel confined by gender stereotyping. Moreover, the functionalist approach does not convincingly explain why men should be assigned categorically to the instrumental role and women to the expressive role.

Conflict Response

Viewed from a conflict perspective, the functionalist approach masks the underlying power relations between men and women. Parsons and Bales never explicitly presented the expressive and instrumental roles as being of unequal value to society, yet their inequality is quite evident. Although social institutions may pay lip service to women's expressive skills, men's instrumental skills are more highly rewarded, whether in terms of money or prestige. Consequently, according to feminists and conflict theorists, any division of labor by gender into instrumental and expressive tasks is far from neutral in its impact on women.

Conflict theorists contend that the relationship between females and males has traditionally been one of unequal power, with men in a dominant position over women. Men may originally have

Conflict theorists emphasize that men's work is uniformly valued, while women's work (whether unpaid labor in the home or wage labor) is devalued. This woman is assembling computer parts in a factory in Austin, Texas.

become powerful in preindustrial times because their size, physical strength, and freedom from childbearing duties allowed them to dominate women physically. In contemporary societies, such considerations are not so important, yet cultural beliefs about the sexes are long established, as anthropologist Margaret Mead and feminist sociologist Helen Mayer Hacker (1951, 1974) both stressed. Such beliefs support a social structure that places males in controlling positions.

Conflict theorists, then, see gender differences as a reflection of the subjugation of one group (women) by another group (men). If we use an analogy to Marx's analysis of class conflict, we can say that males are like the bourgeoisie, or capitalists; they control most of the society's wealth, prestige, and power. Females are like the proletariat, or workers; they can acquire valuable resources only by following the dictates of their bosses. Men's work is uniformly valued; women's work (whether unpaid labor in the home or wage labor) is devalued.

Feminist Perspective

A significant component of the conflict approach to gender stratification draws on feminist theory. Although use of the term *feminist theory* is comparatively recent, the critique of women's position in society and culture goes back to some of the earliest works that have influenced sociology. Among the most important are Mary Wollstonecraft's *A Vindication of the Rights of Women* (originally published in 1792), John Stuart Mill's *The Subjection of Women* (originally published in 1869), and Friedrich Engels's *The Origin of the Family, Private Property, and the State* (originally published in 1884).

Engels, a close associate of Karl Marx, argued that women's subjugation coincided with the rise of private property during industrialization. Only when people moved beyond an agrarian economy could males enjoy the luxury of leisure and withhold rewards and privileges from women. Drawing on the work of Marx and Engels, many contemporary feminist theorists view women's subordination as part of the overall exploitation and injustice that they see as inherent in capitalist societies. Some

FIGURE 34-1 Matrix of Domination

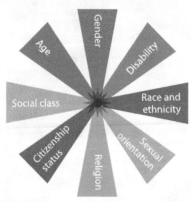

Source: Developed by author.

The matrix of domination illustrates how several social factors, including gender, social class, and race and ethnicity, can converge to create a cumulative impact on a person's social standing.

radical feminist theorists, however, view the oppression of women as inevitable in *all* male-dominated societies, whether they are labeled capitalist, socialist, or communist (L. Feuer 1989; Tuchman 1992; Tucker 1978: 734–759).

Feminist sociologists would find little to disagree with in the conflict theorists' perspective, but are more likely to embrace a political agenda. Feminists would also argue that until recently, the very discussion of women and society, however well meant, was distorted by the exclusion of women from academic thought, including sociology. We have noted the many accomplishments of Jane Addams and Ida Wells-Barnett, but they generally worked outside the discipline, focusing on what we would now call applied sociology and social work. At the time, their efforts, while valued as humanitarian, were seen as unrelated to the research and conclusions being reached in academic circles, which of course were male academic circles (Andersen 2007; J. Howard 1999).

Contemporary feminists recognize the differential treatment of some women, not only because of their gender, but also because of their race, ethnicity, and socioeconomic status. Simply put, Whites dominate these poor, non-White women because they are non-White; men dominate them because they are women; and the affluent dominate them because they are poor. The African American feminist theorist Patricia Hill Collins (2000) has termed the convergence of social forces that contributes to the subordinate status of these low-status women the **matrix of domination** (Figure 34-1).

Gender, race, and social class are not the only sources of oppression in the United States, though they profoundly affect women and people of color. Other forms of categorization and stigmatization that might be included in the matrix are sexual orientation, religion, disability, and age. If we apply the matrix to the world as a whole, we might add citizenship status or perceived colonial or neocolonial status to the list (Winant 2006).

Though feminists have addressed themselves to the needs of minority women, these women are oppressed much more by their race and ethnicity than by their gender. The question for Latinas (Hispanic women), African American women, Asian American women, and Native American women appears to be whether they should unite with their brothers against racism or challenge them for their sexism. The answer is that our society must eradicate both sexism and racism (Beisel and Kay 2004; Breines 2007; C. Epstein 1999).

The discussion of gender roles among African Americans has always provoked controversy. Advocates of Black nationalism contend that feminism only distracts women from participating fully in the African American struggle. The existence of feminist groups among Blacks, in their view, simply divides the Black community, thereby serving the dominant White majority. In contrast, Black feminists such as bell hooks (1994) argue that little is to be gained by accepting the gender-role divisions of the dominant society, which place women in a separate, subservient position. Though the media commonly portray Black women in a negative light—as illiterates, welfare queens, or prostitutes—Black feminists emphasize that it is not solely Whites and the White-dominated media who focus on such negative images. Black men (most recently, Black male rap artists) have also portrayed Black women in a negative way (Raybon 1989; Threadcraft 2008).

Historically, Native Americans stand out as an exception to the patriarchal tradition in North America. At the time of the European settlers' arrival, Native American gender roles varied greatly from tribe to tribe. Southern tribes, for reasons unclear to today's scholars, were usually matriarchal and traced their descent through the mother. European missionaries, who sought to make the native peoples more like Europeans, set out to transform this arrangement, which was not entirely universal. Like members of other groups, some Native American women have resisted gender stereotypes (Marubbio 2006).

Latinas are usually considered as part of either the Hispanic or feminist movements, and their distinctive experience ignored. In the past, they have been excluded from decision making in the two social institutions that most affect their daily lives: the family and the church. Particularly in the lower class, the Hispanic family suffers from the pervasive tradition of male domination. And the Catholic Church relegates women to supportive roles, while reserving the leadership positions for men (Browne 2001; De Anda 2004).

Prior to this module, much of our discussion has focused on the social effects of race and ethnicity, coupled with poverty, low incomes, and meager wealth. The matrix of domination highlights the confluence of these factors with gender discrimination, which we must include to fully understand the plight of women of color.

use your **sociological imagination**

Which elements of the matrix of domination privilege you? Which place you at a disadvantage?

Interactionist Approach

While functionalists and conflict theorists who study gender stratification typically focus on macro-level social forces and institutions, interactionist researchers tend to examine gender stratification on the micro level of everyday behavior. The key to this approach is the way gender is socially constructed in everyday interactions. We "do gender" by reinforcing traditionally masculine and feminine actions. For example, a man "does masculinity" by opening a door for his girlfriend; she "does femininity" by consenting to his assistance. Obviously, the social construction of gender goes beyond these relatively trivial rituals. Interactionists recognize, too, that people can challenge traditional gender roles. A female golfer who uses the men's tees and a man who actively arranges a birthday luncheon at work are redoing gender (Deutsch 2007; West and Zimmerman 1987).

One continuing subject of investigation is the role of gender in cross-sex conversations (sometimes referred to as "crosstalk"), specifically the idea that men interrupt women more than women interrupt men. Interestingly, empirical research does

summing up

Table **34-2** Sociological Perspectives on Gender

Theoretical Perspective	Emphasis
Functionalist	Gender differentiation contributes to social stability
Conflict	Gender inequality is rooted in the female–male power relationship
Feminist	Women's subjugation is integral to society and social structure
Interactionist	Gender distinctions and "doing gender" are reflected in people's everyday behavior

not clearly support this assertion. True, people in positions of authority or status—who are much more likely to be male than female—dominate interpersonal conversations. That does not necessarily mean that women per se cannot be heard, however. Future research results may deemphasize the clichéd advice that women must speak up and focus instead on the situational structures that cast men in dominant positions (Cameron 2007; Hyde 2005; Tannen 1990).

Table 34-2 summarizes the major sociological perspectives on gender.

MODULE 34 | Recap and Review

Summary

Gender is an ascribed status that provides a basis for social differentiation. This module examines the social construction of gender and theories of stratification by gender.

1. In the United States, the social construction of gender continues to define significantly different expectations for females and males.

2. **Gender roles** show up in our work and behavior and in how we react to others. Throughout history, these roles have constricted women much more than they have men.

3. Though men may exhibit a variety of different gender roles, or **multiple masculinities,** society reinforces their traditional role of dominating women.

4. Anthropological research points to the importance of cultural conditioning in defining the social roles of males and females.

5. Functionalists maintain that sex differentiation contributes to overall social stability, but conflict theorists charge that the relationship between females and males is one of unequal power, with men dominating women. This dominance shows up in people's everyday interactions.

6. Many women experience differential treatment, not only because of their gender but because of their race, ethnicity, and social class. This convergence of social forces is called the **matrix of domination.**

7. As an example of their micro-level approach to the study of gender stratification, interactionists have analyzed men's verbal dominance over women through conversational interruption.

Thinking Critically

1. Compare the social construction of gender with the social construction of race.

2. Which aspects of the functionalist and conflict perspectives on gender make the most sense to you? Explain.

Key Terms

Expressiveness

Gender role

Homophobia

Instrumentality

Matrix of domination

Multiple masculinities

Many people, both male and female, find it difficult to conceive of women as a subordinate and oppressed group. Yet take a look at the political structure of the United States: women remain noticeably underrepresented. As of mid-2009, for example, only 6 of the nation's 50 states had a female governor (Arizona, Connecticut, Hawaii, Michigan, North Carolina, and Washington).

Women have made slow but steady progress in certain political arenas. In 1981, out of 535 members of Congress, there were only 21 women: 19 in the House of Representatives and 2 in the Senate. In contrast, the Congress that held office in mid-2010 had 90 women: 73 in the House and 17 in the Senate. Yet the membership and leadership of Congress remain overwhelmingly male (Center for American Women and Politics 2010).

In October 1981, Sandra Day O'Connor was sworn in as the nation's first female Supreme Court justice. Still, no woman has ever served as president of the United States, vice president, or chief justice of the Supreme Court.

Our society is run by male-dominated institutions, yet with the power that flows to men come responsibility and stress. Men have higher reported rates of certain types of mental illness than women, and a greater likelihood of death due to heart attack or stroke. The pressure on men to succeed, and then to remain on top in the competitive world of work, can be especially intense. That is not to suggest that gender stratification is as damaging to men as it is to women. But it is clear that the power and privilege men enjoy are no guarantee of personal well-being.

 use your sociological imagination

Think of organizations or institutions you belong to whose leadership positions are customarily held by men. What would those organizations be like if they were led by women?

Sexism and Sex Discrimination

Just as African Americans are victimized by racism, women in our society are victimized by sexism. **Sexism** is the ideology that one sex is superior to the other. The term is generally used to refer to male prejudice and discrimination against women. In Module 31, we noted that Blacks can suffer from both individual acts of racism and institutional discrimination. **Institutional discrimination** was defined as the denial of opportunities and equal rights to individuals and groups that results from the normal operations of a society. In the same sense, women suffer from both individual acts of sexism (such as sexist remarks and acts of violence) and institutional sexism.

It is not simply that particular men in the United States are biased in their treatment of women. All the major institutions of our society—including the government, armed forces, large corporations, the media, universities, and the medical establishment—are controlled by men. These institutions, in their normal, day-to-day operations, often discriminate against women and perpetuate sexism. For example, if the central office of a nationwide bank sets a policy that single women are a bad risk for loans—regardless of their incomes and investments—that bank will discriminate against women in state after state. It will do so even at branches where loan officers hold no personal biases toward women, but are merely "following orders."

The Status of Women Worldwide

A detailed overview of the status of the world's women, issued by the United Nations in 2001, noted that women and men live in two different worlds. In too many nations women are denied equal pay, sexually harassed at work, or dismissed from their jobs because they are pregnant. These abuses happen even in places where such treatment is prohibited by law. Women who assert their rights are routinely ignored or even punished for their protests. To achieve gender equality, the report concludes, society must hold the powerful accountable to women (United Nations Development Fund for Women 2009).

This critique applies to Western as well as non-Western countries. Although Westerners tend to view some societies—for example, Muslim countries—as being particularly harsh toward women, that perception is actually an overgeneralization. Muslim countries are exceedingly varied and complex and do not often fit the stereotypes created by the Western media. For a detailed discussion of the status of Muslim women today, see the Sociology in the Global Community box.

Regardless of culture, however, women everywhere suffer from second-class status. It is estimated that women grow half the world's food, but they rarely own land. They constitute one-third of the world's paid labor force, but are generally found

Sociology in the Global Community

The Head Scarf and the Veil: Complex Symbols

The wearing of a veil or head scarf by women is common to many but not all Middle Eastern societies. However, Muslim women are not alone in their observance of certain standards for dress. All Muslims, men and women alike, are expected to cover themselves and avoid revealing clothes designed to accentuate the body's contours or emphasize its physical beauty. The Koran does permit Muslims to wear revealing garments in private, with their families or with members of the same sex.

The Prophet Muhammad recommended that women cover all of their bodies except for the face, hands, and feet. The Koran adds that a woman's headcovering should fall over the neck and upper chest. A variety of women's outergarments comply with these guidelines for modest attire; collectively, they are referred to as the *hijab*. Face veils are dictated by cultural tradition, however—not by Islam.

> In effect, the veil represents a rejection of the beauty myth, which is so prevalent in Western societies.

In effect, the veil represents a rejection of the beauty myth (see Module 24), which is so prevalent in Western societies. By covering themselves almost completely, Muslim women assure themselves and their families that their physical appearance will not play a role in their contacts outside the family. Rather, these women will be known only for their faith, their intellect, and their personalities.

In the 20th century, the veil was politicized by modernization movements that pitted Western cultural values against traditional Islamic values. In Turkey, for instance, in the early 20th century, government officials attempted to subordinate traditional ethnic and religious influences to their nationalistic goals. Though women weren't forbidden to wear the veil, they were not allowed to veil themselves in public places like schools. Not surprisingly, many Muslims resented these forced social changes.

In the United States today, Muslim women select from an array of traditional garments, including a long, loose tailored coat and a loose black overgarment that is worn with a scarf or perhaps a face veil. However, they are just as apt to wear an overblouse and a long skirt or loose pants, which they can buy at local clothing stores.

Researchers have identified three perspectives on the *hijab* among Muslim women in the United States and other non-Islamic countries. Younger, better-educated women who support wearing the *hijab* in public draw on Western ideas of individual rights, arguing in favor of veiling as a form of personal expression. In contrast, older, less-well-educated women who support the *hijab* do so without referring to Western ideology; they cannot see why veiling should be an issue. A third group of women, of all ages and educational backgrounds, opposes the *hijab*.

In some non-Muslim countries, notably France, officials have come under fire for banning the *hijab*, or the head scarf, in public schools. The custom generally has not been an issue in the United States, though one 11-year-old had to go to federal court to establish her right to wear a head scarf at school in

The head scarf—an expression of modesty, a woman's right as an individual, or a sign of oppression?

Muskogee, Oklahoma. Interestingly, the U.S. Department of Justice supported her lawsuit.

LET'S DISCUSS

1. Consider life in a society in which women wear veils. Can you see any advantages, from the woman's point of view? From the man's?

2. Do you find the Western emphasis on physical beauty oppressive? If so, in what ways?

Sources: Al-Jadda 2006; Gurbuz and Gurbuz-Kucuksari 2009; Haq 2009; Killian 2003; C. Murphy 2009; Selod 2008b.

---

in the lowest-paying jobs. Single-parent households headed by women, which appear to be on the rise in many nations, are typically found in the poorest sections of the population. The feminization of poverty has become a global phenomenon. As in the United States, women around the world are underrepresented politically.

Despite these challenges, women are not responding passively. They are mobilizing, individually and collectively. Given the significant underrepresentation of women in government offices and national legislatures, however, the task is difficult, as we shall see in Module 47.

Not surprisingly, there is a link between the wealth of industrialized nations and the poverty of women in developing countries. Viewed from a conflict perspective or through the lens of Immanuel Wallerstein's world systems analysis, the economies of developing nations are controlled and exploited by industrialized countries and multinational corporations based in those countries. Much of the exploited labor in developing nations, especially in the nonindustrial sector, is performed by women. Women workers typically toil long hours for low pay, but contribute significantly to their families' incomes (Chubb et al. 2008).

FIGURE 35-1 **Gender Inequality in Industrial Nations**

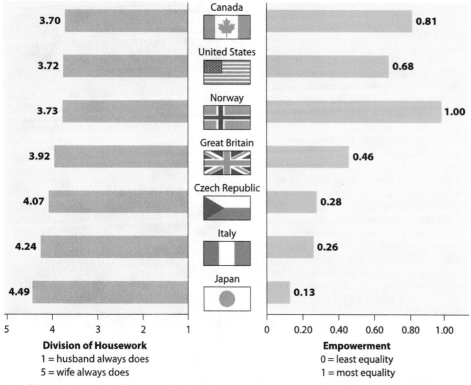

		Division of Housework	Empowerment
Canada		3.70	0.81
United States		3.72	0.68
Norway		3.73	1.00
Great Britain		3.92	0.46
Czech Republic		4.07	0.28
Italy		4.24	0.26
Japan		4.49	0.13

Division of Housework
1 = husband always does
5 = wife always does

Empowerment
0 = least equality
1 = most equality

Notes: Housework includes laundry, grocery shopping, dinner preparation, and care for sick family members. Empowerment includes the proportions of women in parliament, in management, and in professional/technical positions, as well as gender inequality in income.
Source: Adapted from Fuwa 2004:757.

Striking differences exist in women's empowerment—that is, the percentage of women in leadership positions—from one country to the next (right). Yet there is much less difference in the division of housework, even in the same countries (left).

In industrial countries, women's unequal status can be seen in the division of housework, as well as in the jobs they hold and the pay they earn. Sociologist Makiko Fuwa (2004) analyzed gender inequality in 22 industrial countries using data from the

International Social Survey Programme. Fuwa looked first at how couples divided their housework. Then she compared that data to society-wide measures of women's presence in high-status occupations, as well as their wages relative to men's. Figure 35-1 shows that while gender differences in empowerment vary widely from one country to the next, equality between the sexes is rare.

Women in the Workforce of the United States

More than 30 years ago, the U.S. Commission on Civil Rights (1976:1) concluded that the passage in the Declaration of Independence proclaiming that "all men are created equal" has been taken too literally for too long—especially with respect to women's opportunities for employment. In this section we will see how gender bias has limited women's opportunities for employment outside the home, at the same time that it forces them to carry a disproportionate burden inside the home.

Labor Force Participation

Women's participation in the paid labor force of the United States increased steadily throughout the 20th century and into the 21st century (Figure 35-2). Today, millions of women—married or single, with or without children, pregnant or recently having given birth—are working in the labor force. Overall, 60 percent of adult women in the United States were in the labor force in 2008, compared to 41 percent in 1970 (Bureau of the Census 2009a:375, 377). (The data for men are 73 percent in 2008, compared to 76 percent in 1970.)

Still, women entering the job market find their options restricted in important ways. Particularly damaging is occupational segregation, or confinement to sex-typed "women's jobs." For example, in 2008, women accounted for 98 percent of all dental hygienists and 84 percent of all librarians. Entering such sex-typed occupations places women in "service" roles that parallel the traditional gender-role standard under which housewives "serve" their husbands.

Women are *underrepresented* in occupations historically defined as "men's jobs," which often carry much greater financial rewards and prestige than women's jobs. For example, in 2008, women accounted for approximately 46 percent of the paid labor force of the United States, yet they constituted only 10 percent of civil engineers, 28 percent of computer systems analysts, and 31 percent of physicians (Table 35-1).

trend|spotting

Working Mothers

Women in the labor force, either working or seeking employment, is an established fact in the United States. So too is the participation of women with young children. Such was not always the case, however. Forty years ago only 30 percent of married mothers with children under age 6 were working outside the home. By 1995—just 25 years later—that proportion had more than doubled. For married mothers, work outside the home has been the norm ever since.

This rising trend has also affected single mothers, whose labor force participation has always been high. In 1970 the proportion of single mothers of preschoolers who worked outside the home was 52 percent—22 percent higher than for married mothers of young children. Today the proportion has climbed to 72 percent.

Another way to look at these statistics is to note the narrowing gap between the two groups' participation rates. Today, a married woman with at least one child under age 6 is *more likely to be working* than a single mother was in 1970.

FIGURE 35-2 Trends in U.S. Women's Participation in the Paid Labor Force, 1890–2008

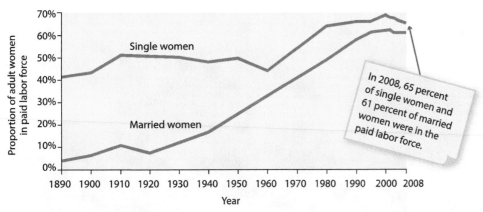

Sources: Bureau of the Census 1975, 2009a:377.

Such occupational segregation is not unique to the United States but typical of industrial countries. In Great Britain, for example, only 29 percent of computer analysts are women, while 81 percent of cashiers and 90 percent of nurses are women (Cross and Bagilhole 2002).

Women from all groups and men from minority groups sometimes encounter attitudinal or organizational bias that prevents them from reaching their full potential. As we saw in Module 31, the term **glass ceiling** refers to an invisible barrier that blocks the promotion of a qualified individual in a work environment because of the individual's gender, race, or ethnicity. A study of the *Fortune* 500 largest corporations in the United States

showed that in 2008, barely 15 percent of the seats on their boards of directors were held by women. Furthermore, less than 7 percent of the top earners were female (Catalyst 2009a, 2009b; Kalev 2009).

This type of inequality is not unique to the United States. Worldwide, women hold less than 1 percent of corporate managerial positions. In recognition of the underrepresentation of women on boards of directors, the Norwegian legislature established minimum quotas for the number of female board members. As the architects of the plan put it, "instead of assuming what people *can't* do at work, provide opportunities for employees to prove what they can do." The goal was not complete equity for women, but 40 percent representation by 2008. The percentage in Norway now stands at 36—much higher than Europe's average of 9 percent. About one in six of Norway's biggest companies have failed to meet the quota, however, and a handful still have no women on their boards (Center for Corporate Diversity 2008; Fouché 2008; Goering 2008).

Compensation

He works. She works. Both are physicians—a high-status occupation with considerable financial rewards. He makes $140,000. She makes $88,000.

These median earnings for physicians in the United States were released by the Census Bureau in 2004. They are typical of the results of the bureau's detailed study of occupations and income. Take air traffic controllers. He makes $67,000; she makes $56,000. Or housekeepers: he makes $19,000; she makes $15,000. What about teachers' assistants? He makes $20,000; she makes $15,000. Statisticians at the bureau looked at the median earnings for no fewer than 821 occupations ranging from dishwasher to chief executive. After adjusting for workers' ages, education, and work experience, they came to an unmistakable conclusion: across the board, there is a substantial gender gap in the median earnings of full-time workers.

Men do not always earn more than women for doing the same work. Researchers at the Census Bureau found 2 occupations out of 821 in which women typically earn about 1 percent more income than men: hazardous materials recovery and telecommunications line installation. These two occupations employed less than 1 out of every 1,000 workers the bureau studied. Forecasting analyses show no convincing evidence that the wage gap is narrowing.

Table **35-1** U.S. Women in Selected Occupations: Women As a Percentage of All Workers in the Occupation

Underrepresented		Overrepresented	
Aircraft pilots	3%	High school teachers	56%
Firefighters	5	Cashiers	76
Civil engineers	10	Social workers	79
Police officers	15	Elementary teachers	81
Clergy	15	File clerks	84
Chefs and head cooks	17	Librarians	84
Gaming service workers	21	Tellers	85
Dentists	27	Registered nurses	92
Computer systems analysts	28	Word processors and typists	93
Physicians	31	Receptionists	94
Mail carriers	33	Child care workers	96
Lawyers	34	Dental hygienists	98

Note: Women constitute 47 percent of the entire labor force.

Source: Data for 2008 reported in Bureau of the Census 2009a:387–389.

Give Me a Male Boss, Please

As women increased their presence in the managerial ranks from 19.7 percent in 1972 to 50.8 percent in 2008, the desirability of having a male supervisor became a topic of casual conversation. Numerous studies suggest that compared to all the other social factors present in the workplace, the boss's gender has little effect on the nature and quality of the manager–employee relationship. However, that fact does not prevent potential workers—male or female—from preferring a male boss. National opinion polls consistently show that, in general—that is, without reference to particular people—workers prefer to take orders from a man by a two-to-one margin. If anything, women are more likely than men to prefer a male supervisor.

This preference is so strong that many people are willing to accept less pay to get a male boss. Researchers at the University of Chicago's business school asked college students who were about to graduate to consider hypothetical job opportunities at consulting firms. The positions varied in terms of their starting salary, location, paid holidays, and the boss's sex. The results showed that students' choices matched their stated preferences for

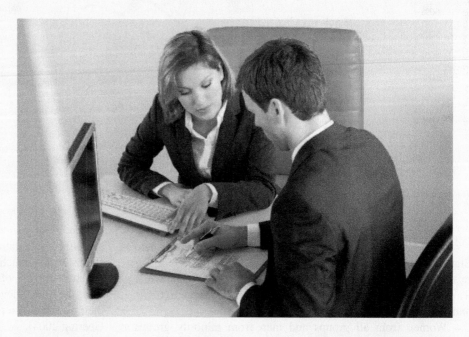

> National opinion polls consistently show that, in general, workers prefer to take orders from a man by a two-to-one margin.

salary, location, and holidays. Surprisingly, the boss's sex turned out to be a far more important variable than the other three, whether students were male or female. In a variety of scenarios describing both salary and the boss's characteristics, students chose to take a 22 percent reduction in starting salary to get a male boss.

LET'S DISCUSS

1. Have you ever worked for a female boss? If so, were you comfortable taking orders from her? Did you notice any differences in the way your boss was treated, compared to men on her level?

2. What might explain the strong preference for a male boss? Do you expect this preference to remain stable or disappear over time? Explain.

Sources: Bureau of the Census 2009a:386; Bureau of Labor Statistics 2003; Caruso et al. 2009; N. Gibbs 2009:31; Powell 2010; Whittaker 2006.

What accounts for these yawning wage gaps between men and women in the same occupation? Scholars at the Census Bureau studied the following characteristics of men and women in the same occupation:

- Age and degree of formal education
- Marital status and the presence of children at home
- Specialization within the occupation (for example, family practice versus surgical practice)
- Years of work experience
- Hours worked per year

Taking all these factors into consideration reduced the pay gap between men and women by only 3 cents. Women still earned 80 cents for every dollar earned by men. In sum, the disparity in pay between men and women cannot be explained by pointing to women's career choices (Government Accountability Office 2003; Weinberg 2004, 2007).

Legally, sex discrimination in wage payments is difficult to prove. Witness the case of former Goodyear worker Lilly Ledbetter, who learned 19 years after she was hired that she was being paid less than men doing the same job. Ledbetter sued and was awarded damages, only to have the Supreme Court overturn the decision on the grounds that she made her claim more than six months after the first discriminatory paycheck was issued. Congress relaxed this restriction in 2009 (Pear 2009).

Not all the obstacles women face in the workplace originate with management. Unfortunately, many workers, both male and female, would prefer not to work for a woman (Research Today: Give Me a Male Boss, Please).

While women are at a disadvantage in male-dominated occupations, the same is not true for men in female-dominated occupations.

Sociologist Michelle Budig (2002) examined a national database containing career information on more than 12,000 men, collected over the course of 15 years. She found that men were uniformly advantaged in female occupations. Though male nurses, grade school teachers, and librarians may experience some scorn in the larger society, they are much more likely than women to be encouraged to become administrators. Observers of the labor force have termed this advantage for men in female-dominated occupations the *glass escalator*—quite a contrast to the glass ceiling (J. Jacobs 2003; C. L. Williams 1992, 1995).

Social Consequences of Women's Employment

Today, many women face the challenge of trying to juggle work and family. Their situation has many social consequences. For one thing, it puts pressure on child care facilities, public financing of day care, and even the fast-food industry, which provides many of the meals women used to prepare themselves. For another, it raises questions about what responsibility male wage earners have in the household.

Who does the housework when women become productive wage earners? Studies indicate that there is a clear gender gap in the performance of housework, although it has been narrowing (see Figure 35-1). Women do more housework and spend more time on child care than men do, whether on a workday or a nonworkday. Taken together, then, a woman's workday on and off the job is much longer than a man's (Sayer et al. 2004).

Sociologist Arlie Hochschild (1989, 1990, 2005) has used the phrase **second shift** to describe the double burden—work outside the home followed by child care and housework—that many women face and few women share equitably. Unfortunately, today's workplace is becoming a 24/7 virtual office thanks to the advent of mobile information technologies. As these devices take over what little personal time employees have left, the physical toll on women becomes even more burdensome.

What is life like for these women? On the basis of interviews with and observations of 52 couples over an eight-year period, Hochschild reports that the wives (and not their husbands) drive home from the office while planning domestic schedules and play dates for children—and then begin their second shift. Drawing on national studies, she concludes that women spend 15 fewer hours each week in leisure activities than their husbands. In a year, these women work an extra month of 24-hour days because of the second shift; over a dozen years, they work an extra year of 24-hour days. Hochschild found that the married couples she studied were fraying at the edges, and so were their careers and their marriages. With such reports in mind, many feminists have advocated greater governmental and corporate support for child care, more

FIGURE 35-3 **Why Leave Work?**

Five Top Reasons for Leaving

Women	Reason	Men
44%	Family time	12%
16%	Change in career	29%
23%	Earn a degree, other training	25%
17%	Work not enjoyable, satisfying	24%
*	Not interested in field	18%
17%	Moved away	*

* Not one of top 5 reasons

Note: Based on a representative Harris Interactive survey of "highly qualified" workers, defined as those with a graduate degree, a professional degree, or a high honors undergraduate degree.
Source: Figure adapted from Sylvia Ann Hewlett and Carolyn Burk Luce, 2005. "Off-Ramps and On-Ramps: Keeping Talented Women on the Road to Success," *Harvard Business Review,* March 2005. Copyright © 2005 by the Harvard Business School Publishing Corporation, all rights reserved. Reprinted by permission of *Harvard Business Review.*

flexible family leave policies, and other reforms designed to ease the burden on the nation's families (Eby et al. 2010).

The greater amounts of time women put into caring for their children, and to a lesser degree into housework, take a special toll on women who are pursuing careers. In a survey published in the *Harvard Business Review,* about 40 percent of women indicated that they had voluntarily left work for months or years, compared to only 24 percent of men. As Figure 35-3 shows, women were much more likely than men to take time off for family reasons.

Though women in the United States have a long way to go toward equality in housework, they are doing as well as or better than women in most other countries, including industrial nations. By one measure, 30 percent of the couples in U.S. households share most of the housework, compared to 4 percent in Japan, 25 percent in Great Britain, 27 percent in Sweden, and 32 percent in Canada (Geist 2005).

⬤ Emergence of a Collective Consciousness

Feminism is the belief in social, economic, and political equality for women. The feminist movement of the United States was born in upstate New York, in a town called Seneca Falls, in the summer of 1848. On July 19, the first women's rights convention began, attended by Elizabeth Cady Stanton, Lucretia Mott, and other pioneers in the struggle for women's rights. This first wave of *feminists,* as they are currently known, battled ridicule and scorn as they fought for legal and political equality for women. They were not afraid to risk controversy on behalf of their cause; in 1872, Susan B. Anthony was arrested for attempting to vote in that year's presidential election.

Abigail E. Drevs, *Former Program and Volunteer Coordinator, Y-ME Illinois*

For two and a half years Abigail Drevs served as the program and volunteer coordinator for the Illinois affiliate of Y-ME National Breast Cancer Organization. Y-ME's mission is to provide support and educational outreach through workshops and peer-led support groups, to ensure that no one faces breast cancer alone.

As the coordinator, Drevs was responsible for recruiting, training, and retaining the volunteers who staff the organization's support groups. She also presented workshops about breast cancer and how to detect it early. To make sure that services were available to all and that funding was being managed effectively, she met with community leaders and organizations, corporate partners, and medical institutions. "A typical workweek, in one word, was juggling," she says. "In a small nonprofit, few people do the work of many."

Occasionally, Drevs traveled to conferences to network with other organizations dedicated to working with certain populations of breast cancer survivors, including young women. These organizations have banded together to develop a pilot program that will address young women's concerns with intimacy and infertility after breast cancer.

In Chicago, Drevs strove to raise the awareness of breast cancer among African American women from all walks of life. "As a middle-class white woman, the issue of race had been a very academic one in my experience," she says. "I read Studs Terkel and took racial disparities curricula, but never truly understood the issues until I became immersed in the community." Drevs's experience with Y-ME helped her to understand the position of thousands of underinsured African American women in that city: "limited access to health care, distrust of the system, and the importance of their community and social networks."

Asked what insights she has drawn from her training in sociology, Drevs replies, "It reaffirmed my belief that no one perspective is the only perspective. From fundamental social theory to social conflict to developing nations, there are many ways to explain something,

and oftentimes, there is something that can be gained from each perspective."

Drevs is now working for her alma mater, Dartmouth College, as the program manager for young alumni, students, and diversity at the Office of Alumni Relations. Her advice to current students of sociology: "Even if you don't major in this, make sure to take it with you wherever you go. Many of the world's problems can be traced to not communicating properly and not understanding another group's perspective. A good basis in sociology can serve you well, no matter what you do."

LET'S DISCUSS

1. Do some research on breast cancer. Does the survival rate differ among different racial and ethnic groups? What about different social classes? Why are education and early detection important?

2. Relate what you have learned about breast cancer to what you have learned about gender. What social patterns does your research illustrate?

Ultimately, the early feminists won many victories, among them the passage and ratification of the Nineteenth Amendment to the Constitution, which granted women the right to vote in national elections beginning in 1920. But suffrage did not lead to other reforms in women's social and economic position, and in the early and middle 20th century the women's movement became a much less powerful force for social change.

The second wave of feminism in the United States emerged in the 1960s and came into full force in the 1970s. In part, the movement was inspired by three pioneering books arguing for women's rights: Simone de Beauvoir's *The Second Sex,* Betty Friedan's *The Feminine Mystique,* and Kate Millett's *Sexual Politics.* In addition, the general political activism of the 1960s led women—many of whom were working for Black civil rights or against the war in Vietnam—to reexamine their own powerlessness. The sexism often found even within allegedly progressive and radical political circles convinced many women that they needed to establish a movement for women's liberation (Breines 2007; Freeman 1973, 1975).

As more and more women became aware of sexist attitudes and practices, including attitudes they themselves had accepted through socialization into traditional gender roles, they began to challenge male dominance. A sense of sisterhood, much like the class consciousness that Marx hoped would emerge in the proletariat, became evident. Individual women identified their interests with those of the collectivity *women.* No longer were women happy in submissive, subordinate roles ("false consciousness" in Marxist terms).

National surveys done today, however, show that while women generally endorse feminist positions, they do not necessarily accept the label *feminist.* Some 57 percent of women considered themselves feminists in 1987; the proportion had dropped to about 25 percent in 2001. Feminism as a unified political cause, requiring one to accept a similar stance on everything from abortion to sexual harassment to pornography to welfare, has fallen out of favor. Both women and men prefer to express their views on these complex issues individually, rather than under a convenient umbrella like feminism. Still, feminism is very much alive in the growing acceptance of women in nontraditional roles, and even the basic acknowledgment that a married mother not only can work outside the home but perhaps *belongs* in the labor force. A majority of women say that given the choice, they would prefer to work outside the home rather than stay home and take care of a house and family, and about one-quarter of women prefer *Ms.* to *Miss* or *Mrs.* (Feminist Majority Foundation 2007; Robison 2002).

The women's movement has undertaken public protests on a wide range of issues. Feminists have endorsed passage of the equal rights amendment, government subsidies for child care (see Module 15), affirmative action for women and minorities (see Module 43), federal legislation outlawing sex discrimination in education (see Module 42), greater representation of women in government (see Module 47), and the right to a legal abortion (discussed in the Social Policy section of this module).

social policy and Gender Stratification

The Battle over Abortion from a Global Perspective

Few issues seem to stir as much intense conflict as abortion. A critical victory in the struggle for legalized abortion in the United States came in 1973, when the Supreme Court granted women the right to terminate pregnancies. This ruling, known as *Roe v. Wade*, was based on a woman's right to privacy. The Court's decision was generally applauded by pro-choice groups, which believe women should have the right to make their own decisions about their bodies and should have access to safe and legal abortions. It was bitterly condemned by those opposed to abortion. For these pro-life groups, abortion is a moral and often a religious issue. In their view, human life begins at the moment of conception, so that its termination through abortion is essentially an act of murder.

Understanding the Issue

The debate that has followed *Roe v. Wade* revolves around prohibiting abortion altogether or, at the very least, limiting it. In 1979, for example, Missouri required parental consent for minors wishing to obtain an abortion, and the Supreme Court upheld the law. Parental notification and consent have become especially sensitive issues in the debate. Pro-life activists argue that the parents of teenagers should have the right to be notified about—and to permit or prohibit—abortions. In their view, parental authority deserves full support at a time when the traditional nuclear family is embattled. However, pro-choice activists counter that many pregnant teenagers come from troubled families where they have been abused. These young women may have good reason to avoid discussing such explosive issues with their parents.

In the United States, people support a woman's right to a legal abortion, but with reservations. According to a 2009 national survey, 46 percent say that abortion should be legal in most or all cases; 44 percent say it should be illegal in most or all cases. There is no gender difference in opinion on this issue: women are just as likely as men to embrace a right-to-life orientation. In contrast, on most social issues, women take a more liberal position than men. For example, women are much more likely than men to favor gun control—see the Social Policy section in Module 25 (Pew Research Center 2009).

The United States is not alone in debating abortion. Latin American countries typically have the strictest measures against the practice, but occasionally changes occur. In 2006, while protesters took to the streets, the Nicaraguan government joined five other states (Chile, East Timor, El Salvador, Malta, and Vatican City) in outlawing all forms of abortion, including procedures performed to save a pregnant woman's life. And in 2007, Mexico loosened decade-old restrictions to permit legal abortions during the first three months, for any reason (R. Carrol 2006; Ellingwood 2008).

Applying Sociology

Sociologists see gender and social class as the defining issues surrounding abortion. That is, the intense conflict over abortion reflects broader differences over women's position in society. Feminists involved in defending abortion rights typically believe that men and women are essentially similar. They support women's full participation in work outside the home and oppose all forms of sex discrimination. Feminists also claim that pregnancy and childbirth have been socially constructed by male-centered health care systems and patriarchal religious traditions. In contrast, most antiabortion activists believe that men and women are fundamentally different. In their view, men are best suited to the public world of work, while women are best suited to the demanding and crucial task of rearing children. These activists are troubled by women's growing participation in work outside the home, which they view as destructive to the family, and ultimately to society (Lorber 2005).

In regard to social class, the first major restriction on the legal right to terminate a pregnancy affected poor people. In 1976, Congress passed the Hyde Amendment, which banned the use of Medicaid and other federal funds for abortions. The Supreme Court upheld this legislation in 1980. State laws also restrict the use of public funds for abortions (Figure 35-4).

Another obstacle facing the poor is access to abortion providers. In the face of vocal pro-life sentiment, fewer and fewer hospitals throughout the world are allowing physicians to perform abortions, except in extreme cases. To avoid controversy, many medical schools have ceased to offer training in the procedure. Moreover, some doctors who work in clinics, intimidated by death threats and murders, have stopped performing abortions. For poor people in rural areas, this reduction in service makes it more difficult to locate and travel to a facility that will accommodate their wishes. Viewed from a conflict perspective, this is one more financial burden that falls especially heavily on low-income women.

Finally, some antiabortion activists have charged that family-planning agencies and health care professionals are targeting young African American women for abortions. These pro-life proponents use the emotion-laden phrase "womb lynchings" to call attention to the issue. Abortion

FIGURE 35-4 Restrictions on Public Funding for Abortion

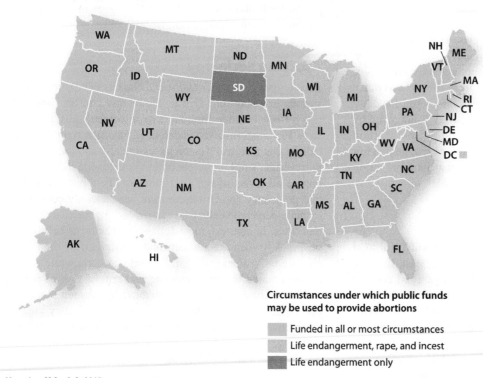

Circumstances under which public funds may be used to provide abortions

- Funded in all or most circumstances
- Life endangerment, rape, and incest
- Life endangerment only

Note: As of March 9, 2010.
Source: NARAL Pro-Choice America 2010.

rights advocates counter that the campaign falsely portrays young Black women as naive and not in control of their own decisions (Dewan 2010).

Initiating Policy

In 1973 the Supreme Court supported the general right to terminate a pregnancy by a narrow 5–4 majority. Although pro-life activists continue to hope for an overruling of *Roe v. Wade,* they have focused in the interim on weakening the decision through tactics such as limiting the use of fetal tissue in medical experiments and prohibiting certain late-term abortions, which they term "partial-birth" abortions. The Supreme Court continues to hear cases involving such restrictions. In 2005, speculation arose over a potential narrowing of the applicability of *Roe v. Wade* following the appointment of new justices, who may hold more conservative positions than those they replaced.

In 2010, the pro-choice versus pro-life controversy almost derailed passage of health care reform. To secure an additional 13 votes from Democratic congressional representatives who

oppose abortion, President Obama reluctantly agreed to sign an executive order requiring that federal funds not be used to support abortion. The order stated that federal funds would not be used to pay for abortions in the new, federally run community health centers that would be set up under the legislation. It also stipulated that federal funds would not subsidize that portion of health insurance policies that covers the termination of pregnancies. Individuals may purchase such insurance under the new legislation, but the government will not pay for it.

What is the policy in other countries? As in the United States, many European nations responded to public opinion and liberalized abortion laws beginning in the 1970s. However, many of those nations limit the procedure to the first 12 weeks of a pregnancy. (The United States, in contrast, allows abortions up to about the 24th week and beyond.) Inspired by the strong antiabortion movement in the United States, antiabortion activists in Europe have become more outspoken, especially in Great Britain, France, Portugal, Spain, Italy, and Germany.

The policies of the United States are intertwined with those of developing nations. From the 1980s through January 2009, members of Congress who opposed abortion successfully blocked foreign aid to countries that might use the funds to encourage abortion. Yet developing nations generally have the most restrictive abortion laws. As Figure 35-5 shows, it is primarily in Africa, Latin America, and parts of Asia that women are not allowed to terminate a pregnancy on request. As might be expected, illegal abortions are most common in those nations. An estimated quarter of the world's women live in countries where abortion is illegal or is permitted only if a woman's life is in jeopardy. Indeed, the rate of abortions in countries with legal restrictions on the procedure matches the rate in countries that

(continued)

FIGURE 35-5 **The Global Divide on Abortion**

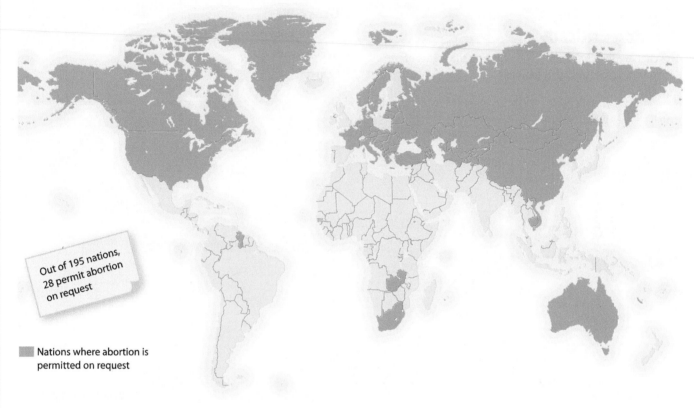

Out of 195 nations, 28 permit abortion on request

■ Nations where abortion is permitted on request

Note: Data current as of November 2007.
Source: Developed by the author based on United Nations Population Division 2007.

permit it. Hence, 40 percent of abortions worldwide—about 16 million procedures each year—are performed illegally (P. Baker 2009; Guttmacher Institute 2008).

TAKE THE ISSUE WITH YOU

1. How easy do you think it is for a young adult woman to obtain an abortion? What do you think should be the first step she takes in considering one?

2. Do you think teenage girls should be required to get their parents' consent before having an abortion? Why or why not?

3. Under what circumstances should abortions be allowed? Explain your reasoning.

MODULE 35 | **Recap and Review**

Summary

This module examines the status of women as an oppressed minority in the United States and around the world.

1. Women around the world suffer from **sexism** and **institutional discrimination.**

2. In the United States today, almost as many women as men participate in the paid labor force, but women are underrepresented in managerial positions and underpaid compared to men with the same jobs.

3. As women have taken on more and more hours of paid employment outside the home, they have been only

partially successful in getting their husbands to take on more homemaking duties, including child care.

4. Many women agree with the positions of the feminist movement but reject the label *feminist.*

5. The issue of abortion has bitterly divided the United States (as well as other nations), pitting pro-choice activists against pro-life activists.

Thinking Critically

1. What are the challenges to comparing the status of women across different nations?

2. How would you argue that women have come either very far or not far enough in their labor force participation?

3. Today, is feminism more likely to produce social change or respond to social change? Explain.

Key Terms

Feminism

Glass ceiling

Institutional discrimination

Second shift

Sexism

Mastering This Chapter: Stratification by Gender

taking sociology with you

1 For a day or two, watch for examples of people "doing gender" on your campus. Record your sightings in a journal and compare them with those of your classmates.

2 Find out what percentage of the faculty members at your college are women. What percentage of the women has tenure, compared to the men? What percentage holds full professorships? Do the percentages vary much from one department to another, and if so, why?

3 Use your school's alumni network to get in touch with graduates who have entered the workforce. Are mothers of young children having difficulty balancing work and parenting? Do both men and women feel they have a chance to get ahead? Are both men and women well compensated?

key terms

Expressiveness Concern for the maintenance of harmony and the internal emotional affairs of the family.

Feminism The belief in social, economic, and political equality for women.

Gender role Expectations regarding the proper behavior, attitudes, and activities of males and females.

Glass ceiling An invisible barrier that blocks the promotion of a qualified individual in a work environment because of the individual's gender, race, or ethnicity.

Homophobia Fear of and prejudice against homosexuality.

Institutional discrimination The denial of opportunities and equal rights to individuals and groups that results from the normal operations of a society.

Instrumentality An emphasis on tasks, a focus on more distant goals, and a concern for the external relationship between one's family and other social institutions.

Matrix of domination The cumulative impact of oppression because of race and ethnicity, gender, and social class, as well as religion, sexual orientation, disability, age, and citizenship status.

Multiple masculinities A variety of male gender roles, including nurturing-caring and effeminate-gay roles, that men may play along with their more pervasive traditional role of dominating women.

Second shift The double burden—work outside the home followed by child care and housework—that many women face and few men share equitably.

Sexism The ideology that one sex is superior to the other.

self-quiz

Read each question carefully and then select the best answer.

1. Both males and females are physically capable of learning to cook and sew, yet most Western societies determine that women should perform these tasks. This illustrates the operation of
   a. gender roles.
   b. sociobiology.
   c. homophobia.
   d. comparable worth.

2. An important element in traditional views of proper "masculine" and "feminine" behavior is fear of homosexuality. This fear, along with accompanying prejudice, is referred to as
   a. lesbianism.
   b. femme fatalism.
   c. homophobia.
   d. claustrophobia.

3. The most crucial agents of socialization in teaching gender roles in the United States are
   a. peers.
   b. teachers.
   c. media personalities.
   d. parents.

4. Research by anthropologists Margaret Mead and Peggy Reeves Sanday has shown that
   a. biology is the most important factor in determining the social roles of males and females.

b. cultural conditioning is the most important factor in determining the social roles of males and females.

c. biology and cultural conditioning have an equal impact in determining the social roles of males and females.

d. biology and cultural conditioning have a negligible impact in determining the social roles of males and females.

5. Which sociological perspective acknowledges that it is not possible to change gender roles drastically without dramatic revisions in a culture's social structure?
   a. functionalist perspective
   b. conflict perspective
   c. interactionist perspective
   d. both a and b

6. The term *sexism* is generally used to refer to
   a. female prejudice and discrimination against men.
   b. male prejudice and discrimination against women.
   c. female discrimination against men and male discrimination against women equally.
   d. discrimination between members of the same sex.

7. Which of these statements is true?
   a. More boys than girls take AP exams.
   b. Women in the United States are more likely than men to attend college.

c. Women in the United States are less likely than men to obtain doctoral degrees.

d. all of the above

8. Which sociological perspective distinguishes between instrumental and expressive roles?
   a. functionalist perspective
   b. conflict perspective
   c. interactionist perspective
   d. labeling theory

9. Contemporary feminists recognize the differential treatment of some women, not only because of their gender, but also because of their
   a. race.
   b. ethnicity.
   c. socioeconomic status.
   d. all of the above

10. The sense of sisterhood that became evident during the rise of the contemporary feminist movement resembled the Marxist concept of
   a. alienation.
   b. dialectics.
   c. class consciousness.
   d. false consciousness.

11. Talcott Parsons and Robert Bales contend that women take the _____, emotionally supportive role in the family and that men take the _____, practical role, with the two complementing each other.

12. A significant component of the _____ approach to gender stratification draws on feminist theory.

13. It is not simply that particular men in the United States are biased in their treatment of women. All the major institutions of our society—including the government, the armed forces, large corporations, the media, the universities, and the medical establishment—are controlled by men. This situation is symptomatic of institutional _____.

14. Women from all groups and men from minority groups sometimes encounter attitudinal or organizational bias that prevents them from reaching their full potential. This is known as the_____ _____.

15. Sociologist Arlie Hochschild has used the phrase _____ _____ to describe the double burden that many women face and few men share equitably: work outside the home followed by child care and housework.

16. Within the general framework of their theory, _____ sociologists maintain that gender differentiation has contributed to overall social stability.

17. Through the rise of contemporary _____, women are developing a greater sense of group solidarity.

18. _____ contributes significantly to rigid gender-role socialization, since many people stereotypically associate male homosexuality with femininity and lesbianism with masculinity.

19. The term _____ _____ _____ was coined by feminist theorist Patricia Hill Collins to describe the convergence of social forces that contributes to the subordinate status of poor, non-White women.

20. The author of the pioneering argument for women's rights, *The Feminine Mystique*, is_____ _____.

Answers

1 (a); 2 (c); 3 (d); 4 (b); 5 (d); 6 (b); 7 (b); 8 (a); 9 (d); 10 (c); 11 expressive, instrumental; 12 conflict; 13 discrimination; 14 glass ceiling; 15 second shift; 16 functionalist; 17 feminism; 18 Homophobia; 19 matrix of domination; 20 Betty Friedan

thinking about movies

La Mission (Peter Bratt, 2009)

An intimate portrayal of the vibrant culture of the Mission District in San Francisco, *La Mission* focuses on community leader Che Rivera (Benjamin Bratt). Che, a single father, is dedicated to raising his son Jesse (Jeremy Ray Valdez), with whom he has become very close since the death of Jesse's mother. When he learns that his son is gay, however, he reacts violently and eventually shuns Jesse. The culture of masculinity into which he was born prevents Rivera from coming to terms with his son's sexual orientation.

This movie shows how homosexuality is mistakenly associated with femininity. Che's gender-role socialization has shaped his perspective on gay people, leading to his prejudice and homophobia.

For your consideration

1. What are some of the illustrations of masculinity in the film, and how do they inform your understanding of gender-role socialization?

2. In what ways does the film show cross-cultural perspectives on gender roles?

Boys Don't Cry (Kimberly Peirce, 1999)

This film is based on the true story of Brandon Teena (Hillary Swank), a transgendered person whose identity cuts across the conventional male–female boundary line. Brandon, who was born with the body of a woman, prefers to live as a man. Disguising his female form, he assumes a man's gender role and moves to the small town of Falls City, Nebraska. Reveling in the acceptance he finds there, he makes friends and enters into a romantic relationship. After being jailed on a minor charge, however, his sex is exposed. In a tragic confrontation, Brandon feels the wrath of those who do not tolerate his alternative lifestyle.

This movie shows the social construction of gender, demonstrating that a person's identity as a man or woman is a social role, not a biological fact. Brandon's dress, speech, and behavior are what constitute his male identity. The violence he suffers attests to the rigidity of gender-role socialization and gender norms.

For your consideration

1. What does it take for Brandon to play the role of a man, and what does that say about the social construction of gender?

2. Why does Brandon's gender incite such violence in others? How might the answer to this question change depending on whether you take a functionalist or an interactionist view?

Currently, over 95 percent of all men and women in the United States marry at least once during their lifetimes. Historically, the most consistent aspect of family life in this country has been the high rate of marriage. In fact, despite the high rate of divorce, there are some indications of a miniboom in marriages of late.

In this module, we will examine various aspects of love, marriage, and parenthood in the United States and contrast them with cross-cultural examples. Though we're used to thinking of romance and mate selection as strictly a matter of individual preference, sociological analysis tells us that social institutions and distinctive cultural norms and values also play an important role.

trend|spotting

Cougars on the Rise

Typically, people choose someone of the same age as a romantic partner. In the most common deviation from this pattern, the husband is older than the wife. Yet today, the number of marriages that involve a much older woman—at least 10 years older—is growing. In fact, there is at least one online dating service that is dedicated to matching older women, dubbed "cougars," with younger men. According to sociologist Andrew Beveridge, although this type of couple represents only 1.3 percent of all marriages, that percentage is double that of 1960.

A similar trend can be seen among dating couples. According to an AARP survey, 20 percent of single women ages 40 to 69 said they were dating or had recently dated a man who was at least five years younger. And an informal tally by one dating service, published in the New York Times, indicates a rapid increase in the percentage of women over 40 who want to date men much younger than they are.

Professor Sandra L. Caron of the University of Maine has studied the reasons for this new trend. She notes that unlike many younger women, mature women are self-sufficient and don't need to look for an older, better educated man to support them. She finds that, in general, women who marry much younger men have happy marriages, although they may be insecure about their ages. That insecurity is probably misplaced. University of Washington sociologist Pepper Schwartz says she thinks young men are attracted to older women who are sexually free and don't make the demands that younger women do. As men become more accustomed to the idea of women earning more money than they do, the social barriers between young men and older women begin to melt away.

Courtship and Mate Selection

In the past, most couples met their partners through family, friends, or their neighborhood or workplace. Today, however, many couples meet on the Internet. According to a national survey done in 2010, the Internet is second only to friends as a source of romantic partners—ahead of family, workplace, and neighborhood. Significantly, online networking is just as important to mate-seekers in their 40s and 50s as to those under age 30. It is especially important to gays and lesbians, given the limited number of meeting places available to them: 61 percent of same-sex couples meet online, compared to 23 percent of heterosexual couples (Rosenfeld 2010).

Internet romance is only the latest courtship practice. In the central Asian nation of Uzbekistan and many other traditional cultures, courtship is defined largely through the interaction of two sets of parents, who arrange marriages for their children. Typically, a young Uzbekistani woman will be socialized to eagerly anticipate her marriage to a man whom she has met only once, when he is presented to her family at the time of the final inspection of her dowry. In the United States, in contrast, courtship is conducted primarily by individuals who have a romantic interest in each other. In our culture, courtship often requires these individuals to rely heavily on intricate games, gestures, and signals. Despite such differences, courtship—whether in the United States, Uzbekistan, or elsewhere—is influenced by the norms and values of the larger society (Carol J. Williams 1995).

One unmistakable trend in mate selection is that the process appears to be taking longer today than in the past. A variety of factors, including concerns about financial security and personal independence, has contributed to this delay in marriage. Most people are now well into their 20s before they marry, both in the United States and in other countries (Figure 40-1).

Aspects of Mate Selection

Many societies have explicit or unstated rules that define potential mates as acceptable or unacceptable. These norms can be distinguished in terms of endogamy and exogamy. **Endogamy** (from the Greek *endon*, "within") specifies the groups within which a spouse must be found and prohibits marriage with others. For example, in the United States, many people are expected to marry within their racial, ethnic, or religious group, and are strongly discouraged or even prohibited from marrying outside the group. Endogamy is intended to reinforce the cohesiveness

FIGURE 40-1 Median Age at First Marriage in Eight Countries

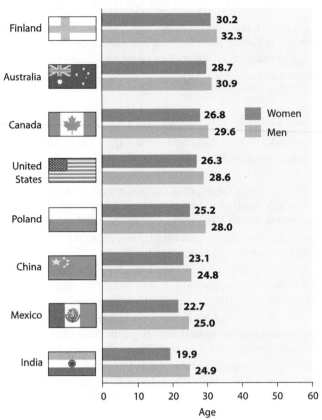

Finland — Women 30.2, Men 32.3
Australia — Women 28.7, Men 30.9
Canada — Women 26.8, Men 29.6
United States — Women 26.3, Men 28.6
Poland — Women 25.2, Men 28.0
China — Women 23.1, Men 24.8
Mexico — Women 22.7, Men 25.0
India — Women 19.9, Men 24.9

Source: United Nations Statistics Division 2008.

Think about It

Why do people marry earlier in India than in Finland?

Although most interracial couples are not as visible as Seal and Heidi Klum, such unions are becoming increasingly common and accepted. They are also blurring the definitions of race. Will the children of these couples be considered Black or White? Why do you think so?

of the group by suggesting to the young that they should marry someone "of their own kind."

In contrast, **exogamy** (from the Greek *exo,* "outside") requires mate selection outside certain groups, usually one's own family or certain kinfolk. The **incest taboo,** a social norm common to virtually all societies, prohibits sexual relationships between certain culturally specified relatives. For those of us in the United States, this taboo means that we must marry outside the nuclear family. We cannot marry our siblings, and in most states we cannot marry our first cousins.

Endogamous restrictions may be seen as preferences for one group over another. In the United States, such preferences are most obvious in racial barriers. Until the 1960s, some states outlawed interracial marriage. Nevertheless, the number of marriages between African Americans and Whites in the United States has increased more than nine times in recent decades, jumping from 51,000 in 1960 to 481,000 in 2009. Marriage across ethnic lines is even greater among Hispanics: 35 percent of all married Hispanics have a non-Hispanic spouse. But while

these examples of racial exogamy are noteworthy, endogamy is still the social norm in the United States (Bureau of the Census 1998, 2009a:54).

Another factor that influences the selection of a marriage partner is **homogamy,** the conscious or unconscious tendency to select a mate with personal characteristics similar to one's own. The "like marries like" rule can be seen in couples with similar personalities and cultural interests. However, mate selection is unpredictable. Though some people may follow the homogamous pattern, others observe the "opposites attract" rule: one person is dependent and submissive—almost childishly so—while the other is dominant and controlling.

Recently, the concept of homogamy has been incorporated into the process of seeking a date or marital partner online. The Internet dating site eHarmony, which claims to be the first to use a "scientific approach" to matching people based on a variety of abilities and interests, says that it "facilitates" 46 marriages a day. Sociologist Pepper Schwartz, who works as a consultant for the competing site PerfectMatch.com, has developed a 48-question survey that covers everything from prospective mates' decision-making style to their degree of impulsivity (Gottlieb 2006; Kalmijn 1998).

The Love Relationship

Today's generation of college students seems more likely to hook up or cruise in large packs than to engage in the romantic dating relationships of their parents and grandparents. Still, at some point in their adult lives, the great majority of today's students will meet someone they love and enter into a long-term relationship that focuses on creating a family.

Parents in the United States tend to value love highly as a rationale for marriage, so they encourage their children to develop intimate relationships based on love and affection. Songs, films, books, magazines, television shows, and even cartoons and comic books reinforce the theme of love. At the same time, our society expects parents and peers to help a person confine his or her search for a mate to "socially acceptable" members of the opposite sex.

Though most people in the United States take the importance of falling in love for granted, the coupling of love and marriage is by no means a cultural universal. Many of the world's cultures give priority in mate selection to factors other than romantic feelings. In societies with *arranged marriages* engineered by parents or religious authorities, economic considerations play a significant role. The newly married couple is expected to develop a feeling of love *after* the legal union is formalized, if at all.

Even where arranged marriage is the norm, new media technologies have changed the mating game. Today, when young people exchange phone numbers, a flurry of short text messages is more likely to follow than a series of extended phone conversations. In India, where most young people defer to their parents' wishes when they marry, much of this text messaging is recreational. Still, it can test the limits of traditional dating norms, by reducing the formality of social interactions between men and women (Giridharadas 2008).

In some societies, neither the parents nor the bride has a say in whom she marries. Since at least the 12th century, men in the central Asian nation of Kyrgyzstan have literally kidnapped their future wives from the street in a custom known as *ala kachuu,* which translates roughly as "grab and run." In its most benign form, this custom is a kind of elopement in which the man whisks off his girlfriend. Men do it to avoid the bride-price that parents often demand in return for their consent. But, as of 2005, one-third of the brides in Kyrgyzstan had been abducted against their will. Many of them—perhaps 80 percent—eventually assent to the kidnapping, often at their parents' urging. For these women, romantic love does not precede marriage, though love may well develop over time (Craig Smith 2005).

 use your sociological imagination

Your parents and/or a matchmaker are going to arrange a marriage for you. What kind of mate will they select? Will your chances of having a successful marriage be better or worse than if you selected your own mate?

Variations in Family Life and Intimate Relationships

Within the United States, social class, race, and ethnicity create variations in family life. Studying these variations will give us a more sophisticated understanding of contemporary family styles in our country.

Social Class Differences

Various studies have documented the differences in family organization among social classes in the United States. In the upper class, the emphasis is on lineage and maintenance of family position. If you are in the upper class, you are not simply a member of a nuclear family but rather a member of a larger family tradition (think of the Rockefellers or the Kennedys). As a result, upper-class families are quite concerned about what they see as proper training for children.

Lower-class families do not often have the luxury of worrying about the "family name"; they must first struggle to pay their bills and survive the crises often associated with a life of poverty. Such families are more likely to have only one parent at home, which creates special challenges in child care and financial management. Children from lower-class families typically assume adult responsibilities—including marriage and parenthood—at an earlier age than children from affluent homes. In part, that is because they may lack the money needed to remain in school.

Social class differences in family life are less striking today than they once were. In the past, family specialists agreed that the contrasts in child-rearing practices were pronounced. Lower-class families were found to be more authoritarian in rearing children and more inclined to use physical punishment. Middle-class families were more permissive and more restrained in punishing their children. And compared to lower-class families, middle-class families tended to schedule more of their children's time, or even to overstructure it. However, these differences may have narrowed as more and more families from all social classes turned to the same books, magazines, and even television talk shows for advice on rearing children (Kronstadt and Favreault 2008; Luster et al. 1989).

Among the poor, women often play a significant role in the economic support of the family. Men may earn low wages, may be unemployed, or may be entirely absent from the family. In 2008, 29 percent of all families headed by women with no husband present fell below the government poverty line. In comparison, the poverty rate for married couples was only 5.5 percent. The disproportionate representation of female-headed households among the poor is a persistent and growing trend, referred to by sociologists as the *feminization of poverty* (see Module 28; DeNavas-Walt et al. 2009:14).

Many racial and ethnic groups appear to have distinctive family characteristics. However, racial and class factors are often closely related. In examining family life among racial and ethnic minorities, keep in mind that certain patterns may result from class as well as cultural factors.

Racial and Ethnic Differences

The subordinate status of racial and ethnic minorities in the United States profoundly affects their family lives. For example, the lower incomes of African Americans, Native Americans, most Hispanic groups, and selected Asian American groups make creating and maintaining successful marital unions a difficult task. The economic restructuring of the past 60 years, described by sociologist William Julius Wilson (1996, 2009) and others, has especially affected people living in inner cities and desolate rural areas, such as reservations. Furthermore, the immigration policy of the United States has complicated the successful relocation of intact families from Asia and Latin America.

The African American family suffers from many negative and inaccurate stereotypes. It is true that, in a significantly higher proportion of Black than White families, no husband is present in the home (Figure 40-2). Yet Black single mothers often belong to stable, functioning kin networks, which mitigate the pressures of sexism and racism. Members of these networks—predominantly female kin such as mothers, grandmothers, and aunts—ease financial strains by sharing goods and services. In addition to these strong kinship bonds, Black family life has emphasized deep religious commitment and high aspirations for achievement (DuBois [1909] 1970; F. Furstenberg 2007).

Like African Americans, Native Americans draw on family ties to cushion many of the hardships they face. On the Navajo reservation, for example, teenage parenthood is not regarded as the crisis that it is elsewhere in the United States. The Navajo trace their descent matrilineally. Traditionally, couples reside with the wife's family after marriage, allowing the grandparents to help with the child rearing. While the Navajo do not approve of teenage parenthood, the deep emotional commitment of their extended families provides a warm home environment for children, even when no father is present or involved (Dalla and Gamble 2001).

Sociologists also have taken note of differences in family patterns among other racial and ethnic groups. For example, Mexican American men have been described as exhibiting a sense of virility, personal worth, and pride in their maleness that is called **machismo.** Mexican Americans are also described as being more familistic than many other subcultures. **Familism** refers to pride in the extended family, expressed through the maintenance of close ties and strong obligations to kinfolk outside the immediate family. Traditionally, Mexican Americans have placed proximity to their extended families above other needs and desires.

Although familism is often seen as a positive cultural attribute, it may also have negative consequences. Sociologists who have studied the relatively low college application rates of Hispanic students have found they have a strong desire to stay at home. Even the children of college-educated parents express this preference, which diminishes the likelihood of their getting a four-year degree and dramatically reduces the possibility that they will apply to a selective college (Desmond and Turley 2009).

These family patterns are changing, however, in response to changes in Latinos' social class standing, educational achievements, and occupations. Like other Americans, career-oriented Latinos in search of a mate but short on spare time are turning to Internet sites. As Latinos and other groups assimilate into the

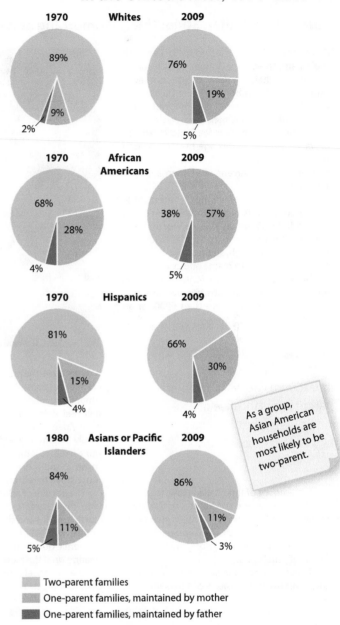

FIGURE 40-2 **Rise of Single-Parent Families in the United States, 1970–2009**

As a group, Asian American households are most likely to be two-parent.

☐ Two-parent families
☐ One-parent families, maintained by mother
☐ One-parent families, maintained by father

Note: Families are groups with children under 18. Early data for Asian Americans are for 1980. Hispanics can be of any race. Not included are unrelated people living together with no children present. All data exclude the 11 percent of children in nonparental households. *Sources:* Bureau of the Census 2008a:56, 2010b:Table EG10.

dominant culture of the United States, their family lives take on both the positive and negative characteristics associated with White households (Landale and Oropesa 2007).

● Child-Rearing Patterns

The Nayars of southern India acknowledge the biological role of fathers, but the mother's eldest brother is responsible for her children. In contrast, uncles play only a peripheral role in child care

Family Life, Italian Style: Thirty-Something and Living with Mom

Bamboccioni—adult children who live with their parents—are no longer socially unacceptable in Italy. In fact, they're not even unusual. In December 2009, the Italian government released new data showing that 40 percent of Italian men between ages 30 and 34 live with their parents. So do 20 percent of Italian women in this age bracket. Among those a little older, ages 35 to 39, 17.5 percent of men and 9.3 percent of women live with their parents.

This state of affairs is not a recent phenomenon. What is new is that 80 percent of these adult children say they cannot afford to leave their parents' homes. Salaries in Italy are low but rents are high, so these not-so-young adults linger on with mama and papa. As one of them, a 30-year-old biologist, put it, "We are the €1,000-per-month generation—who can afford spending more than €800 for an apartment?"

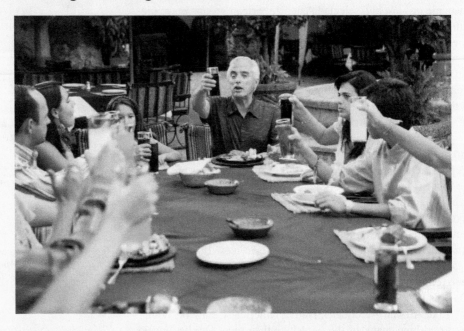

> About 40 percent of *bamboccioni* live with their parents not because of financial need, but because they enjoy the company.

The amount of time Italians take to graduate from college also contributes to the trend. Many are still studying for their degree in their late 20s. As in the United States, most find that living alone before graduation is financially impossible.

About 40 percent of *bamboccioni* live with their parents not because of financial need, but because they enjoy the company. Others feel responsible for their aging parents. Among the women ages 35 to 40, more than half feel it is a duty. Sociologist Giampiero dalla Zuanna says their commitment to the family means the elderly in Italy are much more likely to remain in their own homes than those in northern Europe, many of whom must move to retirement communities.

The pattern of adult children staying home with their parents is not unique to Italy. In North America and throughout Europe, young people are feeling the impact of the recent economic downturn. Many are delaying childbearing until their job prospects improve.

One relatively unnoticed factor that is contributing to the trend is parents' greater longevity. Today, more parents survive long enough for their children to become adults, and remain healthy enough to maintain a home for them.

LET'S DISCUSS

1. Do you or someone you know live at home with parents? If so, do you see the situation as similar to that of the *bamboccioni*?

2. In the United States, what other factors might contribute to adult children choosing to live with their parents?

Sources: Haub and Kent 2009; Momigliana 2010; S. Roberts 2010.

---

in the United States. Caring for children is a universal function of the family, yet the ways in which different societies assign this function to family members can vary significantly. Even within the United States, child-rearing patterns are varied. We'll take a look here at parenthood and grandparenthood, adoption, dual-income families, single-parent families, and stepfamilies.

Parenthood and Grandparenthood

The socialization of children is essential to the maintenance of any culture. Consequently, parenthood is one of the most important (and most demanding) social roles in the United States. Sociologist Alice Rossi (1968, 1984) has identified four factors that complicate the transition to parenthood and the role of

socialization. First, there is little anticipatory socialization for the social role of caregiver. The normal school curriculum gives scant attention to the subjects most relevant to successful family life, such as child care and home maintenance. Second, only limited learning occurs during the period of pregnancy itself. Third, the transition to parenthood is quite abrupt. Unlike adolescence, it is not prolonged; unlike the transition to work, the duties of caregiving cannot be taken on gradually. Finally, in Rossi's view, our society lacks clear and helpful guidelines for successful parenthood. There is little consensus on how parents can produce happy and well-adjusted offspring—or even on what it means to be well-adjusted. For these reasons, socialization for parenthood involves difficult challenges for most men and women in the United States.

One recent development in family life in the United States has been the extension of parenthood, as single adult children continue to live at home or return home after college. In 2009, 33 percent of men and 22 percent of women in their 20s lived with their parents. Some of these adult children were still pursuing an education, but in many instances, financial difficulties lay at the heart of these living arrangements. While rents and real estate prices have skyrocketed, salaries for younger workers have not kept pace, and many find themselves unable to afford their own homes. (This problem, along with the trend toward adult children living with their parents, is not unique to the United States: see the Sociology in the Global Community box above.) Moreover, with many marriages now ending in divorce—most commonly in the first seven years of marriage—divorced sons and daughters often return to live with their parents, sometimes with their own children (Bureau of the Census 2010b:Table A2).

Is this living arrangement a positive development for family members? Social scientists have just begun to examine the phenomenon, sometimes called the "boomerang generation" or the "full-nest syndrome" in the popular press. One survey in Virginia seemed to show that neither the parents nor their adult children were happy about continuing to live together. The children often felt resentful and isolated, but the parents suffered too: learning to live without children in the home is an essential stage of adult life and may even be a significant turning point for a marriage (*Berkeley Wellness Letter* 1990; Mogelonsky 1996).

In some homes, the full nest holds grandchildren. In 2009, 7 million children, or 9 percent of all children in the United States, lived in a household with a grandparent. In about a third of these homes, no parent was present to assume responsibility for the youngsters. Special difficulties are inherent in such relationships, including legal custodial concerns, financial issues, and emotional problems for adults and youths alike. It is not surprising that support groups such as Grandparents as Parents have emerged to provide assistance (Bureau of the Census 2010b:Table C4).

Adoption

In a legal sense, **adoption** is a "process that allows for the transfer of the legal rights, responsibilities, and privileges of parenthood" to a new legal parent or parents (E. Cole 1985:638). In many cases, these rights are transferred from a biological parent or parents (often called birth parents) to an adoptive parent or parents. At any given time, about 2 million adults in the United States are raising adopted children (Jo Jones 2009).

Viewed from a functionalist perspective, government has a strong interest in encouraging adoption. Policymakers, in fact, have both a humanitarian and a financial stake in the process. In theory, adoption offers a stable family environment for children who otherwise might not receive satisfactory care. Moreover, government data show that unwed mothers who keep their babies tend to be of lower socioeconomic status and often require public assistance to support their children. The government can lower its social welfare expenses, then, if children are transferred to

When nine-year-old Blake Brunson shows up for a basketball game, so do his *eight* grandparents—the result of his parents' remarriages. Blended families can be very supportive to children, but what message do they send to them on the permanency of marriage?

economically self-sufficient families. From an interactionist perspective, however, adoption may require a child to adjust to a very different family environment and parental approach to child rearing.

About 4 percent of all people in the United States are adopted, about half of whom were adopted by persons not related to them at birth. There are two legal methods of adopting an unrelated person: the adoption may be arranged through a licensed agency, or in some states it may be arranged through a private agreement sanctioned by the courts. Adopted children may come from the United States or from abroad. In 2009 over 12,700 children entered the United States as the adopted children of U.S. citizens. Figure 40-3 shows how the countries of origin have changed over time. International adoptions began to decline in 2004 after a long and steady increase. Recently China, the source for about one-fourth of overseas adoptions, tightened the rules for foreign adoptions, effectively reducing their number. Applicants for adoption who are single, obese, or older than 50 are now automatically disqualified.

The 2010 earthquake in Haiti drew attention to the foreign perspective on international adoptions, which is not always positive. When well-meaning people from the United States arrived in Haiti to rescue alleged orphans and arrange for their adoption in other countries, government officials objected. Some of the children, it turned out, were not orphans; their parents were simply too poor to care for them. For the governments of overstressed developing nations, adoption can be both a solution and a problem.

Adoption is controversial, not only abroad, but at home. In some cases, those who adopt children are not married. In 1995, an important court decision in New York held that a couple does not need to be married to adopt a child. Under this ruling, unmarried heterosexual couples, lesbian couples, and gay couples can all adopt children in New York. Today, most states permit gay and lesbian couples to adopt. Florida is the only state that explicitly forbids it; five others (Arkansas, Michigan, Mississippi, Nebraska, and Utah) prohibit couples who are not legally married from adopting (National Gay and Lesbian Task Force 2008).

FIGURE 40-3 Foreign-Born Adoptees by Top 10 Countries of Origin, 1989 and 2009

1989	Country	Rank	Country	2009
3,544	S. Korea	1	China	3,001
736	Colombia	2	Ethiopia	2,277
648	India	3	Russia	1,586
465	Philippines	4	S. Korea	1,080
253	Chile	5	Guatemala	756
252	Paraguay	6	Ukraine	610
222	Peru	7	Vietnam	481
202	Guatemala	8	Haiti	330
201	China	9	India	297
131	Honduras	10	Kazakhstan	295
Total 6,654				Total 14,862

Number of children

Source: Department of State 2001, 2010.

Think about It

Why did so many foreign-born adopted children come from these countries in particular? Why did the children's countries of origin change so much from 1989 to 2009?

For every child who is adopted, many more remain the wards of state-sponsored child protective services. At any given time, around half a million children in the United States are living in foster care. Every year, about 58,000 of them are adopted; another 123,600 are eligible and waiting to be adopted (Department of Health and Human Services 2010a).

Dual-Income Families

The idea of a family consisting of a wage-earning husband and a wife who stays at home has largely given way to the dual-income household. Among married people between ages 25 and 34, 96 percent of the men and 69 percent of the women were in the labor force in 2007 (Bureau of the Census 2008a:375).

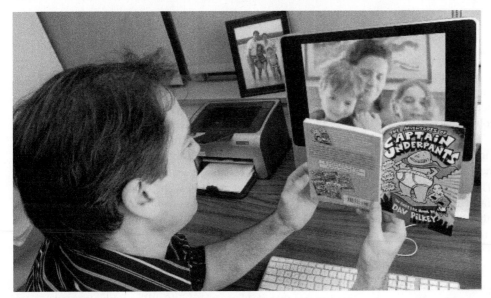

Miles Harvey reads to his children via Skype. Harvey, who is happily married, lives 900 miles from his family in Chicago. He accepted a job in New Orleans for economic reasons.

Why has there been such a rise in the number of dual-income couples? A major factor is economic need, coupled with a desire by both men *and* women to pursue their careers. Evidence of this trend can be found in the rise in the number of married couples living apart for reasons other than marital discord. The 3.6 million couples who now live apart represent 1 out of every 33 marriages. More than half of them live farther than 100 miles apart, and half of those live 1,000 or more miles apart. Of course, couples living apart are nothing new; men have worked at transient jobs for generations as soldiers, truck drivers, or traveling salesmen. Now, however, the woman's job is often the one that creates the separation. The existence of such household arrangements reflects an acceptance of the egalitarian family type (Holmes 2009; Silverman 2009).

 use your **sociological imagination**

What personal experience do you have with child rearing by grandparents, adoption, or dual-income families? Describe what you observed using sociological concepts.

Single-Parent Families

The 2004 *American Idol* winner Fantasia Barrino's song "Baby Mama" offers a tribute to young single mothers—a subject she knows about. Barrino was 17 when she became pregnant with her daughter. Though critics charged that the song sends the wrong message to teenage girls, Barrino says it is not about encouraging teens to have sex. Rather, she sees the song as an anthem for young mothers courageously trying to raise their children alone (Cherlin 2006).

In recent decades, the stigma attached to unwed mothers and other single parents has significantly diminished. **Single-parent families,** in which only one parent is present to care for the children, can hardly be viewed as a rarity in the United States. In 2009, a single parent headed about 24 percent of White families with children under 18, 34 percent of Hispanic families with children, and 62 percent of African American families with children (see Figure 40-2).

Interestingly, since 1995 the greatest increase in unwed motherhood has occurred among women in their 20s and 30s. This age group still constitutes a smaller proportion of unwed mothers than teens. In 2007, however, 45 percent of births to women in their 20s were to unmarried women (Ventura 2009).

The lives of single parents and their children are not inevitably more difficult than life in a traditional nuclear family. It is as inaccurate to assume that a single-parent family is necessarily deprived as it is to assume that a two-parent family is always secure and happy. Nevertheless, life in a single-parent family can be extremely stressful, in both economic and emotional terms. A family headed by a single mother faces especially difficult problems when the mother is a teenager.

Why might low-income teenage women wish to have children and face the obvious financial difficulties of motherhood? Viewed from an interactionist perspective, these women tend to have low self-esteem and limited options; a child may provide a sense of motivation and purpose for a teenager whose economic worth in our society is limited at best. Given the barriers that many young women face because of their gender, race, ethnicity, and class, many teenagers may believe they have little to lose and much to gain by having a child.

According to a widely held stereotype, "unwed mothers" and "babies having babies" in the United States are predominantly African American. However, this view is not entirely accurate. African Americans account for a disproportionate

 use your **sociological imagination**

What special challenges have you witnessed in stepfamilies? What about advantages they may experience? Describe what you observed using sociological concepts.

Most households in the United States do not consist of two parents living with their unmarried children.

share of births to unmarried women and teenagers, but the majority of all babies born to unmarried teenage mothers are born to White adolescents. Moreover, since 1980, birthrates among Black teenagers have generally declined (J. Martin et al. 2009).

Although 84 percent of single parents in the United States are mothers, the number of households headed by single fathers more than quadrupled from 1987 to 2008. Though single mothers often develop social networks, single fathers are typically more isolated. In addition, they must deal with schools and social service agencies that are more accustomed to women as custodial parents (Bureau of the Census 1994, 2009a:58).

Stepfamilies

Approximately 45 percent of all people in the United States will marry, divorce, and then remarry. The rising rates of divorce and remarriage have led to a noticeable increase in stepfamily relationships.

The exact nature of blended families has social significance for adults and children alike. Certainly resocialization is required when an adult becomes a stepparent or a child becomes a stepchild and stepsibling. Moreover, an important distinction must be made between first-time stepfamilies and households where there have been repeated divorces, breakups, or changes in custodial arrangements.

In evaluating the rise of stepfamilies, some observers have assumed that children would benefit from remarriage because they would be gaining a second custodial parent, and would potentially enjoy greater economic security. However, after reviewing many studies of stepfamilies, sociologist Andrew J. Cherlin (2008a:800) concluded that "the well-being of children in stepfamilies is no better, on average, than the well-being of children in divorced, single-parent households."

Stepparents can play valuable and unique roles in their stepchildren's lives, but their involvement does not guarantee an improvement in family life. In fact, standards may decline. Studies suggest that children raised in families with stepmothers are likely to have less health care, education, and money spent on their food than children raised by biological mothers. The measures are also negative for children raised by stepfathers, but only half as negative as in the case of stepmothers. These results don't mean that stepmothers are "evil"—it may be that the stepmother holds back out of concern for seeming too intrusive, or she relies mistakenly on the biological father to carry out parental duties (Schmeeckle 2007; Schmeeckle et al. 2006).

MODULE 40 | **Recap and Review**

Summary

People select mates in a variety of ways: in some societies, marriages are arranged, while in others, people select their own mates.

1. Some societies require mates to be chosen within a certain group (**endogamy**) or outside certain groups (**exogamy**). Consciously or unconsciously, many people look for a mate with similar personal characteristics (**homogamy**).

2. In the United States, family life varies with social class, race, and ethnicity.

3. Currently, in the majority of all married couples in the United States, both husband and wife work outside the home.

4. **Single-parent families** account for an increasing proportion of U.S. families.

Thinking Critically

1. How do both cultural and socioeconomic factors contribute to the following trends: later age of first marriage, the increasing number of extended-family households, and the "boomerang generation"?

2. Explain mate selection from the functionalist and interactionist perspectives.

Key Terms

Adoption

Endogamy

Exogamy

Familism

Homogamy

Incest taboo

Machismo

Single-parent family

Divorce

In the United States, the pattern of family life includes commitments both to marriage and to self-expression and personal growth. Needless to say, the tension between those competing commitments can undermine a marriage, working against the establishment of a lasting relationship. This approach to family life is distinctive to the United States. In some nations, such as Italy, the culture strongly supports marriage and discourages divorce. In others, such as Sweden, people treat marriage the same way as cohabitation, and both arrangements are just as lasting (Cherlin 2009).

Statistical Trends in Divorce

Just how common is divorce? Surprisingly, this is not a simple question; divorce statistics are difficult to interpret. The media frequently report that one out of every two marriages ends in divorce, but that figure is misleading. It is based on a comparison of all divorces that occur in a single year (regardless of when the couples were married) with the number of new marriages in the same year.

In many countries, divorce began to increase in the late 1960s but then leveled off; since the late 1980s, it has declined by 30 percent (Figure 41-1, shows the pattern in the United States). This trend is due partly to the aging of the baby boomer population and the corresponding decline in the proportion of people of marriageable age. But it also indicates an increase in marital stability in recent years (Coontz 2006).

Getting divorced obviously does not sour people on marriage. About 63 percent of all divorced people in the United States have remarried. Women are less likely than men to remarry because many retain custody of their children after a divorce, which complicates a new adult relationship (Bianchi and Spain 1996; Saad 2004).

Some people regard the nation's high rate of remarriage as an endorsement of the institution of marriage, but it does lead to the new challenges of a kin network composed of both current and prior marital relationships. Such networks can be particularly complex if children are involved or if an ex-spouse remarries.

Factors Associated with Divorce

Perhaps the most important factor in the increase in divorce over the past hundred years has been the greater social *acceptance* of divorce. It is no longer considered necessary to endure an unhappy marriage. More important, various religious denominations have relaxed their negative attitudes toward divorce, so that most religious leaders no longer treat it as a sin.

The growing acceptance of divorce is a worldwide phenomenon. A decade ago, Sunoo, South Korea's foremost matchmaking service, had no divorced clients. Few Koreans divorced; those who did felt social pressure to resign themselves to the single life. But in one recent seven-year period, South Korea's divorce rate doubled. Today, 15 percent of Sunoo's membership are divorced (Onishi 2003; United Nations Statistics Division 2009:Table 23).

In the United States, several factors have contributed to the growing social acceptance of divorce:

- Most states have adopted more liberal divorce laws in the past three decades. No-fault divorce laws, which allow a couple to end their marriage without fault on either side (by specifying adultery, for instance), accounted for an initial surge in the divorce rate after they were introduced in the 1970s, but appear to have had little effect beyond that.

- Divorce has become a more practical option in newly formed families, since families tend to have fewer children now than in the past.

- A general increase in family incomes, coupled with the availability of free legal aid to some poor people, has meant that more couples can afford costly divorce proceedings.

- As society provides greater opportunities for women, more and more wives are becoming less dependent on their husbands, both economically and emotionally. They may feel more able to leave a marriage if it seems hopeless.

What about the stress of separation caused by military duty? Forced transfer overseas, the tension of war, new duties at home, and anxiety over a spouse's return might seem a recipe for marital failure. The Research Today box considers military marriages' vulnerability while the husband or wife is away at war.

Impact of Divorce on Children

Divorce is traumatic for all involved, but it has special meaning for the more than 1 million children whose parents divorce each year. Of course, for some of these children, divorce signals the welcome end to a very dysfunctional relationship. Perhaps that is why a national study that tracked 6,332 children both before and after their parents' divorce found that their behavior did not suffer from the marital breakups. Other studies have shown greater unhappiness among children who live amidst parental conflict than among children whose parents are divorced. Still, it would be simplistic to assume that children are automatically better off following the breakup of their parents' marriage. The interests of the parents do not necessarily serve children well (Zi 2007).

FIGURE 41-1 Trends in Marriage and Divorce in the United States, 1920–2009

The divorce rate has generally risen since 1920, while the marriage rate has declined.

Sources: Bureau of the Census 1975:64; *National Vital Statistics Reports* 2010.

Diverse Lifestyles

Marriage is no longer the presumed route from adolescence to adulthood. In fact, it has lost much of its social significance as a rite of passage. The nation's marriage rate has declined since 1960 because people are postponing marriage until later in life, and because more couples, including same-sex couples, are deciding to form partnerships without marriage.

MAPPING LIFE NATIONWIDE

FIGURE 41-2 Unmarried-Couple Households by State

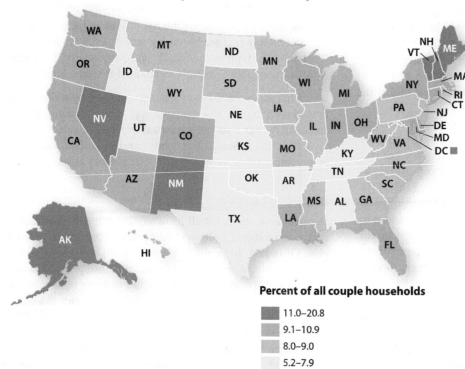

Percent of all couple households

- 11.0–20.8
- 9.1–10.9
- 8.0–9.0
- 5.2–7.9

Note: Data are for 2000 and include both opposite-sex and same-sex partners. U.S. average is 9.1 percent.
Source: Simmons and O'Connell 2003:4.

Cohabitation

In the United States, testing the marital waters by living together before making a commitment is a common practice among marriage-wary 20- and 30-somethings. The tremendous increase in the number of male–female couples who choose to live together without marrying, a practice called **cohabitation,** is one of the most dramatic trends of recent years.

About half of all *currently* married couples in the United States say that they lived together before marriage. This percentage is likely to increase. The number of unmarried-couple households in the United States rose 600 percent in the 1960s and increased another 72 percent between 1990 and 2000. Presently over 8 percent of opposite-sex couples are unmarried. Cohabitation is more common among African Americans and American Indians than among other racial and ethnic groups; it is least common among Asian Americans. Figure 41-2 shows regional variations in cohabitation (Peterson 2003; Simmons and O'Connell 2003).

In much of Europe, cohabitation is so common that the general sentiment seems to be "Love, yes; marriage, maybe." In Iceland, 62 percent of all children are born to single mothers; in France, Great Britain, and Norway, about 40 percent. Government policies in these countries make few legal distinctions between married and unmarried couples or households. Perhaps as a result, partnerships between cohabiting adults are not necessarily brief or lacking in commitment. Children born to a cohabiting couple in Sweden, for example, are less likely than children born to a cohabiting couple in the United States to see their parents break up (Cherlin 2009; Lyall 2002; M. Moore 2006).

People commonly associate cohabitation with younger couples. But according to a study done in Los Angeles, working couples are almost twice as likely to cohabit as college students. And census data show that in 2003, 45 percent of unmarried couples had one or more children present in the household. These cohabitants are more like spouses than dating partners. Moreover, in contrast to the common perception that people who cohabit have never been married,

Divorce and Military Deployment

Whenever soldiers talk about the hardships of foreign deployment, separation from their families and the toll on their marital relationships are the main topic. Too often, military couples marry just before a deployment, following a brief romance. Then, when they are suddenly separated, the relationship begins to fall apart. To keep wives from worrying or to reduce their own homesickness, many soldiers avoid calling home. Those couples who do communicate by phone, letter, or e-mail often argue; some talk about divorce. Impulsively, a soldier may throw his wedding ring away. A wife struggling to manage on her own may empty the family's bank account.

Yet many couples make heroic efforts to hold together despite the hardship. Those who are left home continue to care for their families, coping with life as a single parent and comforting children who miss their father or mother. They will themselves to overcome loneliness and anxiety. For these couples, every new deployment is a challenge; being apart doesn't get easier as they get older.

On balance, does overseas deployment affect the divorce rate among military couples? Current research delivers a mixed message. One long-term study published recently indicates that the longer the deployment, the lower the risk of divorce. Studies of soldiers who served in the Vietnam War and the 1991 Persian Gulf War came to the same conclusion. Yet 2009 data show that the current divorce rate among those in the military is 3.6 percent a year—slightly higher than the national rate of 3.4 percent. Furthermore, 23 percent of soldiers stationed in Iraq in 2009 say they plan to divorce or separate after returning home, compared to 12 percent in 2003.

There were other negative findings of the study. Female service members were found to be twice as likely as male service members to end their marriages. Moreover, enlisted service members were more likely than officers to end their marriages. This second disparity may be due to the fact that officers tend to be older than enlisted personnel, and older couples are less likely than younger couples to divorce.

Studies of the impact of overseas deployment on couples' children have not been reassuring. In 2007, an Army-funded study found that the rate of child neglect among military families was almost four times higher when husbands were deployed than when they were home. Physical abuse of children in those

Welcome home! Military families reunite after a long, anxious separation.

cases was nearly twice as high when husbands were away. Given these findings, one can only hope that support programs for families separated by war will be strengthened.

How can we explain the resiliency of some service members' marriages in the face of war? Although wartime separation is undeniably stressful for couples, the researchers speculated that it might also benefit them, perhaps through higher earnings (combat pay) or the potential for career advancement. Moreover,

> 23 percent of soldiers stationed in Iraq in 2009 say they plan to divorce or separate after returning home.

many couples reported finding meaning and fulfillment in the deployment, which they saw as an important service to the nation. Finally, the spouses who are left behind are not totally isolated. The military provides strong social support, along with health care, child care, and housing subsidies. All these forms of

support offer some protection from the impact of stress.

There is a need for further research on this topic. The information that researchers have covers only the short term and pertains only to those soldiers who remained in the military. Could the long-term impact on military couples be more telling? Could the outcome be different for those who leave the military soon after a war? And might soldiers consider marriage more carefully than the average person, knowing that their futures are uncertain? As with even the most detailed research, this study's conclusions raise new questions for scientific investigation.

LET'S DISCUSS

1. Do you know any married couples who have been separated by military deployment overseas? If so, how did they cope? What was the effect on their children?

2. Can you think of some other reasons why military marriages might survive the strain of war as well as they do?

Sources: Block 2009; Bowman 2009; D. Gibbs et al. 2007; Karney and Crown 2007; Krauss 1993; T. Perry 2007; Priest 2008; RAND 2007; A. Stone and Bello 2009; Wheller 2009; Zoroya 2009.

researcher report that about half of all people involved in cohabitation in the United States have been previously married. Cohabitation serves as a temporary or permanent alternative to matrimony for many men and women who have experienced their own or their parents' divorces (Jason Fields 2004; Popenoe and Whitehead 1999).

Periodically, legislators attempt to bolster the desirability of a lifelong commitment to marriage. In 2002, President George W. Bush backed funding for an initiative to promote marriage among those who receive public assistance. Under the Healthy Marriage Initiative, the federal government created a resource center that promoted marriage-related programs. Critics charged that the effort was underfunded or an inappropriate mission for the federal government. Still, the Obama administration has indicated a desire to continue the initiative, although the worsening economy may jeopardize its funding (Jayson 2009).

Remaining Single

Looking at TV programs today, you would be justified in thinking that most households are composed of singles. Although that is not the case, it is true that more and more people in the United States are postponing entry into a first marriage. Over one out of three households with children in the United States is a single-parent household. Even so, fewer than 4 percent of women and men in the United States are likely to remain single throughout their lives (Bureau of the Census 2008a).

The trend toward maintaining a single lifestyle for a longer period is related to the growing economic independence of young people. This trend is especially significant for women. Freed from financial needs, women don't necessarily need to marry to enjoy a satisfying life. Divorce, late marriage, and longevity also figure into this trend.

There are many reasons why a person may choose not to marry. Some singles do not want to limit their sexual intimacy to one lifetime partner. Some men and women do not want to become highly dependent on any one person—and do not want anyone depending heavily on them. In a society that values individuality and self-fulfillment, the single lifestyle can offer certain freedoms that married couples may not enjoy. Even divorced parents may not feel the need to remarry. Sociologist Andrew J. Cherlin (2009) contends that a single parent who connects with other adults, such as grandparents, to form a solid, supportive relationship for child rearing should not feel compelled to re-partner.

Nevertheless, remaining single represents a clear departure from societal expectations; indeed, it has been likened to "being single on Noah's Ark." A single adult must confront the inaccurate view that he or she is always lonely, is a workaholic, or is immature. These stereotypes help to support the traditional assumption in the United States and most other societies that to be truly happy and fulfilled, a person must get married and raise a family. To counter these societal expectations, singles have formed numerous support groups (Hertz 2006; Lundquist 2006).

Marriage without Children

There has been a modest increase in childlessness in the United States. According to census data, about 16 to 17 percent of women will now complete their childbearing years without having borne any children, compared to 10 percent in 1980. As many as 20 percent of women in their 30s expect to remain childless (Biddlecom and Martin 2006).

Childlessness within marriage has generally been viewed as a problem that can be solved through such means as adoption and artificial insemination. More and more couples today, however, choose to not have children and regard themselves as child-free rather than childless. They do not believe that having children automatically follows from marriage, nor do they feel that reproduction is the duty of all married couples. Childless couples have formed support groups (with names like No Kidding) and set up Web sites.

Economic considerations have contributed to this shift in attitudes; having children has become quite expensive. According to a government estimate made for 2008, the average middle-class family will spend $221,190 to feed, clothe, and shelter a child from birth to age 18. If the child attends college, that amount could double, depending on the college chosen. In 1960, parents spent only 2 percent of their income on child care and education; now they spend 16 percent, reflecting the rising dependence on nonfamily child care (see the Social Policy section in Module 15). Aware of the financial pressures, some couples are weighing the advantages of a child-free marriage (Lino and Carlson 2009).

Childless couples are beginning to question current practices in the workplace. While applauding employers' efforts to provide child care and flexible work schedules, some nevertheless express concern about tolerance of employees who leave early to take children to doctors, ball games, or after-school classes. As more dual-career couples enter the paid labor force and struggle to balance career and familial responsibilities, conflicts with employees who have no children may increase (Biddlecom and Martin 2006).

 use your **sociological imagination**

What would happen to our society if many more married couples suddenly decided to not have children? How would society change if cohabitation and/or singlehood became the norm?

Lesbian and Gay Relationships

Twenty-one-year-old Parke, a junior in college, grew up in a stable, loving family. A self-described fiscal conservative, he credits his parents with instilling in him a strong work ethic. Sound like an average child of an average family? The only break with traditional expectations in this case is that Parke is the son of a lesbian couple (P. Brown 2004).

The lifestyles of lesbians and gay men are varied. Some live in long-term, monogamous relationships; others live alone or with roommates. Some remain in "empty-shell" heterosexual marriages and do not publicly acknowledge their homosexuality. Others live with children from a former marriage or with adopted children. Based on election exit polls, researchers for the National Health and Social Life Survey and the Voter News Service estimate that 2 to 5 percent of the adult population identify themselves as either gay or lesbian. An analysis of the 2000 Census shows a minimum of at least 600,000 gay households, and a gay and lesbian adult population approaching 10 million (E. Laumann et al. 1994b:293; David M. Smith and Gates 2001).

Gay and lesbian couples face discrimination on both a personal and a legal level. Their inability to marry denies them many rights that married couples take for granted, from the ability to make decisions for an incapacitated partner to the right to receive government benefits to dependents, such as Social Security payments. Though gay couples consider themselves families just like the straight couples who live down the street, they are often treated as if they are not.

Precisely because of such inequities, many gay and lesbian couples are now demanding the right to marry. In the Social Policy section that follows, we will examine the highly controversial issue of gay marriage.

 use your sociological imagination

Which of the four different lifestyles described in this module do you think would be most and least acceptable to your friends? Why?

social policy and the Family

Gay Marriage

In the United States, attitudes toward marriage are complex. As always, society and popular culture suggest that a young man or woman should find the perfect mate, settle down and marry, have children, and live happily ever after. But young people are also bombarded by messages implying the frequency of adultery and the acceptability of divorce. In this atmosphere, the idea of same-sex marriage strikes some people as only the latest of many attacks on traditional marriage. To others, it seems an overdue acknowledgment of the formal relationships that faithful, monogamous gay couples have long maintained.

Understanding the Issue

What has made gay marriage the focus of national attention? Events in two states brought the issue to the forefront. In 1999, Vermont gave gay couples the legal benefits of marriage through civil union, but stopped short of calling the arrangement a marriage. Then, in 2003, the Massachusetts Supreme Court ruled 4–3 that under the state's constitution, gay couples have the right to marry—a ruling the U.S. Supreme Court has refused to review. Now, with gay married couples in this state passing their 5th anniversaries and approaching their 10th, scholars are beginning to study their experiences compared to those of opposite-sex couples.

Recently, national surveys of attitudes toward gay marriage in the United States have shown an almost even split among the public. A 2009 survey showed that 53 percent oppose allowing gay men and lesbians to marry. However, 57 percent favor allowing them to enter legal unions—arrangements that give gay couples many of the same rights as marriage (E. Kelley and Bazar 2010).

(continued)

FIGURE 41-3 Gay Marriage by State

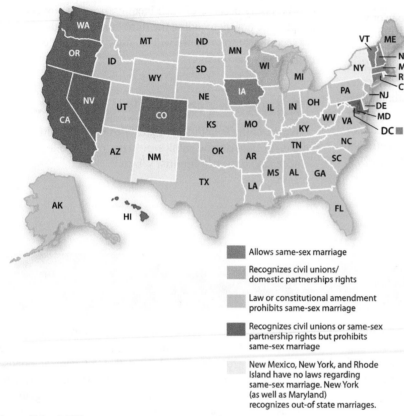

Allows same-sex marriage

Recognizes civil unions/domestic partnerships rights

Law or constitutional amendment prohibits same-sex marriage

Recognizes civil unions or same-sex partnership rights but prohibits same-sex marriage

New Mexico, New York, and Rhode Island have no laws regarding same-sex marriage. New York (as well as Maryland) recognizes out-of state marriages.

Source: Clabaugh 2010.

Applying Sociology

Functionalists have traditionally seen marriage as a social institution that is closely tied to human reproduction. Same-sex marriage would at first appear not to fit that arrangement. But many same-sex couples are entrusted with the socialization of young children, whether or not their relationship is recognized by the state. Functionalists also wonder whether religious views toward marriage can be ignored. The courts have focused on civil marriage, but religious views are hardly irrelevant, even in a country like the United States, which observes a separation between religion and the state. Indeed, religious teachings have led even some staunch supporters of gay rights to oppose same-sex marriage on spiritual grounds.

Conflict theorists have charged that denial of the right to marry reinforces the second-class status of gays and lesbians. Some have compared the ban against gay marriage to past policies that until 1967 banned interracial marriage in 32 states. Figure 41-3 illustrates the different ways same-sex partnerships are treated today in different states.

Interactionists generally avoid the policy question and focus instead on the nature of same-sex households. They ask many of the same questions about gay partner relations and child rearing that they ask about conventional couples. Of course, much less research has been done on same-sex households than on other families, but the studies published to date raise the same issues as those that apply to conventional married couples, plus a few more. For gay couples, the support or opposition of family, co-workers, and friends looms large (Dundas and Kaufman 2000; Dunne 2000).

Initiating Policy

The United States is not the first nation to consider this issue. Recognition of same-sex partnerships is common in Europe, including legal recognition of same-sex marriage in Belgium, the Netherlands, Norway, Portugal, Spain, and Sweden. Today, as many as 8 percent of all marriages in the Netherlands are same-sex. The trend is toward recognition in North America as well, since gay couples can marry legally in Canada.

Many nations strongly oppose such measures, however. For example, when Kofi Annan, then secretary general of the United Nations (UN), proposed extending the benefits that married UN employees receive to employees' same-sex partners in 2004, so many countries rose in protest that he reneged. Annan decided that such benefits would extend only to those UN employees whose member nations extend the same benefits to their citizens (Cowell 2005; Maggie Farley 2004; Wines 2005).

In the United States, many local jurisdictions have passed legislation allowing for the registration of domestic partnerships, and have extended employee benefits to those relationships. Under such policies, a **domestic partnership** may be defined as two unrelated adults who share a mutually caring relationship, reside together, and agree to be jointly responsible for their dependents, basic living expenses, and other common necessities. Domestic partnership benefits can apply to couples' inheritance, parenting, pensions, taxation, housing, immigration, workplace fringe benefits, and health care. Even though the most passionate support for domestic partnership legislation has come from lesbian and gay activists, the majority of those eligible for such benefits would be cohabiting heterosexual couples.

In the United States, marriage has traditionally been under the jurisdiction of state lawmakers. But recently, pressure has been mounting for national legislation. The Defense of Marriage Act, passed in 1996, provided that no state is obliged to recognize same-sex marriages performed in another state. However, some legal scholars doubt that the law could withstand a constitutional challenge, since it violates a provision in the Constitution that requires states to recognize one another's laws. In 2003, therefore, opponents of gay marriage proposed a constitutional amendment that would limit marriage to heterosexual couples. The measure was introduced in the Senate in 2006, but failed to receive sufficient support to come to a vote.

Within the United States, state courts in California, Iowa, and Massachusetts have ruled that there is no state law that precludes same-sex marriage. In California, 18,000 same-sex couples were married before voters amended the state constitution to prohibit such marriages in the future. As of mid-2010, the District of Columbia and five states (Connecticut, Iowa, Massachusetts, New Hampshire, and Vermont) were issuing marriage licenses to same-sex couples. In August 2010, a federal court weighed in for the first time on gay marriage, ruling that California's ban on same-sex marriage was unconstitutional. Ultimately the Supreme Court will consider the issue. Gay rights activists claim their movement is gathering momentum, but opponents argue that their high-profile actions have galvanized conservatives who wish to define marriage as the union of one man and one woman.

TAKE THE ISSUE WITH YOU

1. If marriage is good for heterosexual couples and their families, why isn't it good for homosexual couples and their families?

2. How can interactionist studies of gay couples and their families inform policymakers who are dealing with the issue of gay marriage? Give a specific example.

3. Who are the stakeholders in the debate over gay marriage, and what do they stand to gain or lose? Whose interest do you think is most important?

MODULE 41 | Recap and Review

Summary

Divorce and alternatives to traditional marriage such as cohabitation now represent common choices of family style.

1. Among the factors that contribute to the rising divorce rate in the United States are greater social acceptance of divorce and the liberalization of divorce laws in many states.

2. More and more people are living together without marrying, a practice known as **cohabitation.** People are also staying single longer, and some married couples are deciding not to have children.

3. The gay marriage movement, which would confer equal rights on gay and lesbian couples and their dependents, is strongly apposed by conservative religious and political groups.

Thinking Critically

1. In a society that maximizes the welfare of all family members, how easy should it be for couples to divorce? How easy should it be to get married?

2. How is romantic cohabitation similar to marriage? How is it different? Could gay and lesbian couples achieve all the benefits of marriage without actually marrying?

Key Terms

Cohabitation

Domestic partnership

Nineteenth-century educators would be amazed at the scale of schools in the United States in the 21st century. For example, California's public school system, the largest in the nation, currently enrolls as many children as there were in secondary schools in the entire country in 1950 (Bureau of the Census 1975:368; 2009a).

In many respects, today's schools, when viewed as an example of a formal organization, are similar to factories, hospitals, and business firms. Like those organizations, schools do not operate autonomously; they are influenced by the market of potential students. This statement is especially true of private schools, but could have broader impact if acceptance of voucher plans and other school choice programs increases. The parallels between schools and other types of formal organizations will become more apparent as we examine the bureaucratic nature of schools, teaching as an occupation, and the student subculture (K. Dougherty and Hammack 1992).

● Bureaucratization of Schools

It simply is not possible for a single teacher to transmit culture and skills to children of varying ages who will enter many diverse occupations. The growing number of students being served by school systems and the greater degree of specialization required within a technologically complex society have combined to bureaucratize schools.

Max Weber noted five basic characteristics of bureaucracy, all of which are evident in the vast majority of schools, whether at the elementary, secondary, or even college level:

1. **Division of labor.** Specialized experts teach particular age levels and specific subjects. Public elementary and secondary schools now employ instructors whose sole responsibility is to work with children with learning disabilities or physical impairments.

2. **Hierarchy of authority.** Each employee of a school system is responsible to a higher authority. Teachers must report to principals and assistant principals and may also be supervised by department heads. Principals are answerable to a superintendent of schools, and the superintendent is hired and fired by a board of education.

3. **Written rules and regulations.** Teachers and administrators must conform to numerous rules and regulations in the performance of their duties. This bureaucratic trait can become dysfunctional; the time invested in completing required forms could instead be spent in preparing lessons or conferring with students.

4. **Impersonality.** As class sizes have swelled at schools and universities, it has become more difficult for teachers to give personal attention to each student. In fact, bureaucratic norms may actually encourage teachers to treat all students in the same way, despite the fact that students have distinctive personalities and learning needs.

5. **Employment based on technical qualifications.** At least in theory, the hiring of instructors is based on professional competence and expertise. Promotions are normally dictated by written personnel policies; people who excel may be granted lifelong job security through tenure.

Functionalists take a generally positive view of the bureaucratization of education. Teachers can master the skills needed to work with a specialized clientele, since they no longer are expected to cover a broad range of instruction. The chain of command within schools is clear. Students are presumably treated in an unbiased

Despite efforts to establish positive relationships among students and between teachers and students, many young people view their schools as impersonal institutions.

fashion because of uniformly applied rules. Finally, security of position protects teachers from unjustified dismissal. In general, then, functionalists stress that the bureaucratization of education increases the likelihood that students, teachers, and administrators will be dealt with fairly—that is, on the basis of rational and equitable criteria.

In contrast, conflict theorists argue that the trend toward more centralized education has harmful consequences for disadvantaged people. The standardization of educational curricula, including textbooks, will generally reflect the values, interests, and lifestyles of the most powerful groups in our society, and may ignore those of racial and ethnic minorities. In addition, the disadvantaged, more so than the affluent, will find it difficult to sort through complex educational bureaucracies and to organize effective lobbying groups. Therefore, in the view of conflict theorists, low-income and minority parents will have even less influence over citywide and statewide educational administrators than they have over local school officials (Bowles and Gintis 1976; Katz 1971).

Sometimes schools can seem overwhelmingly bureaucratic, with the effect of stifling rather than nourishing intellectual curiosity in students. This concern has led many parents and policymakers to push for school choice programs—allowing parents to choose the school that suits their children's needs, and forcing schools to compete for their "customers."

In the United States, another significant countertrend to the bureaucratization of schools is the availability of education over the Internet. Increasingly, colleges and universities are reaching out via the Web, offering entire courses and even majors to students in the comfort of their homes. Online curricula provide flexibility for working students and others who may have difficulty attending conventional classes because of distance or disability. Research on this type of learning is just beginning, so the question of whether teacher–student contact can thrive online remains to be settled. Computer-mediated instruction may also have an impact on instructors' status as employees, which we will discuss next, as well as on alternative forms of education like homeschooling.

 use your **sociological imagination**

How would you make your school less bureaucratic? What would it be like?

Teachers: Employees and Instructors

Whether they serve as instructors of preschoolers or of graduate students, teachers are employees of formal organizations with bureaucratic structures. There is an inherent conflict in serving

as a professional in a bureaucracy. The organization follows the principles of hierarchy and expects adherence to its rules, but professionalism demands the individual responsibility of the practitioner. This conflict is very real for teachers, who experience all the positive and negative consequences of working in bureaucracies (see Table 19-1).

A teacher undergoes many perplexing stresses every day. While teachers' academic assignments have become more specialized, the demands on their time remain diverse and contradictory. Conflicts arise from serving as an instructor, a disciplinarian, and an employee of a school district at the same time. In too many schools, discipline means dealing with violence (see Research Today box). Burnout is one result of these stresses: between a quarter and a third of new teachers quit within their first three years, and as many as half leave poor urban schools in their first five years (Wallis 2008).

Given these difficulties, does teaching remain an attractive profession in the United States? In 2009, 4.1 percent of first-year college students indicated that they were interested in becoming elementary school teachers, and 4.4 percent, high school teachers. These figures are dramatically lower than the 11 percent of first-year male students and 37 percent of first-year female students who held those occupational aspirations in 1966 (Pryor et al. 2007:122, 76; 2009:30).

Undoubtedly, economic considerations enter into students' feelings about the attractiveness of teaching. In 2008 the average salary for all public elementary and secondary school teachers in the United States was reported at $51,009, placing teachers somewhere near the average of all the nation's wage earners. In most other industrial countries, teachers' salaries are higher in relation to the general standard of living. Of course, teachers' salaries vary considerably from state to state (Figure 43-1), and even more from one school district to another. Nevertheless, the economic reward for teaching is miniscule compared to some career options: the CEO of a major corporation makes more money in a day than the average teacher makes in a year.

The status of any job reflects several factors, including the level of education required, financial compensation, and the respect given the occupation by society. The teaching profession (see Table 27-1) is feeling pressure in all three of these areas. First, the level of formal schooling required for teaching remains high, and the public has begun to call for new competency examinations. Second, the statistics just cited demonstrate that teachers' salaries are significantly lower than those of many professionals and skilled workers. Third, the overall prestige of the teaching profession has declined in the past decade. Many teachers have become disappointed and frustrated and have left the educational world for careers in other professions (Bureau of the Census 2009a:162).

Research Today

Violence in the Schools

Littleton, Colorado; Red Lake, Minnesota; Jonesboro, Arkansas; West Paducah, Kentucky; Pearl, Mississippi; Edinboro, Pennsylvania; Springfield, Oregon—these are now more than just the names of small towns and medium-size cities. They resonate with the sound of gunshots, of kids killing kids on school grounds. As a result, people no longer perceive schools as safe havens. But how accurate is that impression?

Studies of school violence put the recent spate of school killings in perspective:

- A child has less than a one in 1.6 million chance of being killed at school.
- In 2007, 36 percent of high school students reported being in a fight, and one-third of these fights took place on school property.
- Fewer students are now being found with guns in school.
- Since 1992, the number of homicides at schools has ranged between 13 and 34 per year.
- Among people under age 19, for every homicide that takes place at school, 87 occur away from home.

Schools, then, are safer than neighborhoods, but people are still unnerved by the perception of an alarming rise in schoolyard violence generated by heavy media coverage of recent incidents. Some conflict theorists object to the

> A child has less than a one in 1.6 million chance of being killed at school.

huge outcry about recent violence in schools. After all, they note, violence in and around inner-city schools has a long history. It seems that only when middle-class White children are the victims does school violence become a plank on the national policy agenda. When violence hits the middle class, the problem is viewed not as an extension of delinquency, but as a structural issue in need of legislative remedies, such as gun control (see the Social Policy section in Module 25).

Feminists observe that virtually all the offenders in these incidents are male, and in some instances, such as the case in Jonesboro, the victims are disproportionately female. The precipitating factor in the violence is often a broken-off dating relationship—yet another example of the violence of men against women (or in this case, boys against girls).

Increasingly, efforts to prevent school violence are focusing on the ways in which the socialization of young people contributes to violence. For example, the American Medical Association has invested in a violence prevention

curriculum for elementary school students that teaches social skills related to anger management, impulse control, and empathy.

Some people believe that a key ingredient in the prevention of violence, in or out of school, is greater parental supervision of and responsibility for their children. In her book *A Tribe Apart,* Patricia Hersch documents the lives of eight teens growing up in a Virginia suburb over a three-year period. Her conclusion: children need meaningful adult relationships in their lives. And former Secretary of Education Richard Riley cites studies showing that youths who feel connected to their parents and schools are less likely than others to engage in high-risk behaviors.

LET'S DISCUSS

1. Has a shooting or other violent episode ever occurred at your school? If so, how did students react? Do you feel safer at school than at home, as experts say you are?
2. What steps have administrators at your school taken to prevent violence? Have they been effective, or should other steps be taken?

Sources: American Medical Association 2009; Dinkes et al. 2009; Donohue et al. 1998; Hersch 1998; National Center for Education Statistics 2002.

Student Subcultures

An important latent function of education relates directly to student life: schools provide for students' social and recreational needs. Education helps toddlers and young children to develop interpersonal skills that are essential during adolescence and adulthood. In their high school and college years, students may meet future husbands and wives and establish lifelong friendships.

When people observe high schools, community colleges, or universities from the outside, students appear to constitute a cohesive, uniform group. However, the student subculture is actually quite complex and diverse. High school cliques and social groups may crop up according to race, social class, physical attractiveness, placement in courses, athletic ability, and leadership roles in the school and community. In his classic community study of "Elmtown," August B. Hollingshead (1975) found some 259 distinct cliques in a single high school. The cliques, whose average size was five, were centered on the school itself, on recreational activities, and on religious and community groups.

Amid these close-knit and often rigidly segregated cliques, gay and lesbian students are particularly vulnerable. Peer group pressure to conform is intense at this age. Although coming to terms with one's sexuality is difficult for all adolescents, it can be downright dangerous for those whose sexual orientation does not conform to societal expectations.

Teachers and administrators are becoming more sensitized to these issues. Perhaps more important, some schools are creating gay–straight alliances (GSAs), school-sponsored support groups that bring gay teens together with sympathetic straight peers. Begun in Los Angeles in 1984, these programs numbered nearly 3,000 nationwide in 2005; most were founded after the murder of Matthew Shepard, a gay college student, in 1998. In some districts parents have objected to these organizations, but the same court rulings that protect the right of conservative Bible groups to meet on school grounds also protect GSAs. In 2003, the gay–straight movement reached a milestone when the New York City public schools moved an in-school program for gays, bisexuals, and transgender students to a separate school of their

FIGURE 43-1 **Average Salary for Teachers**

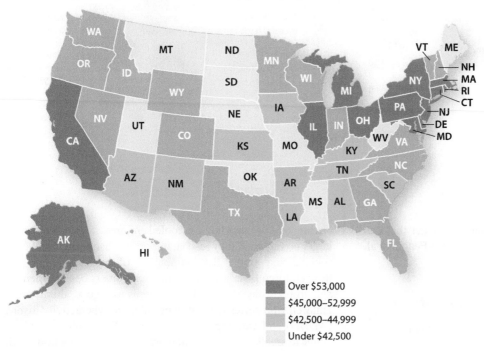

Over $53,000

$45,000–52,999

$42,500–44,999

Under $42,500

Note: Data released in 2008 for 2006–2007.
Source: Di Carlo and Johnson 2008.
State averages for teacher salaries range from a low of $35,378 in South Dakota to a high of $63,640 in Massachusetts.

Each college student is eventually exposed to these competing subcultures and must determine which (if any) seems most in line with his or her feelings and interests.

The typology used by the researchers reminds us that school is a complex social organization—almost like a community with different neighborhoods. Of course, these four subcultures are not the only ones evident on college campuses in the United States. For example, one might find subcultures of Vietnam veterans or former full-time homemakers at community colleges and four-year commuter institutions. And as more and more students from minority groups decide to continue their formal education beyond high school, subcultures based on race and ethnicity will become more evident. As Figure 43-2 shows, college campuses are becoming increasingly diverse.

Sociologist Joe R. Feagin has studied a distinctive collegiate subculture: Black students at predominantly White universities. These students must function academically and socially within universities where there are few Black faculty members or administrators, where harassment of Blacks by campus police is common, and where curricula place little emphasis on Black contributions. Feagin (1989:11) suggests that "for minority students life at a predominantly White college or university means long-term encounters with pervasive whiteness." In Feagin's view, Black students at such institutions experience both blatant and subtle

own. The Harvey Milk High School was named in memory of San Francisco's first openly gay city supervisor, who was assassinated in 1978 (Gay, Lesbian and Straight Education Network 2010).

We can find a similar diversity of student groups at the college level. Burton Clark and Martin Trow (1966) and more recently, Helen Lefkowitz Horowitz (1987) have identified four distinctive subcultures among college students:

1. The *collegiate* subculture focuses on having fun and socializing. These students define what constitutes a "reasonable" amount of academic work (and what amount of work is "excessive" and leads to being labeled as a "grind"). Members of the collegiate subculture have little commitment to academic pursuits. Athletes often fit into this subculture.

2. The *academic* subculture identifies with the intellectual concerns of the faculty and values knowledge for its own sake.

3. The *vocational* subculture is interested primarily in career prospects and views college as a means of obtaining degrees that are essential for advancement.

4. Finally, the *nonconformist* subculture is hostile to the college environment and seeks ideas that may or may not relate to academic studies. This group may find outlets through campus publications or issue-oriented groups.

Student subcultures are more diverse today than in the past. Many adults are returning to college to obtain further education, advance their careers, or change their line of work.

FIGURE 43-2 **College Campuses by Race and Ethnicity: Then, Now, and in the Future**

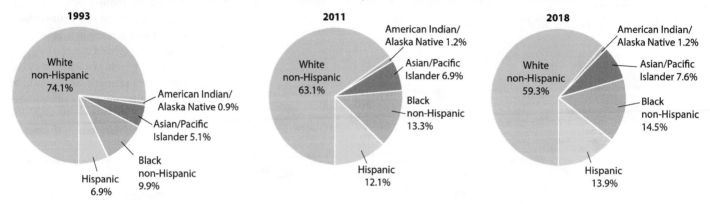

Note: Percentages do not add to 100 due to rounding error.
Source: National Center for Education Statistics 2009a.

racial discrimination, which has a cumulative impact that can seriously damage the students' confidence (see also Feagin et al. 1996).

 use your **sociological imagination**

What distinctive subcultures can you identify at your college?

Homeschooling

When most people think of school, they think of bricks and mortar and the teachers, administrators, and other employees who staff school buildings. But for an increasing number of students in the United States, home is the classroom and the teacher is a parent. About 1.5 million students are now being educated at home. That is about 3 percent of the K–12 school population. For these students, the issues of bureaucratization and social structure are less significant than they are for public school students (Grady et al. 2010).

In the 1800s, after the establishment of public schools, families that taught their children at home lived in isolated environments or held strict religious views that were at odds with the secular environment of public schools. But today, homeschooling is attracting a broader range of families not necessarily tied to organized religion. Poor academic quality, peer pressure, and school violence are motivating many parents to teach their children at home. In addition, some immigrants choose homeschooling as a way to ease their children's transition to a new society. For example, the growing Arab American population recently joined the movement toward homeschooling (MacFarquhar 2008; National Center for Education Statistics 2009b).

While supporters of homeschooling believe children can do just as well or better in homeschools as in public schools, critics

counter that because homeschooled children are isolated from the larger community, they lose an important chance to improve their socialization skills. But proponents of homeschooling claim their children benefit from contact with others besides their own age group. They also see homeschools as a good alternative for children who suffer from attention-deficit/hyperactivity disorder (ADHD) and learning disorders (LDs). Such children often do better in smaller classes, which present fewer distractions to disturb their concentration.

Quality control is an issue in homeschooling. While homeschooling is legal in all 50 states, 10 states require no notification that a child will be homeschooled, and another 14 require notification only. Other states may require parents to submit their children's curricula or test scores for professional evaluation. Despite the lack of uniform standards, a research review by the Home School Legal Defense Association (2005) reports that homeschooled students score higher than others on standardized tests, in every subject and every grade.

Who are the people who are running homeschools? In general, they tend to have higher-than-average incomes and educational levels. Most are two-parent families, and their children watch less television than average—both factors that are likely to support superior educational performance. The same students, with the same support from their parents, would probably do just as well in the public schools. As research has repeatedly shown, small classes are better than big classes, and strong parental and community involvement is key (R. Cox 2003:28).

Whatever the controversy over homeschooling in the United States, it is much less serious than in some other nations. In 2010 the U.S. Immigration and Naturalization Service began granting political asylum to German families who homeschool their children, in violation of their country's constitution. German parents can be fined and imprisoned for homeschooling their children (Francis 2010).

No Child Left Behind Act

The consensus was clear: too many public schools in the United States were failing to educate their students—failing to meet even minimum performance standards. In the 2000 presidential election campaign, President George W. Bush had promised to "leave no child behind" if he were elected. The president had advocated an educational reform plan that he had instituted in the Texas public schools while he was governor of that state. In 2001, the U.S. House of Representatives voted 381–41, and the Senate 87–10, to approve the president's No Child Left Behind (NCLB) Act, an initiative designed to improve the performance of public schools in the United States. The NCLB increased federal standards of accountability for states, school districts, and schools, and gave parents more flexibility in choosing which schools their children would attend.

The apparent consensus for educational reform soon disappeared, however. Supporters charged that the act was not being enforced stringently enough; others felt the legislation went too far. What does this state of affairs say about the NCLB in particular, and about the school reform movement in general?

Understanding the Issue

The NCLB must be viewed in the context of the United States' unusual educational system. In this country, unlike most others, public schools are locally run and financed, albeit with some federal and state aid. The United States does not have a national education program that follows a common curriculum. Until the 1940s, in fact, the federal government had very little involvement with public education. But in the 1990s, public concern over poor student performance in the United States, compared to that of other countries, led to the establishment of national educational standards.

The NCLB built on those national standards, and for the first time set penalties for failure to meet them. States are now required to conduct annual assessments of all public school students, grades K–12. The resulting performance data must be cross-tabulated by students' race, ethnicity, gender, social class, and disability. Schools whose students do not perform well on the required tests are subject to restructuring, and their students are eligible to transfer to different schools. Theoretically, the testing requirements and the penalties associated with substandard performance should reduce the achievement gap between advantaged and disadvantaged students, allowing the nation to "leave no child behind." The program's ambitious goal is for every student in the nation to be proficient in reading and mathematics by the year 2014.

The NCLB has created a national debate about how best to offer high-quality schooling to all children. Some critics have charged that the program has no substance—that the required testing is just an academic exercise. Others charge that it over-emphasizes reading and math at the expense of other subjects, such as art, music, and social studies. Indeed, many principals have reworked their curricula and staff to emphasize the subjects that are tested under the NCLB. Finally, state and local educators have complained bitterly about federal intrusion into local schools. They insist that they need more federal funding if they are to have any hope of complying with the act (Schneider and Keesler 2007).

Applying Sociology

From a functionalist point of view, the development of common curricular objectives promotes social integration. Because the NCLB requires scores to be broken out by gender, race, income, ethnicity, and disability, it prevents schools from disguising low achievement by disadvantaged students. The result should be better educational achievement across the board. Conflict theorists support the need to educate all students, regardless of their socioeconomic status, but they question the wisdom of pursuing that goal through testing programs.

Even before the NCLB, educational testing was a hot issue. From preschool screening through entry-level professional examinations, the practice has always been controversial. Recall Diane Ravitch's critique of "teaching to the test" in the book excerpt that opened this chapter. Ravitch would contend that measuring educational outcomes only through scores on multiple-choice tests ignores or belittles many important goals. Other critics have raised serious questions about the reliability and validity of such tests. Recall from Module 5 that **validity** refers to the degree to which a measure or scale truly reflects the phenomenon under study. Does an aptitude test really measure the likelihood of future academic success, for instance? **Reliability** refers to the extent to which a measure provides consistent results. If an exam supposedly measures a student's readiness to study high school algebra, it should yield the same result, no matter who administers and scores it.

Reliability and validity are major issues in constructing any test; rarely are these concerns totally resolved. Scholars who design standardized tests are constantly tweaking the questions to improve the tests' reliability and validity. From preschool to graduate and professional programs, the reliability and validity of tests affect everything from the allocation of funds to admissions decisions in highly competitive programs. With high-stakes testing—testing that determines

(continued)

whether a public school closes or remains open, for instance—these issues become even more important.

Initiating Policy

National policy efforts like the NCLB overlay a patchwork of state and local programs. Educational reformers have yet to come up with a solution that fits all schools in all states. Former Representative Dick Gephardt, a Democrat who voted for the act, has complained that the program does not do what it claimed it would: "We were all fooled into it. It is a fraud." Still, many educators see the NCLB as their best hope so far for improving the nation's schools. According to Peggy Hinckley, an Indiana School superintendent, "We are living in a results-oriented society. Everybody is looking for results and we will do whatever we can to achieve them" (Dobbs 2004:29; Schrag 2004:40).

In 2007, an independent commission advocated maintaining the 2014 goals, even though by its own estimate, only a small portion of the nation's schools would reach the objectives. By that time, only 13 percent of the nation's eighth graders are expected to reach the mathematics objectives. A maximum of 33 percent of all third graders are expected to meet the reading objectives. Indeed, several states have purposefully been moving very slowly toward meeting the objectives, assuming they would be revised downward. As of 2009, however, there was little indication that Congress planned to move in that direction (Dillon 2008; Tommy Thompson and Barnes 2007:69).

By 2010, President Obama had resisted calls to abandon the NCLB, and his administration proposed judging the

Reflecting disappointment over the performance of public schools, the School District of Philadelphia turned management of several schools over to Mastery, a local operator of charter schools.

results of the program on more comprehensive criteria, including graduation rates and individual progress as well as test scores. In addition, the administration planned to spend over $4 billion to make over the nation's 5,000 lowest-performing schools over three years (Cruz 2010).

TAKE THE ISSUE WITH YOU

1. What are the public schools like in the community where you live? Are some schools in trouble because of high-stakes testing? Does the school system have adequate funding, or are administrators forced to cut corners to stay within budget?

2. What do you think of the practice of restructuring or closing schools whose students do not perform well on national tests? What will be the short-term effect on individual students? The long-term effect on students and schools?

3. Can you think of a better way to improve the nation's public schools?

MODULE 43 | Recap and Review

Summary

Most schools in the United States are organized like formal organizations such as factories and hospitals.

1. Weber's five basic characteristics of bureaucracies are all evident in schools.

2. Teachers are professionals who serve as part of a bureaucracy. There is an inherent conflict in combining those two different roles.

3. Schools provide for students' social and emotional needs as well as their educational needs. Student subcultures within high schools and colleges are complex and varied.

4. Homeschooling has become a viable alternative to traditional public and private schools. In some countries homeschooling is illegal.

5. No Child Left Behind is a controversial initiative designed to improve the performance of public schools by increasing federal accountability standards. Critics charge that the program is underfunded, that it overemphasizes reading and math, and that the tests used to assess performance are flawed. In 2010 the Obama administration widened the criteria used to evaluate school performance.

Thinking Critically

1. Select two functions of education and suggest how they could be fulfilled through homeschooling.

2. What student subcultures can you identify on your campus? Which have the highest and lowest social status? How would functionalists, conflict theorists, and interactionists view the existence of student subcultures on a college campus?

Key Terms

Reliability

Validity

The collective nature of religion has led to many forms of religious association. In modern societies, religion has become increasingly formalized. Specific structures such as churches and synagogues have been constructed for religious worship; individuals have been trained for occupational roles within various fields. These developments make it possible to distinguish clearly between the sacred and secular parts of one's life—a distinction that could not be made easily in earlier times, when religion was largely a family activity carried out in the home.

Four Basic Forms of Organization

Sociologists find it useful to distinguish among four basic forms of organization: the ecclesia, the denomination, the sect, and the new religious movement, or cult. We can see differences among these four forms of organization in their size, power, degree of commitment that is expected from members, and historical ties to other faiths.

Ecclesiae

An **ecclesia** (plural, *ecclesiae*) is a religious organization that claims to include most or all members of a society and is recognized as the national or official religion. Since virtually everyone belongs to the faith, membership is by birth rather than conscious decision. Examples of ecclesiae include Islam in Saudi Arabia and Buddhism in Thailand. However, significant differences exist within this category. In Saudi Arabia's Islamic regime, leaders of the ecclesia hold vast power over actions of the state. In contrast, the Lutheran Church in contemporary Sweden holds no such power over the Riksdag (parliament) or the prime minister.

Generally, ecclesiae are conservative, in that they do not challenge the leaders of a secular government. In a society with an ecclesia, the political and religious institutions often act in harmony and reinforce each other's power in their relative spheres of influence. In the modern world, ecclesiae are declining in power.

Denominations

A **denomination** is a large, organized religion that is not officially linked to the state or government. Like an ecclesia, it tends to have an explicit set of beliefs, a defined system of authority, and a generally respected position in society. Denominations claim as members large segments of a population. Generally, children accept the denomination of their parents and give little thought to membership in other faiths. Denominations also resemble ecclesiae in that they make few demands on members.

However, there is a critical difference between these two forms of religious organization. Although the denomination is considered respectable and is not viewed as a challenge to the secular government, it lacks the official recognition and power held by an ecclesia (Doress and Porter 1977).

The United States is home to a large number of denominations. In good measure, this diversity is a result of our nation's immigrant heritage. Many settlers brought with them the religious commitments native to their homelands. Some Christian denominations in the United States, such as the Roman Catholics, Episcopalians, and Lutherans, are the outgrowth of ecclesiae established in Europe. New Christian denominations also emerged, including the Mormons and Christian Scientists. Within the past generation, immigrants have increased the number of Muslims, Hindus, and Buddhists living in the United States.

Although by far the largest denomination in the United States is Roman Catholicism, at least 24 other Christian faiths have 1 million or more members. Protestants collectively accounted for about 34 percent of the nation's adult population in 2008, compared to 25 percent for Roman Catholics and 2 percent for Jews. There are also 5 million Muslims in the United States, and large numbers of people adhere to Eastern faiths such as Buddhism (3 million) and Hinduism (1 million) (Britannica Online 2010; Kosmin and Keysar 2009; Lindner 2008). The Research Today box takes a look at Islam in the United States.

Sects

A **sect** can be defined as a relatively small religious group that has broken away from some other religious organization to renew what it considers the original vision of the faith. Many sects, such as that led by Martin Luther during the Reformation, claim to be the "true church," because they seek to cleanse the established faith of what they regard as extraneous beliefs and rituals (Stark and Bainbridge 1985). Max Weber ([1916] 1958:114) termed the sect a "believer's church," because affiliation is based on conscious acceptance of a specific religious dogma.

Sects are fundamentally at odds with society and do not seek to become established national religions. Unlike ecclesiae and denominations, they require intensive commitments and demonstrations of belief by members. Partly owing to their outsider status, sects frequently exhibit a higher degree of religious fervor and loyalty than more established religious groups. Recruitment focuses mainly on adults, and acceptance comes through conversion.

Sects are often short-lived. Those that survive may become less antagonistic to society over time and begin to resemble denominations. In a few instances, sects have endured over several

Islam in the United States

The growing presence of Islam in the United States is promoting better understanding of the significant diversity *within* Islam. Throughout the world, including the United States, Muslims are divided into a variety of sects, such as Sunni and Shia (or Shiite). These divisions sometimes result in antagonism, just as rivalries between Christian denominations can cause friction. Yet the Islamic faith is expressed in many different ways, even among Sunnis or Shia. To speak of Muslims as either Sunni or Shia would be like speaking of Christians as either Roman Catholic or Baptist.

The great majority of Muslims in the United States are Sunni Muslims—literally, those who follow the *Sunnah,* or way of the Prophet. Compared to other Muslims, Sunnis tend to be more moderate in their religious orthodoxy. The Shia, who come primarily from Iraq and Iran, are the second-largest group. Shia Muslims are more attentive to guidance from accepted Islamic scholars than are Sunnis. In sufficient numbers, these two Muslim groups will choose to worship separately, even if they must cross ethnic or linguistic lines to do so. That certainly is the case in U.S. cities with large and varied Muslim communities.

Estimating the number of Muslim Americans in the United States is even more difficult than estimating the number of Arab Americans (see Module 31). There are no census data on Muslim Americans, and Islamic institutions such as mosques tend to operate autonomously. Even the most scientific analyses of the topic vary widely in their estimates. Based on the most recent studies, we can say that there are between 3 million and 5.7 million or more Muslims in the United States. About two-thirds of those residents are native-born citizens. In terms of ethnic and racial background, the estimated breakdown of Muslim Americans is as follows:

- 20–42 percent African American
- 24–33 percent South Asian (Afghan, Bangladeshi, Indian, and Pakistani)
- 12–32 percent Arab
- 15–22 percent "other" (Bosnian, Iranian, and Turk, as well as White and Hispanic converts)

All scholars agree that the Muslim population in the United States is growing rapidly, through both immigration and religious conversion.

From these data, we can determine that African Americans who embrace Islam form a significant segment of the Muslim American community. The history of Black American Islam began in the 17th century, when members of some Muslim tribes were forcibly transported to the American colonies. An estimated 10 percent of African slaves were Muslim. Today's Black Islamic community emerged in the 20th century, however, based on the teachings of

In the United States, Muslim Americans must focus strongly on their faith to survive within the permissive mainstream culture. This Islamic school allows Muslim girls to play basketball without compromising their modesty.

Elijah Muhammad. The Nation of Islam, a sect that focuses on the condition of Blacks in the United States as well as on the teachings of the Qur'an, was formed by Muhammad's followers. Today, African American adherents of Islam reflect a variety of orientations, some unique to the United States and others tied to the larger Muslim community.

> To many Muslim Americans, the popular culture of the United States celebrates money and sex.

Though mosques are becoming more common in the United States, these houses of worship attract a different kind of attention than a traditional church with a steeple. To many people in the United States, the mosque represents not religious freedom and diversity but a "foreign threat." Some communities have attempted to block the construction of Muslim religious centers. In return for a permit, local authorities may require that the buildings be stripped of the usual cultural symbols, perhaps even the traditional dome. On college campuses, administrators have responded more constructively to growing numbers of Muslim students, by hiring part-time imams (prayer leaders) to minister to their needs, dedicating space for daily prayer, and providing for Muslim dietary restrictions.

How does being Muslim in the United States differ from being Muslim in an Islamic country? In the United States, Muslim Americans reflect the diversity of the worldwide Islamic faith, but they practice their faith in a nation where Christianity is the dominant cultural influence. Some Islamic scholars argue that the democracy, religious diversity, and freedom of expression that Muslims experience in the United States have encouraged a stronger, more correct Islamic practice, uninhibited by the government interference that is characteristic of many Islamic states.

Other scholars contend that what makes the Muslim American experience unique is that followers must focus even more strongly on their religion in order to survive in a culture that is so permissive. Indeed, U.S. culture encourages many behaviors that are prohibited by Islamic law or cultural tradition. To many Muslim Americans, the popular culture of the United States celebrates money and sex. Muslim Americans, then, feel both the freedom to practice their faith as they choose and the pressure to remain Muslim.

LET'S DISCUSS

1. Is there a mosque in your community or a Muslim congregation on your campus? If so, are the members primarily Sunni or Shia? Immigrants or African Americans?

2. Should communities be allowed to block the construction of mosques or dictate their appearance? Would your answer be the same if your community tried to block the construction of a church or temple?

Sources: Grossman 2008; Leonard 2003; McCloud 1995; Pew Forum on Religion and Public Life 2008, 2009; Selod 2008a.

Characteristic	Ecclesia	Denomination	Sect	New Religious Movement (or Cult)
Size	Very large	Large	Small	Small
Wealth	Extensive	Extensive	Limited	Variable
Religious services	Formal, little participation	Formal, little participation	Informal, emotional	Variable
Doctrines	Specific, but interpretation may be tolerated	Specific, but interpretation may be tolerated	Specific, purity of doctrine emphasized	Innovative, pathbreaking
Clergy	Well-trained, full-time	Well-trained, full-time	Trained to some degree	Unspecialized
Membership	By virtue of being a member of society	By acceptance of doctrine	By acceptance of doctrine	By an emotional commitment
Relationship to the state	Recognized, closely aligned	Tolerated	Not encouraged	Ignored or challenged

Source: Adapted from Vernon 1962; see also Chalfant et al. 1994.

generations while remaining fairly separate from society. Sociologist J. Milton Yinger (1970:226–273) uses the term **established sect** to describe a religious group that is the outgrowth of a sect, yet remains isolated from society. Hutterites, Jehovah's Witnesses, Seventh-Day Adventists, and Amish are contemporary examples of established sects in the United States.

New Religious Movements or Cults

In 1997, 38 members of the Heaven's Gate cult were found dead in Southern California after a mass suicide timed to occur with the appearance of the Hale-Bopp comet. They believed the comet hid a spaceship on which they could catch a ride once they had broken free of their "bodily containers."

Partly as a result of the notoriety generated by such groups, the popular media have stigmatized the word *cult,* associating it with the occult and the use of intense and forceful conversion techniques. The stereotyping of cults as uniformly bizarre and unethical has led sociologists to abandon the term and refer instead to a *new religious movement (NRM).* While some NRMs exhibit strange behavior, many do not. They attract new members just like any other religion, and often follow teachings similar to those of established Christian denominations, though with less ritual.

Sects are difficult to distinguish from cults. A **new religious movement (NRM)** or **cult** is generally a small, secretive religious group that represents either a new religion or a major innovation of an existing faith. NRMs are similar to sects in that they tend to be small and are often viewed as less respectable than more established faiths. Unlike sects, however, NRMs normally do not result from schisms or breaks with established ecclesiae or denominations. Some cults, such as those focused on UFO sightings, may be totally unrelated to existing faiths. Even when a cult does accept certain fundamental tenets of a dominant faith—such as a belief in Jesus as divine or in Mohammad as a messenger of God—it will offer new revelations or insights to

justify its claim to being a more advanced religion (Stark and Bainbridge 1979, 1985).

Like sects, NRMs may be transformed over time into other types of religious organization. An example is the Christian Science Church, which began as a new religious movement under the leadership of Mary Baker Eddy. Today, this church exhibits the characteristics of a denomination. In fact, most major religions, including Christianity, began as cults. NRMs may be in the early stages of developing into a denomination or new religion, or they may just as easily fade away through the loss of members or weak leadership (R. Schaefer and Zellner 2011).

Comparing Forms of Religious Organization

How can we determine whether a particular religious group falls into the sociological category of ecclesia, denomination, sect, or NRM? As we have seen, these types of religious organization have somewhat different relationships to society. Ecclesiae are recognized as national churches; denominations, although not officially approved by the state, are generally widely respected. In contrast, sects and NRMs are much more likely to be at odds with the larger culture.

Still, ecclesiae, denominations, and sects are best viewed as types along a continuum rather than as mutually exclusive categories. Table 46-1 summarizes some of the primary characteristics of the ideal types. Since the United States has no ecclesiae, sociologists studying this country's religions have focused on the denomination and the sect. These religious forms have been pictured on either end of a continuum, with denominations accommodating to the secular world and sects protesting against established religions. Although NRMs also are included in the table, they lie outside the continuum, because they generally define themselves in terms of a new view of life rather than in terms of existing religious faiths. In fact, one of the most controversial NRMs, the Church of Scientology, may not fully qualify as a religion (see the Research Today box).

Research Today

The Church of Scientology: Religion or Quasi-Religion?

From the public statements of entertainers Tom Cruise, Kirstie Alley, and John Travolta to representations on *South Park*, probably no faith has come under as much scrutiny in the past 60 years, or been more misunderstood, than the Church of Scientology. Scientology bears little if any relationship to any other organized religious group, either historically or ideologically. Indeed, its detractors—and there are many, as we will see—question whether it should even be considered a religion.

The Church of Scientology was founded and continues to be based on the voluminous writings of L. Ron Hubbard (1911–1986). Hubbard described a spiritual system that he called Dianetics, in which the individual strives to achieve a heightened, positive state of mind. Essential to Dianetics is a process known as auditing, which is usually the first step in becoming a Scientologist. Auditing is a form of personal counseling in which the auditor, always a church member, measures a person's mental state using an Electropsychometer ("E-Meter"), a device developed by Hubbard.

> Scientology bears little if any relationship to any other organized religious group, either historically or ideologically.

Members of the Church of Scientology call it the only major new religion to have emerged in the 20th century. They consider their faith to be similar to the Judeo-Christian and Eastern religions, particularly Buddhism.

Skeptics find this claim to be far-fetched. The fact that an organization has declared its doctrine to be a religion does not make it so, they counter. Indeed, some scholars treat the Church of Scientology as a **quasi-religion,** a category that includes organizations that may see themselves as religious but may be seen by others as "sort of religious." Included in this category are Maharishi Mahesh Yogi's Transcendental Meditation (TM), introduced in 1958, and the New Age movements.

Though research on the Church of Scientology is admittedly limited, scholars are moving toward accepting it as a religion. Scientology is a body of belief that offers an explanation for the world, a purpose for humankind, and answers to issues like salvation and the afterlife. Acknowledging this body of belief as a religion, however, would not mean that scholars regard it as an accurate worldview, any more than they might consider Episcopalian or Hindu doctrine to be accurate.

Organizationally, many scholars of religion find Scientology's method of financing its operations problematic. Most religious organizations seek voluntary contributions toward their operating expenses, along with payment for specific services, such as child care programs and youth activities. They do not construe these monies as direct payments for instruction in their doctrine. In contrast, the Church of Scientology's doctrine includes the concept of "reciprocity," meaning that members are expected to pay for the spiritual benefits they receive through auditing and training.

Religion or quasi-religion? Founded in the 20th century, the Church of Scientology (shown here in Los Angeles, California) is a successful and growing organization.

an Electropsychometer? If you were considering becoming a Scientologist, what questions would you ask your auditor about this device?

2. Do you agree that Scientology should be considered a religion? Why or why not?

Sources: Bromley and Bracey Jr. 1998; Hubbard 1950; Religious Tolerance 2007; R. Schaefer and Zellner 2011.

LET'S DISCUSS

1. What do you think of the practice of measuring a person's mental state with

---

Sociologists look at religion from an organizational perspective, which tends to stress the stability of religious adherence, but there are other ways to view religion. From an individual perspective, religion and spirituality are remarkably fluid. People often change their places of worship or move from one denomination to another. In many countries, including the United States, churches, temples, and mosques operate in a highly competitive market (Pew Forum on Religion and Public Life 2008; A. Wolfe 2008).

One sign of this fluidity is the rapid rise of still another form of religious organization, the electronic church. Facilitated by cable television and satellite transmission, *televangelists* (as they are called) direct their messages to more people—especially in

the United States—than are served by all but the largest denominations. While some televangelists are affiliated with religious denominations, most give viewers the impression that they are dissociated from established faiths.

At the close of the 1990s, the electronic church began to take on another dimension: the Internet. Today, rather than going to a service in person, many people shop online for a church or faith. Surfers can go to GodTube.com, a video-sharing and social-networking Web site, for spiritually oriented content. Even the Second Life virtual world (described in Module 16) has a rich spiritual landscape, with functioning congregations of Buddhist, Jewish, Muslim, and Christian avatars (Kiper 2008; MacDonald 2007; Simon 2007).

From a sociological point of view, the nation of India is large and complex enough that it might be considered a world of its own. Four hundred languages are spoken in India, 16 of which are officially recognized by the government. Besides the two major religions that originated there—Hinduism and Buddhism—several other faiths animate this society. Demographically the nation is huge, with over a billion residents. This teeming country is expected to overtake China as the most populous nation in the world in about three decades (Third World Institute 2007).

The Religious Tapestry in India

Hinduism and Islam, the two most important religions in India, were described and 411. Islam arrived in India in A.D. 1000, with the first of many Muslim invasions. It flowered there during the Mogul empire (1526–1857), the period when the Taj Mahal was built. Today, Muslims account for 13 percent of India's population; Hindus make up 83 percent.

The presence of one dominant faith influences how a society views a variety of issues, even secular ones. For example, India has emerged as a leader in biotechnology, due at least partly to the Hindu faith's tolerance of stem cell research and cloning—techniques that have been questioned in nations where Christianity dominates. Hinduism is open to the latest biomedical techniques, as long as no evil is intended. The only legal prohibition is that fetuses cannot be terminated for the purpose of providing stem cells. Because of its respect for life in all forms, Hinduism has no major conflict with engineered life-forms of any kind, such as clones (Religion Watch 2006; Sengupta 2006).

Another religion, the Sikh faith, originated in the 15th century with a Hindu named Nanak, the first of a series of gurus (prophets). Sikhism shows the influence of Islam in India, in that it is monotheistic (based on a belief in one god rather than many). It resembles Buddhism in its emphasis on meditation and spiritual transcendence of the everyday world. *Sikhs* (learners) pursue their goal of spiritual enlightenment through meditation with the help of a guru.

Sikh men have a characteristic mode of dress that makes them easy to identify. They do not cut their beards or hair, and they wrap their heads in turbans. (Because of their distinctive dress, the 400,000 Sikhs who live in the United States are often mistaken—and discriminated against—as Muslims.) Sikhs are highly patriotic. Though their 20 million members

make up just 2 percent of India's population, they account for 25 percent of India's army. Their presence in the military gives them a much larger voice in the governance of the country than might be expected, given their numbers (Fausset 2003; Watson 2005).

Another faith that has been influential beyond its numbers in India is Jainism (pronounced *Jinism*). This religion was founded six centuries before the birth of Christ—about the same time as Buddhism—by a young Hindu named Mahavira. Offended by the Hindu caste system—the rigid social hierarchy that reduces some people to the status of outcastes based solely on their birth—and by the numerous Hindu deities, Mahavira left his family and his wealth behind to become a beggar monk. His teachings attracted many followers, and the faith grew and flourished until the Muslim invasions of the 12th century.

According to the Jain faith, there is no god; each person is responsible for his or her spiritual well-being. By following a strict code of conduct, Jains believe they can ultimately free their souls from the endless cycle of death and rebirth and attain *nirvana* (spiritual enlightenment). Jains are required to meditate; forswear lying and stealing; limit their personal wealth; and practice self-denial, chastity, and nonviolence. Because they will not knowingly harm other living beings, including plants and animals, Jains shun meat, fish, or even vegetables whose harvest kills the entire plant, such as carrots and potatoes. They will not work in the military, in farming or fishing, or in the manufacture or sale of alcohol and drugs. Though the Jains are a relatively small group (about 4 million),

Adherents of the Hindu religion participate in fire worship at a celebration in Kerala, India. The Hindu faith is enormously influential in India, the country where most Hindus live.

they exercise considerable influence in India through their business dealings and charitable contributions.

Another group that forms a small segment of the faithful, Christians, also plays a disproportionate role in the country's social safety net. Christian schools, hospitals, and other social service organizations serve non-Christians as well as Christians. Interestingly, hundreds of priests who were trained at churches in India have since immigrated to the United States to ease the shortage of priests there. Together with Jains and Buddhists, Christians make up 4 percent of India's population (Embree 2003; Goodstein 2008).

Religion and the State in India

Religion was influential in India's drive to overturn British colonialism. The great Mohandas K. Gandhi (1869–1948) led the long struggle to regain India's sovereignty, which culminated in its independence in 1947. A proponent of nonviolent resistance, Gandhi persuaded Hindus and Muslims, ancient enemies, to join in defying British domination. But his influence as a peacemaker could not override the Muslims' demand for a separate state of their own. Immediately after independence was granted, India was partitioned into two states, Pakistan for the Muslims and India for the Hindus. The new arrangement caused large-scale migrations of Indians, especially Muslims, from one nation to the other, and sparked boundary disputes that continue to this day. In many areas Muslims were forced to abandon places they considered sacred. In the chaotic months that followed, centuries of animosity between the two groups boiled over into riots, ending in Gandhi's assassination in January 1948.

Today, India is a secular state that is dominated by Hindus (see Figure 45-1). Though the government is officially tolerant of the Muslim minority, tensions between Hindus and Muslims remain high in some states. Conflict also exists among various Hindu groups, from fundamentalists to more secular and ecumenical adherents (Embree 2003).

Many observers see religion as the moving force in Indian society. As in so many other parts of the world, religion is being redefined in India. To the dismay of Sikh spiritual leaders, increasing numbers of young Sikh men are trimming their long hair and abandoning the traditional turban. To show that the 300-year-old tradition is still cool in the 21st century, Sikh leaders now offer a CD-ROM called "Smart Turban 1.0" (Gentleman 2007b).

social policy and Religion

Religion in the Schools

Should public schools be allowed to sponsor organized prayer in the classroom? How about Bible reading, or just a collective moment of silence? Can athletes at public schools offer up a group prayer in a team huddle? Should students be able to initiate voluntary prayers at school events? Each of these situations has been an object of great dissension among those who see a role for prayer in the schools and those who want to maintain strict separation of church and state.

Another controversy concerns the teaching of theories about the origin of humans and the universe. Mainstream scientific thinking holds that humans evolved over billions of years from one-celled organisms, and that the universe came into being 15 billion years ago as a result of a big bang. These theories are challenged by people who hold to the biblical account of the creation of humans and the universe some 10,000 years ago—a viewpoint known as **creationism.** Creationists, many of whom are Christian fundamentalists, want their belief taught in the schools as the only one—or at the very least, as an alternative to the theory of evolution.

Who has the right to decide these issues, and what is the "right" decision? Religion in the schools is one of the thorniest issues in U.S. public policy today.

Understanding the Issue

The issues just described go to the heart of the First Amendment's provisions regarding religious freedom. On the one hand, the government must protect the right to practice one's religion; on the other, it cannot take any measures that would seem to establish one religion over another (separation of church and state).

(continued)

In the key case of *Engle v. Vitale,* the Supreme Court ruled in 1962 that the use of nondenominational prayer in New York schools was "wholly inconsistent" with the First Amendment's prohibition against government establishment of religion. In finding that organized school prayer violated the Constitution—even when no student was required to participate—the Court argued, in effect, that promoting religious observance was not a legitimate function of government or education. Subsequent Court decisions have allowed *voluntary* school prayer by students, but forbid school officials to *sponsor* any prayer or religious observance at school events. Despite these rulings, many public schools still regularly lead their students in prayer recitations or Bible readings. Other states have enacted "moments of silence" during the public school day, which many see as prayer in disguise (Robelon 2007).

School prayer is not the only issue that pits religion against public schools. Unlike Europeans, many people in the United States seem highly skeptical of evolutionary theory, which is taught as a matter of course in science classes. In 2007 a national survey showed that 43 percent of adults believe that God created humans in their present form. Another 38 percent believe that humans developed their present form with divine guidance. Only 14 percent believe that humans developed without divine guidance. And only 18 percent of respondents believe the central tenet of evolutionary theory, that human beings developed over millions of years from less advanced forms of life (Gallup 2009c).

The controversy over whether the biblical account of creation should be presented in school curricula recalls the famous "monkey trial" of 1925. In that trial, high school biology teacher John T. Scopes was convicted of violating a Tennessee law making it a crime to teach the scientific theory of evolution in public schools. Today, creationists have gone beyond espousing fundamentalist religious doctrine; they are attempting to reinforce their position regarding the origins of humanity and the universe with quasi-scientific data.

In 1987, the Supreme Court ruled that states could not compel the teaching of creationism in public schools if the primary purpose was to promote a religious viewpoint. In response, those who believe in the divine origin of life have recently advanced a concept called **intelligent design (ID),** the idea that life is so complex that it could only have been created by intelligent design. Though this concept is not based explicitly on the biblical account of creation, fundamentalists feel comfortable with it. Supporters of intelligent design consider it a more accurate account of the origin of life than Darwinism and hold that, at the very least, ID should be taught as an alternative to the theory of evolution. But in 2005, in *Kitzmiller v. Dove Area*

People on both sides of the debate between science and creationism invoke the name of Albert Einstein. Evolutionists emphasize the need for verifiable scientific data, like that which confirmed Einstein's groundbreaking scientific theories. Advocates of intelligent design quote the Nobel Prize–winning physicist's assertion that religion and science should coexist.

School District, a federal judge ended a Pennsylvania school district's plans to require teachers to present the concept in class. In essence, the judge found ID to be "a religious belief," a subtler but similar approach to creationism in that both find God's fingerprints in nature. The issue continues to be hotly debated and is expected to be the subject of future court cases (Clemmitt 2005; W. Tierney and Holley 2008).

Applying Sociology

Supporters of school prayer and of creationism feel that strict Court rulings have forced too great a separation between what Émile Durkheim called the *sacred* and the *profane.* They insist that the use of nondenominational prayer can in no way lead to the establishment of an ecclesia in the United States. Moreover, they believe that school prayer—and the teaching of creationism—can provide the spiritual guidance and socialization that many children today do not receive from parents or regular church attendance. Many communities also believe that schools should transmit the dominant culture of the United States by encouraging prayer.

Opponents of school prayer and creationism argue that a religious majority in a community might impose viewpoints specific to its faith at the expense of religious minorities. These critics question whether school prayer can remain truly voluntary. Drawing on the interactionist perspective and small-group research, they suggest that children will face enormous social pressure to conform to the beliefs and practices of the majority.

Initiating Policy

Public school education is fundamentally a local issue, so most initiatives and lobbying have taken place at the local or state level. Federal courts have taken a hard line on religion in the schools. In a decision that the Supreme Court reversed in 2004, a federal appeals court ruled that reciting the phrase "under God" during the Pledge of Allegiance that opens each school day violates the U.S. Constitution (Religion News Service 2003).

Religion–school debates show no sign of ending. The activism of religious fundamentalists in the public school system raises the question: Whose ideas and values deserve a hearing in classrooms? Critics see this campaign as one step toward sectarian religious control of public education. They worry that at some point in the future, teachers may not be able to use books or make statements that conflict with fundamentalist interpretations of the Bible. For advocates of a liberal education and of intellectual (and religious) diversity, this is a genuinely frightening prospect (Wilgoren 2005).

TAKE THE ISSUE WITH YOU

1. Was there organized prayer in any school you attended? Was creationism part of the curriculum?
2. Do you think that promoting religious observance is a legitimate function of education?
3. How might a conflict theorist view the issue of organized school prayer?

MODULE 46 | Recap and Review

Summary

Religious organizations grow and evolve over time and in reaction to social changes.

1. Four basic types of religious organizations are the **ecclesia,** the **denomination,** the **sect,** and the **new religious movement,** or **cult.**

2. Advances in communication have led to a new type of church organization, the electronic church. Televangelists now preach to more people than belong to many denominations, and every day millions of people use the Internet for religious purposes.

3. India is a secular state that is dominated by a religious majority, the Hindus. The creation of a separate nation, Pakistan, for the Muslim minority following India's independence in 1947 did not end the centuries-old strife between the two groups, which has worsened with political polarization.

4. Today, the question of how much religion, if any, should be permitted in the U.S. public schools is a matter of intense debate.

Thinking Critically

1. What do you think attracts people to new religious movements?

2. Aside from differences in religious affiliation, how does religious life in India differ from religious life in the United States?

Key Terms

Creationism

Denomination

Ecclesia

Established sect

Intelligent design

New religious movement (NRM) or cult

Quasi-religion

Sect

Power and Authority

In any society, someone or some group—whether it be a tribal chief, a dictator, or a parliament—makes important decisions about how to use resources and how to allocate goods. One cultural universal, then, is the exercise of power and authority. Inevitably, the struggle for power and authority involves **politics,** which political scientist Harold Lasswell (1936) tersely defined as "who gets what, when, and how." In their study of politics and government, sociologists are concerned with social interactions among individuals and groups and their impact on the larger political and economic order.

The social institution that is responsible for implementing and achieving society's goals is the **political system.** Each country has a unique political system that is founded on a recognized set of procedures. The political system interacts closely with the **economic system,** the social institution through with goods and services are produced, distributed, and consumed. As we will see throughout the next four modules, the political and economic systems are inextricably intertwined, and together they regulate power and authority within society.

Power

Power lies at the heart of a political system. According to Max Weber, **power** is the ability to exercise one's will over others. To put it another way, whoever can overcome the resistance of others and control their behavior is exercising power. Power relations can involve large organizations, small groups, or even people in an intimate association.

Because Weber developed his conceptualization of power in the early 1900s, he focused primarily on the nation-state and its sphere of influence. Today scholars recognize that the trend toward globalization has brought new opportunities, and with them new concentrations of power. Power is now exercised on a global as well as a national stage, as countries and multinational corporations vie to control access to resources and manage the distribution of capital (R. Schaefer 2008b; Sernau 2001).

There are three basic sources of power within any political system: force, influence, and authority. **Force** is the actual or threatened use of coercion to impose one's will on others. When leaders imprison or even execute political dissidents, they are applying force; so, too, are terrorists when they seize or bomb an embassy or assassinate a political leader.

In the 21st century, force has taken on new meaning as nations clamp down on use of the Internet to oppose the central government or assert freedom of expression, human rights, and minority or religious views. When a military coup overthrew the democratically elected government of Thailand in September 2006, for example, citizens lost access to Web sites that criticized the takeover. As of 2008, 16 nations maintained selective to pervasive political controls on Internet content (Figure 47-1). Censorship of online content is just as much a use of force as closing down a newspaper or arresting dissidents (Deibert et al. 2008; OpenNet Initiative 2008; Zittrain and Palfrey 2008).

Influence, on the other hand, refers to the exercise of power through a process of persuasion. A citizen may change his or her view of a Supreme Court nominee because of a newspaper editorial, the expert testimony of a law school dean before the Senate Judiciary Committee, or a stirring speech by a political activist at a rally. In each case, sociologists would view such efforts to persuade people as examples of influence. Now let's take a look at the third source of power, *authority.*

Types of Authority

The term **authority** refers to institutionalized power that is recognized by the people over whom it is exercised. Sociologists commonly use the term in connection with those who hold legitimate power through elected or publicly acknowledged positions. A person's authority is often limited. Thus, a referee has the authority to decide whether a penalty should be called during a football game, but has no authority over the price of tickets to the game.

Max Weber ([1913] 1947) developed a classification system for authority that has become one of the most useful and frequently cited contributions of early sociology. He identified three ideal types of authority: traditional, rational-legal, and charismatic. Weber did not insist that only one type applies to a given society or organization. All can be present, but their relative importance will vary. Sociologists have found Weber's typology valuable in understanding different manifestations of legitimate power within a society.

Traditional Authority Until the middle of the past century, Japan was ruled by a

FIGURE 47-1 Filtering Information: Political Content

- ■ Pervasive
- ■ Substantial
- ■ Selective
- ■ Suspected
- □ No evidence
- □ No data (not tested for filtering)

Note: "No data" (see the beige portions of the map) does not necessarily indicate an absence of filtering.
Sources: OpenNet Initiative 2010; see also Deibert et al. 2008; Faris and Villeneuve 2008.
This map highlights nations that filter or restrict content that expresses views that oppose those of the current government, or are related to human rights, freedom of expression, minority rights, and religious movements.

revered emperor whose absolute power was passed down from generation to generation. In a political system based on **traditional authority,** legitimate power is conferred by custom and accepted practice. A king or queen is accepted as ruler of a nation simply by virtue of inheriting the crown; a tribal chief rules because that is the accepted practice. The ruler may be loved or hated, competent or destructive; in terms of legitimacy, that does not matter. For the traditional leader, authority rests in custom, not in personal characteristics, technical competence, or even written law. People accept the ruler's authority because that is how things have always been done. Traditional authority is absolute when the ruler has the ability to determine laws and policies.

Rational-Legal Authority The U.S. Constitution gives Congress and our president the authority to make and enforce laws and policies. Power made legitimate by law is known as **rational-legal authority.** Leaders derive their rational-legal authority from the written rules and regulations of political systems, such as a constitution. Generally, in societies based on rational-legal authority, leaders are thought to have specific areas of competence and authority but are not thought to be endowed with divine inspiration, as in certain societies with traditional forms of authority.

Charismatic Authority Joan of Arc was a simple peasant girl in medieval France, yet she was able to rally the French people and lead them into major battles against English invaders. How was this possible? As Weber observed, power can be legitimized by the *charisma* of an individual. The term **charismatic authority** refers to power made legitimate by a leader's exceptional personal or emotional appeal to his or her followers.

Charisma lets a person lead or inspire without relying on set rules or traditions. In fact, charismatic authority is derived more from the beliefs of followers than from the actual qualities of leaders. So long as people perceive a charismatic leader such as Jesus, Joan of Arc, Gandhi, Malcolm X, or Martin Luther King Jr. as having qualities that set him or her apart from ordinary citizens, that leader's authority will remain secure and often unquestioned.

Observing charismatic authority from an interactionist perspective, sociologist Carl Couch (1996) points out that the growth of the electronic media has facilitated the development of charismatic authority. During the 1930s and 1940s, the heads of state of the United States, Great Britain, and Germany all used radio to issue direct appeals to citizens. Now, television and the Internet allow leaders to "visit" people's homes and communicate with them. In both Taiwan and South Korea in 1996, troubled political leaders facing reelection campaigns spoke frequently to national audiences and exaggerated military threats from neighboring China and North Korea, respectively.

As we noted earlier, Weber used traditional, rational-legal, and charismatic authority as ideal types. In reality, particular leaders and political systems combine elements of two or more of these forms. Presidents Franklin D. Roosevelt, John F. Kennedy, and Ronald Reagan wielded power largely through the rational-legal basis of their authority. At the same time, they were unusually charismatic leaders who commanded the personal loyalty of large numbers of citizens.

Types of Government

Each society establishes a political system through which it is governed. In modern industrial nations, these formal systems of government make a significant number of critical political decisions. We will survey five basic types of government here: monarchy, oligarchy, dictatorship, totalitarianism, and democracy.

Monarchy

A **monarchy** is a form of government headed by a single member of a royal family, usually a king, queen, or some other hereditary ruler. In earlier times, many monarchs claimed that God had granted them a divine right to rule. Typically, they governed on the basis of traditional forms of authority, sometimes accompanied by the use of force. By the beginning of the 21st century, however, monarchs held genuine governmental power in only a few nations, such as Monaco. Most monarchs now have little practical power; they serve primarily ceremonial purposes.

Oligarchy

An **oligarchy** is a form of government in which a few individuals rule. A rather old method of governing that flourished in ancient Greece and Egypt, oligarchy now often takes the form of military rule. In developing nations in Africa, Asia, and Latin America, small factions of military officers will forcibly seize power, either from legally elected regimes or from other military cliques.

Strictly speaking, the term *oligarchy* is reserved for governments that are run by a few selected individuals. However, the People's Republic of China can be classified as an oligarchy if we stretch the meaning of the term. In China, power rests in the hands of a large but exclusive ruling *group,* the Communist Party. In a similar vein, drawing on conflict theory, one might argue that many industrialized nations of the West should be considered oligarchies (rather than democracies), since only a powerful

North Korea has a totalitarian government whose leadership attempts to control all aspects of people's lives. This billboard, a blatant example of government propaganda, portrays the country's ruthless leader as a benevolent father figure.

few—leaders of big business, government, and the military—actually rule. In Module 48, we will examine the *elite model* of the U.S. political system in greater detail.

Dictatorship and Totalitarianism

A **dictatorship** is a government in which one person has nearly total power to make and enforce laws. Dictators rule primarily through the use of coercion, which often includes torture and executions. Typically, they *seize* power rather than being freely elected (as in a democracy) or inheriting power (as in a monarchy). Some dictators are quite charismatic and manage to achieve a certain popularity, though their supporters' enthusiasm is almost certainly tinged with fear. Other dictators are bitterly hated by the people over whom they rule.

Frequently, dictators develop such overwhelming control over people's lives that their governments are called *totalitarian.* (Monarchies and oligarchies may also achieve this type of dominance.) **Totalitarianism** involves virtually complete government control and surveillance over all aspects of a society's social and political life. Germany during Hitler's reign, the Soviet Union in the 1930s, and North Korea today are classified as totalitarian states.

Democracy

In a literal sense, **democracy** means government by the people. The word *democracy* originated in two Greek roots—*demos,* meaning "the populace" or "the common people," and *kratia,* meaning "rule." Of course, in large, populous nations such as the United States, government by the people is impractical at the national level. Americans cannot vote on every important issue that comes before Congress. Consequently, popular rule is generally maintained through **representative democracy,** a form of government in which certain individuals are selected to speak for the people.

The United States is commonly classified as a representative democracy, since the elected members of Congress and state legislatures make our laws. However, critics have questioned how representative our democracy really is. Do Congress and the state legislatures genuinely represent the masses? Are the people of the United States legitimately self-governing, or has our government become a forum for powerful elites? We will explore these issues in Module 48. First, however, we will turn to a central aspect of social relations: conflict.

● War and Peace

Too often conflict becomes ongoing and violent, engulfing innocent bystanders as well as intentional participants. Sociologists Theodore Caplow and Louis Hicks (2002:3) have defined **war** as conflict between organizations that possess trained combat forces equipped with deadly weapons. This meaning is broader than the legal definition, which typically requires a formal declaration of hostilities.

War

Sociologists approach war in three different ways. Those who take a *global view* study how and why two or more nations become engaged in military conflict. Those who take a *nation-state view* stress the interaction of internal political, socioeconomic, and cultural forces. And those who take a *micro view* focus on the social impact of war on individuals and the groups they belong to (Kiser 1992).

The internal decision-making process that leads to war has been much studied. During the Vietnam War, Presidents Johnson and Nixon both misled Congress, painting a falsely optimistic picture of the likely outcome. Based on their intentional distortions, Congress appropriated the military funds the two administrations requested. But in 1971 the *New York Times* published a set of classified documents now known as "The Pentagon Papers," which revealed the real prospects for the war. Two years later—over Nixon's veto—Congress passed the War Powers Act, which requires the president to notify Congress of the reasons for committing combat troops to a hostile situation (Patterson 2003).

Although the decision to go to war is made by government leaders, public opinion plays a significant role in its execution. By

1971, the number of U.S. soldiers killed in Vietnam had surpassed 50,000, and antiwar sentiment was strong. Surveys done at that time showed the public was split roughly equally on the question of whether war was an appropriate way to settle differences between nations (Figure 47-2). This division in public opinion continued until the United States became involved in the Gulf War following Iraq's invasion of Kuwait in 1990. Since then, U.S. sentiment has been more supportive of war as a means of resolving disputes.

A major change in the composition of the U.S. military is the growing presence of women. Over 197,000 women, or about 14 percent of active U.S. military forces, are now in uniform, serving not just as support personnel but as an integral part of combat units. The first casualty of the war in Iraq, in fact, was Private First Class Lori Piestewa, a member of the Hopi tribe and a descendant of Mexican settlers in the Southwest (Bureau of the Census 2008a:328).

From a micro view, war can bring out the worst as well as the best in people. In 2004, graphic images of the abuse of Iraqi prisoners by U.S. soldiers at Iraq's Abu Ghraib prison shocked the world. For social scientists, the deterioration of the guards' behavior brought to mind Philip Zimbardo's mock prison experiment, done in 1971. Although the results of the experiment, highlighted in the opening excerpt of Chapter 5, have been applied primarily to civilian correctional facilities, Zimbardo's study was actually funded by the Office of Naval Research. In July 2004, the U.S. military began using a documentary film about the experiment to train military interrogators to avoid mistreatment of prisoners (Zarembo 2004; Zimbardo 2004).

Peace

Sociologists have considered **peace** both as the absence of war and as a proactive effort to develop cooperative relations among nations. While we will focus here on international relations, we should note that in the 1990s, 90 percent of the world's armed conflicts occurred *within* rather than between states. Often, outside powers became involved in these internal conflicts, either as supporters of particular factions or in an attempt to broker a peace accord. In at least 28 countries where such conflicts occurred—none of which would be considered core nations in world systems analysis—at least 10,000 people died (Kriesberg 1992; Dan Smith 1999).

Another way of picturing the relative peacefulness of nations around the world is the Global Peace Index (Figure 47-3). This index is based on 24 indicators, including organized internal conflict, violent crime, political instability, the potential for terrorist acts, and a nation's level of military expenditures compared to its neighbors'. Currently, New Zealand is at the top of the index (very peaceful); Somalia, Afghanistan, and Iraq are at the bottom. The United States ranks 83 on this list of 144 nations, between Ukraine and Kazakhstan.

Sociologists and other social scientists who draw on sociological theory and research have tried to identify conditions that deter war. One of their findings is that international trade may act as a deterrent to armed conflict. As countries exchange goods, people, and then cultures, they become more integrated and less likely to threaten each other's security. Viewed from this perspective,

FIGURE 47-2 U.S. Public Opinion on the Necessity of War, 1971–2007

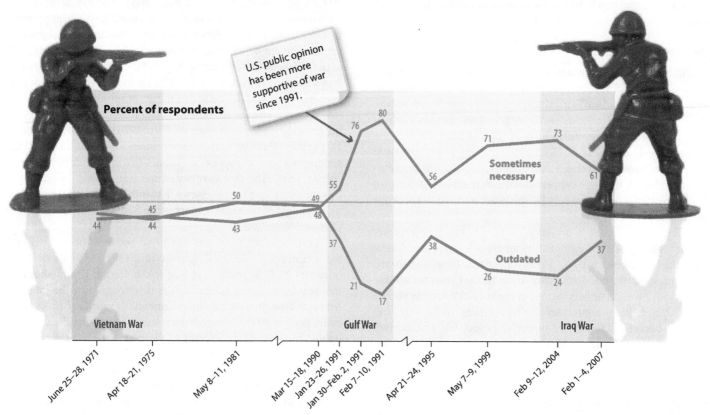

Percent of respondents

U.S. public opinion has been more supportive of war since 1991.

Sometimes necessary

Outdated

44 · 45 · 50 · 49 · 55 · 76 · 80 · 56 · 71 · 73 · 61

44 · 44 · 43 · 48 · 37 · 21 · 17 · 38 · 26 · 24 · 37

Vietnam War · Gulf War · Iraq War

June 25–28, 1971 · Apr 18–21, 1975 · May 8–11, 1981 · Mar 15–18, 1990 · Jan 23–26, 1991 · Jan 30–Feb. 2, 1991 · Feb 7–10, 1991 · Apr 21–24, 1995 · May 7–9, 1999 · Feb 9–12, 2004 · Feb 1–4, 2007

Note: Respondents replied to the following question: "Some people feel that war is an outmoded way of settling differences between nations. Others feel that wars are sometimes necessary to settle differences. With which point of view do you agree?"
Source: Gallup 2009d.

not just trade but immigration and foreign exchange programs have a beneficial effect on international relations.

Another means of fostering peace is the activity of international charities and activist groups called nongovernmental organizations (NGOs). The Red Cross and Red Crescent, Doctors Without Borders, and Amnesty International donate their services wherever they are needed, without regard to nationality. In the past decade or more, these global organizations have been expanding in number, size, and scope. By sharing news of local conditions and clarifying local issues, they often prevent conflicts from escalating into violence and war. Some NGOs have initiated cease-fires, reached settlements, and even ended warfare between former adversaries.

Finally, many analysts stress that nations cannot maintain their security by threatening violence. Peace, they contend, can best be maintained by developing strong mutual security agreements between potential adversaries (Etzioni 1965; Shostak 2002).

In recent years, the United States has begun to recognize that its security can be threatened not just by nation-states, but

A representative of the International Red Crescent Society delivers an aid parcel in the southern Iraqi town of Safwan. The Red Crescent provides emergency aid to victims of war and disaster in Muslim communities. Such nongovernmental organizations (NGOs) help to bind countries together, promoting peaceful relations.

by political groups that operate outside the bounds of legitimate authority. Indeed, terrorism is now considered the foremost threat to U.S. security—one the U.S. military is unaccustomed to fighting.

FIGURE 47-3 **Global Peace Index**

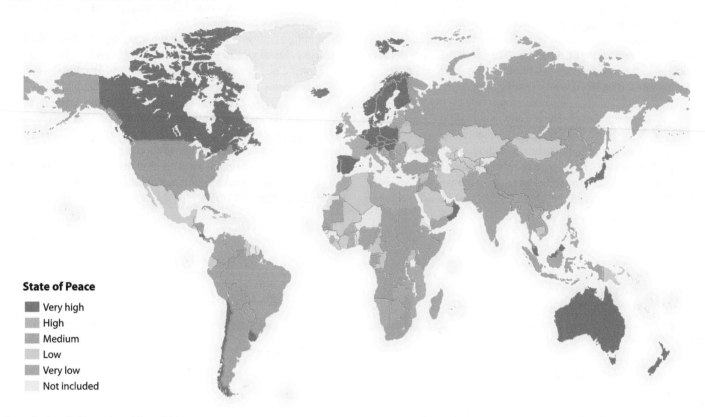

State of Peace

- Very high
- High
- Medium
- Low
- Very low
- Not included

Source: Institute for Economics and Peace 2010.

 use your **sociological imagination**

Do you hear much discussion of how to promote worldwide peace, or do the conversations you hear focus more on ending a particular conflict?

Terrorism

Acts of terror, whether perpetrated by a few or by many people, can be a powerful political force. Formally defined, **terrorism** is the use or threat of violence against random or symbolic targets in pursuit of political aims. For terrorists, the end justifies the means. They believe the status quo is oppressive, and desperate measures are essential to end the suffering of the deprived. Convinced that working through the formal political process will not effect the desired political change, terrorists insist that illegal actions—often directed against innocent people—are needed. Ultimately, they hope to intimidate society and thereby bring about a new political order.

An essential aspect of contemporary terrorism involves use of the media. Terrorists may wish to keep secret their individual identities, but they want their political messages and goals to receive as much publicity as possible. Drawing on Erving

Global terrorism is just that—global in scope and impact. In March 2010, two female suicide bombers from the Caucasus region took 40 lives on the Moscow subway to call attention to their homeland's struggle for political independence from Russia.

Goffman's dramaturgical approach, sociologist Alfred McClung Lee has likened terrorism to the theater, where certain scenes are played out in predictable fashion. Whether through calls to the media, anonymous manifestos, or other means, terrorists typically admit responsibility for and defend their violent acts.

Sociologists and others have studied the role of different factors in the development of terrorism. They find that both democratic and repressive regimes can facilitate terrorism, although in different ways. The likelihood of violence is higher in youthful populations and among alienated groups, especially expatriate (overseas) communities (P. Davis and Cragin 2009).

Since September 11, 2001, governments worldwide have renewed their efforts to fight terrorism. Although the public generally regards increased surveillance and social control as a necessary evil, these measures have nonetheless raised governance issues. For example, some citizens in the United States and elsewhere have questioned whether measures such as the USA Patriot Act of 2001 threaten civil liberties. Citizens also complain about the heightened anxiety created by the vague alerts issued by the federal government from time to time. Worldwide, immigration and the processing of refugees have slowed to a crawl, separating families and preventing employers from filling job openings. As these efforts to combat political violence illustrate, the term *terrorism* is an apt one (R. Howard and Sawyer 2003; Lee 1983; R. Miller 1988).

Like many other aspects of society, terrorism can be viewed from a feminist perspective. That is, terrorism and terrorist movements can be seen symbolically as enactments of masculinity. Thus, organizers and leaders of terrorism are even more likely to be male than members of conventional political organizations. Terrorist acts by women, such as female suicide bombers, are so rare that they attract significant media and societal attention (Ferber and Kimmel 2008).

MODULE 47 | Recap and Review

Summary

Every society must have a **political system** to allocate valued resources.

1. There are three basic sources of **power** within any political system: **force, influence,** and **authority.**

2. Max Weber identified three ideal types of authority: **traditional, rational-legal,** and **charismatic.**

3. There are four basic types of government: **monarchy, oligarchy, dictatorship,** and **democracy.**

4. **War** may be defined as conflict between organizations that possess trained combat forces equipped with deadly weapons—a definition that includes conflict with terrorist organizations.

Thinking Critically

1. On your campus, what are some examples of the three types of authority?

2. Contrast the use of power in a dictatorship with its use in a democracy, as defined by Max Weber.

3. What is the greatest threat to world peace, and how would you counter it?

Key Terms

Authority

Charismatic authority

Democracy

Dictatorship

Economic system

Force

Influence

Monarchy

Oligarchy

Peace

Political system

Politics

Power

Rational-legal authority

Representative democracy

Terrorism

Totalitarianism

Traditional authority

War

The sociocultural evolution approach developed by Gerhard Lenski categorizes preindustrial society according to the way in which the economy is organized. The principal types of preindustrial society, as you recall, are hunting-and-gathering societies, horticultural societies, and agrarian societies.

As we noted in Module 17, the *Industrial Revolution*—which took place largely in England during the period 1760 to 1830—brought about changes in the social organization of the workplace. People left their homesteads and began working in central locations such as factories. As the Industrial Revolution proceeded, a new form of social structure emerged: the **industrial society,** a society that depends on mechanization to produce its goods and services.

Two basic types of economic system distinguish contemporary industrial societies: capitalism and socialism. As described in the following sections, capitalism and socialism serve as ideal types of economic system. No nation precisely fits either model. Instead, the economy of each individual state represents a mixture of capitalism and socialism, although one type or the other is generally more useful in describing a society's economic structure.

Capitalism

In preindustrial societies, land functioned as the source of virtually all wealth. The Industrial Revolution changed all that. It required that certain individuals and institutions be willing to take substantial risks in order to finance new inventions, machinery, and business enterprises. Eventually, bankers, industrialists, and other holders of large sums of money replaced landowners as the most powerful economic force. These people invested their funds in the hope of realizing even greater profits, and thereby became owners of property and business firms.

The transition to private ownership of business was accompanied by the emergence of the capitalist economic system. **Capitalism** is an economic system in which the means of production are held largely in private hands and the main incentive for economic activity is the accumulation of profits. In practice, capitalist systems vary in the degree to which the government regulates private ownership and economic activity (D. Rosenberg 1991).

Immediately following the Industrial Revolution, the prevailing form of capitalism was what is termed **laissez-faire** ("let them do"). Under the principle of laissez-faire, as expounded and endorsed by British economist Adam Smith (1723–1790), people could compete freely, with minimal government intervention in the economy. Business retained the right to regulate itself and operated essentially without fear of government interference (Smelser 1963).

Two centuries later, capitalism has taken on a somewhat different form. Private ownership and maximization of profits still remain the most significant characteristics of capitalist economic systems. However, in contrast to the era of laissez-faire, capitalism today features government regulation of economic relations. Without restrictions, business firms can mislead consumers, endanger workers' safety, and even defraud the companies' investors—all in the pursuit of greater profits. That is why the government of a capitalist nation often monitors prices, sets safety and environmental standards for industries, protects the rights of consumers, and regulates collective bargaining between labor unions and

trend|spotting

Occupational Growth and Decline

One of the most closely watched trends in the U.S. economy is the growth or decline of particular occupations. In good economic times and bad, people want to know where the jobs of the future will be. As a result, the Bureau of Labor Statistics regularly projects job growth over the next 10 years.

In the United States today, most new job openings are expected to require little formal education, or at most on-the-job training. Construction laborers, groundskeepers, and food preparers are three occupations that are expected to see a large increase in employment. Skilled occupations such as nurses, accountants, and teachers from preschool through high school are also expected to see strong growth.

The fastest-growing occupations—those that show the highest growth proportionately—are almost all skilled occupations, most of them in health and medicine. They include biomedical engineers—expected to grow 72 percent over the next 10 years—health aides, physician assistants, and physical therapists. Skilled non-health-related occupations, such as financial examiners and computer software engineers, are also expected to grow.

Finally, there is the other side of the ledger—occupations that are declining in number. The steepest decline, down 33 percent, is expected to occur among sewing machine operators. Other occupations that are expected to see big job losses are farmers, postal workers, telemarketers, switchboard operators, and door-to-door sales workers.

management. Yet under capitalism as an ideal type, government rarely takes over ownership of an entire industry.

Contemporary capitalism also differs from laissez-faire in another important respect: capitalism tolerates monopolistic practices. A **monopoly** exists when a single business firm controls the market. Domination of an industry allows the firm to effectively control a commodity by dictating pricing, quality standards, and availability. Buyers have little choice but to yield to the firm's decisions; there is no other place to purchase the product or service. Monopolistic practices violate the ideal of free competition cherished by Adam Smith and other supporters of laissez-faire capitalism.

Some capitalistic nations, such as the United States, outlaw monopolies through antitrust legislation. Such laws prevent any business from taking over so much of the competition in an industry that it controls the market. The U.S. federal government allows monopolies to exist only in certain exceptional cases, such as the utility and transportation industries. Even then, regulatory agencies scrutinize officially approved monopolies to protect the public. The protracted legal battle between the Justice Department and Microsoft, owner of the dominant operating system for personal computers, illustrates the uneasy relationship between government and private monopolies in capitalistic countries.

For more than a century, the board game of Monopoly has entertained millions of people around the world. In the game, players strive to dominate the fictitious economy, gleefully bankrupting other players. Ironically, Monopoly was actually developed to demonstrate the weaknesses of capitalist economies, such as excessive rents and the tendency for money to accumulate in the hands of a few.

Conflict theorists point out that although *pure* monopolies are not a basic element of the economy of the United States, competition is still much more restricted than one might expect in what is called a *free enterprise system*. In numerous industries, a few companies largely dominate the field and keep new enterprises from entering the marketplace.

During the severe economic downturn that began in 2008, the United States moved even further away from the laissez-faire ideal. To keep major financial institutions from going under, the federal government invested hundreds of millions of dollars in distressed banking, investment, and insurance companies. Then, in 2009, the government bailed out the failing automobile industry, taking a 60 percent interest in General Motors. The Canadian government took another 12 percent.

As we have seen in earlier modules, globalization and the rise of multinational corporations have spread the capitalistic pursuit of profits around the world. Especially in developing countries, governments are not always prepared to deal with the sudden influx of foreign capital and its effects on their economies. One particularly striking example of how unfettered capitalism can harm developing nations is found in the Democratic Republic of the Congo (formerly Zaire). Congo has significant deposits of the metal columbite-tantalite—coltan, for short—which is used in the production of electronic circuit boards. Until the market for cell phones, pagers, and laptop computers heated up, U.S. manufacturers got most of their coltan from Australia. But at the height of consumer demand, they turned to miners in Congo to increase their supply.

Predictably, the escalating price of the metal—as much as $400 a kilogram at one point, or more than three times the average Congolese worker's yearly wages—attracted undesirable attention. Soon the neighboring countries of Rwanda, Uganda, and Burundi, at war with one another and desperate for resources to finance the conflict, were raiding Congo's national parks, slashing and burning to expose the coltan beneath the forest floor. Indirectly, the sudden increase in the demand for coltan was financing war and the rape of the environment. U.S. manufacturers have since cut off their sources in Congo in an effort to avoid abetting the destruction. But their action has only penalized legitimate miners in the impoverished country (Austin 2002; Friends of the Congo 2009).

The Federal Reserve's Board of Governors confers with the presidents of regional reserve banks. The 12-member board, which meets behind closed doors, exerts economic power by controlling key interest rates. Because of the Fed's involvement in economic regulation—a function much publicized during the economic downturn that began in 2008—the United States is not considered a laissez-faire economy.

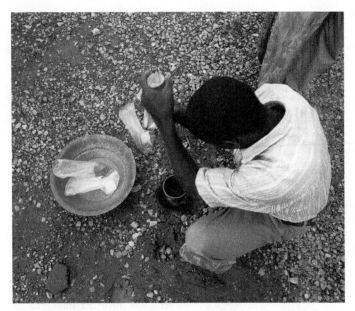

A worker mines for coltan with sweat and a stick. The sudden increase in demand for the metal by U.S. computer manufacturers caused incursions into Congo by neighboring countries hungry for capital to finance a war. Too often, globalization can have unintended consequences for a nation's economy and social welfare.

 use your **sociological imagination**

Which aspects of capitalism do you personally appreciate? Which do you find worrisome?

Socialism

Socialist theory was refined in the writings of Karl Marx and Friedrich Engels. These European radicals were disturbed by the exploitation of the working class that emerged during the Industrial Revolution. In their view, capitalism forced large numbers of people to exchange their labor for low wages. The owners of an industry profit from the labor of workers primarily because they pay workers less than the value of the goods produced.

As an ideal type, a socialist economic system attempts to eliminate such economic exploitation. Under **socialism,** the means of production and distribution in a society are collectively rather than privately owned. The basic objective of the economic system is to meet people's needs rather than to maximize profits. Socialists reject the laissez-faire philosophy that free competition benefits the general public. Instead, they believe that the central government, acting as the representative of the people, should make basic economic decisions. Therefore, government ownership of all major industries—including steel production, automobile manufacturing, and agriculture—is a primary feature of socialism as an ideal type.

In practice, socialist economic systems vary in the extent to which they tolerate private ownership. For example, in Great Britain, a nation with some aspects of both a socialist and a capitalist economy, passenger airline service is concentrated in the government-owned corporation British Airways. Yet private airlines are allowed to compete with it.

Socialist nations differ from capitalist nations in their commitment to social service programs. For example, the U.S. government provides health care and health insurance to the elderly and poor through the Medicare and Medicaid programs. But socialist countries typically offer government-financed medical care to *all* citizens. In theory, the wealth of the people as a collectivity is used to provide health care, housing, education, and other key services to each individual and family.

Marx believed that socialist societies would eventually "wither away" and evolve into *communist* societies. As an ideal type, **communism** refers to an economic system under which all property is communally owned and no social distinctions are made on the basis of people's ability to produce. In recent decades, the Soviet Union, the People's Republic of China, Vietnam, Cuba, and nations in Eastern Europe were popularly thought of as examples of communist economic systems. However, this usage represents an incorrect application of a term with sensitive political connotations. All nations known as communist in the 20th century actually fell far short of the ideal type (Walder and Nguyen 2008).

By the early 1990s, Communist parties were no longer ruling the nations of Eastern Europe. As of 2010, however, China, Cuba, Laos, North Korea, and Vietnam remained socialist societies ruled by Communist parties. Even in those countries, however, capitalism had begun to make inroads. In China, fully 25 percent of the country's production originated in the private business sector. (See the case study Capitalism in China, for a fuller discussion.)

As we have seen, capitalism and socialism serve as ideal types of economic systems. In reality, the economy of each industrial society—including the United States, the European Union, and Japan—includes certain elements of both capitalism and socialism (Table 49-1). Whatever the differences—whether a society more closely fits the ideal type of capitalism or socialism—all industrial societies rely chiefly on mechanization in the production of goods and services.

The Informal Economy

In many countries, one aspect of the economy defies description as either capitalist or socialist. In the **informal economy,** transfers of money, goods, or services take place but are not reported to the government. Examples of the informal economy include trading services with someone—say, a haircut for a computer lesson; selling goods on the street; and engaging in illegal transactions, such as gambling or drug deals. The informal economy also includes off-the-books work in landscaping, street vending, child care, and housecleaning. Participants in this type of economy avoid taxes and government regulations.

In the United States, the informal economy accounts for about 8 percent of total economic activity. In other industrial nations it varies, from 11 percent in Great Britain to 18 percent in Belgium and 25 percent in Greece. In developing nations, the informal economy represents a much larger (40 to 60 percent) and often unmeasured part of total economic activity. Yet because this sector of the economy

Sociology in the Global Community

Working Women In Nepal

Nepal, a small and mountainous Asian country of about 27 million people, has a per capita gross domestic product (GDP) of just $1,040 per year. (The comparable figure in the United States is $45,850.) But gross domestic product seriously understates the true production level in Nepal, for several reasons. Among the most important is that many Nepalese women work in the informal economy, whose activities are not included in the GDP.

Because women's work is undervalued in this traditional society, it is also underreported and underestimated. Official figures state that women account for 27 percent of GDP and form 40 percent of the labor force. But Nepalese women are responsible for 60 percent of additional nonmarket production—that is, work done in the informal economy—and 93 percent of the housework (see the companying figure).

> **Because women's work is undervalued in this traditional society, it is also underreported and underestimated.**

Gender Contributions to GDP and Household Maintenance in Nepal

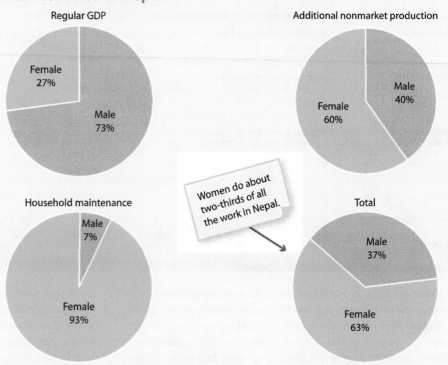

Regular GDP: Female 27%, Male 73%

Additional nonmarket production: Female 60%, Male 40%

Household maintenance: Male 7%, Female 93%

Women do about two-thirds of all the work in Nepal.

Total: Male 37%, Female 63%

Source: Survey by M. Acharya as cited in Mahbub ul Haq Human Development Centre 2000:54.

Most female workers cultivate corn, rice, and wheat on the family farm, where they spend hours on labor-intensive tasks such as fetching water and feeding livestock. Because much of the food they raise is consumed at home, however, it is considered to be nonmarket production. At home, women concentrate on food processing and preparation, caregiving, and other household tasks, such as clothes making. Childbearing and rearing and elder care are particularly crucial activities. Yet none of these chores are considered part of GDP; instead, they are dismissed as "women's work," both by economists and by the women themselves.

The figures on housework and nonmarket production in Nepal come from an independent economic study. To compile them, researchers had to adapt the conventional accounting system by adding a special account dedicated to household maintenance activities. When they did so, women's "invisible work" suddenly became visible and valuable. Not just in Nepal, but in every country, economists need to expand their definitions of work and the labor force to account for the tremendous contributions women make to the world economy.

LET'S DISCUSS

1. In your family, is "women's work" taken for granted? Have you ever tried to figure out what it would cost your family to pay for all the unpaid work women do?

2. Why is recognizing women's work important? How might life for both men and women change if the true economic value of women's work were recognized?

Sources: Acharya 2000; Haub and Kent 2009; Mahbub ul Haq Human Development Centre 2000:54–57.

---

depends to a large extent on the labor of women, work in the informal economy is undervalued or even unrecognized the world over. The Sociology in the Global Community box above explains how the informal economy operates in Nepal (T. Barnes 2009).

Functionalists contend that bureaucratic regulations sometimes contribute to the rise of an informal, underground, economy. In the developing world, governments often set up burdensome business regulations that overworked bureaucrats must administer. When requests for licenses and permits pile up, delaying business projects, legitimate entrepreneurs find they need to go

underground to get anything done. Despite its apparent efficiency, this type of informal economy is dysfunctional for a country's overall political and economic well-being. Since informal firms typically operate in remote locations to avoid detection, they cannot easily expand when they become profitable. And given the limited protection for their property and contractual rights, participants in the informal economy are less likely than others to save and invest their income.

Whatever the functions an informal economy may serve, it is in some respects dysfunctional for workers. Working conditions

Table **49-1** Characteristics of the Three Major Economic Systems

Economic System	Characteristics	Contemporary Examples
Capitalism	Private ownership of the means of production Accumulation of profits the main incentive	Canada Mexico United States
Socialism	Collective ownership of the means of production Meeting people's needs the basic objective	Germany Russia Sweden
Communism	Communal ownership of all property No social distinctions made on basis of people's ability to produce	Cuba North Korea Vietnam

Note: Countries listed in column 3 are typical of one of the three economic systems, but not perfectly so. In practice, the economies of most countries include a mix of elements from the three major systems.

in these illegal businesses are often unsafe or dangerous, and the jobs rarely provide any benefits to those who become ill or cannot continue to work. Perhaps more significant, the longer a worker remains in the informal economy, the less likely that person is to make the transition to the regular economy. No matter how efficient or productive a worker, employers expect to see experience in the formal economy on a job application. Experience as a successful street vendor or self-employed cleaning person does not carry much weight with interviewers (Venkatesh 2006).

case study | Capitalism in China

Today's China is not the China of past generations; it is expected to become the world's largest economy by 2020. (Figure 49-1 shows the world's largest economies over the past 20 years.) In this country where the Communist Party once dominated people's lives, few now bother to follow party proceedings. Instead, after a decade of rapid economic growth, most Chinese are more interested in acquiring the latest consumer goods. Ironically, it was party officials' decision to transform China's economy by opening it up to capitalism that reduced the once-omnipotent institution's influence (*The Economist* 2006a).

The Road to Capitalism

When the communists assumed leadership of China in 1949, they cast themselves as the champions of workers and peasants and the enemies of those who exploited workers, namely landlords and capitalists. Profit making was outlawed, and those who engaged in it were arrested. By the 1960s, China's economy was dominated by huge state-controlled enterprises, such as factories. Even private farms were transformed into community-owned organizations. Peasants essentially worked for the government, receiving payment in goods based on their contribution to the collective good. In addition, they could receive a small plot of land on which to produce food for their families or for exchange with others. But, while the centralization of production for the benefit of all seemed to make sense ideologically, it did not work well economically.

In the 1980s, the government eased restrictions on private enterprise somewhat, permitting small businesses with no more than seven employees. But business owners could not hold policymaking positions in the party, at any level. Late in the decade, party leaders began to make market-oriented reforms, revising the nation's legal structure to promote private business. For the first time, private entrepreneurs were allowed to compete with some state-controlled businesses. By the mid-1990s, impressed with the results of the experiment, party officials had begun to hand some ailing state-controlled businesses over to private entrepreneurs, in hopes they could be turned around (D. Bell 2008).

The Chinese Economy Today

Today, the entrepreneurs who weathered government harassment during the Communist Party's early years are among the nation's wealthiest capitalists. Some even hold positions on government advisory boards. The growing free-market economy they spawned has brought significant inequality to Chinese workers, however, especially between urban and rural workers. Though the move toward market-driven development has been slowing, questions are still being raised about the accumulation of wealth by a few (Sicular et al. 2006).

Chinese capitalists have had to compete with multinational corporations, which can operate more easily in China now, thanks to government economic reforms. General Motors (GM) first became interested in China in 1992, hoping to use the nation's low-cost labor to manufacture cars for overseas markets. But more and more, foreign-owned enterprises like GM are selling to the Chinese market. By 2009 the Chinese were buying more automobiles than people were in the United States (Kahn 2003; Miles 2009).

FIGURE 49-1 World's Largest Economies, 2008

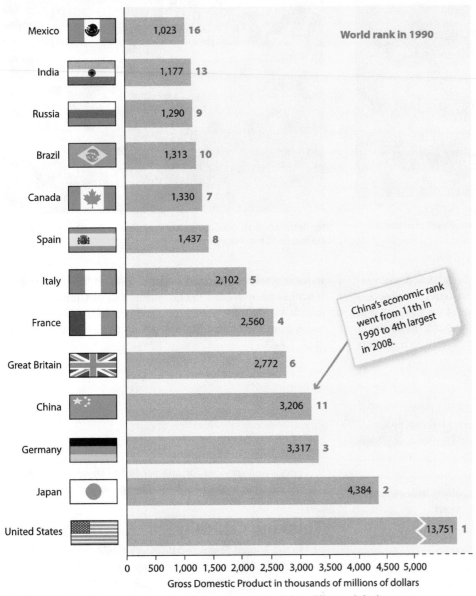

World rank in 1990

Country	GDP	Rank
Mexico	1,023	16
India	1,177	13
Russia	1,290	9
Brazil	1,313	10
Canada	1,330	7
Spain	1,437	8
Italy	2,102	5
France	2,560	4
Great Britain	2,772	6
China	3,206	11
Germany	3,317	3
Japan	4,384	2
United States	13,751	1

China's economic rank went from 11th in 1990 to 4th largest in 2008.

Gross Domestic Product in thousands of millions of dollars

0   500   1,000   1,500   2,000   2,500   3,000   3,500   4,000   4,500   5,000

Note: Data standardized in terms of estimated purchasing power parity to eliminate differences in buying power.
Sources: World Bank, 2007:194–196; 2010b:230–232.

Chinese Workers in the New Economy

For Chinese workers, the loosening of state control over the economy has meant a rise in occupational mobility, which was severely limited in the early days of Communist Party rule. The new markets created by private entrepreneurs are allowing ambitious workers to advance their careers by changing jobs or even cities. On the other hand, many middle-aged urban workers have lost their jobs to rural migrants seeking higher wages. Moreover, the privately owned factories that churn out lawn chairs and power tools for multinational corporations offer limited opportunities and very long hours. Wages average $120 to $200 a month for a six-day workweek.

Serious social problems have accompanied China's massive economic growth. Because safety is not a priority in many businesses, workers suffer from high injury rates. Harsh working conditions contribute to rapid turnover in the labor force. There is no pension system in China, so retirees must struggle to find other ways to support themselves. Pollution is common in urban areas, and environmental problems are extraordinary (Barboza 2008; French 2008).

For the average worker, party membership is less important now than in the past. Instead, managerial skill and experience are much in demand. Hong Kong sociologist Xiaowei Zang (2002) surveyed 900 workers in a key industrial city and found that party members still had an advantage in government and state-owned companies, where they earned higher salaries than other workers. But in private businesses, seniority and either managerial or entrepreneurial experience were what counted. As might be expected, being male and well educated also helped.

Women have been slower to advance in the workplace than men. Traditionally, Chinese women have been relegated to subservient roles in the patriarchal family structure. Communist Party rule has allowed them to make significant gains in employment, income, and education, although not as quickly as promised. For rural women in China, the growth of a market economy has meant a choice between working in a factory or on a farm. Still, despite recent economic changes, emerging research shows that Chinese women receive lower wages than men who work in the same job sectors (Wang and Cai 2006).

With the growth of a middle class and increased education, many Chinese are seeking the same opportunities as their

(continued)

On this seemingly endless assembly line in Dehui City, China, factory workers process chicken parts. China's huge economy will soon become the world's largest.

For better or worse, the expansion of capitalism in China has linked U.S. businesses to that expanding economy.

Western counterparts. The struggle has been particularly visible in the Chinese people's desire for open, unrestricted access to the World Wide Web. In most countries of the world, a Web search for images of Tiananmen Square will call up photos of the 1989 crackdown on student protesters, in which soldiers in tanks attacked unarmed students. But, on the other side of what has been dubbed the Great Firewall of China, the same search yields only photos of visiting diplomats—including those from the United States—posing in the square (Deibert et al. 2008).

MODULE 49 | Recap and Review

Summary

A society's **economic system** has an important influence on social behavior and on other social institutions.

1. With the Industrial Revolution, a new form of social structure emerged: the **industrial society.**

2. Systems of **capitalism** vary in the degree to which the government regulates private ownership and economic activity, but all emphasize the profit motive.

3. The basic objective of **socialism** is to eliminate economic exploitation and meet people's needs. Marx believed that **communism** would evolve naturally out of socialism.

4. In developing nations, the **informal economy** represents a significant part of total economic activity. Yet because this sector depends largely on women's work, it is undervalued.

5. In the 1980s, the Chinese Communist Party began allowing Chinese entrepreneurs to experiment with capitalist ventures. Today multinational corporations are capitalizing on China's huge workforce to produce goods and services for sale not just to those in industrial nations, but to the people of China.

Thinking Critically

1. In the United States, what factors might encourage the growth of the informal economy? Are those factors related to the country's economic system?

2. Why do you think China's economy has grown as fast as it has?

Key Terms

Capitalism

Communism

Industrial society

Informal economy

Laissez-faire

Monopoly

Socialism

As the entire nation is well aware, the costs of health care have skyrocketed in the past 35 years. In 1997, total expenditures for health care in the United States crossed the trillion-dollar threshold—more than four times the 1980 total (Figure 53-1). In 2000, the amount spent on health care equaled that spent on education, defense, prisons, farm subsidies, food stamps, and foreign aid combined. By the year 2018, total expenditures for health care in the United States are expected to exceed $4.4 trillion. The rising costs of medical care are especially burdensome

in the event of catastrophic illnesses or confinement to a nursing home. Bills of tens of thousands of dollars are not unusual in the treatment of cancer, Alzheimer's disease, and other chronic illnesses requiring custodial care.

The health care system of the United States has moved far beyond the days when general practitioners living in a neighborhood or community typically made house calls and charged modest fees for their services. How did health care become a big business involving nationwide hospital chains and marketing campaigns? How have these changes reshaped the interactions between doctors, nurses, and patients? We will address these questions in this module.

A Historical View

Today, state licensing and medical degrees confer an authority on medical professionals that is maintained from one generation to the next. However, health care in the United States has not always followed this model. The "popular health movement" of the 1830s and 1840s emphasized preventive care and what is termed "self-help." Strong criticism was voiced of "doctoring" as a paid occupation. New medical philosophies or sects established their own medical schools and challenged the authority

FIGURE 53-1 **Total Health Care Expenditures in the United States, 1970–2019 (Projected)**

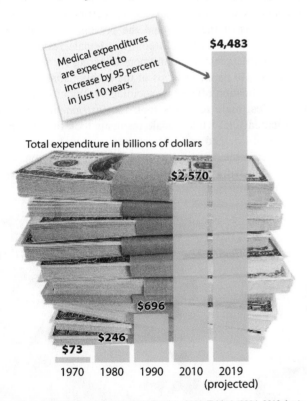

Medical expenditures are expected to increase by 95 percent in just 10 years.

$4,483

Total expenditure in billions of dollars

$2,570

$696

$246

$73

| 1970 | 1980 | 1990 | 2010 | 2019 (projected) |

Sources: Centers for Medicare and Medicaid Services 2010: Table 1 (2004–2019 data); Health Care Financing Administration 2001 (1970–1990 data).

Think about It

What social changes in the United States might account for the rise in health care costs from $73 billion in 1970 to almost 2.6 trillion in 2010?

HOSPITAL
INTENSIVE BILLING UNIT

and methods of more traditional doctors. By the 1840s, most states had repealed medical licensing laws.

In response, through the leadership of the American Medical Association (AMA), founded in 1848, "regular" doctors attacked lay practitioners, sectarian doctors, and female physicians in general. Once they had institutionalized their authority through standardized programs of education and licensing, they conferred it on all who successfully completed their programs. The authority of the physician no longer depended on lay attitudes or on the person occupying the sick role; increasingly, it was built into the structure of the medical profession and the health care system. As the institutionalization of health care proceeded, the medical profession gained control over both the market for its services and the various organizational hierarchies that govern medical practice, financing, and policymaking. By the 1920s, physicians controlled hospital technology, the division of labor of health personnel, and, indirectly, other professional practices such as nursing and pharmacy (R. Coser 1984).

Physicians, Nurses, and Patients

Traditionally, physicians have held a position of dominance in their dealings with both patients and nurses. The functionalist and interactionist perspectives offer a framework for understanding the professional socialization of physicians as it relates to patient care. Functionalists suggest that established physicians and medical school professors serve as mentors or role models who transmit knowledge, skills, and values to the passive learner—the medical student. Interactionists emphasize that students are molded by the medical school environment as they interact with their classmates.

Both approaches argue that the typical training of physicians in the United States leads to rather dehumanizing physician–patient encounters. As Dr. Lori Arviso Alvord writes in *The Scalpel and the Silver Bear,* "I had been trained by a group of physicians who placed much more emphasis on their technical abilities and clinical skills than on their abilities to be caring and sensitive" (Alvord and Van Pelt 1999:13). Despite many efforts to formally introduce a humanistic approach to patient care into the medical school curriculum, patient overload and cost-cutting by hospitals have tended to undercut positive relations. Moreover, widespread publicity about malpractice suits and high medical costs has further strained the physician–patient relationship. Interactionists have closely examined compliance and negotiation between physician and patient. They concur with Talcott Parsons's view that the relationship is generally asymmetrical, with doctors holding a position of dominance and controlling rewards.

Just as physicians have maintained dominance in their interactions with patients, they have controlled interactions with nurses. Despite their training and

professional status, nurses commonly take orders from physicians. Traditionally, the relationship between doctors and nurses has paralleled the male dominance of the United States: most physicians have been male, while virtually all nurses have been female.

Like other women in subordinate roles, nurses have been expected to perform their duties without challenging the authority of men. Psychiatrist Leonard Stein (1967) refers to this process as the *doctor–nurse game.* According to the rules of this "game," the nurse must never openly disagree with the physician. When she has recommendations concerning a patient's care, she must communicate them indirectly, in a deferential tone. For example, if asked by a hospital's medical resident, "What sleeping medication has been helpful to Mrs. Brown in the past?" (an indirect request for a recommendation), the nurse will respond with a disguised recommendation, such as "Pentobarbital 100 mg was quite effective night before last." Her careful response allows the physician to authoritatively restate the same prescription as if it were *his* idea.

Like nurses, female physicians have traditionally found themselves in a subordinate position because of gender. In fall 2009, 48 percent of all new medical school students in the United States were female, along with 35 percent of all faculty members at medical schools. A study of male and female medical residents suggests that the increasing number of women physicians may alter the traditional doctor–patient relationship. Male residents were found to be more focused on the intellectual challenges of medicine and the prestige associated with certain medical specialties. In contrast, female residents were more likely to express a commitment to caring for patients and devoting time to them. In terms of the functionalist analysis of gender stratification offered by sociologists Talcott Parsons and Robert Bales, male residents took the *instrumental,* achievement-oriented role, while female residents took the *expressive,* interpersonal-oriented role. As women continue to enter and move higher in the hierarchies of the medical profession, sociological studies will surely be done to see whether these apparent

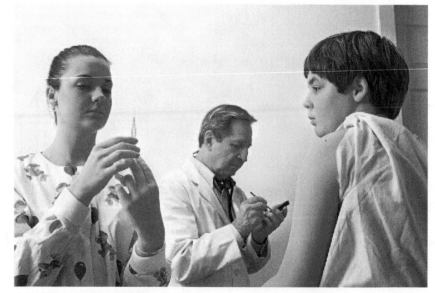

As if the status differences between nurses and physicians were not clear to all, the cheery uniform of nurses and the formal white doctor's coat reinforce the distinction.

gender differences persist (Association of American Medical Colleges 2009a: Chart 2, 2009b).

Patients have traditionally relied on medical personnel to inform them of health care issues, but increasingly they are turning to the media for health care information. Recognizing this change, pharmaceutical firms are advertising their prescription drugs directly to potential customers through television and magazines. The Internet is another growing source for patient information. Medical professionals are understandably suspicious of these new sources of information. A study published in the *Journal of the American Medical Association* in 2001 found that health information on the Internet is often incomplete and inaccurate, even on the best sites. Nevertheless, there is little doubt that Web research is transforming an increasing proportion of patient–physician encounters, as patients arrive for their doctor's appointments armed with the latest printout from the Internet (Berland 2001; Gerencher 2007).

Finally, consumers today get more than their health care information in new ways. Over the past decade, they have discovered a new way to access traditional medicine: going to the store (see the Research Today box).

Medical Technology and Telemedicine

Technological advances touch all aspects of society, including medicine. To reverse paralysis, doctors have inserted microchips in patients' limbs. These space-age devices respond to the electrical impulses the brain sends out to initiate movement. Someday, microchips may even replace chemical medications.

Robotics is another up-and-coming medical technology. Already, voice-activated robotic instruments are being used in heart surgery. NASA is currently developing a robotic probe that can locate brain tumors.

Both these technologies raise the possibility of doing medicine from a distance. To activate microchips or robots, medical personnel do not need to be standing next to a patient. Soon, remote monitoring may supplement the familiar bedside monitor.

use your **sociological imagination**

If you were a patient, would you put yourself entirely in the physician's hands? Or would you do some research about your illness on your own? If you were a doctor, would you want your patient checking medical information on the Internet? Explain your positions.

Alternatives to Traditional Health Care

In traditional forms of health care, people rely on physicians and hospitals for the treatment of illness. Yet at least one out of every three adults in the United States attempts to maintain good health or respond to illness through the use of alternative health care techniques. For example, in recent decades interest has been growing in *holistic* (also spelled *wholistic*) medical principles, first developed in China. **Holistic medicine** refers to therapies in which the health care practitioner considers the person's physical, mental, emotional, and spiritual characteristics. The individual is regarded as a totality rather than a collection of interrelated organ systems. Treatment methods include massage, chiropractic medicine, acupuncture (which involves the insertion of fine needles into surface points), respiratory exercises, and the use of herbs as remedies. Nutrition, exercise, and visualization may also be used to treat ailments that are generally treated through medication or hospitalization (Sharma and Bodeker 1998).

Practitioners of holistic medicine do not necessarily function totally outside the traditional health care system. Some have medical degrees and rely on X-rays and EKG machines for diagnostic assistance. Others who staff holistic clinics, often referred to as *wellness clinics*, reject the use of medical technology. The recent resurgence of holistic medicine comes amid widespread recognition of the value of nutrition and the dangers of overreliance on prescription drugs (especially those used to reduce stress, such as Valium).

The medical establishment—professional organizations, research hospitals, and medical schools—has generally served as a stern protector of traditionally accepted health care techniques. However, a major breakthrough occurred in 1992 when the federal government's National Institutes of Health—the nation's major funding source for biomedical research—opened an Office of Alternative Medicine, empowered to accept grant requests. NIH-sponsored national surveys conducted in 2002 and 2007 found that one in four adults in the United States had used some form of "complementary and alternative medicine" during the previous month or year. Examples included acupuncture, folk medicine, meditation, yoga, homeopathic treatments, megavitamin therapy, and chiropractic treatment. When prayer was included as an alternative or complementary form of medicine, the proportion of adults who used alternative medicine rose to over 62 percent (Figure 53-3).

On the international level, the World Health Organization (WHO) has begun to monitor the use of alternative medicine around the world. According to WHO, 80 percent of people who live in

Health Care, Retail Style

Greeting cards are in aisle 7; vaccinations, in aisle 4. Today, over 1,200 health clinics are located in retail stores throughout the United States, including Walgreens, CVS, and Walmart. Staffed by nurse-practitioners and nurses with advanced degrees, these in-store clinics treat a limited menu of complaints, including sore throats, ear infections, pinkeye, and noncomplicated respiratory conditions. And the nurses do write prescriptions.

What are the implications of these new clinics for traditional health care? Having a regular physician is becoming less and less common in the United States, given the many people who lack health insurance, as well as the frequent changes in corporate health plans. Like it or not, the physician you see this year simply may not be available to you next year. Under these circumstances, retail medical care may not pose much of a challenge to traditional medical practices.

> For three acute conditions—sore throat, middle ear infection, and urinary tract infection—retail clinics delivered the same or better-quality care than traditional medical settings.

What about the quality of care offered at in-store clinics? Recently, researchers compared the care delivered in retail clinics to the care available in doctors' offices, urgent care departments, and emergency rooms. For three acute conditions—sore throat, middle ear infection, and urinary tract infection—they found that retail clinics delivered the same or better-quality care than traditional medical settings, including preventive care during or after the first visit. Costs were much lower, especially compared to those in emergency rooms.

In-store clinics are another example of **McDonaldization,** the process through which the principles of the fast-food restaurant are coming to dominate more and more sectors of society (see Module 19). McDonaldization offers the benefit of clearly stated services and prices, but the drawback of impersonality. Family doctors note that 40 percent of clinic patients have a family physician. Yet, given the shortcomings of health care delivery in the United States, it is difficult to argue against an innovative new method of providing health care.

LET'S DISCUSS

1. Have you ever been treated at an in-store clinic? If so, were you satisfied with the care you received? What about the price you paid—was it reasonable?

2. Evaluate the emergence of clinics from a functionalist and then a conflict perspective. On balance, do you think these clinics are a benefit to society?

Sources: Pickert 2009; RAND 2010; Ritzer 2011.

---

the poorest countries in the world use some form of alternative medicine, from herbal treatments to the services of a faith healer. In most countries, these treatments are largely unregulated, even though some of them can be fatal. For example, kava kava, an herbal tea used in the Pacific Islands to relieve anxiety, can be toxic to the liver in concentrated form. But other alternative treatments have been found to be effective in the treatment of serious diseases, such as malaria and sickle-cell anemia. WHO's goal is to compile a list of such practices, as well as to encourage the development of universal training programs and ethical standards for practitioners of alternative medicine. To date, the organization has published findings on about 100 of the 5,000 plants believed to be used as herbal remedies (McNeil 2002).

The Role of Government

Not until the 20th century did health care receive federal aid. The first significant involvement was the 1946 Hill-Burton Act, which provided subsidies for building and improving hospitals, especially in rural areas. A far more important change came with the enactment in 1965 of two wide-ranging government assistance programs: Medicare, which is essentially a compulsory health insurance plan for the elderly, and Medicaid, which is a noncontributory federal and state insurance plan for the poor. These programs greatly expanded federal involvement in health care financing for needy men, women, and children.

Given the high rates of illness and disability among elderly people, Medicare has had a huge impact on the health care system. Initially, Medicare simply reimbursed health care providers such as physicians and hospitals for the billed costs of their services. However, in 1983, as the overall costs of Medicare increased dramatically, the federal government introduced a price-control system. Under this system, private hospitals often transfer patients whose treatment may be unprofitable to public facilities. In fact, many private hospitals have begun to conduct "wallet biopsies"—that is, to investigate the financial status of

FIGURE 53-3 **Use of Complementary and Alternative Medicine**

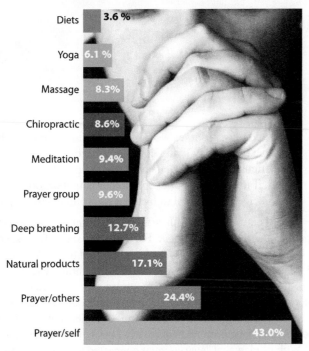

Diets	3.6%
Yoga	6.1%
Massage	8.3%
Chiropractic	8.6%
Meditation	9.4%
Prayer group	9.6%
Deep breathing	12.7%
Natural products	17.1%
Prayer/others	24.4%
Prayer/self	43.0%

Note: Data from 2007 survey, except for prayer data from 2002 survey.
Source: Barnes et al. 2004, 2008.

potential patients. Those judged undesirable are then refused admission or dumped. Although a federal law passed in 1987 made it illegal for any hospital receiving Medicare funds to dump patients, the practice continues (E. Gould 2007; D. Light 2004).

The expansion of health insurance coverage enacted by Congress in 2010 raised the hope of improved health care. It also brought severe criticism from the Tea Party movement, whose members charged that legislators were spending money they did not have. The costs of the legislation, Tea party members warned, would lead inevitably to higher taxes.

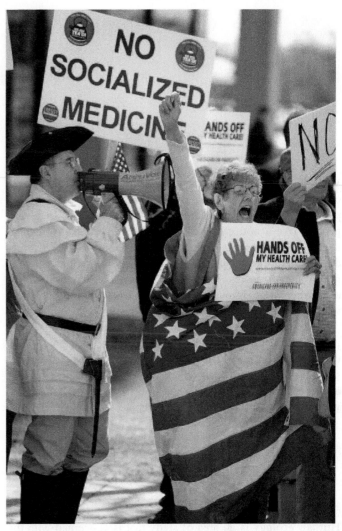

Tea Party members protest the passage of health care reform outside a congressional representative's office in Schaumburg, Illinois. Although the legislation would help millions of Americans who lack health insurance, opponents worry that the cost would be prohibitive.

MODULE 53 | Recap and Review

Summary

The health care system in the United States is a complex and expensive social institution that has evolved from relatively simple roots.

1. The preeminent role of physicians in the U.S. health care system gives them a position of dominance in their dealings with nurses and patients.

2. Many people use alternative health care techniques such as **holistic medicine** and self-help groups.

Thinking Critically

1. Explain the dominance of physicians in the health care system from a conflict perspective.

2. In the United States, a nation with a world-renowned medical system, why do so many people seek alternative forms of health care?

Key Terms

Holistic medicine

McDonaldization

54 | Sociological Perspectives on the Environment

We have seen that the environment people live in has a noticeable effect on their health. Those who live in stressful, overcrowded places suffer more from disease than those who do not. Likewise, people have a noticeable effect on their environment. Around the world, increases in population, together with the economic development that accompanies them, have had serious environmental consequences. We can see signs of despoliation almost everywhere: our air, our water, and our land are being polluted, whether we live in St. Louis, Mexico City, or Lagos, Nigeria.

Though environmental problems may be easy to identify, devising socially and politically acceptable solutions to them is much more difficult. In this section we will see what sociologists have to say about the trade-off between economic growth and development and its effects on the environment. In the section that follows we will look more closely at specific environmental problems.

Effects of Growth and Development

Human Ecology

Human ecology is an area of study that is concerned with the interrelationships between people and their environment. As the environmentalist Barry Commoner (1971:39) put it, "Everything is connected to everything else." Human ecologists focus on how the physical environment shapes people's lives and on how people influence the surrounding environment.

In an application of the human ecological perspective, sociologists and environmentalists have identified several relationships between the environment and people. Among them are the following:

1. **The environment provides the resources essential for life.** These include air, water, and materials used to create shelter, transportation, and needed products. If human societies exhaust these resources—for example, by polluting the water supply or cutting down rain forests—the consequences could be dire.

2. **The environment serves as a waste repository.** More so than other living species, humans produce a huge quantity and variety of waste products—bottles, boxes, papers, sewage, garbage, and so on. Various types of pollution have become more common because human societies are generating more wastes than the environment can safely absorb.

3. **The environment "houses" our species.** It is our home, our living space, the place where we reside, work, and play. At times we take this truism for granted, but not when day-to-day living conditions become unpleasant and difficult. If our air is "heavy," if our tap water turns brown, if toxic chemicals seep into our neighborhood, we remember why it is vital to live in a healthful environment.

There is no shortage of illustrations of the interconnectedness of people and their environment. For example, scientific research has linked pollutants in the physical environment to people's health and behavior. The increasing prevalence of asthma, lead poisoning, and cancer have all been tied to human alterations to the environment. Similarly, the rise in melanoma (skin cancer) diagnoses has been linked to global warming. And ecological changes in our food and diet have been related to early obesity and diabetes.

With its view that "everything is connected to everything else," human ecology stresses the trade-offs inherent in every decision that alters the environment. In facing the environmental challenges of the 21st century, government policymakers and environmentalists must determine how they can fulfill humans' pressing needs for food, clothing, and shelter while preserving the environment as a source of resources, a waste repository, and our home.

Conflict View of the Environment

In Module 29 we drew on world systems analysis to show how a growing share of the human and natural resources of developing countries is being redistributed to the core industrialized nations.

To make a point about climate change, in 2009, Mohammed Nasheed, president of a small island nation in the Indian Ocean, held an underwater cabinet meeting in the waters that surround his low-lying homeland. Forecasters project that his country, the Maldives, will be under water by the end of this century due to climate change. Nasheed has called on all countries of the world to reduce their carbon dioxide emissions.

This process only intensifies the destruction of natural resources in poorer regions of the world. From a conflict perspective, less affluent nations are being forced to exploit their mineral deposits, forests, and fisheries in order to meet their debt obligations. The poor turn to the only means of survival available to them: they plow mountain slopes, burn plots in tropical forests, and overgraze grasslands (World Bank 2010b).

Brazil exemplifies this interplay between economic troubles and environmental destruction. Each year more than 5.7 million acres of forest are cleared for crops and livestock. The elimination of the rain forest affects worldwide weather patterns, heightening the gradual warming of the earth. These socioeconomic patterns, with their harmful environmental consequences, are evident not only in Latin America but in many regions of Africa and Asia.

Although deforestation of the rain forest has long been a concern, only in the past few years have policymakers begun to listen to the indigenous peoples who live in these areas. In 2008, native peoples from Brazil, the Congo, and Indonesia convened to make the case that wealthier countries should compensate them for conservation of the tropical rain forests. Preservation of the rain forests may make sense at the global level, but for many local peoples, it limits their efforts to cultivate crops or graze cattle (Barrionuevo 2008).

Conflict theorists are well aware of the environmental implications of land use policies in the Third World, but they contend that focusing on the developing countries is ethnocentric. Who, they ask, is more to blame for environmental deterioration: the poverty-stricken and "food-hungry" populations of the world or the "energy-hungry" industrialized nations? These theorists point out that the industrialized nations of North America

and Europe account for only 12 percent of the world's population but are responsible for 60 percent of worldwide consumption. The money their residents spend on ocean cruises each year could provide clean drinking water for everyone on the planet. Ice-cream expenditures in Europe alone could be used to immunize every child in the world. Thus, conflict theorists charge, the most serious threat to the environment comes from the global consumer class (Gardner et al. 2004; Shah 2009).

Allan Schnaiberg (1994) further refined this analysis by shifting the focus from affluent consumers to the capitalist system as the cause of environmental troubles. In his view, a capitalist system creates a "treadmill of production" because of its inherent need to build ever-expanding profits. This treadmill necessitates the creation of increasing demand for products, the purchase of natural resources at minimal cost, and the manufacturing of products as quickly and cheaply as possible—no matter what the long-term environmental consequences.

Environmental Justice

In autumn 1982, nearly 500 African Americans participated in a six-week protest against a hazardous waste landfill in North Carolina. Their protests and legal actions against the dangerous cancer-causing chemicals continued until 2002, when decontamination of the site finally began. This 20-year battle could be seen as yet another "not in my backyard" (NIMBY) event. But today, the Warren County struggle is viewed as a transformative moment in contemporary environmentalism: the beginning of the *environmental justice* movement (Bullard 1993; McGurty 2000; North Carolina Department of Environment and Natural Resources 2008).

Environmental justice is a legal strategy based on claims that racial minorities are subjected disproportionately to environmental hazards. Some observers have heralded environmental

From the perspective of developing nations, many calls for the reduction of greenhouse gases unfairly target countries that are just beginning to industrialize.

Sociology in the Global Community

The Mysterious Fall of the Nacirema

Chapter 3 opened with anthropologist Horace Miner's description of the strange rituals practiced by the Nacirema (*American* spelled backward). Sixteen years after Miner first described the culture, American Studies scholar Neil B. Thompson wrote a follow-up article, "The Mysterious Fall of the Nacirema," that was in effect the culture's epitaph.

The Nacirema, Thompson wrote, were master engineers who had created extensive networks of "narrow ribbons, called streets," which covered the landscape. From the air, the ribbons around major population centers could be seen to be very elaborate. The purpose of these networks, Thompson speculated, might have been to promote the centralization of government or to separate "persons of lower caste" from others, in neighborhoods referred to as "ottehgs."

A special group of highly privileged priests, called the "ssenisub community," directed such massive projects. The priests lived in gated areas secured by electronic alarm systems. The ssenisub enjoyed complete freedom in creating their vast engineering marvels. "There is no evidence," Thompson wrote, "to suggest that any restraints—moral, sociological, or

> Looking back over the past 300 "solar cycles" of the culture, Thompson noted that the Nacirema had devoted a great deal of time and attention to changing the color of the air and water.

engineering—were placed on their self-determined enterprises."

Looking back over the past 300 "solar cycles" of the culture, Thompson noted that the Nacirema had devoted a great deal of time and attention to changing the color of the air and water. For the first 250 cycles they had little success, "but during the short period before the fall of the culture, they mastered their art magnificently," changing the water from bluish-green to reddish-brown and the air from blue to grayish-yellow.

To accomplish this great engineering feat, the Nacirema built huge plants near large cities. "These plants constantly produced a variety of reagents ... which were then pumped into the rivers and lakes or released into the atmosphere in the form of hot gases." To solve the problem of what to do with the by-products of these processes, the Nacirema distributed them to people's homes, where they were kept for a short time before being sent to a landfill.

Thompson wrote his article in 1972. To date, archeologists have not been able to explain the demise of this fascinating culture.

LET'S DISCUSS

1. Have you ever visited a foreign culture and been struck by something that seemed odd to you, but perfectly normal to everyone else? If so, did you discuss your reaction with others? Could they see your point of view?

2. If all of us could step back and take an objective look at what we are doing to the environment, would our society change for the better? Why or why not?

Sources: Miner 1956; N. Thompson 1972.

---

justice as the "new civil rights of the 21st century" (Kokmen 2008:42). Since the start of the environmental justice movement, activists and scholars have discovered other environmental disparities that break along racial and social class lines. In general, poor people and people of color are much more likely than others to be victimized by the everyday consequences of our built environment, including the air pollution from expressways and incinerators.

Sociologists Paul Mohai and Robin Saha (2007) examined over 600 identified hazardous waste treatment, storage, and disposal facilities in the United States. They found that non-Whites and Latinos make up 43 percent of the people who live within one mile of these dangerous sites. Skeptics often argue that minorities move near such sites because of low housing prices. However, two recent longitudinal (long-term) research studies, done over 30- and 50-year periods found that toxic facilities tend to be located in minority communities (Mohai et al. 2009:413).

Following reports from the Environmental Protection Agency (EPA) and other organizations documenting the discriminatory location of hazardous waste sites, President Bill Clinton issued an executive order in 1994 that requires all federal agencies to ensure that low-income and minority communities have access to better information about their environment and an opportunity to participate in shaping government policies that affect their health. Initial efforts to implement the policy, along with increased activity by the environmental justice movement, aroused

widespread opposition because of the delays it imposes in establishing new industrial sites. Some observers question the wisdom of an order that slows economic development in areas that are in dire need of employment opportunities. Others point out that such businesses employ few unskilled or less skilled workers, and only make the environment less livable (Laszewski 2008; A. Szasz 1994; D. Taylor 2000).

The environmental justice movement has become globalized, for several reasons. In many nations, activists have noticed similar patterns in the location of hazardous waste sites. These groups have begun to network across international borders, to share their tactics and remedies. Their unified approach is wise, because the offending corporations are often multinational entities (see Module 29); influencing their actions, much less prosecuting them, is difficult. As we have noted before, the global warming debate often focuses criticism on developing nations like China and India, rather than on established industrial giants with a long history of greenhouse gas emissions (Mohai et al. 2009; Shah 2009).

Sociologists, then, have emphasized both the interconnectedness of humans and the environment and the divisiveness of race and social class in their work on humans and their alteration of the environment. Scientists, too, have taken different approaches, disagreeing sharply on the likely outcomes of environmental change. And, when their disagreements threaten to affect government policy and economic regulations, they become highly politicized. For some perspective on this struggle between environmental preservation and economic self-interest, let's revisit the Nacirema, introduced in the opening excerpt for Chapter 3. The Sociology in the Global Community box, doore, presents this unusual culture through the eyes of environmentalists.

Environmental Problems

Unfortunately, the environmental problems caused by unbridled development have effects far beyond the places where they are created. Witness Muhammad Ali, a Bangladeshi man who has had to flee floodwaters five times in the past decade. Scientists believe that global warming is to blame, both for worsening monsoons and for the raging waters of the Jamuna River, swollen by abnormally high glacier melt from the Himalayas. Every time the river floods, Ali tears down his house, made of tin and bamboo, and moves to higher ground. But he is running out of land to move to. "Where we are standing, in five days it will be gone," he says. "Our future thinking is that if this problem is not taken care of, we will be swept away" (Goering 2007).

Increasingly, people are recognizing the need to address such challenges to the environment. Yet in the United States, survey respondents do not see environmental issues as the most pressing of problems, and they often balk at proposed solutions. Little wonder, given that, in a 2010 national survey, nearly half the respondents were unsure of the evidence presented by scientists, and 48 percent thought the seriousness of global warming was exaggerated. Only 10 percent of those surveyed expected that they would see the effects of global warming in their lifetime (Newport 2010).

We will discuss the enormous challenge of global warming in this section, along with three broad areas of environmental concern. Two of them, air and water pollution, are thought to be contributors to global warming.

Air Pollution

Worldwide, more than 1 billion people are exposed to potentially health-damaging levels of air pollution. Unfortunately, in cities around the world, residents have come to accept smog and polluted air as normal. Urban air pollution is caused primarily by emissions from automobiles and secondarily by emissions from electric power plants and heavy industries. Smog not only limits visibility; it can lead to health problems as uncomfortable as eye irritation and as deadly as lung cancer. Such problems are especially severe in developing countries. The World Health Organization estimates that up to 700,000 premature deaths *per year* could be prevented if pollutants were brought down to safer levels (Carty 1999; World Resources Institute 1998).

People are capable of changing their behavior, but they are also unwilling to make such changes permanent. During the 1984 Olympics in Los Angeles, residents were asked to carpool and stagger their work hours to relieve traffic congestion and improve the quality of the air athletes would breathe. These changes resulted in a remarkable 12 percent drop in ozone levels. But when the Olympians left, people reverted to their normal behavior and the ozone levels climbed back up. Similarly, in the 2008 Olympics, China took drastic action to ensure that Beijing's high levels of air pollution did not mar the games. Construction work in the city ceased, polluting factories and power plants closed down, and roads were swept and sprayed with water several times a day. This temporary solution hardly solved China's ongoing problem, however (*The Economist* 2008b).

On an everyday basis—that is, when cities are not holding down their emissions because of global sports events—air pollution is still a serious issue in the United States. Today, 6 out of every 10 people in the United States live in communities with dangerously high levels of air pollution, either short-term or year-round. Solutions range from community efforts to clean up power plants and enforce or strengthen air quality standards to individual actions, like driving less often or using less electricity (American Lung Association 2009; *The Economist* 2008b).

Water Pollution

Throughout the United States, dumping of waste materials by industries and local governments has polluted streams, rivers, and lakes. Consequently, many bodies of water have become unsafe for drinking, fishing, and swimming. Around the world, pollution of the oceans is an issue of growing concern. Such pollution results regularly from waste dumping and is made worse by fuel leaks from shipping and occasional oil spills. When the oil tanker *Exxon Valdez* ran aground in Prince William Sound, Alaska, in 1989, its cargo of more than 11 million gallons of crude oil spilled into the sound and washed onto the shore, contaminating 1,285 miles of shoreline. All together, about 11,000 people joined in a massive cleanup effort that cost over $2 billion. Globally, tanker oil spills occur regularly. Much more dramatic has been the oil spilled from BP's Deepwater Horizon oil platform in 2010, with estimates of the oil spill beginning at *sixteen times* that of the *Exxon Valdez* (ITOPF 2006; Shapley 2010).

Less dramatic than large-scale accidents or disasters, but more common in many parts of the world, are problems with the basic water supply. Worldwide, over 1.1 billion people lack safe and adequate drinking water, and 2.5 billion have no acceptable means of sanitation—a problem that further threatens the quality of water supplies. The health costs of unsafe water are enormous.

Water scarcity in and of itself is another critical issue. For centuries, competition for limited supplies of water has led to

FIGURE 54-1 Increase in Carbon Dioxide Emissions

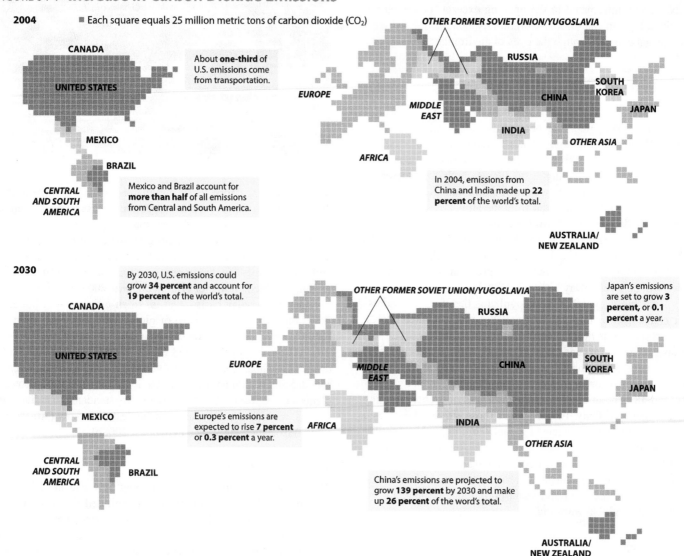

2004   ▪ Each square equals 25 million metric tons of carbon dioxide (CO₂)

About **one-third** of U.S. emissions come from transportation.

Mexico and Brazil account for **more than half** of all emissions from Central and South America.

In 2004, emissions from China and India made up **22 percent** of the world's total.

2030

By 2030, U.S. emissions could grow **34 percent** and account for **19 percent** of the world's total.

Japan's emissions are set to grow **3 percent**, or **0.1 percent** a year.

Europe's emissions are expected to rise **7 percent** or **0.3 percent** a year.

China's emissions are projected to grow **139 percent** by 2030 and make up **26 percent** of the word's total.

Source: Mufson 2007:6.

Throughout the world, carbon dioxide emissions are expected to increase over the coming generation. However, new global agreements may stem the projected increases.

conflict. Today, for example, the continuing war over the Darfur region of the Sudan is fueled by a growing population and a shrinking water supply. In many of the world's poorest regions, particularly in Africa, millions of people spend much of their day simply searching for water. Obviously, their time and labor could be better used in creating a self-sustaining environment (Pacific Institute 2010a, 2010b; Velasquez-Manoff 2009).

Global Warming

Based primarily on complex computer models, scientists have made hundreds of projections of global warming. The term *global warming* refers to the significant rise in the earth's surface temperatures that occurs when industrial gases like carbon dioxide

turn the planet's atmosphere into a virtual greenhouse. These *greenhouse gas emissions,* which also include methane, nitrous oxide, and ozone, trap heat in the lower atmosphere. Even one additional degree of warmth in the globe's average surface temperature can increase the likelihood of wildfires, shrinkage of rivers and lakes, expansion of deserts, and torrential downpours, including typhoons and hurricanes. As Figure 54-1 shows, scientists now track and project carbon dioxide emissions around the world (Lynas 2008).

Although scientific concern over global warming has heated up, climate change remains low on policymakers' list of concerns. The problem seems abstract, and in many countries, officials think that the real impact of any action they may take depends on decisive action by other nations. The Kyoto Protocol

(1997) was intended to reduce global emissions of heat-trapped gases, which can contribute to global warming and climate change. To date, 190 countries are party to the accord, but the United States has failed to ratify it. Opponents of the protocol argue that doing so would place the nation at a disadvantage in the global marketplace.

In 2009, shortly after Barack Obama became president, the United States pledged to become involved in negotiating a new, broader agreement. Besides reducing greenhouse emissions, the proposed agreement would give technical assistance to developing countries struggling to cope with climate change. However, the 2009 summit, held in Copenhagen, served only to reinforce the global divide over how to address climate change. Europeans were unhappy that their countries seemed to be the only ones with binding objectives to reduce carbon emissions. Poorer nations objected to being left out of many of the critical negotiations. Environmental groups gave a cautious nod of approval, but with goals stretching to 2050, the summit's lasting impact will be difficult to assess (Broder 2009; E. Rosenthal 2009; United Nations Framework Convention on Climate Change 2010).

In writing about the global environment, activists often assert, "We're all in this together." Though we are all in this together, the reality is that globally, the most vulnerable countries tend to be the poorest. Developing nations are more likely than others to have economies that are built on limited resources or on a small number of crops vulnerable to drought, flood, and fluctuations in worldwide demand (Nordhaus and Shellenberger, 2007; Revkin 2007).

We can view global warming from the point of view of world systems analysis. Historically, core nations have been the major emitters of greenhouse gases. Today, however, manufacturing has moved to semi-periphery and periphery nations, where greenhouse gas emissions are escalating. Ironically, many of the forces that are now calling for a reduction in the human activity that contributes to global warming are located in core nations, which have contributed disproportionately to the problem. We want our hamburgers, but we decry the destruction of the rain forests to create grazing land for cattle. We want inexpensive clothes and toys, but we condemn developing countries for depending on coal-fired power plants, which are expected to increase 46 percent by 2030. The challenge of global warming, then, is closely tied to global inequality (M. Jenkins 2008; Roberts et al. 2003).

What are the causes of this global environmental crisis? Some observers, such as Paul Ehrlich and Anne Ehrlich, see the pressure of world population growth as the central factor in environmental deterioration. They argue that population control is essential in preventing widespread starvation and environmental decay. Barry Commoner, a biologist, counters that the primary cause of environmental ills is the increasing use of technological innovations that are destructive to the environment—among them plastics, detergents, synthetic fibers, pesticides, herbicides, and chemical fertilizers. Conflict theorists see the despoliation of the environment through the lens of world systems analysis. And interactionists stress efforts by informed individuals and groups to reduce their carbon footprint—that is, their daily or even lifetime production of greenhouse gases—through careful selection of the goods they consume (Carbon Trust 2010; Commoner 1990, 2007; Ehrlich and Ellison 2002).

 ## use your **sociological imagination**

As you think about all the problems facing our society, how often do you consider global warming? How often do your friends give it much thought?

The Impact of Globalization

Globalization can be both good and bad for the environment. On the negative side, it can create a race to the bottom, as polluting companies relocate to countries with less stringent environmental standards. Similarly, globalization allows multinationals to reap the resources of developing countries for short-term profit. From Mexico to China, the industrialization that often accompanies globalization has increased pollution of all types.

Yet globalization can have a positive impact, as well. As barriers to the international movement of goods, services, and people fall, multinational corporations have an incentive to carefully consider the cost of natural resources. Overusing or wasting resources makes little sense, especially when they are in danger of depletion (Kwong 2005).

One reflection of the interplay between globalization and the environment is the emergence of *environmental refugees.*

"Two can live as carbon-neutral as one."

To combat global warming, increasing numbers of people are seeking to achieve net-zero carbon emissions, both by avoiding emissions when possible—for example, by walking rather than driving—and through offsets (such as planting trees).

Vacation in an unspoiled paradise! Increasingly, people from developed countries are turning to ecotourism as an environmentally friendly way to see the world. The new trend bridges the interests of environmentalists and businesspeople, especially in developing countries. These birdwatchers are vacationing in Belize.

Europe in particular is beginning to see an influx of such immigrants from developing nations. According to a European Union report, global warming can be viewed as a "threat multiplier" that exacerbates prolonged droughts and a shortage of arable land, and along with them, poverty, poor health, and poor living conditions. Viewed through the lens of world systems analysis, periphery countries may become overburdened by environmental problems, precipitating either migrations to industrial nations or conflicts that cause mass displacements of their populations. "Europe must expect substantially increased migratory pressure" from these environmental refugees, the report concludes (Traynor 2008).

Against these potentially negative effects of globalization we must note the potential for new

social policy and the Environment

Environmentalism

On April 22, 1970, in a dramatic manifestation of growing grassroots concern over preservation of the environment, an estimated 25 million people turned out to observe the nation's first Earth Day. Two thousand communities held planned celebrations, and more than 2,000 colleges and 10,000 schools hosted environmental teach-ins. In many parts of the United States, citizens marched on behalf of specific environmental causes. That same year, the activism of these early environmentalists convinced Congress to establish the Environmental Protection Agency. The Clean Air, Clean Water, and Endangered Species acts soon followed (Brulle and Jenkins 2008).

Understanding the Issue

Sociologist Manual Castells (2010a:72) has declared environmentalism "the most comprehensive, influential movement of our time." Several social trends helped to mobilize the environmental movement. First, the activist subculture of the 1960s and early 1970s encouraged people, especially young people, to engage in direct action regarding social issues. Second, the dissemination of scientific knowledge about serious environmental problems like oil spills and air pollution alarmed many Americans. And third, the growing popularity of outdoor recreation increased the number of people who were concerned about the environment. In this climate of broad-based interest in environmental issues, many organizations that had once focused narrowly on the conservation of natural resources evolved into full-fledged environmental groups (Dunlap and Mertig 1991).

Today, Earth Day has been enshrined on the calendars of city councils, zoos, and museums worldwide. Environmental

issues have also moved up the agenda of mainstream political parties. Increasingly, efforts to publicize environmental concerns and create support for action have moved to the Internet. Although times have changed, two beliefs continue to galvanize environmentalists: the environment is in dire need of protection, and the government must take strong action in response. Although environmentalists recognize that they must "think locally" and monitor their own carbon footprints, they also see preservation of the environment as a global challenge. They note that while significant progress has been made toward environmental protection, government regulation of the environment has been curtailed in some ways (Brulle and Jenkins 2008; Rootes 2007; Sieber et al. 2006).

The general public has a mixed reaction to environmental issues. Many people question the scientific arguments behind the theory of global warming. And although the economic cost of environmental protection has always been an issue, the broad economic downturn that began in 2008 tipped the balance of public opinion in favor of economic growth. In 2009, for the first time since Americans were first asked about the trade-off between the economy and the environment, a majority of people gave economic growth priority over the environment (Figure 54-2). In times of economic stress, the public puts off or ignores environmental concerns. Not surprisingly, the debate over the environmental movement grew more partisan between 2000 and 2010: Democrats became more sympathetic and Republicans more antagonistic (Dunlap 2010).

Today's college students also show less interest in the environment than students of past decades. In 2009, less than 30 percent of first-year college students in the United States

FIGURE 54-2 The Environment Versus the Economy

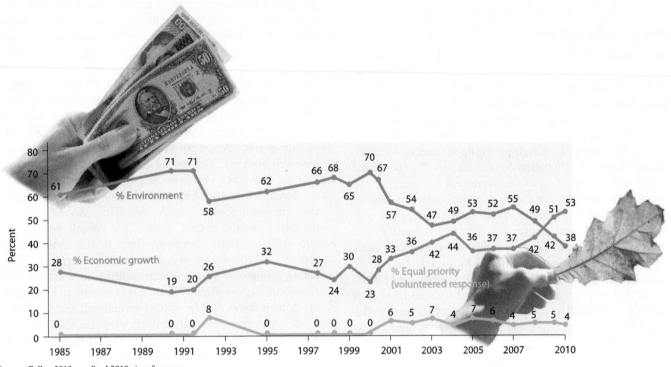

% Environment

% Economic growth

% Equal priority (volunteered response)

Percent

80 70 60 50 40 30 20 10 0

1985 1987 1989 1991 1993 1995 1997 1999 2001 2003 2005 2007 2010

Source: Gallup 2010; see Saad 2010c in references.

FIGURE 54-3 Are U.S. Teens Green Enough?

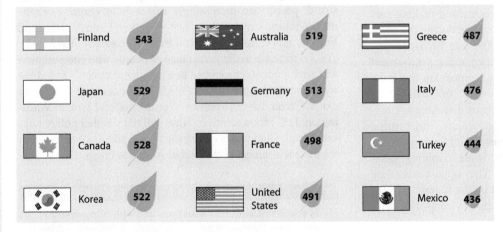

Finland	543	Australia	519	Greece	487
Japan	529	Germany	513	Italy	476
Canada	528	France	498	Turkey	444
Korea	522	United States	491	Mexico	436

Note: Mean score for 15-year-old students' knowledge of environmental issues = 543.
Source: Organisation for Economic Co-operation and Development 2009b:40.

wanted to clean up the environment—down from 42.5 percent in 1972 (see Figure 12-2). And as Figure 54-3 shows, U.S. high school students' interest in the issue does not compare favorably with that of teens in other major countries. In a 30-nation comparative study, 15-year-olds in the United States tied those in another country for 22nd place in their knowledge of environmental issues.

The contemporary environmental movement has evolved in several directions. At the local level, the number of grassroots organizations that deal with perceived environmental hazards has increased markedly. Indeed, some observers contend that the movement has become so specialized and fragmented, we can no longer speak of a single movement. At the same time, the largest and most powerful environmental organizations have become increasingly bureaucratic. Led by relatively well-paid professional management, they often focus on particular issues, such as air or water pollution, wildlife preservation, or energy conservation. These national organizations work for social change through educational efforts, lobbying, lawsuits, and electoral politics. In contrast, smaller environmental groups distrust virtually all major social institutions, and sometimes resort to sabotage or other illegal tactics. Consequently, the environmental movement is now more fragmented than it was in the 1970s (E. Johnson 2008; McCloskey 1991; Rootes 2007).

Applying Sociology

Even those who support environmentalists' goals are troubled by the fact that nationwide, the most powerful environmental organizations are predominantly White, male-dominated, and affluent. One study notes that while women are overrepresented in the environmental movement (particularly in grassroots environmental groups), men continue to hold most of the high-profile upper-management positions in mainstream national organizations. The perceived middle-class orientation of the movement is especially relevant given the class, racial, and ethnic factors associated with environmental hazards. As we saw earlier in the context of environmental justice, low-income communities and areas with significant minority populations are more likely than affluent White communities to be located near waste sites. Sociologists Liam Downey and Brian Hawkins (2008) found that an average Black household with an income of $50,000 to $60,000 a year coped with higher levels of pollution than an average White household with an income of less than $10,000 a year.

Viewed from a conflict perspective, it is significant that some environmental organizations accept funding from oil companies, chemical giants, and other powerful corporations. Perhaps as a result, the environmental movement has often emphasized limited reform rather than profound structural change. For example, activists may recommend making cars more energy-efficient instead of drastically reducing the number of vehicles on the road (Navarro 2009; Sale 1996).

Like any social movement, the environmental movement has aroused resistance. In this case, the opposition has itself become a social movement. The "wise-use" (or "sustainable-use") movement, founded in 1988, argues that we must balance our need for clean air, unspoiled waters, and pristine wilderness with our need for jobs, energy, and tourism. Wise-use advocates hope to open *all* public lands to mining, grazing, logging, and energy development. They oppose what they view as the special privileges granted by the federal government, through which Native Americans can control or limit development on reservation lands.

Another source of opposition comes from those who promote other issues with remedies that would seem to thwart environmental interests. For example, some question the environmentalists' move to replace fossil fuels such as coal and oil with biofuels such as ethanol. They complain that diverting corn and other crops into fuel production will raise food prices, hampering their efforts to reduce global hunger (Helvarg 1994; Pontin 2007).

Initiating Policy

The global economic downturn that began in 2008 has been a mixed blessing for environmentalists. As noted earlier, public opinion in the United States currently favors economic growth over environmental protection. Yet at the same time, the recession has sharply reduced the use of fossil fuels such as coal and oil. Moreover, the federal government's efforts to stimulate economic activity have emphasized the creation of green-collar jobs. By one estimate, every $1 billion invested in well-conceived green programs generates over 30,000 jobs and $450 million in cost savings per year. More specific environmental measures, such as raising federal gas mileage standards for automobiles, face a tough battle in Congress (Houser et al. 2009).

Environmentalism has moved onto a much bigger stage than the one it occupied on the first Earth Day. In 2008, for the first time, the leaders of the G8 economic powers (the United States, Japan, Germany, Great Britain, France, Italy, Canada, and Russia) set an explicit long-term target for eliminating greenhouse gases, which scientists have long warned were warming the planet. "Long-term" may be an understatement: their target date for cutting greenhouse gases in half is 2050. Environmentalists sharply criticized the G8's failure to set specific goals for the nearer term. The challenge is significant, given the fact that G8 emissions *increased* 35 percent over the preceding 15 years (Stolberg 2008).

Conventional wisdom holds that concern for environmental quality is limited to wealthy industrialized nations. However, the results of a 47-nation survey show that, around the world, people are increasingly reluctant to ignore environmental issues. Concern has risen sharply in Latin America and Europe, as well as in Japan and India. The survey also noted a general increase in the percentage of people who cite pollution and environmental problems as a top global threat. Around the world, many people blame the United States, and to a lesser extent China, for environmental problems, and look to Washington, D.C., for a solution. Time will tell whether policymakers in the United States or elsewhere will address their concern for the environment (Pew Global Attitudes Project 2007).

TAKE THE ISSUE WITH YOU

1. In your community, how would you act locally to preserve the environment? Describe your community's environmental problems and explain how you would seek to solve them.

2. How do you see the trade-off between the economy and the environment? Which is more important? Is it possible to improve both at the same time? Explain.

3. Thinking globally about the environment, list what you consider the most pressing priorities. How important are world hunger and economic justice compared to global warming, clean air and water, and economic development? Are some of your priorities related? In what way?

jobs in what are called green industries. Installing solar panels, weatherizing homes, brewing biofuels, building hybrid cars, growing organic foods, manufacturing organic garments, and erecting giant wind turbines are all classified as *green-collar* *jobs*. However, skeptics question how many such jobs will be created, and to what degree they will offset job losses in pollution-prone industries like oil, gas, and coal mining (S. Greenhouse 2008b; R. Pinderhughes 2008).

MODULE 54 | Recap and Review

Summary

The human ecological perspective suggests that the environment serves three basic functions: it provides essential resources, serves as a waste repository, and houses our species.

1. Conflict theorists charge that the most serious threat to the environment comes from Western industrialized nations.

2. **Environmental justice** addresses the disproportionate subjection of minorities to environmental hazards.

3. Four broad areas of environmental concern include air and water pollution, global warming, and globalization. Although globalization can contribute to environmental woes, it can also have beneficial effects.

4. Environmentalism is a social movement that is dominated by wealthy White people from industrialized countries. Increasingly, however, people of all races, ethnicities, social classes, and nationalities are becoming concerned about global warming and the threat it poses to our planet's health.

Thinking Critically

1. How are the physical and human environments connected in your neighborhood or community?

2. Which issue is more significant in your local community, air or water pollution? Why?

Key Terms

Environmental justice

Human ecology

Although such factors as the physical environment, population, technology, and social inequality serve as sources of change, it is the *collective* effort of individuals organized in social movements that ultimately leads to change. Sociologists use the term **social movements** to refer to organized collective activities to bring about or resist fundamental change in an existing group or society (Benford 1992). Herbert Blumer (1955:19) recognized the special importance of social movements when he defined them as "collective enterprises to establish a new order of life."

In many nations, including the United States, social movements have had a dramatic impact on the course of history and the evolution of the social structure. Consider the actions of abolitionists, suffragists, civil rights workers, and activists opposed to the war in Vietnam. Members of each social movement stepped outside traditional channels for bringing about social change, yet each had a noticeable influence on public policy. In Eastern Europe, equally dramatic collective efforts helped to topple Communist regimes in a largely peaceful manner, in nations that many observers had thought were "immune" to such social change (Ramet 1991).

Though social movements imply the existence of conflict, we can also analyze their activities from a functionalist perspective. Even when they are unsuccessful, social movements contribute to the formation of public opinion. Initially, people thought the ideas of Margaret Sanger and other early advocates of birth control were radical, yet contraceptives are now widely available in the United States. Moreover, functionalists view social movements as training grounds for leaders of the political establishment. Such heads of state as Cuba's Fidel Castro and South Africa's Nelson Mandela came to power after serving as leaders of revolutionary movements. Poland's Lech Walesa, Russia's Boris Yeltsin, and the Czech playwright Václav Havel all led protest movements against Communist rule and later became leaders of their countries' governments.

Because social movements know no borders, even nationalistic movements like those led by Castro and Walesa are deeply influenced by global events. Increasingly, social movements are taking on an international dimension from the start. Global enterprises, in particular, lend themselves to targeting through international mobilization, whether they are corporations like McDonald's or governmental bodies like the World Trade Organization. Global activism is not new, however; it began with the writing of Karl Marx, who sought to mobilize oppressed peoples in other industrialized countries. Today, activist networking is facilitated by the Internet and by relatively cheap travel costs. Participation in transnational activism is much wider now than in the past, and passions are quicker to ignite (Della Porta and Tarrow 2005; Tarrow 2005).

 use your **sociological imagination**

What social movements are most visible on your campus? In the community where you live?

In 2008 the ceremonial Olympic torch relay became the focus of protests by the human rights movement. In San Francisco, human rights activists denounced China's repression of free speech and religion in Tibet.

The Emergence of Social Movements

How and why do social movements emerge? Obviously, people are often discontented with the way things are. But what causes them to organize at a particular moment in a collective effort to effect change? Sociologists rely on two explanations for why people mobilize: the relative deprivation and resource mobilization approaches.

Relative Deprivation Approach

Those members of a society who feel most frustrated and disgruntled by social and economic conditions are not necessarily the worst off in an objective sense. Social scientists have long recognized that what is most significant is the way in which people *perceive* their situation. As Karl Marx pointed out, although the misery of the workers was important to their perception of their oppressed state, so was their position *in relation to* the capitalist ruling class (Marx and Engels [1847] 1955).

The term **relative deprivation** is defined as the conscious feeling of a negative discrepancy between legitimate expectations and present actualities (J. Wilson 1973). In other words, things aren't as good as you hoped they would be. Such a state may be characterized by scarcity rather than a complete lack of necessities (as we saw in the distinction between absolute and relative poverty in Module 28). A relatively deprived person is dissatisfied because he or she feels downtrodden relative to some appropriate reference group. Thus, blue-collar workers who live in two-family houses on small plots of land—though hardly at the bottom of the economic ladder—may nevertheless feel deprived in comparison to corporate managers and professionals who live in lavish homes in exclusive suburbs.

In addition to the feeling of relative deprivation, two other elements must be present before discontent will be channeled into a social movement. People must feel that they have a *right* to their goals, that they deserve better than what they have. For example, the struggle against European colonialism in Africa intensified when growing numbers of Africans decided that it was legitimate for them to have political and economic independence. At the same time, the disadvantaged group must perceive that its goals cannot be attained through conventional means. This belief may or may not be correct. Whichever is the case, the group will not mobilize into a social movement unless there is a shared perception that members can end their relative deprivation only through collective action (Morrison 1971).

Critics of this approach have noted that people don't need to feel deprived to be moved to act. In addition, this approach fails to explain why certain feelings of deprivation are transformed into social movements, whereas in similar situations, no collective effort is made to reshape society. Consequently, in recent years, sociologists have paid increasing attention to the forces needed to bring about the emergence of social movements (Alain 1985; Finkel and Rule 1987; Orum and Dale 2009).

 use your **sociological imagination**

Why might well-off people feel deprived?

Resource Mobilization Approach

It takes more than desire to start a social movement. It helps to have money, political influence, access to the media, and personnel. The term **resource mobilization** refers to the ways in which a social movement utilizes such resources. The success of a movement for change will depend in good part on what resources it has and how effectively it mobilizes them. In other words, recruiting adherents and marshalling resources is critical to the growth and success of social movements (Gamson 1989; Tilly 1964, 2003; Walder 2007).

Sociologist Anthony Oberschall (1973:199) has argued that to sustain social protest or resistance, there must be an "organizational base and continuity of leadership." As people become part of a social movement, norms develop to guide their behavior. Members of the movement may be expected to attend regular meetings of organizations, pay dues, recruit new adherents, and boycott "enemy" products or speakers. An emerging social movement may give rise to special language or new words for familiar terms. In recent years, social movements have been responsible for such new terms of self-reference as *Blacks* and *African Americans* (to replace *Negroes*), *senior citizens* (to replace *old folks*), *gays* (to replace *homosexuals*), and *people with disabilities* (to replace *the handicapped*).

Leadership is a central factor in the mobilization of the discontented into social movements. Often, a movement will be led by a charismatic figure, such as Dr. Martin Luther King Jr. As Max Weber described it in 1904, *charisma* is that quality of an individual that sets him or her apart from ordinary people. Of course, charisma can fade abruptly, which helps to account for the fragility of certain social movements (A. Morris 2000).

Yet many social movements do persist over long periods because their leadership is well organized and ongoing. Ironically, as Robert Michels (1915) noted, political movements that

Two members of People for the Ethical Treatment of Animals (PETA) protest the killing of animals for fur coats. Social movements like PETA seek public attention for the positions they espouse.

It's time

In 1842, a Roman Catholic became president of the University of Notre Dame.

In 1875, a woman became president of Wellesley College.

In 1886, a Jew became president of Yeshiva University.

In 1926, a Black person became president of Howard University.

AND IN 1988, the Gallaudet University presidency belongs to a DEAF person.

To show OUR solidarity behind OUR mandate for a deaf president of OUR university, you are invited to participate in a historic RALLY!

Gallaudet Univ. → TUESDAY, MARCH 1st
Football Field → 12:30–3:00 pm
BE THERE: signs, pickets, symbols and all

Gallaudet University in Washington, D.C., is the only four-year liberal arts college for deaf students in the United States. A leaflet (left) was distributed in 1988 as part of a successful effort by students, faculty, and alumni to force the appointment of the university's first deaf president. In 2007, after that president's retirement, students protested once again over the election process (right). The mobilization of resources is one key to the success of a social movement.

are fighting for social change eventually take on some of the aspects of bureaucracy that they were organized to protest. Leaders tend to dominate the decision-making process without directly consulting followers. The bureaucratization of social movements is not inevitable, however. More radical movements that advocate major structural change in society and embrace mass actions tend not to be hierarchical or bureaucratic (Fitzgerald and Rodgers 2000).

Why do certain individuals join a social movement while others who are in similar situations do not? Some of them are recruited to join. Karl Marx recognized the importance of recruitment when he called on workers to become *aware* of their oppressed status and to develop a class consciousness. Like theorists of the resource mobilization approach, Marx held that a social movement (specifically, the revolt of the proletariat) would require leaders to sharpen the awareness of the oppressed. They would need to help workers to overcome feelings of **false consciousness,** or attitudes that do not reflect workers' objective position, in order to organize a revolutionary movement. Similarly, one of the challenges faced by women's liberation activists of the late 1960s and early 1970s was to convince women that they were being deprived of their rights and of socially valued resources.

Gender and Social Movements

Sociologists point out that gender is an important element in understanding social movements. In our male-dominated society, women find it more difficult than men to assume leadership positions in social movement organizations. Though women often serve disproportionately as volunteers in these movements, their work is not always recognized, nor are their voices as easily heard as men's. Gender bias causes the real extent of their influence to be overlooked. Indeed, traditional examination of the

sociopolitical system tends to focus on such male-dominated corridors of power as legislatures and corporate boardrooms, to the neglect of more female-dominated domains such as households, community-based groups, and faith-based networks. But efforts to influence family values, child rearing, relationships between parents and schools, and spiritual values are clearly significant to a culture and society (Ferree and Merrill 2000; Noonan 1995).

Scholars of social movements now realize that gender can affect even the way we view organized efforts to bring about or resist change. For example, an emphasis on using rationality and cold logic to achieve goals helps to obscure the importance of passion and emotion in successful social movements. It would be difficult to find any movement—from labor battles to voting rights to animal rights—in which passion was not part of the consensus-building force. Yet calls for a more serious study of the role of emotion are frequently seen as applying only to the women's movement, because emotion is traditionally thought of as being feminine (Ferree and Merrill 2000; V. Taylor 1999, 2004).

 use your **sociological imagination**

Try to imagine a society without any social movements. Under what conditions could such a society exist? Would you want to live in it?

New Social Movements

Beginning in the late 1960s, European social scientists observed a change in both the composition and the targets of emerging social movements. Previously, traditional social movements had focused on economic issues, often led by labor unions or by people who shared the same occupation. However, many social movements that have become active in recent decades—including

Women and New Social Movements In India

In the more than 60 years since India gained its independence from Great Britain, a variety of new social movements has emerged. These grassroots efforts deal primarily with women's rights, discrimination against the *Dalits* (untouchables), environmental issues, and farming problems. Though they tend to be most visible in the media when their demonstrations occur in cities, most of these movements are based in India's vast rural areas, where about 70 percent of the nation's 1.2 billion people live.

Sociologists and other scholars have emphasized the central role that women play in starting these movements and creating social networks with activists in neighboring villages and adjacent states. Sometimes these movements connect to form nationwide networks through the assistance of the Women's Development Program (WDP). Founded by UNICEF in 1984, the WDP helps women to improve their quality of life, freeing them from dependence on slow and cumbersome government bureaucracies.

> The initial goal of the movement was to provide drought relief for villagers, but the deeper goal was to empower rural areas.

One notable social movement occurred in the Indian textile industry. In the mid-1980s, 5,000 striking textile workers came home from Mumbai to mobilize support in their rural villages and gather food for strikers in the city. As the strike wore on, some remained in their villages and sought employment on government drought-relief projects. However, there weren't enough jobs for rural residents, much less for these new migrants from Mumbai.

This experience was the origin of a new social movement in rural India. With unemployment threatening an expanded population in rural areas, activists formed what came to be called the *Shoshit, Shetkari, Kashtakari, Kamgar, Mukti Sangharsh (SSKKMS),* which means "exploited peasants, toilers, workers, liberation struggle." The initial goal of the movement was to provide drought relief for villagers, but the deeper goal was to empower rural areas.

The SSKKMS was unusual compared to other social movements in India: about half its participants and many of its leaders were women. This was no accident, for the movement also sought to address gender inequities. Some men have joined the women of the SSKKMS in their political activism, using direct-action tactics such as roadblocks.

Women have also marched on government offices to demand that at least a third of the seats in Parliament and the state assemblies be reserved for them. And they have begun to improve their families' lot through microfinance programs (see Module 50). Clearly, Indian women's traditional role of maintaining their households' health and nutrition is critical to their families' survival. Thus, their leadership in seeking improved living conditions is winning them new respect in India's patriarchal society. From the environment to the voting booth, from untouchables' rights to workers' rights, women's social movements are an increasingly common feature of Indian politics.

LET'S DISCUSS

1. Why do you think so many of India's women participate in new social movements? Describe their goals.

2. What would happen if "powerless" people in the United States formed a similar social movement? Would it succeed? Why or why not?

Sources: Bystydzienski and Sekhon 1999; Daley-Harris 2002; Desai 1996; Haub and Kent 2009; Ray 1999; Sengupta 2009; Subramaniam 2006; Working Women's Forum 2010.

---

the contemporary women's movement, the peace movement, and the environmental movement—do not have the social class roots typical of the labor protests in the United States and Europe over the past century (Tilly 1993, 2004).

The term **new social movements** refers to organized collective activities that address values and social identities, as well as improvements in the quality of life. These movements may be involved in developing collective identities. Many have complex agendas that go beyond a single issue, and even cross national boundaries. Educated, middle-class people are significantly represented in some of these new social movements, such as the women's movement and the movement for lesbian and gay rights. The Sociology in the Global Community box above describes some new social movements in India.

New social movements generally do not view government as their ally in the struggle for a better society. While they typically

Table **55-1**	Contributions to Social Movement Theory

Approach	Emphasis
Relative deprivation approach	Social movements are especially likely to arise when expectations are frustrated.
Resource mobilization approach	The success of social movements depends on which resources are available and how effectively they are used.
New social movement theory	Social movements arise when people are motivated by value issues and social identity questions.

do not seek to overthrow the government, they may criticize, protest, or harass public officials. Researchers have found that members of new social movements show little inclination to accept established authority, even scientific or technical authority. This characteristic is especially evident in the environmental and anti–nuclear power movements, whose activists present their own experts to counter those of government or big business (Garner 1996; Polletta and Jasper 2001; A. Scott 1990).

The environmental movement is one of many new movements with a worldwide focus (see the Social Policy section in Module 54). In their efforts to reduce air and water pollution, curtail global warming, and protect endangered animal species, environmental activists have realized that strong regulatory measures within a single country are not sufficient. Similarly, labor union leaders and human rights advocates cannot adequately address exploitative sweatshop conditions in a developing country if a multinational corporation can simply move the factory to another country, where workers earn even less. Whereas traditional views of social movements tended to emphasize resource mobilization on a local level, new social movement theory offers a broader, global perspective on social and political activism.

Table 55-1 summarizes the sociological approaches that have contributed to social movement theory. Each has added to our understanding of the development of social movements.

Communications and the Globalization of Social Movements

Today, through global text-messaging and the Internet, social activists can reach a large number of people around the world almost instantaneously, with relatively little effort and expense. The Internet's listservs and chat rooms—a new form of social networking—allow organizers of social movements to enlist like-minded people without face-to-face contact, or even simultaneous interaction (Calhoun 1998; Kavada 2005).

Moreover, television and the Internet, as contrasted with books and newspapers, often convey a false sense of intimacy

reinforced by immediacy. We seem to be personally hurt by the death of Princess Diana or moved by the troubles of the Kennedy family. Therefore, the latest technology brings us together to act and react in an electronic global village (Della Porta and Tarrow 2005; Garner 1999).

This sense of online togetherness extends to social movements, which more and more are being mounted on the Web. Through the instantaneous communication that is possible over the Internet, Mexican Zapatistas and other groups of Indigenous Peoples can transform their cause into an international lobbying effort, and Greenpeace organizers can link environmental activists throughout the world via video recorded on members' cell phones.

Sociologists have begun to refer to such electronic enhancement of established social movements as *computer-mediated communication (CMC)*. Electronic communication strengthens a group's solidarity, allowing fledgling social movements to grow and develop faster than they might otherwise. Thus the face-to-face contact that once was critical to a social movement is no longer necessary (Castells 2010b; Niezen 2005).

The new global communications technology also helps to create enclaves of similarly minded people. Alex Steffen (2008), editor of *World Changing* (see the chapter-opening excerpt), notes that the Internet is changing the way people relate to one another across vast distances, allowing small, focused audiences to become part of a global conversation. In doing so, they may find a common purpose. These social connections happen because of the Internet's technological structure. Web sites are not autonomous and independent; they are connected by a global electronic network. One Web site generally lists a variety of other sites that serve as links. For example, seeking information on domestic partnerships may lead you to an electronic enclave that is supportive of cohabitation between men and women or, alternatively, to an enclave that is supportive of gay and lesbian couples. New developments in communications technology have clearly broadened the way we interact with one another (Calhoun 1998).

In the 21st century, technology links people in even the remotest areas. In 2008 Mongolia's capital was rocked by protests over election fraud; two years later, by angry demands for better distribution of the nation's mining wealth. In both cases, the protests were swelled by people from rural areas, mobilized by the Internet.

Summary

Social movements are more structured than other forms of collective behavior and persist over longer periods.

1. A group will not mobilize into a social movement without a shared perception that its **relative deprivation** can be ended only through collective action.

2. The success of a social movement depends in good part on effective **resource mobilization.**

3. **New social movements** tend to focus on more than just economic issues and often cross national boundaries.

4. Advances in communications technology—especially the Internet—have had a major impact on social movements.

Thinking Critically

1. What might be some drawbacks of global communications technology?

2. What aspects of traditional gender roles explain the roles that women and men typically play in social movements?

Key Terms

False consciousness

New social movement

Relative deprivation

Resource mobilization

Social movement